BOOKS BY ROSS RUSSELL

The Sound (1961)
Jazz Style in Kansas City and the Southwest (1971)
Bird Lives! The High Life and Hard Times of Charlie Parker (1973)

ROSS RUSSELL

Da Capo Press • New York

BIRD LIVES!

The High Life and Hard Times of

Charlie (Yardbird) Parker

for Albert Goldman

Library of Congress Cataloging in Publication Data

Russell, Ross.
  Bird lives: the high life and hard times of Charlie (Yardbird)
Parker / Ross Russell.
     p.   cm.
  Originally published: New York: Charterhouse, 1973.
  Includes bibliographical references (p.) and discography (p.).
  ISBN 0-306-80679-7 (alk. paper)
  1. Parker, Charlie, 1920–1955. 2. Jazz musicians—United States—
Biography. I. Title.
ML419.P4R9 1996
788.7′3165′092—dc20   95-43925
[B]   CIP

First Da Capo Press edition 1996

This Da Capo Press paperback edition of *Bird Lives!* is an
unabridged republication of the edition published in New York
in 1973. It is reprinted by arrangement with the author.

Designed by The Etheredges

Published by Da Capo Press, Inc.
A Subsidiary of Plenum Publishing Corporation
233 Spring Street, New York, N.Y. 10013

Manufactured in the United States of America

PHOTO CREDITS

Credit is given for the photographic section, acknowledged here
by the number of the individual pictures:

1 — Robert Reisner collection; 2 — Reisner collection;
3 — *Jazz Hot*, Paris; 4 — *Jazz Tempo*, Hollywood;
5 — Don Lanphere, Billy Shaw Artists; 6 — Reisner collection;
7 — Reisner collection; 8 — Dial Records by Ray Whitten;
9 — Don Lanphere; 10 — Billy Shaw Artists;
11 — Mark Gardner; 12 — *Orkester Journalen*, Stockholm;
13 — *Orkester Journalen*; 14 — Reisner collection;
15 — Dial Records by Ray Whitten; 16 — Tony Williams;
17 — *Orkester Journalen*; 18 — Mark Gardner;
19 — Billy Shaw Artists; 20 — Reisner collection;
21 — *Orkester Journalen*; 22 — Richard Dickert; 23 — *Down Beat*, Chicago;
24 — *Orkester Journalen*; 25 — Dial Records by Ray Whitten;
26 — *Jazz Tempo*; 27 — Dial Records;
28 — Dial Records by Ray Whitten; 29 — *Jazz Hot*;
30 — Howard Moorehead; 31 — Verve Records;
32 — Aram Avakian, courtesy of *Jazz Hot*; 33 — Mark Gardner,
Klactoveesedstene, Faversham, Kent, England.

Contents

At Billy Berg's: An Obbligato   1

PART I

1 *Heavenly City*   29
2 *Getting Straight*   35
3 *Kansas City Mystique*   46
4 *Trials of Manhood*   57
5 *Modes*   66
6 *The Making of a Jazzman*   76

PART II

7 *Woodshedding in the Ozarks*   89
8 *The Apple*   97

9 *Hootie* 109

10 *The Band That Played the Blues* 117

11 *The Bebop Laboratory* 130

12 *The Last of the Big Bands* 145

13 *The Street* 162

14 *A Dizzy Atmosphere* 178

PART III

15 *The Independent Record Derby* 191

16 *Yardbird in Lotus Land* 199

17 *Sparrow's Last Jump* 218

18 *Relaxin' at Camarillo* 228

19 *Klactoveesedstene* 242

20 *Bird at Work* 255

21 *Birdland* 269

PART IV

22 *Travels with a Genius* 281

23 *A Queer Night in Brussels* 300

24 *The Jazz Baroness* 311

25 *King Pleasure* 322

26 *Down and Out in New York* 333

27 *At the Hotel Stanhope* 348

28 *Coda: Six Pretty Horses Pullin' Me* 359

Acknowledgments 375

Bibliography 381

Discography 384

Index 389

At Billy Berg's:
An Obbligato

Inside the one-story stucco building that houses the night club, in the part farthest removed from the bandstand—in the men's room to be exact—a man is listening to music through a set of earphones. He is a tall man with pale ivory skin and raven hair brushed back in neat waves from a high, prideful forehead, and he is dressed immaculately in cocoa-brown trousers, with knife pleats and wide cuffs, a narrow belt of rubbed pigskin, a cream-colored sports shirt with a softly rolled collar, no tie, and a lapel-less band jacket cut from fawn-colored camel's-hair. His name is Dean Benedetti, and he is a kind of amateur recording engineer. His job is to take musical notes by means of a portable recording machine.

1

The music that Dean Benedetti can hear through the earphones is being picked up by a small, sensitive microphone hung from a fastening in the padded leatherette shell of the bandstand outside. From the microphone a wire, of very fine gauge, its color matching that of the interior decor of the night club, runs along walls, facings, moldings, and door frames until it reaches the men's room. There Dean has come to an understanding with the elderly Negro who dispenses towels and shoe laces to the customers of the night club. The men's room is larger than most, equipped with a mirror and three each of wash basins, urinals, and toilet stalls. To the door of one of the stalls has been hung an OUT OF ORDER sign. Inside, on the closed lid of the toilet, Benedetti sits with the portable recording machine cradled in his lap, the headphones clamped to his ears, monitoring the music coming from the bandstand.

Tonight Dean's arrangements are a little complicated. Ordinarily he likes to work from a table in the main room of a night club. Tonight he has run into difficulties. The business agent of the musicians' union, which forbids unauthorized recording of live performances, has complained to the management and Dean has been asked to leave. Luckily, this happened thirty minutes before the opening set. After making a show of quitting the premises, Dean returned through a service entrance and carried out emergency arrangements. He is an old hand at this kind of thing. In the course of his musical note-taking Dean has been thrown out of clubs too numerous to mention. It has happened to him in New York, Boston, and Chicago. Dean always travels with spare wire leads, fastenings, and hand tools.

In the toilet stall he is comfortable and secure. Union officials, waiters, bouncers, the owner of the night club (a man named Billy Berg) cannot interfere with his work. To be able to make musical notes unmolested is important to Dean. When the music reaches a pitch and excitement mounts, the decibel meter must be watched carefully and the gain-control knob constantly adjusted to the volume being put into the machine. If he fails to do this the valuable tapes will be overcut and the notes distorted.

As the opening set of the evening begins, Dean listens closely, identifying each of the men in the band by turn. As yet no tape is running through the recording heads. Dean hears an opening figure played by the drummer, Stan Levey, followed by a series of round, mellow notes that walk up the fingerboard of the contrabass, played by Ray Brown. Then the pianist, Al Haig, joins in and the rhythm section is all together, setting up its sinuous, driving beat. The band is opening with a tune titled *A Night in Tunisia*. After a few measures, gonglike notes, seemingly out of time, but actually setting up a second rhythmic line and adding to the tension, are played by a vibraphone. That is Milt Jackson.

Dean Benedetti waits for the entry of the wind instruments. He is ready to start the machine. A trumpet is heard. It seems to burp, gargle, and falter. But that is just a musical put-on, one of Dizzy's little tricks. Instantly the trumpet recovers from the fake false start and soars into the upper register with faultless control. All of the instrumental voices are familiar. It is child's play for a man with Benedetti's ear to identify the various players. Even if Dean were unfamiliar with the personnel of the band, he would have no trouble in sorting out Dizzy Gillespie from all of the trumpet players or Al Haig from all of the pianists playing jazz in America. Before abandoning his own instrument, the alto saxophone, and settling on his present vocation, Dean was a member of the jazz community, not one of its principal figures by any means, but a minor one with status. He has a comprehensive knowledge of jazz instrumental style.

Now a saxophone joins the trumpet, and immediately Dean starts the machine running. This was what he was waiting for—the saxophone. In the earphones he hears a group of lush, quivering notes, and knows that something is amiss. The sounds do not come from an alto saxophone but a tenor. No tenor saxophonist was scheduled to appear with the band tonight. Dean recognizes the player. It is a man named Eli "Lucky" Thompson, last heard of as being at liberty in these parts.

Dean has no difficulty in identifying the player by the vibrato and phrasing. The style is a variation of Don Byas out of Coleman Hawkins. A tenor saxophonist has been substituted for the alto saxophonist, the man Dean came to record. He stops the tape at once. Charlie Parker, the easiest of all contemporary jazzmen to identify because of the power and clarity of his tone, cannot be heard, even in the ensemble parts, therefore is not on the bandstand. Something is wrong.

It is his custom to record only the Parker parts. Solos by other musicians, even those as eminent in the new movement as Dizzy Gillespie and Al Haig, let alone Lucky Thompson, do not merit Dean's time or materials. In his view these men are just barely good enough to occupy the same bandstand with Charlie Parker, of interest only because of their supporting roles. Benedetti places the recording machine on the lid of the toilet seat and closes the stall. Bird has missed the opening set.

In another part of the club, adjoining a corridor where empty beer cases are stacked, is a single, long, narrow, cheerless dressing room, shared by whatever talent is booked into the club. It resembles dressing rooms in night clubs all over America. A silver star on the door has drifted awry. The walls are beaverboard nailed to two-by-four studs and painted light green. The paint has begun to peel, and on the heads of the nails the paint has chipped away completely, so that the nail heads shine in the light. Instrument cases are stacked at one end of the dressing room. An enormous molded leather-sheathed case for the bass violin leans against the fiberboard carry-all for the vibraphone. There is a separate pile of smaller, black fiberboard cases for the bass drum, the snare, the tom-toms, and other accessories of the percussion outfit. In another corner winter overcoats that the musicians (none of whom has ever been to California) have ill-advisedly brought from New York are hung from wire hooks attached to the walls and old, rusted, bent coat hangers swinging from a lopsided crosspiece of pine round.

The dressing room door with its crooked star stands ajar. Inside, under the glare of neon fixtures that run along the top of a tarnished mirror, seated at the painted plywood counter where artists apply make-up and prepare for their performances, is a man with his back to the door. He has close-cropped hair that curls closely to the head. His body is strong and solid, the body of a workman, a stevedore, or a teamster. The man is hunched over the counter in a way that suggests intense concentration on the task before him. The man might be assembling the parts of a watch, but this is not what he is doing. The man is eating.

Pushed to the back edge of the make-up counter are the remains of the complete De Luxe Mexican dinner that is featured on the menu at Billy Berg's. It is called the *Comida Conquistador* and costs $4.75. Its various platters, saucers, and side dishes are a shambles of food thoroughly picked over and almost completely consumed. The meal has been washed down with three bottles of an imported Mexican beer called Tecate. The empty bottles stand nearby. Before the man at the counter lies a duplicate complete De Luxe *Comida Conquistador* dinner, hot and steaming. Its array of dishes has been set out in some sort of order, so that the eater can get at everything without having to reach or look up. There is a combination platter containing an enchilada, tamale, taco, and tostada, pats of butter, side dishes of refried beans, Spanish rice, flour tortillas, and small oval-shaped dishes of home-made salsa brava and guacamole. All of this food is rapidly following the first meal into the stomach of the eater. He eats working-man style, without niceties, in silence and with total concentration, with chewing and drinking noises, sounds of gratification, the clatter of a fork against crockery, the thump of the beer bottle as he plunks it down on the counter. From time to time he turns his head and listens to the music coming from the main room of the night club, where the band is playing without him.

Dean Benedetti appears at the dressing room door, makes the required pause, and softly calls, "Bird?" The response comes quickly, although the seated man neither turns nor looks up from the plates, but carries on with the tempo of his eating, between bites saying, "Hey, Dean!" Then he swallows, takes a long pull at the Mexican beer and adds, "Hey, man, dig this crazy Mex stuff!" The speaking voice is soft and has a pleasing lilt. It is well down in the baritone register of voices, on the husky side, but vibrant and alive, a voice with distinction that having heard once, you would not forget. It is a voice with music in it.

Benedetti steps across the threshold and is officially admitted. He is not a Mexican-food enthusiast. To Bird he says, "It don't kill me." The *don't* is deliberate. Errors in grammar and Dean's acquired, specialized, limited vocabulary are all part of the efforts he is making to become a white Negro. The high-school education received at Susanville, California, before entering the music profession, is an obstacle to his progress in the social group he esteems. In order to be in, it is necessary to master the argot of the black ghetto and jazz club. The musicians Dean has admired and seeks to emulate have all been black, and few of their generation have gone very far in school. The classes they attended met in other places—in bars, cabarets, dance halls, pads, dressing rooms, and all-night cafeterias —where the chief object for study was the playing of jazz.

Bird turns in his chair and glances down the corridor leading to the kitchen. He says, "Man, what's happening? Where's the waiter?"

Benedetti is supposed to do something about this. Benedetti says, "Listen, Bird, you ain't gonna scoff no more now, not after them two whole Mexican meals!"

"Trying to score me a bottle of booze," Bird explains. "See here, this is the first chance I had to eat since last night on the train. They carried a dining car, you know. It was on one of them big Santa Fe trains." Bird does not raise his head, but his eyes slide across the mirror toward Benedetti. "My old man used to work on them dining cars. Out of Kaycee, you know. He used to make this run, out to the Coast . . ." The sentence runs down. This is one of the few things he can remember now about his father, except that he could dance and play the piano a little. The food is more important, and the booze, which has not arrived.

Bird tells Benedetti to see to the booze. He continues to eat, head over the plates, fork sawing off three-inch sections of enchilada, one hand working the glass with the Mexican beer, which is being used as a chaser for the food. The beer is pale amber in color, and the beads stay on it a long time. Music seeps back into the dressing room. An elaborate phrase is being worked out by the saxophonist. The style is rhapsodic. The phrase does not hold Bird's attention. The tortillas are quartered and folded neatly and quickly with the deft motions of a man making a hand-rolled cigarette, only one-handed. The hands are broad and the fingers plump, the little finger almost as long as the forefinger, so that the hands look square and flat. The ends of the fingers taper, and the first joints of the fingers are wrinkled. They are hands that have undergone a great deal of discipline and training. Their movements are smooth and fast. They are the hands of a magician, or a pickpocket.

The waiter comes at last, a waiter in a starched jacket with a fifth of Gordon's gin, a clean highball glass, a bowl of ice cubes, and a choice of mixers. There are also revised checks for the food and beer, and a bar check for the bottle of liquor. "Mr. Berg say for you to sign these." The waiter speaks English with a Mexican accent.

Bird turns with a dramatic gesture and fixes the waiter with a stare. "My good man!" he exclaims. "Do you mean to tell me that these amenities are not on the house?"

The waiter says, "Mr. Berg, he say for you to please sign these checks."

Bird goes into his bag and finds a new speaking voice. It carries a strong undertone of surprise, almost of shock. The words are weighted and pompous. "It is customary in night clubs in the eastern states," Bird is saying, "to extend these courtesies to the *artist*." *Artist* is the key word. There is no implied hostility toward the waiter, who, like himself, is a member of the working class. The innuendo is directed toward the guilty party, the manager of the night club.

All of this goes over the head of the waiter. "You no sign?"

"Kindly leave the checks," Bird says in a peremptory voice. "Everything will be taken care of."

"You talk to Mr. Berg?"

"In due course," Bird assures the waiter. "I will take the matter up with Mr. Berg, personally." The name of the night club owner is made to sound like Mickey Mouse.

Dubiously the waiter leaves the checks, and, as an after-thought, a pencil. The waiter goes out and Dean Benedetti says, "Dig that kinda shit!"

"Yes, indeedy," Bird says. "The house is cheap." *Cheap* is cast in its own special tone of contempt. Bird has the trick of making words plastic, like musical notes. He picks up and examines the checks, studying the printing and serial numbers and the entries, as if he wants to see how such things are managed in California. Then he gathers the slips with the fingers of one hand and kneads them into a small wad of paper. With a smooth, supple movement of the wrist he flicks the wad of paper so that it strikes the corner of the dressing room wall where the beaverboard is joined. The wad does a double carom off the surfaces of the wall and flies into a metal waste basket standing in the corner.

"Two cushions and into the basket," Benedetti says, like a sports commentator.

Bird chuckles merrily and goes back to the final mop-up of the *Comida Conquistador*. The sound of the band playing in the main room of the night club continues to seep back through the walls of the dressing room. The band finishes *Dizzy Atmosphere* and goes into a blues at medium tempo called *Now's the Time*, and that is followed by *Confirmation*. After *Confirmation* comes another new tune called *Ornithology*. Bird listens with a third ear. He is familiar with all of these tunes because he wrote them. Some were written as long as five years ago, when he was an unknown musician in the reed section of a territorial band operating out of Kansas City under the leadership of a pianist named Jay McShann. Bird is able to detect any innovations played by the musicians on the bandstand as they take their solos, but hears nothing he has not heard before. Before coming to California Bird worked with the same band on Fifty-second Street, and, as he is aware, the musicians are all among the best in the new movement, but they seem to have exhausted their supply of musical ideas. Bird dips one of the tortillas into a bowl of salsa brava, which is the color of red paint and is made of tomatoes and many kinds of peppers. The salsa brava makes Bird's eyes water. He washes the food down with the last of the beer. "Dean," he says, "have a look at my sax case." His voice is offhand and functional again, but the same rich vibrato remains. "See what's happening with them reeds."

"Yes, indeedy," Benedetti says with enthusiasm. Dean locates the sax case in the pile of musical luggage. On the outside the case is much-traveled and battered. Benedetti unlocks the clasp and lays back the lid. Inside everything is clean and glistening. Snugly fitted into the red velvet nest lies the main section of a Selmer E-flat alto. There is a fine balance between its tubular part and the involved system of levers, keys, and buttons that makes up the working mechanism. The tube tapers into a brass bell that is engraved with the ornate crest of the manufacturer. The engraved letters show the registered number of the instrument and its place of manufacture—Paris, France. The horn is a genuine French Selmer, handcrafted by a firm employing the world's most-skilled instrument makers. "Looks like the same reeds you had back at the Three Deuces," Dean says. "Same box of Ricos."

"How about the mouthpiece?" Bird asks. "What's in the mouthpiece?"

Dean uncaps the mouthpiece. Clamped to the stationary part is a Rico number five reed. A number five is the stiffest reed made. It is the reed giving the biggest and most impressive sound on the saxophone. It is also the reed that requires the most sheer blowing power, and the reed that lends itself least to flexibility and speed of execution. A number five Rico reed is ordinarily used for brass band work where single, contrapuntal notes are wanted to fill in behind the heavier instruments. It is seldom if ever used by dance band or jazz musicians. It is a stiff, unyielding, unforgiving reed. It is very hard to control. "Rico number five," Dean Benedetti says. "Want me to change it for you?"

"Leave it in," Bird tells him.

Bird lights a cigarette. His eyes wander in the direction of the main room of the club, and he listens idly to the music from inside. "The five is cool," Bird says. *Cool* is a word he likes. It denotes all good qualities, and situations under control. Bird pushes the dinner plates to the back of the make-up counter and uncaps the fifth of Gordon's gin. He dumps the dregs of the beer into an empty platter and refills the glass with gin. The clean highball glass, the ice, and the mixers are ignored. Bird then drinks off the clear, warm gin. He drinks it off as if it were a dose of Bromo Seltzer, slowly and purposefully, pausing once to gulp for air. His eyes mist and brighten. Then he lies back on the chair like a big cat surfeited with food, breathing slowly and luxuriously. He smokes the cigarette. It turns to ash, a half an inch at a time. Beads of perspiration gather on his forehead and over the strong, prominent cheekbones that suggest a remote and fractional Indian ancestry.

Bird's color is a medium, coffee-bean brown. His skin is as smooth as a baby's skin. He is somewhere in his middle twenties. If he has white blood, it does not show. He is a Negro, of American working-class stock, with perhaps a small percentage of American Indian blood. His hair is black and somewhere between being kinky and curly. It is worn short because this is well before the time of the Afro. The nose thickens and broadens at the tip and fans out like the good African nose it is. The most African feature is the jaw, which is long and heavy, a powerful jaw with solid bone in it. Bird's eyes are brown, full, placid, luminous, like the eyes of a deer. He listens to the music seeping through the walls of the dressing room with professional interest. From *Ornithology* the band has gone into *Billie's Bounce*, which he also composed. He breathes slowly and deeply, and has the air of a man not about to hurry. The physical man is satisfied and quiescent—*cool*. Now it is time for another man to prepare.

Bird sits back in the rickety dressing room chair and refills the emptied glass of gin, studying the play of light through the clear liquid. He lights another cigarette and says, "Dean. The ax."

Benedetti slides the instrument case across the counter. The cigarette remains wedged between Bird's lips. He assembles the saxophone, part by part, into a whole instrument. Bird lifts the neckpiece and runs his fingers over the swanlike curve, as he might the calf of a woman's leg, fitting this part onto the main section. The main section itself is manufactured from three separate curved pieces, but they have been brazed so cleverly by the French craftsmen that it is barely possible to make out the joints where the parts dovetail. When the main section and the neck are joined and the key mechanism, with its intricate system of keys, pads, rods, and levers, is brought into alignment, then it is time for the mouthpiece, which is painstakingly slipped and twisted over the cork shoulder of the neck. Bird adjusts the clamp that holds the reed against the hollow opening into the mouthpiece. He holds the assembled saxophone so that it is reflected in the mirror. Light splashes off the polished metal surfaces. Over the curved metal he can see himself sitting in the chair, holding the saxophone, and the image is picked up and doubled on another, smaller mirror behind, so that he is staring at a whole gallery of identical, telescoping images of a man holding a saxophone, of himself. It is an effect that he likes and digs. He stares into the mirror and smiles— shyly.

"You know one thing, Bird," Dean Benedetti says. "I couldn't even get a squawk out of a Rico five. No kind'a way."

"Aw, now," Bird tells him. "It ain't that difficult, man." Bird fingers the saxophone, strikes a single note, and hands the instrument to Dean. "Let me hear your low B-flat, Dean."

Dean is unwilling to try. Bird urges the horn on him. Dean takes the saxophone, assumes a professional stance, and fingers the keys. Dean knows all about the alto saxophone because it was his main instrument for a number of years when he was with the bands. He has doubled on other reed instruments as well, the tenor and baritone saxes, and the clarinet, but the E-flat alto has been his main instrument. Dean puffs out his pigeon chest and blows as hard as he can. The saxophone gives off a queer noise, unmusical, harsh and hollow, like the wind inside a drainpipe. The reed, clamped in the mouthpiece of the Selmer, the number five Rico, is not quite being brought to the threshold of vibration, and as the result the column of air standing inside the saxophone remains unmoved and unmoving. Benedetti stamps his right heel pettishly against the floor. Benedetti's fingers dance on the buttons. The buttons rattle. The key bars clatter drily. There is no effect whatsoever on the pitch. The same hollow sound of wind inside a drainpipe is repeated. With the number five reed the saxophone will not resonate. It is dead.

Dean gasps for breath. "I can't make it, man," he says in a pinched tone and with a kind of muted hysteria, because this is a test of manhood he had wished to avoid. He remembers the night that someone told him about a saxophone player from Kansas City and he had gone to Minton's Playhouse in Harlem, where jazz musicians were jamming in those days, and listened to Bird for the first time, a black man playing his own instrument, on which Dean had attained a high degree of professional competence, and understood that this competence was as nothing, and that here was the way the instrument was intended to be played. Dean had studied every detail of Bird's method—fingering, breathing, embouchure. He imitated Bird's posture, stance, personal mannerisms, even personal habits. He bought number five reeds and practiced in secret, took Yoga breathing exercises to build up his wind, chewed towels to strengthen his jaws. He still couldn't make it. It was a sheer physical impossibility, like trying to lift twelve hundred pounds. Now the muted hysteria returns. As he sees it, the fault is that he was born white, an ofay, lacking the power and special knowledge of the black players who dominate jazz. He has missed out on their culture. That is the real trouble, the reason he stopped playing, became a man with a portable recording machine, a white Negro speaking the argot of the ghetto and the night club, getting himself thrown out of cabarets and drafty dance halls, riding the Greyhound bus from New York to Hollywood, so that he would have time to set up before Charlie Parker's first West Coast appearance. No one pays him to do this work, not even the man he birddogs. Dean has no visible means of support. It is easy for him to pick up enough money, *gold*, as he calls it, to pay expenses. Each day he rolls a few well-packed, professional-looking cigarettes from a supply of marijuana and peddles them on street corners, in music stores, and in men's rooms of night clubs.

"Like, nothing happening, dad!" he says sheepishly. He tries to fluff it off. "Nothing at all, man! Nothing happening."

But Bird is into him. "Bring it up out of the gut," Bird is saying. "Blow, Dean, blow through the *damn* horn!"

Benedetti keeps trying. Bird is bullying him. Dean knows it is useless to try any longer, and he tells himself that this is the last time he is going to get hung with this scene. He blows until his face is pink. The result is the same. "No way," he says and lays down the horn. "No kind'a way, man!"

"You got to use a lot of diaphragm!" Bird tells him. "Look'a here now, man, I just scoffed them two big dinners and I want to show you one thing . . ." Bird gets up out of the chair and faces Dean and sticks out his stomach and tenses his abdominal muscles. "Go ahead and belt me, Dean. Hit me in the gut, you dig?"

Dean doesn't want to do it. He doesn't want to hit Bird. He shrinks back. Bird calls him a fake, calls him a queer, calls him a "dirty ofay motherfucker," and finally Dean gets sore and doubles up his fist, plants both feet, and strikes out at Bird. Dean drives a right-hand punch into Bird's pushed-out stomach. It is like hitting heavy, tightly-stretched canvas, a tarpaulin or a boat cover.

Dean's fist bounces away. Bird laughs, a big, baritone laugh. Dean sniffs nervously, like a boxer in a gym, and gets himself a good bite of air and strikes again, as hard as he can hit, with his shoulder behind the blow, and the same thing happens, the fist bounces off the belly muscles, and Bird laughs and says, "See what I mean?" Bird sits down in the chair. "There's got to be a foundation. It's got to come from the bottom. After you get the wind up in your throat and mouth you can shape the sound any way you want, make it pretty or loud or soft, but first you got to have the foundation. It's got to come out of the gut."

Dean leans against the dressing room wall. He is breathing hard. "Bird, where you learn all this stuff?" Dean asks. "Where you learn to play the alto saxophone this kind'a way?"

"In Kansas City," Bird says gruffly.

"Did you listen to Lester Young back there?"

"Every night," Bird says. "Every night."

Bird takes the saxophone. He is wearing the trousers to a pin-stripe suit and red web suspenders over a white shirt. The trousers are made of hard twill-like material, and the creases across the backs of the legs and knees look deep, almost pre-set, built into the garment. Bird opens the zipper at the waistband of the trousers to give himself breathing space. The soft flat fingers fall into place on the buttons of the saxophone as if the generations of craftsmen in France had custom-designed the entire mechanism to fit Bird's hands. The cheekbones become prominent. The lower jaw is firmly set. The mouthpiece slides into the teeth and is held there like an object set in concrete. Chest muscles rise against the white shirt and the red suspenders.

Bird splays out both legs, flexing them so that his upper body, balanced on the tilted dressing room chair, is braced three ways to the floor. Then the man and the instrument become one. The fingers fit on the keys. The saxophone itself is an extension of the voice. When the first sounds come they are colored with the vibrato of Bird's own husky baritone, but that quality is much refined and extended. In the upper register the notes are thin and haunting. The quality of the tone is broad, as if two tones were combined, a thin transparent tone and a fat thick tone, one on top of the other, all blended into a single textured fabric of sound.

As the notes bubble out of the bell of the saxophone they carry implications of Bird's own speech, its inflections and rhythms. Heard through the horn, Bird's speech is no longer broken and indirect. When Bird talks he never seems wholly at ease. When he is with people that he knows well, he is apt to be gruff, jolly, and direct, but sometimes he is also shy and withdrawn. With people that he does not know Bird acts out many little roles. Sometimes he is a gangster. He can also be a detective, a plainclothes operative attached to the narcotics squad of one of the large cities. He is also an Amos and Andy radio character, a stereotype like Kingfish, rigged out with cone-pone diction and a jawbreaking vocabulary. He is a Mississippi nigger who has just arrived in town from the Delta, he is a con man and a humble average fellow. The roles that he plays are carefully studied and put together, along with the gestures and turns of speech and inflections that they require, and are used to cope with situations that arise during his encounters with people in the music world. But now he is no longer acting. He is himself. He is the musician that he has struggled and woodshedded and connived to become. He has the saxophone in his mouth. He is ready.

The first notes seem only half struck, like little puffs of sound that might have come from a harmonica or an old parlor organ. They are fleeting, almost grace notes, except that each is clearly outlined, each separate and attached to the next in a determined order.

Outside on the bandstand the tenor saxophonist is playing *Smoke Gets in Your Eyes*, and the tune drifts back into the dressing room. Bird picks up the harmonic line and plays along with the man outside. When the man outside modulates, Bird has already made the chord change, although in a different way. After a few bars Bird begins to play variations on what the other man is playing. The variations become more complicated. Bird paraphrases, inverts, moves up a minor third and continues, weighing the odd combinations of notes and the new chords that are being formed. He revises, edits, echoes. Fragments of *Mean to Me* and *Oh, What a Beautiful Morning* are rephrased so that they become part of the fresh melody that Bird is making out of *Smoke Gets in Your Eyes*, softly and privately as he sits tilted on the dressing room chair. When this no longer interests him he gives the saxophone a final workout from top to bottom. First, there is a fast set of scales, then a huge low B-flat, the only powerful, fortissimo note he has yet played, heavy and final, like the grunt of a hippo. Bird lays the saxophone across the open case. "Dean," he says, "how's the house?"

"You got a lot of fans out there, Bird," Dean says. "The house is packed."

"Yeah?" Bird says.

"It's really packed, man. Like——standing room only. You the greatest, man!"

Bird smiles. This is something of which he likes to be reminded. He smiles his disingenuous little-boy's smile.

"You're the cat they came to hear," Dean is saying. "Not Dizzy, or the others. Bird, they wanna hear Bird. Where's Bird at, that's what they're sayin'. What's happened to Bird? He cut out or broom back to the Apple? Ain't he gonna show? That's what they're sayin' out there!"

Bird considers the effort required to get him where he is, and how few people know anything about him and how many don't or care. The greatest, Dean says, and Dean is his severest critic. Dean knows. Dean is a broken saxophone player. Dean has given up, because it is too late for Dean. It is impossible for Dean to put in the hours, nights, weeks, months, years of trials, try-outs, auditions, woodshedding, road trips, battles of music and tests of manhood that were required to bring the saxophone up to Bird's level.

Dean is also the one musician Bird can never kid with any kind of musical fakery, because Dean has an ear that remembers anything that has ever been played, by Bird or anyone else, on a record or in a night club, like the coda tacked onto the end of a ballad fourteen months ago at a little place called the Downbeat Room in Boston (a club that has since folded due to the non-payment of alcoholic beverage taxes). Dean, whose own playing is nothing, just a carbon copy of everyone else's. The greatest, Dean says, only Bird has to prove it, over and over again, in clubs and in unheated dance halls reeking of cheap perfume and sour sweating bodies where the admission is a dollar and a quarter for studs and chicks are fifty cents and the floor of the men's room is strewn with used condoms, in cabarets and jazz policy clubs and places to jam, night after night, every night of the year, as he has been doing for ten years, ever since he was fifteen years of age and stopped going to high school and became a full-time professional musician in Kansas City. Bird is like a heavyweight champion who cannot afford to lose a single bout. He can afford not to work, not to play, not to show. He can goof, fail to make the scene, but the one thing that he cannot afford to do, ever, is lose.

There is a rap on the door and a short, dark man with a polite, severe, reformed tough-guy's face, wearing a silk suit of midnight blue, appears at the dressing room door and asks, "Which one of you people is Charlie Parker?"

Bird turns so that they are face to face. "Just who are you?"

"I'm Billy Berg," the man in the silk suit says. "I own the joint."

Benedetti backs off a step.

"Good evening, Mr. Billy Berg," Bird says.

"My waiter tells me you've run a tab and haven't signed anything." Berg lifts the cuff of the blue sleeve and consults a gold wrist watch. "You're also forty minutes overdue on the bandstand—after we put your name on the marquee."

"That's right," Bird says affably. "To play a man must eat." He takes a pull of the clear gin standing in the beer glass. "And drink."

"On my time?"

"Mr. Billy Berg, it took me one hour to get to this joint." Bird's tone is harder. "Cab fare was six singles. That's on account of there is no hotel for spades in Hollywood."

"That is something that I regret," Billy Berg says.

They stare at one another.

There is one thing that the owner of a night club cannot do. He cannot play the saxophone. He can report a musician to the union for failure to perform. With due cause he can withhold wages. But he cannot force him to play, and they both know this. Billy Berg does not intend to lose face or to be outstared, but he changes his tone slightly and says, "Have you seen the inside of the club?"

"Not as yet, Mr. Berg," Bird says.

"When you get inside," Billy Berg says, "you will see that this is the only club in Los Angeles with a mixed policy. That policy is not very popular in Hollywood, but that is the way the club is run."

Bird studies the entrepreneur with greater interest.

Billy Berg says, "This band is a gamble for me. The booking office refused to send you out here without an eight-weeks irrevocable contract. If the band bombs I stand to drop a bundle. I can afford that, because the war years have been good, but in that case this kind of a band won't be booked out here again for some time. When you're ready, Mr. Parker, a lot of people are waiting to hear you play."

"Roger," Bird says.

Billy Berg leaves the dressing room.

Dean Benedetti makes a face and says, "Heavy jive, man!"

"Maybe," Bird says. Night club operators are his natural enemies. Once in Cleveland a night club operator tried to beat him out of the band's wages for a week and Bird went out and borrowed a .45 automatic from a numbers man. Then he went back to the club and collected the money in cash. He has been shorted, conned, beat, screwed, and tattooed by night club operators. But there are exceptions. Jim Crow is a big issue with Bird. It is no longer something for the black musician to shrug off. If this is the first mixed club on the Coast, he wants to check it out. He tells Dean, "Maybe the cat is straight. Now, man, would you go out front and ask Diz to play my tune for me?"

"*Rhythm?*"

"No," Bird says. "I want him to play *Cherokee*."

"What tempo?"

"Diz will know."

"Roger!"

Benedetti goes out of the dressing room and disappears down the corridor.

Bird rolls down the sleeves of his shirt. It is yesterday's clean shirt that he put on aboard the Santa Fe train somewhere in New Mexico. The cuffs are soiled. Bird finds a necktie in the drawer where he flung it. It is a red-and-white tie knitted from strong, shiny yarn, and the slip knot, which has been run down the standing part but not unfastened, looks like it has been tied with a pair of pliers. The knot is thick, almost square, and the red and white stripes in the material are stretched out of shape. The tie looks awkward when he puts it on. The thick, bulging knot causes the points of the shirt to flare out. The ends of the tie are too short. They barely reach Bird's midriff, but he pays no attention to this.

Bird adjusts the neckstrap over the baby smooth skin of his neck. He slips into a new brown suede jacket, purchased on credit that afternoon at a hip haberdashery shop on Central Avenue, the main street of the Negro ghetto of Los Angeles, where he was known because of the records he has made. Bird pulls the jacket over his thick, heavy shoulders, failing to notice the wrinkle that remains in the collar. He snaps the clip of the neckstrap into the retaining ring on the back of the saxophone and slowly drinks off the last of the clear gin. He waits for the man outside to finish running chord changes on *Smoke Gets in Your Eyes*. His cigarette has burned down to a short, hot stub. He flips it against the mirror and the cigarette bounces into an empty plate. *Smoke Gets in Your Eyes* comes to an end. Outside there is silence. Bird sits on the dressing room chair. He has the look of an athlete waiting for a race to begin.

When Dean Benedetti reaches the main room *Smoke Gets in Your Eyes* is going into the coda. Lucky Thompson is standing at the front and center of the bandstand, which is at one end of the main room and large enough to accommodate six or seven musicians. The bandstand is a raised dais backed by a shell in the shape of a half dome. The decor—Hollywood *moderne* dating from about 1938—consists of beige imitation leather secured to the shell with large studded upholsterer's nails. Lucky Thompson is a round, sleepy-looking man with a short nose and a receding chin. He holds onto a long, breathy final note, moving the tenor saxophone around bodily to add a touch of shake vibrato. Dean hurries to the foot of the bandstand before the next number can start.

Dizzy Gillespie, the leader, is a man of medium height, wiry, nervous, and bustling with energy. Gillespie wears a double-breasted suit with a plaid pattern. Its breast pocket shows a clean white handkerchief carefully folded in three little rolls. His shirt is unstarched and immaculate. The collar of the shirt has long rolled points. Like exotic petals they reveal a satin tie, satin dipped in all the colors of the rainbow. A jaunty black beret tops the leader off.

"What's happening?" Dizzy wants to know. "What's Bird doing back there?" Under Dizzy's lower lip is a small goatee that bobs up and down as he talks.

"Bird's scoffed," Dean tells Dizzy. "Like double scoffed, man, and he's ready. He wants *Cherokee*."

"Um-mm!" Dizzy says. "Now?" Dizzy consults his gold wrist watch. "We're fifteen minutes over on the set." Dizzy tucks a glistening trumpet under one arm and massages his underlip with the ball of a finger.

"Bird wants *Cherokee*," Dean says.

Dizzy makes a face that says, "To know Bird you got to pay your dues." Dizzy tells Benedetti, "All reet, daddy," and takes the microphone and fixes the crowd with a rogueish grin. Over the microphone he says in his hoarse, friendly voice, "And now, ladies and gentlemen, as a little novelty number for you good people of the Far, Far West, we'd like to play a tune called *Cher-o-kee* . . ." Dizzy's pink tongue darts between puckering lips, like a man trying to dislodge a wayward bit of tobacco. Dizzy fingers the trumpet and riffles the buttons of the pistons. He turns to the others on the bandstand. "All right, men, all reet, *Cherokee*." Dizzy pauses and looks at the drummer and adds significantly, *"Up!"*

The drummer is Stan Levey. In a mixed band featuring black musicians he is an anomaly, a white drummer. Levey sits behind a battery of snares, cymbals, and tom-toms, a pale, athletic man with a craggy face and staring eyes. The band jacket that he wears looks like it has come from the same Broadway tailor as the one worn by Dean Benedetti. Levey tucks the drumsticks into a metal band around the bass drum and picks up a pair of wire brushes. When Levey goes to the wire brushes he is the fastest drummer in jazz, with a widely admired technique. Levey has been through the *Cherokee* routine before. Bird is going to walk on and Bird will want the tempo up, way up, as Dizzy has indicated by the way the word was emphasized as spoken. It is the drummer's responsibility and not the leader's or the soloist's to hold the tempo. Once decided upon, the tempo must stay where it is, must neither slow nor accelerate. That is one of the cardinal principles of the jazz rhythm section. Levey nods and leans forward. He wears a ready-to-spring look. The wrists which hold the wire brushes are loose. The brushes slide down over the head of the snare drum, which is between his knees, almost in his lap. Levey's hands and wrists move and become a blur of movement, a kind of two-handed stirring movement, too fast to see. The sounds of the brushes on the stretched head of the snare drum are a monstrous scratching, as on coarse sandpaper, done at a dazzling speed, so that the sounds run together. The pulse is a compelling four-four.

Cherokee is a long, intricate sixty-four-bar theme with in-volved chord changes. Besides setting and maintaining the tempo, it is Levey's job to close off each bar section and supply the cues for the next. These are all the responsibilities of the drummer and are of the greatest importance to the soloist. The sound of the wire brushes on the head of the snare swirls around the shell enclosing the bandstand and starts to flow out into the main room of the night club. The string bass falls in under the nervous, insistent pulse of the drums. The notes of the chords in *Cherokee* are heard in a series of steady, throb-bing fast fours. The piano enters, played by Al Haig, who looks like a bank clerk and is a music-conservatory graduate. Haig is neat and quiet as he sits at the keyboard in an erect but easy posture. He wears a conservative suit, a tie, and, under the jacket, a gray alpaca sweater. Haig does not play equal-time piano, or steady fours. He belongs to the new wave of chord feeders, especially favored by the new soloists. His chords are well chosen, voiced and shaded, and worked into the texture of the rhythm section of which he is a part.

Gillespie's trumpet and Lucky Thompson's saxophone begin running down the ensemble section of *Cherokee*. Behind them Milt Jackson strikes dissonant, off-time notes on the metal bars of his vibraphone. Everyone is aboard now, and the volume is building. In the main room of the night club people are alerted by the fast tempo. Conversation at the tables comes to a stop. There is an electric feeling of things about to happen. The crowd in the main room has increased until the entrance is blocked, and there are people standing against the black velvet drapes that cover the walls. Many of them are young musicians from name bands working in Hollywood. Shelly Manne, the drummer with the Stan Kenton Orchestra, which is at the Hollywood Palladium, and Jackie Mills, the drummer with the Boyd Raeburn Orchestra, have come to watch Stan Levey. Teddy Napoleon, the pianist with the Gene Krupa Orchestra, and Napoleon's opposite number from the Raeburn band, Dodo Marmarosa, are here to listen to Al Haig. Red Rodney and Tommy Allison, very young trumpet stars with those bands, have attended the opening to hear Dizzy Gillespie. There are also bass players who have come to hear Ray Brown and vibraphone players who have come to hear Milt Jackson. But everyone, drummers, pianists, bass players, vibraphone players, trumpet players, saxophone players, all of them are here to listen to Bird, because what Bird plays will apply to all of the instruments of jazz.

Dean Benedetti, struggling through the crowd now blocking the aisles, hears the first notes of the saxophone. The saxophone is somewhere in the distance, in the back of the club, moving out of the dressing room and down the passageway where the empty cases are stored. The notes are muffled, as if they were issuing from a tunnel, but they are becoming louder and stronger. Dean worms through the crowd and breaks free and runs without dignity for his toilet stall. Dean starts the portable tape machine as the first notes come over the wire.

The notes from the alto saxophone are more emphatic with each step taken by the player. The effect is like a band heard in the distance, a band in a parade that cannot yet be seen but is turning the corner and coming into view and suddenly getting louder. The saxophone moves slowly down the passageway until Bird stands framed in the main room of the night club, like a method actor making an entrance. His face is flushed and shining. The new suede jacket is flung open and the collar wrinkled. Underneath the flaring jacket can be seen the red suspenders. At his throat is the striped tie with its awkward knot.

Notes stream out of the horn, penetrating and multitudinous. The sound has its double edge, the two tones combined in one, the thin transparent tone and the fat thick tone, one on top of the other, blended into a single textured sound. It is at once veiled and clear, cloudy and incandescent. The saxophone is being played with the power of a trumpet, but the sound itself remains an extension of the human voice. The saxophone hums, purrs, sings, slides up and down the registers, talks, snarls, groans, exhorts, declaims, shouts, and cries out.

The notes funnel out of the curved end of the saxophone. When Bird moves the horn moves with him, both in one piece, like a statue turning on a pedestal. Notes rattle down the length of the bar, swing back across the back walls where the crowd is standing against the black velvet drapes, and walk in a broad sweep around the room.

Bird is a fantastical machine-gunner. He is attacking a crowded dugout with musical bullets.

Bird plays through the first sixty-four bars of *Cherokee*. He does not stop for breath. There is wind to spare. His belly muscles are feeding it up to him, and the number five reed is like a bird in his throat. The reed resists, stiffens, bends, flutters in the airstream. The column of air inside the saxophone is alive with song. Bird can feel the food in his gut and the fumes from the gin. He's cool. He's in control. Notes pop out of his fingers and go spinning away in skeins and clusters. The black velvet drapes and the low ceiling hold the sound so that notes pile up, one on top of another, until the entire room is packed and stuffed with sound. Bird can feel it feed back against the column of air inside the horn. The room is bigger than the one at the Three Deuces or any of the clubs on Fifty-second Street, and there are more people. The room of the night club is like a huge saxophone. When Bird strikes hard on a note the room quivers. All of the air inside the room vibrates. Bird bites down on the mouthpiece and plays through an odd scale that enters his head, something he remembers from one of the battles of music from his youth. It leads to the turnaround on *Cherokee*—

a new way to get there. As often happens when he is in full cry, he finds new ways to make the changes, new relationships between the sounds.

Bird spots people in the crowd, young musicians he knows, and sees black faces mixed with the white faces. In the back of the club a young Negro, wearing horn-rimmed glasses and very correct in Oxford gray threads, has climbed to the top of a table so that he can see as well as hear, and yells out the only word that comes to mind and describes the emotion he feels, the good black superlative, *"Motherfucker!"*

Bird picks "motherfucker" out of the air as if it were an "amen" shouted at a revival meeting, and like a skillful evangelist works it into the second chorus of *Cherokee*, a rapid group of descending dactyls. Bird makes a final sweep of the room. A path opens for him through the crowded aisles. He plays his way onto the bandstand. He can feel the thrust and drive of the rhythm section. The bandstand is vibrating. Al Haig feeds him cues for the changes and turnarounds. Levey has two kinds of time going. Bird is on top of them. With a rhythm section like this anything is possible. Bird stares over the curved mouthpiece at the drummer. He feels the kick of Levey's drums. The brushes attached to Levey's hands sizzle. Bird rides up on top of everything.

Dizzy zeroes in. With Dizzy, Bird trades eight-bar phrases. It's called a chase section. Dizzy is almost as fast as Bird and hard to lose. The eight-bar chase becomes a four-bar chase and involves the piano and the vibraphone. The band is moving in unison now. As good as it was before, it is now that much better. Everything is in focus. The music is stated with authority. The element missing has been fitted into place. It's all there, complete and irrevocable. The music of the jazz revolution reaches a new level of everything—concept, tonality, complexity, rhythmic energy.

In the men's room, behind the OUT OF ORDER sign tacked to the door of the toilet stall, Dean Benedetti is glued to his seat. The headphones are clamped hard over his ears. He monitors the sounds of the saxophone that are pulsing through the wire from the bandstand. As the music rises and falls the decibel needle oscillates across the etched scale. When the needle brushes against the red warning mark, Dean cuts the volume back so that he will not overcut the tapes and distort the notes of the saxophone. He hunches over the portable recording machine, being careful not to upset its precarious balance. His face is rigid with concentration. Dean permits himself a faint smile of satisfaction. With his free hand he takes a grease marking pen from the pocket of his band jacket and inscribes the spool: Monday, December 10, 1945, Billy Berg's, Hollywood. It's going to be one of his best spools. Bird on one of his great nights!

Benedetti has caught most of the good nights since Bird first appeared in New York, but he wonders about the nights he missed, nights that nobody recorded, in Kansas City, when Bird was coming up.

PART I

Heavenly City

When Charlie Parker appeared on the jazz scene nobody knew much about him, except that he came from Kansas City. Nobody knew much about Kansas City either. It had no great reputation as a jazz center, nothing to compare with Chicago of the Capone era or New Orleans. Kansas City was an obscure, provincial place, off the well-beaten band routes, beyond the notice of talent scouts, artists-and-repertoire men, and booking agents. Occasionally there was a hint as to the quality of its music. The great pianist Art Tatum, who from time to time worked a Kansas City club as a single, had remarked, "Kansas City is a cellar, a dark place where the best wines are kept. And the music is different there, too."

Sidemen in name bands, in town for a one-nighter and eager to flex their muscles at after-hours jam sessions, had been roughly handled by the local talent. Kansas City saxophonists in particular were a formidable lot. One night in 1934 at a club called the Cherry Blossom the leading saxophonist in jazz, Coleman Hawkins, had been challenged by a trio of Kansas City men—Lester Young, Herschel Evans, and Ben Webster, all unknown at the time—in a session that wore on until late the next day and left Hawkins battered and defeated. It was the first time in the memory of jazzmen that the king of the tenor saxophone had been bested in one of these impromptu cutting sessions. A few months later two astute talent scouts, John Hammond of New York and Joe Glaser of Chicago, went down to see for themselves. To their astonishment, they found Kansas City a honeycomb of night clubs that had been operating without interruption all through Prohibition, as if the Volstead Act did not exist, and all through the hard years of the early 1930s, as if there were no Depression either.

They discovered cabarets, show bars, refurbished speakeasies, music lounges, taverns, bars, honky-tonks, dance halls, saloons, and just plain night clubs—places with names like the Reno and Sunset, the Cherry Blossom, Subway, Hi-Hat, Panama, Greenleaf Gardens, Bar le Duc, Elmer Bean's Club and Lucille's Band Box, College Inn, Amos and Andy, Novelty Club, Bucket of Blood, Boulevard Lounge, Vanity Fair, the Jail (where the men in the band wore striped uniforms), and the Hey-Hay Club (where they dressed in overalls and sat on a farm wagon). All of these clubs had live music. The music began early in the evening and carried straight through the night until dawn, the official closing hour, though seldom enforced. At daybreak roving musicians, finished with their regular jobs, would circulate through the district carrying their instruments and jam until well into the morning. In certain clubs shifts of musicians relieved one another and entertainment continued around the clock. There were boogie-woogie, trios, quartets, skiffle bands with jugs and washboards, small dance bands with a sax and trumpet in the front line supported by a three-man rhythm section, and full-sized dance orchestras with complete brass and reed sections.

There was more music in Kansas City than had been heard in America since the gilt palaces and funky butt dance halls of the Storyville section of New Orleans closed their doors at the beginning of World War I. You heard it on the sidewalks from blues singers, fresh in from one of the cities of the Southwest and self-accompanied on a twelve-string guitar, and from blind gospel shouters jingling their coins to four-four time in a tin cup nailed to a white cane.

As a prime wheat and cattle market, Kansas City was the commercial center for an area extending as far south as Houston and as far west as Denver, encompassing most of the Southwest and a large part of the plains and prairie empire. For that sizable portion of the United States, it was also the entertainment center, a wide-open town that attracted big and little spenders of the Southwest with its alluring array of cabarets, gambling halls, bars, brothels, and restaurants, all organized by a crime syndicate operating openly under the benign despotism of the Democratic political boss, Tom Pendergast. Kansas City was fun town and sin city rolled into one, very much like Las Vegas today. It was also a narcotics center, the headquarters for the distribution of cocaine, morphine, and heroin throughout the Southwest.

Scouts Hammond and Glaser were not concerned with the open display of vice and corruption. Tatum had been right. Kansas City was a storehouse of vintage jazz talent. The leading jazzmen from Texas, Oklahoma, Arkansas, and the Southwest had converged there, attracted by employment opportunities and Pendergast's Depression-proof climate. There were more jobs for musicians than anywhere else in America, and more bands. By eastern standards the jobs paid badly, but the musicians did not complain. The cost of living was low, and they were doing what they loved best. At the Reno Club men in the Count Basie Orchestra were making eighteen dollars a week and working from nine P.M. to six A.M., seven nights a week, and the band was the hottest thing Hammond had ever heard. A remarkable feature of music in Kansas City was that nobody told the musicians what to play or how to play it. Jazz-men were free to create as the spirit moved them. So long as the music was danceable and lively and the visiting firemen were satisfied, the gangsters who ran the clubs did not inter-fere. As the result of favoring conditions—steady work, isola-tion, a concentration of talent, and almost total lack of com-mercial pressures—Kansas City had developed a jazz style of its own. Blues and riff tunes supplied the framework for band performances that relied heavily on improvised solos. Ham-mond and Glaser lost no time in signing the Count Basie Or-chestra, Oran "Hot Lips" Page, Lester Young, Jimmy Rushing, Big Joe Turner, and Pete Johnson to national booking-agency and recording-company contracts. The emigration of Kansas City jazzmen began. Soon they were being heard by the rest of America, and their ideas of rhythm and melody began to color the mainstream of jazz.

Charlie Parker was very much a product of this vigorous grassroots musical culture. Charlie grew up in Kansas City dur-ing the Pendergast era. When the first generation of Kansas City jazzmen, Basie and the others, were being scouted by tal-ent hunters from the sophisticated north, Charlie was already familiar with their playing. They were the carefully studied models upon whose style his own was centered.

Charlie was born Charles Parker, Jr., August 29, 1920, of Afro-American parents in Kansas City, Kansas, a suburb of Kansas City proper. Metropolis and suburb, separated by the Kaw River, one lying in Kansas and the other in Missouri, were part of the same greater urban area, then having a population of about half a million people, fifteen percent of whom were black. His father was Charles Parker, Sr., a native of Memphis, more recently a resident of Kansas City, stranded there at the end of a vaudeville tour. He was a singer and dancer. Charlie's mother, Addie Boyley, was a local girl whom the entertainer had married in her seventeenth year.

When Charlie was eight or nine, without having shown any special musical aptitude beyond blowing across the ends of curtain rods, the Parker family moved across the Kaw River and into a rented frame dwelling at 1516 Olive Street. The new Parker home lay in the heart of the black ghetto and within easy walking distance of the area where the night clubs were concentrated. A boy idling in the vicinity of Twelfth and Vine, fifteen minutes away from the Olive Street address, might have heard the sounds of a jam session coming through the doors of the Sunset Club, where these affairs frequently ran on into the morning hours; at night, of course, he would have heard a great deal more. Here, on the edge of the entertainment district of Kansas City, Charlie spent his formative and impressionable years, from 1928 to 1939, years that coincided exactly with the period of Democratic machine government in Kansas City. In 1928, the year that the Parkers moved in from the suburbs, Tom Pendergast, a boss cut in the pattern of early Irish-American vote manipulators and ballot-box stuffers, seized control of the city hall following a coup involving the city manager. Then began the dozen-odd years of good times, full employment for musicians, and the renaissance of Kansas City jazz. Pendergast continued to run the show until 1939, when he was convicted of defrauding the government of over half a million dollars in income taxes and was sentenced to federal prison. Pendergast's downfall brought an end to prosperity and good times. At once reform elements took over, night clubs closed by the score, and jobs for musicians dried up like Kansas wheat in a drought year. In 1939, a few weeks after Pendergast's conviction for tax fraud, Charlie Parker, Jr., left Kansas City, never to return as a permanent resident. He was the leader of the saxophone section of the Jay McShann Orchestra, the last of the major Kansas City bands. He was married and divorced, the father of a son, a member of the musicians' union, an airily self-confident, intransigent, and precocious young man of nineteen.

Between 1928 and 1939, the Pendergast years, Charlie Parker underwent a metamorphosis from an unexceptional schoolboy studying at Crispus Attucks grammar school to one of the geniuses of American music. Charlie's first recordings, obscure transcriptions made for a small radio station in Wichita where the Jay McShann Orchestra stopped for two weeks on its first major tour, show him to have been on the threshold of a system of musical ideas that was to change the course of jazz style. All of this had been accomplished by the time he was scarcely twenty. Only a careful examination of the musical climate of his native Kansas City will upset the theory, much circulated and too readily come by, that Charlie Parker was a "natural-born genius," somehow sprung full-loined from the brow of a modern Jupiter, divinely inspired and beyond logical explanation. Genius he was, but the nature of that genius is spelled out by the unusual and fully savored circumstances of his environment and by the kind of musical empiricism brought to bear on the material so lavishly made available. Just as surely as Mozart grew out of the musical culture of eighteenth-century Salzburg, with its operas and concert halls, its abundant supply of master players and teachers, its enthusiastic and knowledgeable audiences and princely patrons, Charlie Parker was the product of another, similarly intense and pervasive musical culture—demotic, contemporary, and Afro-American. Kansas City was the last of the black ghettos that evolved a coherent jazz style. There have been no such centers since Charlie Parker's time, jazz having become a non-regional if not universal commodity. Charlie Parker was the last of a breed of jazzmen apprenticed at an early age, styled in emulation of great master players, tempered in the rough-and-tumble school of the jam session, a master of his craft by the end of his teens, disciplined to the exacting requirements of the big swing bands, and, eventually, the maverick who turned his back on the big bands to create, almost single-handedly, the musical revolution of the Forties.

Getting Straight

When the Parkers moved from the suburbs to the house on Olive Street, it was to place Charles, Sr., more closely in touch with events of the entertainment world, for Kansas City was also a regional booking center and turn-around point for vaudeville routes; but things did not work out as expected. Vaudeville was in the process of being killed by the new media of the 1920s, the phonograph record, radio, and sound movies; by the end of the decade it would be dead. Parker's talents as a singer and dancer were small. A few tours with circuses playing the prairie hinterlands kept him going for a year or so. Then he was obliged to seek employment as a Pullman chef. When Charles, Sr., was at home he played the piano, and there was good music to be heard on the phonograph: Louis Armstrong, Bessie Smith, Ma Rainey, Duke Ellington, and Blind Lemon Jefferson. Then his wanderings became more erratic, and his visits home less frequent. About 1931 Charles, Sr., dropped out of the family picture altogether and drifted off into a shadowy existence as a gambler and pimp. Before Charlie finished grammar school the father had left home for good, and Addie Parker became the family breadwinner. "He went off to live with some woman," she said, ". . . so I became mother, father, everything to Charles. He thought he was Mama's little man. He never worked like the other little boys in the neighborhood. He wanted to carry papers, but I wouldn't let him. I thought I could take care of him until he was a man." *

In the protective, permissive, matrifocal soil of the reorganized household Charlie's personality developed like an exotic flower. Mrs. Parker placed her son in nearby Crispus Attucks grammar school and went to work as a domestic in white homes outside the district. The family managed to make ends meet, without Charles, Jr., having to carry papers, just as Mrs. Parker wished. At Crispus Attucks Charlie was a model student and a favorite with his teachers. He was bright, alert, quick, and retentive of memory, and his grades were well above average. It was Mrs. Parker's hope that he might someday become a doctor. Small sums from her earnings were set aside in a savings account toward this fragile hope.

After an unremarkable childhood, as a spoiled and pampered young man of thirteen, Charlie entered Lincoln High School, located at a distance of some ten or fifteen minutes' walk across town. It was a walk with its share of temptations. One detour took schoolboys to the neighborhood of Twelfth and Vine, where frequently the sounds of live music could be heard coming through the doors of the Sunset Club. Lincoln High was typical of black schools in that era, and many today. There was one in every large city of America. It was named after the Great Emancipator. It was overcrowded, run down, lacking in

---

* Interview in *Jazz Review*, Vol. 3, No. 8 (September-October 1960), pp.7–11.

modern facilities, and, according to Charlie's report to his mother, the quality of its instruction was poor. "They don't teach you anything there, mama," Charlie complained. "The teachers are no good." The better-than-average grades from Crispus Attucks soon sagged to lower scholastic levels.

The only subject to interest Charlie was the music elective offered to those who signed up for brass band practice. The music department at Lincoln was an exception to the rest, and in this respect also, Lincoln was typical of black secondary schools. The department was run by a dedicated and competent professional, Alonzo Lewis, who had come to Lincoln in the early Twenties. But the tradition of Lincoln's music department went back much further, to Major N. Clark Smith, a veteran of the Spanish-American war and retired United States Army bandmaster, who had begun building bands on the classic Sousa model in the early years of the century. During Major Smith's time Lincoln marching bands became a regular fixture at parades and important civic functions—became, in fact, the pride of Kansas City, a town that took these matters seriously. Following Major Smith's retirement, Alonzo Lewis took over the department, and the tradition of professionally directed musical instruction and smart, well-trained marching bands continued.

An impressive number of Lincoln graduates had used the Lincoln bands as stepping stones to professional careers. Lamar Wright, cornetist with the Bennie Moten Orchestra, the first Kansas City band to record (for RCA Victor in 1923); Jap Allen, an early rival bandleader; Walter Page, leader of the formidable Oklahoma City Blue Devils and later bassist with the Count Basie Orchestra; alto saxophonist Eli Logan, and bandleader Harlan Leonard were all Lincoln alumni and protégés of Major Smith, as were many others who left no deep mark in jazz but pursued successful careers as sidemen in territorial bands. Lincoln undergraduates were aware of these successes, as today students are aware of eminent alumni in sports, arts, and sciences. Success in one of the few professions then open to black people represented a desirable, indeed one of the highest levels of achievement. When Charlie Parker entered Lincoln another generation of successful musicians was in the making.

As a freshman without previous musical training, Charlie was given a baritone horn, one of the easiest instruments to play, and assigned to a rear rank in the marching band, where he contributed a few simple notes from the bass clef. It was a dull business and not what the pampered freshman had in mind, nothing like the music he heard outside the Sunset Club or when he played stick ball in front of the Lee house on Euclid Street, where the George E. Lee Orchestra rehearsed between road trips. As late as 1950, in a taped interview, Charlie spoke of this early experience with mixed amusement and contempt for the cumbersome baritone horn, "All I did was play *coop, coop—coop, coop.*" An alto horn gave equally uninteresting results. As Mrs. Parker tells the story: "He was given a tuba to play. I didn't go for that; it was so heavy and funny coiled around him with just his head sticking out. So I got him another instrument." The money being set aside for the medical career was used to buy her son the instrument of his choice, a used alto saxophone, not very appropriate for brass band work, but one that would head Charlie in a new direction. "The first horn I got him only cost me forty-five dollars at Mitchell's down on Main Street. . . . I had it overhauled, and it ran into money."

In her willingness to please her son Mrs. Parker had made an ill-advised purchase. After the overhaul the new saxophone still was prone to all manner of malfunctions. Tootie Clarkin, a night club operator who knew Charlie in his first professional period, when the forty-five-dollar saxophone was still in service, remembers "an old sax, made in Paris in 1898, that was like nothing. It had rubber bands and cellophane paper all over it and the valves were always sticking and the pads always leaking . . . he had to hold it sideways to make it blow." Nothing daunted, and seeing that the saxophone had come into the family without a proper case, Mrs. Parker proceeded to make one from pillow ticking, white with blue stripes, bought at a goods store, and stitched firmly together on the family sewing machine.

On campus Charlie's reputation escalated rapidly. At Lincoln High in the early 1930s owning one's own saxophone was the equivalent of driving an imported sports car today. The saxophone, his brashness, and the fact that he had grown to be a big, chunky boy for his thirteen years enabled Charlie to ingratiate himself with a group of juniors and seniors who were organizing an amateur dance band called the Deans of Swing. Charlie was allowed to join as the fourth member of the reed section and became a kind of band mascot. Bassist Gene Ramey, later one of Parker's closest friends and another member of the McShann orchestra, remembers the Deans of Swing and Charlie's ambiguous role:

"Charlie was in a group from K.C., Missouri and I was in one from K.C., Kansas. In those days there were a lot of mock band battles. They were judged by enthusiasm and loyalty rather than musical ability. When you played your home town, you won. The leader of Bird's band was a pianist and singer named Lawrence '88' Keyes, who later became well-known in the East. It was the first band Bird ever worked in, and he seemed to me then just like a happy-go-lucky kid. In fact, the whole outfit was a school band, and Bird was hardly fully grown at the time—he was barely fourteen years old! Bird wasn't doing anything, musically speaking, at that period. In fact, he was the saddest thing in the band, and the other members gave him something of a hard time." *

Once Charlie attached himself to the Deans of Swing all thoughts of earning a high school diploma, let alone a medical degree, were abandoned. With a single-mindedness typical of him in later life, Charlie poured all of his energies into music, reporting his little successes to his mother. She responded with enthusiasm, as she did to all of his achievements. He secured her permission to take part in modest nightly excursions of the Deans to play jobs off-campus. There were such minor "battles of bands" as described by Gene Ramey. Once the Deans played the Gaiety Theatre in the night club area; another time the resourceful Keyes lined up a series of weekend dances at an old

* Interview with Gene Ramey, *Jazz Review*, Vol. 3, No. 9 (November 1960).

dance hall where admission was twenty-five cents per person. In spite of warnings that he was not making passing grades, he continued to neglect his studies. The Deans of Swing became his sole interest in life.

That summer the main topic of conversation among Lincoln undergraduates was the Union Station Massacre, which took place June 17, 1933, during the last week of school. A famous bank robber named Frank Nash, on the nation's list of most-wanted criminals, had been captured at Hot Springs, Arkansas, and was being taken to the federal penitentiary at Leavenworth under a heavy guard of peace officers. The itinerary called for a transfer from trains to cars at Union Station in downtown Kansas City. There the party was ambushed by a hand-picked trio of gangsters, all then residing in Kansas City under the protective cover of the Pendergast machine. Nash's friends included Verne Miller, Adam Richetti, and Pretty Boy Floyd. All ranked high on the most-wanted list published by the FBI. Armed with machine guns and automatic pistols, Richetti, Miller, and Pretty Boy opened fire on the Nash party in the parking lot of the station. When the shootout was over an Oklahoma police chief, two Kansas City detectives, and Special Agent Caffrey of the FBI, as well as the unfortunate and manacled Nash, lay dead or dying. Floyd received a bullet slug in the shoulder and was treated by surgeons at a downtown hospital; then, guarded by Johnny Lazia, the "Al Capone of Kansas City," Pretty Boy Floyd was escorted out the back door of the hospital and given safe conduct to another state.

The episode excited undergraduates at Lincoln. They felt a little proud that Kansas City had outdone any spectacle created by Hollywood. They were a little scared, too. Many of the businesses and all of the night clubs in the Afro-American district were run by gangsters operating under the direct supervision of Lazia. One of the Deans of Swing claimed to have seen Lazia one afternoon alighting from a black Lincoln sedan parked in front of a night club at Eighteenth and Vine, only a few blocks away from the school playground.

When school opened in September there was bad news waiting for Charlie. His freshman report card had contained so many No Passes that he was denied sophomore status. Instead of trying to make good his mistakes, he concentrated on music and the Deans of Swing. This too was frustrating business. He was beginning to see through his role as the band mascot, and realize his musical shortcomings. The Deans were nothing more than a kid band. Nor did they work often enough. (He was further depressed by the sudden death of his best friend, a senior named Robert Simpson, the star trombonist of the Deans.) He needed advanced instruction on the saxophone, but that was not available in the music curriculum. Alonzo Lewis suggested an Albert system clarinet as a good foundation reed instrument. Charlie found the clarinet, once the mainstay of New Orleans bands, a difficult task-master. Anyway it was out of date, long since relegated to a minor role by the advent of larger orchestras with their saxophone choirs, and by the first generation of the great saxophone players.

The change in Charlie's lifestyle, toward which he had been verging during his sophomore year, was brought about by a simple event, a new job for Mrs. Parker. About this time she had the good fortune to obtain regular work as a charwoman at the main offices of the Western Union Telegraph Company in downtown Kansas City. By her standards the pay was good and the job several cuts above her usual employment as a casual domestic. The main offices of the telegraph company closed at midnight, opening again at eight the following morning. It was Mrs. Parker's job to dust, mop, and clean during those hours when the office was not in use. In order to get to work Mrs. Parker would board a streetcar at the corner of Twelfth and Olive at half-past eleven each night, starting off to work when Kansas City folk out for a good time were beginning their nocturnal rounds. Between the hours of midnight and eight the next morning there would be no one at home to supervise Charlie, to see that he studied or went to bed on time. As he by now had learned, these were the hours when activities in the night clubs shifted into high gear. The action started off in a low key at around nine or ten, but no one interested in music visited the clubs at so early an hour. The musicians had not yet warmed to their night's work. They were still shaking off the lethargy that had followed the extraordinary efforts of the night before. For the first hour or two they would play safe, easy numbers, taking no chances, challenging no one to a serious exchange of solos, getting their fingers loose, adjusting reeds and embouchures, building wind, and clearing their minds for the competitive and creative events of the hours ahead. If one wanted to hear Kansas City musicians at their best, it was pointless to arrive before midnight.

In 1935 Kansas City saxophone playing had reached its best level. The town contained a number of resident master players. Ben Webster had returned to Kansas City from a long barnstorming tour throughout the Southwest and had taken over as solo tenor with the Clouds of Joy, giving that orchestra its first powerful reed voice. Lester Young, ex-Oklahoma City Blue Devils, worked at the Reno Club, where Count Basie had reorganized the remnants of the Bennie Moten Orchestra following the sudden death of the leader on an operating table. At Lester's side sat his friend and arch-rival, Herschel Evans, who played like Coleman Hawkins and had come to Kansas City when Troy Floyd's Dreamland Orchestra broke up in San Antonio. Their nightly duels at the Reno were the talk of the town. Ben Webster, Herschel, and Lester, they were the Big Three on tenor. There were others as well, fine players like Dick Wilson with the Clouds; Budd Johnson with George E. Lee; Buck Douglas of the Douglas Brothers Orchestra; Herman Walder with Thamon Hayes; Henry Bridges, Jr.; Buddy Tate and Jimmy Keith, all capable of taking the measure of the top three on an inspired night. Among the alto saxophonists the best were Eddie Barefield, ex-Bennie Moten; Walter Knight; Tommy Douglas; Harlan Leonard and Woody Walder with Thamon Hayes; and Prof Smith, another Texan and Blue Devil alumnus, and co-leader with Basie of the band at the Reno Club. This corps of saxophonists, drawn from all parts of the Southwest, was in fact equal to any that could be mustered from all of the most famous bands in the north and east, as events of the late 1930s were to prove. The Southwest was saxophone country. Kansas City had become *the* saxophone player's town.

And every one of these jazzmen was black. Downtown at the Muehlebach Hotel white musicians played watered-down imitations of Afro-American style and made good money doing it, but the source of the real ideas, the sounds and the rhythms, was the Negro district. The renaissance of Southwestern jazz style that reached its highest level in Kansas City during Charlie's formative years was almost wholly an Afro-American art.

As Charlie saw it, these were the men to emulate and from whom he might learn—just how, he was not yet certain. None gave lessons. None was available for consultation in the daytime. They were asleep then, recovering from the exertions of the night before. They would appear in the late afternoons, dressed in their sharp suits of dark material, with double-breasted vests hung with watch chains. They wore shoes with narrow toes and big tweed touring caps with snaps on the brim, and in the cold weather long black undertaker overcoats like the ones sported by the gangster bosses who ran the night clubs. One would see them walking carelessly through Paseo Park with its shade trees or standing on the corner of Twelfth and Vine, in front of the Sunset Club, talking in their strange musicians' jargon. They used such expressions as *a bum kick* for a bad experience, or *cut*, meaning to get the better of a rival at a blowing session, or *cats with sharp claws* to describe dangerous rivals. Good things were *solid*, and better ones *out of the world*. They called their instruments *axes*. A job was a *gig*, alcohol *juice*, and marijuana cigarettes *mezzirolls* or *sticks*. They joked about Charlie's pillow-ticking carrying case for his saxophone, and toyed with him and called him "kid," "kidman," and "boy." He let it bounce off. The seniors in the Deans of Swing had been doing the same thing all year without getting under his skin. They fended off his questions and made private jokes and jived on in their special inside language and told him to wait until he was eighteen and a member of 627, the colored local of the Musicians' Protective Association in Kansas City. Then it would be time for him. "Who bought them long-stem pants for you, son, your mama?"

Charlie made friends with an armless beggar who could be

found in good weather at the corner of Eighteenth and Paseo. Once the man had been in vaudeville, like Charles, Sr., but now there was no market for his skills—he could deal a hand of cards, sort coins, sketch portraits, and shoot dice, all with his toes. He wore long black knit stockings with the heel and front part cut away. Charlie would unbag his saxophone and play the blues, and the armless man would beat time carefully with a pair of tin spoons. It helped attract a crowd, and put a few coins in the tin cup.

They would be joined by Old Man Virgil, who appeared with a homemade bass constructed of a broomstick, a length of clothesline, and a galvanized wash tub. Virgil twanged away on his crude instrument and sang a blues accompaniment in a mournful voice. He was a big, raggedly dressed old man, weighing well over two hundred pounds, strong and fiercely independent, who lived by himself in a shack on Fifteenth Street west of Paseo. He earned a living collecting junk from waste bins and refuse piles behind stores. The blues and fiddle playing were only a sideline. The old man would begin his collecting rounds each evening along the alleyways of the district, after the pavement had cooled. His conveyance was a sturdy old mason's wheelbarrow with long wooden handles. In it he would pile rags, odd electrical parts, bits of copper and iron, bottles and sacks, to be sorted out at the shack and sold off in lots. Sometimes Charlie would follow Virgil home to help with the sorting. Virgil found out how old he was and told him he had a little time to spend before he could expect to get into the music business.

Charlie Parker had no mind to wait another four years until he was eighteen and old enough to join the union. Hadn't Prof Smith begun as a boy of sixteen, learning to play by hanging out around speakeasies and listening to raggedy little Dallas bands? Charlie had a horn of his own and he meant to master it. He had to get into the clubs. He had to study out the details of handling the horn. There was some kind of way. He had to see how the jazzmen held their horns, worked their embouchures and used their fingers, and how they breathed. He'd heard that Lester and Herschel prepared their own reeds and filed and sandpapered the standard mouthpieces of their instruments in a special way and put pads under the keys to speed up the action. He had to find out. There were a great many details involved with the sounds that came out of the horns. Lester even used false fingering, to get different qualities out of the same note. He had to hear what they played, inside the big clubs, in the late hours of the morning, when they were going strong. He had to get the feel of a rhythm section, like the one in the Basie band, with Basie on piano, Walter Page on bass, and his friend Jesse Price on drums, its beat rising under the soloists like a flood tide. That was the way it was to be done, not by learning notes set down on staffed paper and doing exercises out of a method book, or starting in with an obsolete instrument like the Albert clarinet.

Charlie would stand on the wooden porch of the Olive Street house, dressed in an old black slicker and wearing long pants and a black hat which he pulled down over his ears, hopeful that the hat and the slicker would make him look older than his fourteen years. When his mother boarded the street car to go to work at the Western Union Telegraph Company, he would start out. He had no idea of when he would be back. That would depend upon the adventures of the evening. There was so much to see and hear. He only knew that he would return ahead of his mother, some time in the night or perhaps as dawn lay over the bluffs behind the Missouri River, and that he would slip into bed for a few hours sleep and in all probability miss part of his classes the following day at high school. Those classes no longer seemed of any importance to him, not even the band class under Alonzo Lewis.

Kansas City Mystique

His mother would board the street car and he would watch its lighted windows move across the intersection and hear it clattering and careening along the rails headed west on Twelfth to the downtown section of Kansas City, where the Western Union Telegraph Company had its offices. It would be time for him to start. He would light a cigarette, one of the ten-cent brands that had appeared during the Depression years—part of the grown-up image he was trying to convey—and shoulder the bag his mother had sewn from pillow ticking and containing the alto saxophone, and he would start out. When he got to the corner he could look west on Twelfth, in the direction the street car had taken, and see the cluster of electric signs at Twelfth and Paseo. The electric signs formed a blazing ring of light; everything down there looked almost like it did in the daytime.

The signs were made of coiled neon tubing, which had just come into that part of Kansas City. Some of the newer night clubs had them. The rest had old-fashioned displays with small electric light bulbs spelling out the letters. On some of the signs an arrow of light chased itself around the border. Others flashed off and on. On some of the neon signs the colors flickered and changed from pale blue to the color of orange soda water. There was a big sign over the front of the Sunset Club and another over the Boulevard Lounge, and farther along you saw signs advertising the Lone Star and the Cherry Blossom.

When Charlie was within two or three blocks of the Sunset Club, he would be able to hear the music. It wasn't coming through the walls of the club, or through the open door or the windows, because the door and the windows were kept closed. It was coming over a loudspeaker that Piney Brown, the manager, had built directly above the front door, so that the speaker faced out onto Twelfth Street. The loudspeaker was connected up with the bandstand, and there was also a special microphone behind the bar so that when Joe Turner felt like it he could sing the blues. Joe Turner was the bartender at the Sunset, and was called Big Joe because he was really big, over six feet and one inch tall. Big Joe had light yellow-brown skin and was very handsome, with heavy, sleepy eyes. His voice was something on the order of a trombone, although a little higher in compass, and when he sang the blues he shouted them out. The amplifying system made the voice bigger than life and pumped it out into the street. When Big Joe's blues came pouring out onto the street through the loudspeaker, people loitering and trying to make up their minds what to do would find themselves going into the Sunset Club.

As everybody knew, the band at the Sunset Club was the smallest in Kansas City. It consisted of two pieces. The drummer was named Murl Johnson, and a very good man with the snare and tom-toms. The man who made things go at the Sunset was the piano player, whose name was Pete Johnson. They weren't related. Pete Johnson was called "Roll 'em Pete" because he had worked out a fast way of playing the notes in the bass, eight notes to the bar, with the left hand, which some people said came from Texas and called the boogie-woogie or the dirty dozens. Pete called it the fast blues, and sometimes the railroad blues. He was a stumpy man, almost as broad as tall, like a weight lifter in a sideshow, who wore a double-breasted suit as big as a tent. He had a short neck that turned into two thick wrinkles when he hunched over the piano. Pete's fingers looked like bunches of bananas. You would think them too broad for the keys of the piano, but when he was playing fast the tips of the fingers struck the keys in deft little strokes. The right hand had a life of its own and would play off-time and strange heartbreak chords and even imitate a train whistle while the left hand made the sound of the wheels on the rails. That was the railroad blues. His face was round, brown and smooth, and seemed to wear an expression as if he was always being surprised at whatever came out of the piano and the things his two hands were up to.

With Pete Johnson and Murl Johnson the Sunset didn't need a bass player to fill out the rhythm section. The piano and the drums were a whole section by themselves. That left a good deal of room on the bandstand. On certain nights of the week, when other clubs had closed, musicians working in those places would bring their horns and drop into the Sunset for a drink and talk to Piney Brown, who liked nothing better than good music and was known all over Kansas City as a friend of musicians. Eventually the musicians who had dropped into the Sunset for a drink would find their way to the bandstand. Instrument cases would be flung open and a jam session would start. There were no music stands and no such thing as written music. Sometimes Ben Webster, the big man in the Clouds of Joy, would be there and his tenor saxophone would boom out and fill up the place. Or there might be Jimmy Keith, or Eli Logan, or Walter Knight, or Jim "Daddy" Walker on guitar. Sometimes there would be eight or ten musicians on the bandstand, with hardly room left to move around, and only two of them on Piney Brown's payroll. The musicians would wait their turn and take solos, one after the other, all playing their versions of the same tune. You never knew which nights jam sessions would take place at the Sunset. That depended on who was in town and with what band and the mood of the musicians on a particular night. Once you got within earshot of the Sunset, you could tell what was going on inside from the loudspeaker. If you had a good ear you could call off the names of the musicians who were playing inside without seeing them. A lot of people who listened to music and followed musicians could do that. Charlie was learning that the way a man played his instrument, his style on it, was a kind of signature, as plain as a man's handwriting once you knew it. Every musician had a different tone and a different way of phrasing.

If there was a jam session going on at the Sunset, Charlie would stay and listen. If not, he would continue on his rounds. There was so much for him to hear. You couldn't possibly cover Kansas City in a single night. He found the best places to go and the best times, so that he could hear musicians that interested him the most, and how to get in and out of the clubs and how to avoid trouble. Fourteen-year-olds weren't supposed to be admitted to the clubs, and the bigger ones employed bouncers who would throw you out. His favorite place was the Reno, which musicians called the boss club in Kansas City. It was owned by "Papa Sol" Epstein, who was in with the Pendergast machine and could operate the Reno any way he liked without worrying about closing hours or trouble with the police. The police never went in there. They had orders to stay out. The Reno had a floor show with first-class acts. After the floor shows the band played and there was dancing. That's when you heard the real jazz. After the last floor show there would be a long set ending up at around five-thirty or six in the morning.

The band at the Reno Club was the best in town. It was really the old Bennie Moten band, which Count Basie and Prof Smith had taken over after Moten died having his tonsils taken out. Charlie had heard every one of the other Kansas City bands, the same way that guys at Lincoln tried to see all of the pitchers on the Kansas City baseball team at Ruppert Stadium. Charlie had heard George E. Lee, the Douglas Brothers, Paul Banks, Chauncey Downs, Clarence Love, Dave Lewis, the Jesse

Stone Blues Serenaders, Thamon Hayes's Orchestra, Jap Allen's Cotton Club Orchestra, and of course Andy Kirk and the Twelve Clouds. They were all big dance bands with twelve or thirteen musicians, and appeared at different ballrooms, Paseo Hall or El Torreon at Thirty-first and Gillham. Once a year, in May, all the Kansas City bands appeared on a single night, at a tournament staged for the benefit of Local 627, to help pay for the union building on Highland Avenue. One after another, they would battle each other, set for set, for annual supremacy. The winner was judged by the applause of the dancers.

If Charlie did not find a jam session in progress at the Sunset, he would continue down Twelfth Street, pushed along by the momentum of Pete Johnson's piano playing, his steps light, the upper half of his body weaving gently from side to side in a counter rhythm to his legs and feet. It was different from the feeling he had in the marching band at Lincoln. The brass band made you want to march and perhaps strut a bit, but it didn't get inside you or make your steps lighter or give you the sense of weaving and of two rhythms going at the same time. Nobody could do that better than Pete Johnson, except of course the band at the Reno. He had to go nine blocks down Twelfth as far as Cherry. The Reno stood near the corner and took up the lower floor of a big building, its red brick turned gray and sooty over the years. Charlie would stand in front of the entrance, under the marquee, hearing the music very faintly, and read the sign on the brick wall next to the entrance:

FOUR BIG FLOOR SHOWS EVERY NIGHT
FIVE FIRST CLASS ACTS

CHRISTINE BUCKNER	*World's Fastest Tap Dancer*
HATTIE KNOWLES	*Comedienne*
FRED LOWELL	*Songs and Jokes*
MATTIE HEADMAN	*Blues and Novelty Singer*
SHEPHERD MC NEELY	*Your Master of Ceremonies*

FLOOR SHOWS PROMPTLY AT 10 — 12 — 2 — 4

plus

MUSIC FOR YOUR DANCING PLEASURE UNTIL . . . . ?

by the COUNT BASIE—PROF SMITH BAND OF RHYTHM

No Cover Charge   No Minimum   Drinks from 15¢

Charlie knew better than to use the front entrance. To maintain order, so the police wouldn't come into the club, Papa Sol had hired a former boxer named Rusty, a red-haired man with cauliflower ears, beetle-brows, and a hoarse, croaking voice. Rusty had thrown Charlie out of the club several times, and made it clear that he was not to come back, at least not until he was much older; but there was another and better way. Charlie would walk down Cherry to the alley that led to a paved lot right behind the club. In good weather it would be crowded with people. It was a regular hang-out for all the musicians in town who weren't working on a particular night, and a place where leaders recruited sidemen for jobs. If you kept your ears open you would hear what was going on in the band business—how Andy Kirk got stranded in Tennessee on a tour for the Malco Theater chain and had to wire for fare home, but once back in Kansas City went directly into the Vanity Fair for a long engagement; or about the trouble the Thamon Hayes Orchestra ran into with the gangsters who controlled the union in Chicago after they had made a big hit on their opening week at a new night club. Circulating among the crowd would be fifteen or twenty women, some of them as old as his mother, who solicited men and took them up a long flight of wooden stairs leading to rooms in what was supposed to be a hotel on the second floor. They wore low-cut dresses without brassieres or panties and showed you everything when they walked. In the middle of the back lot stood one of the lunch wagons you saw all over the district at night. They were owned by John Agnos, who had a concession from Tom Pendergast. For ten cents you could buy sandwiches made up from brains or pigs' feet or pigs' snouts, or "short thighs," which were roasted legs of chicken. That was Charlie's favorite. He'd eat two or three every night, using change his mother gave him for spending money, so that he would always have a little something in his pocket for anything that he needed.

Between shows the musicians would come out through a door built in the back of the bandstand. They would take a ten-minute break and move around among the at-liberty men and bandleaders and whores, and patronize the lunch wagon, slapping their chicken legs and sandwiches with hot sauces. Charlie knew all of the musicians by sight: Count Basie, who smiled a lot and could get people laughing with his quiet little jokes; Walter Page, called "Big Four" because of his beat; his half brother, "Lips" Page, the most powerful trumpet player in town; and of course all of the men in the saxophone section that had no rival in Kansas City, bouncy little Jack Washington, who played the baritone, Prof Smith and Herschel Evans, who had Texas accents and looked like school teachers, and Lester Young, a tall, fleshy, handsome man with shining eyes and brushed-back hair.

Lester was Charlie's idol, but admired from afar. Charlie's one special friend was Jesse Price, the drummer, a tall man with high cheekbones and dark, reddish skin, like an old copper kettle. Jesse was part Mohawk Indian and came from Memphis, Charlie's father's home town. Jesse Price had been in vaudeville and toured with Bessie Smith, the Empress of the Blues, and worked on the Mississippi riverboats before coming to Kansas City with Ma Rainey's Georgia Minstrels. Jesse gave the rhythm section its strength and smoothness. He had a soft, high-pitched voice, strange for a big man, and treated Charlie almost like a grown-up. Jesse was a serious man. He didn't jive and joke like the others.

"Charlie, how you doin'?" he would ask in his high-pitched, kindly voice. Or, "How you doin', Yardbird?" That name was beginning to stick, on account of Charlie's liking for chicken. "See you got your horn with you, all wrapped up in the case your mama made." Jesse would pause and smile knowingly. "Come down to sit in with us tonight?" That was their private signal, and meant that things inside were under control. When the intermission was over the musicians would start back, dusting hot sauce and sandwich crumbs from their fingers, and Charlie would mingle with them and Jesse would sneak him through the door at the back of the club. On the bandstand inside Charlie would stumble through chairs and instrument stands, and there would be a period of scraping and confusion. Jesse would sneak him to a steep, narrow set of stairs leading to a little balcony hanging out over the stage. It was dark up there, and Rusty the bouncer never came up—the stairs were too steep for his crooked legs. Neither did the waitresses. They didn't bother any more. It was too difficult to carry trays with mixed drinks up and down the stairs. Once Charlie was safely in the balcony, he was set for the rest of the night.

The bandstand below had been built to hold a much smaller band. Count Basie had to sit at a grand piano placed on the floor, but that didn't seem to bother Basie too much, because he had been a theater-pit pianist in vaudeville and the old silent movies before getting into the jazz business. A hole had been cut through the top of the shell so that Walter Page's bass would fit. The rest of the musicians, Jesse with his drum outfit and the five brass and four saxophones, sat in two rows, the saxes in front, the men so close that each was almost touching his neighbor.

Some nights Charlie would get to the Reno in time for the floor show, usually the one at two A.M. From the balcony, leaning over the front rail, he could look down on the performers. He could have dropped a spitball on the top of Shepherd McNeeley's head if he'd wanted. Heads, hats, hairbands, shoulders, detached hands that seemed to move by themselves, and moving feet. That was all he saw of the performers, although he could hear well enough. You hardly saw anything of the faces of the performers. For the floor shows the band had to play backgrounds and short introductions and provide cues and fill-ins for jokes and patter. It played by bits and snatches and was silent a lot of the time. The most interesting part of the floor show was Christine Buckner's act. She was a thin, nervous woman built like a greyhound. She would dance to a piece like *Nagasaki* or *Tiger Rag*, always played at a fast, crazy tempo. Then you would hear Jesse's drum magic, rolls and flams and rim shots that punctuated the sound of Christine Buckner's taps. The dancer's black skin would shine with sweat and her hard, pointed breasts would jiggle inside the sequin brassiere.

She would dance for ten or twelve minutes straight, milking the audience for applause and building toward a climax. Jesse was the only drummer in Kansas City with hands fast enough to keep up with her. He would hold to her strict time, building the dynamics so that the music seemed to be getting faster and faster, when it actually wasn't.

After the floor show the band would settle down and play "music for the dancing pleasure" of the customers. They sat in booths or at tables around the dance floor, few ever bothering Basie with requests because they had learned that the music would be better without any. The band played a lot of blues and original material called riff numbers, made up by Basie and Prof Smith. One of Charlie's favorites was a tune called *One O'Clock Jump*. Basie would start off with eight bars, as if he were talking to the musicians with the piano, describing the tune and setting down its exact time. Then Walter Page's bass would walk in with the steady flow of fat notes and Jesse would bring the drums up under Big Four and the rhythm section would start laying down the beat upon which the rest of the band waited. You would catch a glint of brass as the trumpets and trombones were raised along the back row. The men in the section would fan the notes with metal derbies. After that the saxes would come in with the bitter-sweet blend of reed sounds—one baritone, two tenors, and one alto—and everything would come together. The whole band would play two or three choruses of the riff, each one a little stronger and heavier, but keeping the same strict beat; then it would be time for the solos.

A trumpet fanfare would leap out of the web of sound with sudden brilliance. It was Walter Page's half brother, Oran, called Lips because of his chops. The long, wide, full lips with their razor edges wrapped themselves around the metal mouthpiece of the trumpet until it was lost in the folds. Lips would blow until the veins stood out on his forehead and the notes bounced back off the farthest ends of the club. He had the biggest sound in Kansas City. When Lips changed to the plunger mute the sound became hot and wicked. Lips usually took the first solo, to get the band loose. Basie sat smiling up from the piano, throwing off little blue phrases that told Lips to keep going. When the trumpet solo was finished there would be a reply from the trombone or one of the reeds, perhaps Prof Smith with his pure, smooth alto cutting through the heavier instruments, or Herschel Evans's buttery-soft notes from the tenor. Then the whole band would be coming on once more, and the balcony where Charlie sat would begin to vibrate. He could feel the pulse coming up through his feet.

If he looked across the beams of the spotlights that shone toward the bandstand, he could see a lavender haze, shimmering like air over a street on a hot summer day. He watched the heavy smoke that curled and wreathed, floating lazily upward, borne along by the waves of music. It had a sharp, pungent odor and made a biting sensation in his nose. It was smoke from sticks of tea that were being passed from one man to another on the bandstand below. After twenty minutes of the set Charlie would feel himself borne along in the pleasant lavender haze. Then the long narrow interior of the Reno Club would grow deeper. The bar, the polished glassware in front of the mirror, the waitresses poised like blackbirds, ready to fly to their customers—the tables, booths, dancers, musicians, orchestra, everything in the Reno Club seemed to be exactly where it belonged, as if it had been there forever and would never change, fixed in time and space, and time itself stopped. He was getting high. Now he could hear the things that he had missed, the miniature sounds—Basie's little blue comments, a silvery skein of notes played by Prof as a counter line to Herschel, muted chortling of screened brass under the saxophone choir, a light scurrying of sticks across the head of the snare drum as Jesse marked off a bar section, wispy little phrases that entered somebody's mind because of something just played. You could get high on the balcony at the Reno, in a single set, without spending a dime.

Then came the best part of all. Lester rose to take a solo. Lester had his own way of holding the big saxophone, off to one side, that he had picked up at the Reno, because the bandstand was so crowded. He would stand up and slouch forward, holding the horn off to his right. And the notes would come pouring out. Charlie would hear the fat, airy notes, the long flowing lines, the big grunting sounds and the light tripping ones. Then he would remove his own horn from its case, adjust the neck-strap, and place his fingers on the keys. The reed would be in his mouth but no sound would come out. Charlie wasn't putting any air into the horn. He was playing along with Lester, only in his head, his fingers moving on the keys the way Lester's fingers moved, hearing the long flowery line, imagining that he was shaping the notes in the same way.

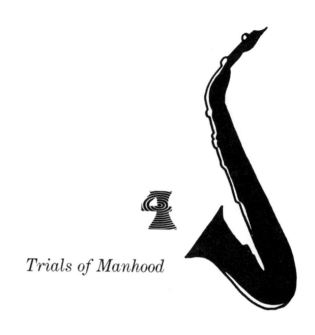

Trials of Manhood

The master saxophonist Charlie had chosen as his model had arrived in Kansas City the year before, after a long tour of duty with territorial bands. Lester Young was then in his twenty-fifth year. Nowadays it seems a little hard to believe that he had behind him seventeen years of professional experience. Lester had begun as a child drummer in a band managed by his father, Billy Young, a Tuskegee graduate. It was called the Billy Young Orchestra and was staffed entirely by members of the Young family. The Young children were taught to sing tunes as soon as they could walk. At the age of five or six they were able to read music and play at least one instrument. Billy played all of the instruments and was featured on trumpet.

Mrs. Young was the band pianist. Brothers and sisters filled in on strings and saxophones. At the age of eight Lester began making regular tours as the band drummer. The musicians wintered in New Orleans, where Lester was born in 1909, and toured nine or ten months of the year with tent shows and small circus companies. With the tent shows they helped attract crowds and sell snake oil and patent medicine. On tour with the circus they were responsible for the pre-show parade and the grand entrance, and furnished accompaniment for clowns, bareback riders, and high-wire acts. It was part of a tradition that went back to the Chautauqua and minstrel show.

In his early teens Lester switched from drums, which had given him a firm grasp of the principles of keeping, and compounding, time, because—as he said—he was lazy and the drummer's outfit was cumbersome to carry about. His next instrument was the alto saxophone. In the Young family band everyone was expected to read music at sight; Lester rebelled against the mandate. He did learn to read, but with great reluctance, and felt that it impeded his flow of ideas. He was a strange, aloof young man, tall and rather fleshy, with dreamy eyes—a born Bohemian. When Lester was about sixteen and beginning to feel his manhood, there had been a bitter conflict with his father and he had resigned from the family band, joining Art Bronson's Bostonians, a territorial dance band operating out of Salina, Kansas.

Along with his father's orthodoxy Lester also rejected the widely imitated saxophone style pioneered by Coleman Hawkins. Lester's models were two white jazzmen, Jimmy Dorsey and Frankie Trumbauer. Their clean technique, pure vibrato-less tone, and melodic sense appealed to Lester. It was pretty. Trumbauer always had "a little story to tell." Lester carried Trumbauer's records around with him, studying the nuances of white saxophone style. When he made his final switch of instruments, from alto to tenor, while he was with the Bostonians, Lester retained something of Trumbauer's airy sound. But Lester was more than just a pretty player. He could punctuate his nice phrases with earth-shaking pedal notes, and he projected a mighty swing.

In those years Lester was beginning to get himself and his ideas together. After the tenure with the Bostonians came a year with King Oliver, the famous New Orleans trumpeter and one of the great figures of jazz, then working out the twilight of a distinguished career as leader of a small band that played one-nighters in the prairie states. Before attaining his majority Lester was recruited by the barnstorming Oklahoma City Blue Devils, the scourge of every band in the Southwest. The Blue Devils thrived on battles of bands. Their reed section smothered rivals under an overwhelming torrent of sound. They were masters of the riff style. Each section bristled with solo talent. They had taken on and beaten the best bands from Kansas City, even Bennie Moten. Had not the Depression intervened, no other band could have touched them. Beginning in 1930 one star after another had left the Blue Devils—Basie, Lips Page, Walter Page, Eddie Durham, Jimmy Rushing—all of them to seek employment in Pendergast's Depression-proof Kansas City. Prof Smith and Lester Young had stayed until the bitter end, until the band went broke on an ill-fated Eastern road trip. Then they had followed the others to Kansas City. Now they were all back together for the job at the Reno, a collection of kindred spirits speaking the same musical language, sharing a mystique acquired over years of jamming and barnstorming together. The idea man and star soloist was Lester Young, destined to become one of the great players of jazz.

When Charlie Parker began hanging around the Reno Club he paid only passing attention to the beautiful, liquid-toned playing of Prof Smith; that influence would come later. Lester Young was his man. Sitting in the balcony, or standing behind the club, Charlie would finger his old saxophone and follow Lester's lines note for note. The modeling of the phrases, the shaping of the notes, the subtle use of dynamics—all of these elements were absorbed by Charlie's inner ear, even though he lacked the technical ability to execute them.

When possible, Charlie would stay over for the jam sessions that followed the last floor show. Then he would have the opportunity to hear Lester engage the best local players and stars with traveling orchestras. The magisterial Coleman

Hawkins might be in Kansas City for the night, or the man known as Rabbit, Johnny Hodges, with the Duke Ellington Orchestra. White jazz stars got down to the Reno to test themselves against the black players. Dick Stabile, leader of a society dance band that played at the Muehlebach Hotel, could surprise people with his jazz ability. Stabile had a clear, singing tone that impressed Charlie. Stabile had modeled his style on that of Rudy Wiedoeft, for many years a popular vaudeville attraction. Charlie had heard Wiedoeft once at a downtown theatre and listened to the wondrous effects achieved by this virtuoso of the C-melody saxophone. All of these players were influences. Charlie became a serious student of saxophone style. From night to night he lived in a world of sound, the good, rich Kansas City sound of saxophones.

The jam sessions at the Reno began around five in the morning, after the last floor show. The men in the Count Basie Orchestra would take a long break. They had been playing almost continuously since nine in the evening. The men would visit the lunch wagon or the bar and then go back to the stage. Jesse Price would readjust his drums, and soon he and Walter Page would have a soft beat loping along. Basie would sit down at the piano bench until he was relieved by Sam Price or Mary Lou Williams from the Clouds of Joy. Then horn players from other clubs or barnstorming bands would begin to drop in, and the stage at the Reno Club would be swarming with musicians waiting to take their solos. On Sunday mornings there was a big affair called a spook breakfast. It was attended by a mixture of business and professional men and night people. Food was served along with beer and mixed drinks, and the jamming might continue until noon, depending upon the general enthusiasm and number of musicians present.

Only established stars dared test themselves in the fast company that gathered at the Reno. There were also minor-league jam sessions at lesser clubs, carried on with the same competitive spirit, where anyone could try his luck. At four or five in the morning the streets would be full of roving musicians carrying saxophones, trumpets, trombones, and guitars. Bassists would hump their awkward, whale-backed instruments and walk with the rest. Pianists had nothing to carry and took their chances with the ancient uprights in the honky-tonks. Drummers relied on a set of house traps, but carried a favorite cymbal, imported from Turkey and purchased at a fancy price at Jenkins's Music Store, and their favorite set of drumsticks. One night at the Subway Club Jesse Price vanquished all of the other drummers in town by playing one hundred and eleven straight choruses of *Nagasaki*, an improvisation that lasted almost an hour.

The musicians drifted from club to club, from door to door, checking on the action inside, welcome wherever they appeared. The institution of the jam session was strongly supported by the small-time gangsters who ran the clubs. The unpredictable nature of the night's events, of who might fall in and what might happen, attracted as many customers as an artist's name featured on a marquee. Many of the club owners hired a house rhythm section as an open invitation to jam sessions. They stood guest musicians to free drinks. Sometimes they supplied meals. At Chief Ellis Burton's Yellow Front Saloon a pot of chili and another of crawdads, a favorite Kansas City seafood delicacy, was kept simmering on a stove in the backroom. Piney Brown, the manager of the Sunset Club, Eddie Spitz at the College Inn, and Milton Morris at the Novelty Club were jazz fans. None of the club owners tried to tell the musicians what to play.

The kitty was a standard fixture in district clubs. A metal receptacle attached to a cardboard-cutout cat, tiger, or spook, the kitty encouraged donations. Some of the kitties were wired for lights and had winking eyes that flashed on and off. The donations were divided among the musicians at the end of the evening. Sometimes gangsters would roll dice to see who fed the kitty. On occasion a black Cadillac with bullet-proof windows would draw up in front of one of the clubs and underworld boss Johnny Lazia and his mob would take over. Guns would be checked and the doors locked. Cigars would be lighted with five- and ten-dollar bills. The kitty would be fattened, and a musician might go home with as much as twenty dollars for his night's fun.

In the memory of the oldest veteran of territorial bands, there had never been a town like Kansas City for jamming. The sessions had much in common with tribal initiation rites. They were constant trials of manhood in which jazzmen were tested. Technical mastery of an instrument was only a beginning. The jammer required a thorough command of standard tunes, blues, and other materials of the time. It was necessary to know the melodic and harmonic character of the material by heart. What counted were fresh ideas. When a man began to repeat himself, he lost his audience. He could not mark time by playing clichés or riff figures. He might improvise on a chord scheme for two or three choruses. He might go on for ten. The giants were known to continue for twenty or thirty without running out of ideas. What counted was the ability to run variations on the changes, to create new melodies, and to control the complicated rhythmic patterns that generate that mysterious ingredient of jazz known as "swing."

One of the most famous jam sessions in Kansas City history took place at the Cherry Blossom at Twelfth and Vine. Charlie missed out on it but heard the story retold many times. The famous Fletcher Henderson Orchestra had been in town to play a one-nighter, to be followed the next night by a similar stand in St. Louis. Stories of the "bad" Kaycee saxophonists had reached Coleman Hawkins, the star of Henderson's reed section and the man credited with being the founding father of jazz saxophone. Hawkins had resolved to put the upstarts in their place and dropped into the Cherry Blossom to jam after the regular job had finished. Within an hour every saxophonist in town had converged on the club. The contest continued through the rest of the night and into the next morning. By noon four were still going: Hawkins, Ben Webster from the Clouds of Joy, and Herschel Evans and Lester Young from the Reno Club band. The eventual winner was Lester Young, who was still fresh and full of ideas by mid-afternoon. It was the first time Coleman Hawkins had been bested in a cutting session and the victory did a great deal for the prestige of Kansas City saxophone players. Coleman Hawkins was said to have burned out the engine of his new Cadillac racing across Missouri to reach St. Louis in time for the next Henderson engagement. After this great victory Lester Young had been nicknamed The President, an allusion to Franklin Delano Roosevelt and the new image being projected from the White House. Later the nickname was shortened to "Pres" and followed Lester throughout his career.

The great infighters were skilled at taking another man's ideas, often his best ones, and standing them on their head, or using them as inspiration for a new set of improvisations. To make things difficult for newcomers, odd riffs might be set behind the soloist, so that he had to create his line with one ear and listen to what was going on behind him with the other. Unnervingly fast tempi and transpositions into seldom-used keys were also sprung on the beginner.

Charlie could not take part in one of the big-league affairs. It would have to be at an impromptu contest open to anyone at the lowest end of the musical pecking order. Although he didn't realize it, his musical ideas were running dangerously ahead of his ability to execute them. What he had picked up amounted to a massive and disorganized smattering, without reference to any coherent method. His fingering had been worked up from visual observation. No one had placed his fingers on the keys for him, as a good reed teacher would have. Such hints as he pried from his idols were suitable only for more advanced players. Charlie's refusal to apply himself at Lincoln, even to his music studies, had closed off a whole area of musical harmony about which he understood almost nothing, and with which he one day would have to reckon.

The exposure to the music was itself invaluable. Charlie's inner ear soaked up the sound and mood of Kansas City jazz. If he didn't know how a note was to be produced, he knew how it should *sound*. Everything was being filed away for future reference, to be sorted out later. Charlie's lonely, questing spirit was being saturated to the core of its being with the Negro idiom of the blues, upon which saxophone playing in Kansas City was actually based.

Charlie's first attempt to jam took place at a club called the High Hat, at Twenty-second and Vine. It was typical of obscure cabarets that had begun as speakeasies. The house band was led by a modishly dressed tenor saxophonist named Jimmy Keith. Others in the band at the High Hat Club included two of Charlie's old comrades from the Deans of Swing, Lawrence Keyes and trumpeter James Ross, now graduated from Lincoln High and working as full-time professional musicians. Keyes and Ross greeted Charlie with friendly nods. That gave him extra confidence. He adjusted the rubber bands around his 1898 saxophone and waited his turn. Charlie knew the chords of the first part of *Up the Lazy River* and the eight-bar bridge of *Honeysuckle Rose*. From these harmonic bits and pieces he planned to put together his improvisation.

When his turn came Charlie mounted the bandstand. Cued by Lawrence Keyes's piano chords and supported by the rhythm section, he played his way gingerly into the solo. Keyes comped painstakingly, and there were encouraging toots from James Ross. Charlie completed two choruses of the hybrid melody. Jimmy Keith, a slender man with a waspish moustache, stood at his side, smiling patronizingly.

Some demon intransigence prompted him to press his luck and attempt an innovation. Perhaps he thought of himself on stage at the Reno and in full command of his instrument. He chose *Body and Soul*, played a whole chorus, then, in the next, tried to double the time. The rhythm section hurriedly doubled up behind him. But the bold rhythmic effects that Charlie imagined ready to fall under his fingers, to the confoundment of Jimmy Keith and the others, failed to dovetail. There were some difficult technical problems involved. Everything came unglued at once. He missed a note, then made a still more fatal lapse of time. The time moved ahead and beyond him. Charlie faltered to a stop. Dead silence fell in the High Hat Club. Lawrence Keyes tried to keep him afloat by repeating the chords of the last bar played. L'il Phil, the drummer, had stopped altogether. The terrible, mounting silence seemed to explode in an outburst of guffaws. Charlie climbed down from the bandstand. His eyes were hot with tears. He packed his horn back in its pillow-ticking case and went home. He cried, and did not play again for three months. An uncertain success had been turned into a minor disaster.

Along with his many other misconceptions Charlie had picked up the idea that all music was somehow played in a single, common key. "I never thought about keys being different or anything like that," he told Lawrence Keyes. Keyes explained the musical facts of life. There was no one universal key. There were a dozen major ones, one for each note on the piano keyboard, half a tone apart, like steps on a ladder. All of Charlie's musical thinking had been based on a naive, wrong assumption.

The revelation was enough to have sidetracked an ordinary career, or at least sent a young musician in search of proper instruction; Charlie was unaware of any abyss yawning beneath his feet. He would work out his own solution to the problems that had occupied European composers for years. Charlie wanted no help from anyone. He knew he had to work it out.

"It's got to be figured out," he told his mother, "some kind of way. . . ."

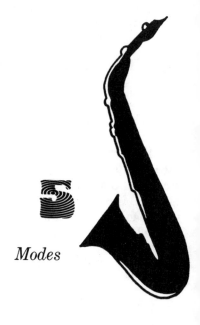

5

Modes

If genius is a capacity for taking infinite pains, it may also be a matter of taking a wrong course and arriving at a new destination. If, as Charlie reasoned, there were twelve major keys, and scales, then he would have to learn all twelve. Had he not been so hard-headed—had he asked—Alonzo Lewis could have told him that jazz was performed in a very few keys, the ones easiest for the wind players. Lawrence Keyes might have told him the same thing. The first major Kansas City band, the famous Bennie Moten Orchestra, the parent organization that had produced Count Basie, had played everything in B-flat, although Moten, a pianist, having come from a ragtime background, could read well enough in other keys. Most Kansas City jazzmen were not comfortable in more than three or four keys. As for the other keys, only schooled musicians could handle them. For most jazzmen they were far country. The aspiring jazzman might better spend his time learning to produce good sounds and assert his mastery of time. All this could have been demonstrated to Charlie Parker in fifteen minutes. Had he asked.

Charlie Parker knew nothing of the system of harmony that rested on the shoulders of Rameau and J. S. Bach. Of its cycle of fifths, its pure mathematical logic, the fruit of painstaking labor by generations of European musicians. Charlie had been told there were twelve keys, one for each of the black and white notes on the piano. Therefore he would learn them. He would begin with the key and scale he knew, the scale of C. Then he would move upward a half tone and learn the scale of D-flat. It was one of those seldom used in jazz, but Charlie didn't know that. Then he would go to D-natural. In that way he would become a musician.

As Charlie progressed, there were difficulties with fingering. He worked out his own adjustments, tinkering with the rubber bands and twine wrappings that kept the old saxophone in its touchy state of playability. Charlie's reed had a tendency to honk at certain intervals of the new scales, as it had that night at the High Hat. He cadged reeds. Charlie stayed with the reeds in the number-one and -two range of the hardness scale. They gave a soft, almost crooning sound. With the harder reeds you had more power and a better cutting edge to your tone. That would be helpful in a jam session. But those stiff reeds were skittish and hard to control. The terrible honk wrenched from the saxophone when he tried the double-time stuff on *Body and Soul* jangled in his memory. He couldn't afford to let that happen again.

Charlie had been told that Lester Young used a hard reed. When asked, Lester just glared at Charlie. The great saxophonist was a difficult man to approach. Lester's reed, its hardness, how it was trimmed with sandpaper and a sharp knife, as well as the shape of Lester's mouthpiece, the way it was worked and hollowed out, were private matters. When Lester was not playing he kept knife, sandpaper, reed, and mouthpiece in his coat pocket. Trade secrets were not handed down all that easily to a kid musician in a back alley. There were a number of them to be guessed at, pried loose, and gathered together. It was part of the difficult school of jazz, and the uneasy relationship between master and apprentice. Lester did tell him, in a gruff tone, that you had "to shape the air," that everything you did, from the bottom of your belly to the tip of your tongue, had to do with the sound you made. It wasn't a matter of notes or pitches, but *sounds*. In order to learn more from experienced musicians you also had to be able to do more. Some professional status was required. The rites called for ever greater degrees of proficiency.

Charlie stuck with his scales. The new one in E-natural had a strange, haunting sound. He tried a twelve-bar blues in E. The effect was odd. It had the quality heard in a singer on Twelfth Street one day, a blind man from the Mississippi who sang the blues in a keening country voice, his tongue fluttering over broken teeth. The blind man played a six-string guitar, and the fourth finger of his left hand, ringed with the neck of a broken whiskey bottle, made crying sounds as it slithered up and down the strings. The effect of playing blues on the saxophone in that key was something that Charlie had never heard before. Resolving to pursue this experiment later, he went on to the scale of F, a welcome key. It had the real Kansas City sound, lusty and honky-tonk, like Pete Johnson ringing the piano at the Sunset Club. A good part of the repertory at the Reno Club was played in F. Charlie was gaining familiarity with the world of different keys. Each had its own personality. Each lent a different mood to the music being played. After F came G-flat, rich, opulent, but difficult—never heard, called-for, or played. Charlie committed it to memory.

Charlie's practice sessions, or "woodshedding," as it was called by jazzmen, took place at home. He rose early in the afternoon, around one o'clock, refreshed after his night's prowl, and, finding his mother still asleep, cooked himself a heavy breakfast. He was a big eater. He had shot up rapidly during his first two years at Lincoln, but now was filling out, growing thick in the chest, and chunky. His face was becoming round, and there was a hint of broadening cheekbones. After breakfast Charlie went upstairs to his room and drew the green shade of the window that looked out over the gardens and clotheslines of the Olive Street neighborhood. Then he removed his horn from its case and began to practice. He always started with the scales that he knew, and went on to the one he was learning. Once he learned a scale he never forgot it. It was locked away inside. There was some advantage to the do-it-yourself method. When you worked things out for yourself, you had it down. The computer memory filed everything away, the "useless" scales along with the useful. The saxophone his mother had bought, and had had repaired, and that still worked by means of cellophane pasted over the leaks and a system of rubber bands over certain levers, had become an amiable genie capable of conjuring up the cool, private world of sounds in which he lived.

Charlie no longer made much pretense of attending Lincoln High. He spent a lot of his free time talking to Old Man Virgil, helping him sort junk and make rounds in the alleys. Once he showed Virgil two reeds that he had pocketed at Jenkins's Music Store while the clerk wasn't looking. Virgil exploded. "That's called shoplifting!" the old man cried like a preacher shouting at his congregation. "You could do two years in the state reformatory for a thing like that! Have it on your record for life! Charlie, it's time you and me had a talk." The old man made Charlie sit facing him in a chair claimed from a furniture store waste bin and hear him out.

"You got no father, so I'm going to set down four rules for you. I'm an old man and I've seen life. The first rule is, *Don't never steal.*" Virgil paused for breath, his eyes hot. "What good are two measly fifty-cent reeds, against time in a reform school? Will you please tell me that?"

"It was pretty dumb," Charlie said.

"Stealing—that's for dummies. The second rule is, *Don't knock no people.* That's mighty easy to do, carry tales and bad-mouth folks. It don't buy you one thing. Always gets back to where it started, and people remember what you said about 'em. Can't no good come of it. Just make up your mind, Charlie, if you can't say nuthin' good about somebody, don't say nuthin'. And you'll strike folks as a whole lot smarter, too.

"I want to talk to you about your music. Heard it all my life up and down these streets, even though I can't play nuthin' but a little blues. You're getting a head start. For colored there ain't all that many doors open to us. With music our people got their own way. In Kansas City you got some of the best musicians in the whole country. Learn everything you can. Keep practicing. The main thing is, stay with it. Stay with your horn. The horn will take you wherever you want to go in this life.

"And the last rule is this. *Get yourself a good woman and stick with her.*" The old man paused. "Now repeat 'em back after me."

Charlie repeated the four rules: *Don't never steal, Don't knock no people, Stay with your horn, Settle down with a good woman.* For several weeks, whenever he saw Old Man Virgil, at the shack, or in the streets or alleys, the junk dealer made him repeat the four rules, like a catechism.

Charlie's former classmates at Lincoln High, with whom he had been a freshman, were now in their junior year and looking forward to graduation. Charlie was still a freshman. He hadn't passed enough courses to advance a single class. Had his I.Q. been measured, it would have been found exceptionally high. He was bright, quick-witted, had a probing mind and an exceptional memory. None of these qualities had been encouraged by any of the teachers at Lincoln. Perhaps he had alienated them by his attitude. Perhaps they were "no good," as he had complained to his mother.

The Deans of Swing were no longer on the campus. Most of the members of the band, including Lawrence Keyes, had graduated. One night Charlie joined his friends to play a dance at Paseo Hall. During the evening the veteran Kansas City bandleader George Ewing Lee sang a few numbers with the Deans. He was a big man with a long, flat face, rich coloring, and strong features, a balladeer rather than a blues singer. He had been called the Cab Calloway of the Middle West. Lee's baritone voice, developed in an era when singers used megaphones instead of microphones, had tremendous carrying power and filled the ballroom.

When the dance was over Lee told the musicians that it was time they joined the Musicians' Protective Association. As one of the charter members of Local 627, he would help. That week Charlie, Keyes, and the others met Lee at union headquarters in the brick building at 1823 Highland Avenue. The young men filled out applications, paid their ten dollars initiation fee, and were interviewed by the president, William Shaw. Observing that the minimum age for union members was eighteen, Charlie advanced his own by four years. Mr. Shaw, taking note of his strapping build and ready assurance, asked no further questions. His fee and application were accepted. It was a major step for Charlie. He felt proud and important. Some of the most respected people in the community were members of Local 627; socially they rated right up there with doctors and lawyers.

As soon as Charlie received his union card, he began looking for a job. According to the grapevine, a saxophone player was needed at a joint called the Greenleaf Gardens. Pay was a dollar twenty-five a night. The band was led by a white pianist, Bill Channing, and played for the beer trade. There wasn't much jazz heard at the Greenleaf Gardens, but it was a job. Charlie applied and, to everyone's surprise but his own, was hired. That was the end of his career at Lincoln High. He became, and for the rest of his life would be, one of the night people.

The job, on the north side of the district, brought him into contact with Gene Ramey again. The bassist, who had contended against the Deans of Swing in battles of music, was working down the street at the Bar le Duc. Ramey was then twenty-two years of age, seven years older than Charlie. A native of Austin, Texas, he had grown up in a strict, middle-class family, learned to play tuba in a brass band, come to Kansas City with his family in 1932, and graduated from high school. Now Ramey was determined to become a jazz musician. He was studying bass with Walter Page of the Count Basie Orchestra.

Gene Ramey and Charlie Parker were opposites in almost every respect. Ramey was a skinny young man who wore spectacles and looked like a divinity student. He had none of Charlie's quick, mercurial qualities or overweening self-assurance. Like many bassists Ramey was a retiring, self-contained, resolute man. The temperament seemed to go with the trade. Good bass players remained in the background, buried in the rhythm section, charged with the unglamorous but exacting job of keeping time, the dependable petty officers of the jazz organization. Their stock in trade was the big sound, the remorseless beat, and smooth-running changes.

In his young friend Ramey detected very little in the way of future promise apart from enthusiasm and a hard-headed determination. There were such odd and interesting ideas as double time and scrambled harmonic schemes that might bear fruit some day, but they would take a lot of working out. Charlie wasn't yet much of a saxophonist. He needed competent instruction, and a better instrument. The worst feature of his playing was the sound he produced. A player's sound was all-important. It was the projection of his innermost spirit. Like a literary style it was the man himself, his hopes, fears, loves, hates, obsessions, his vision of musical beauty. All of these ideas and emotions could be projected by tonal means. Charlie's sound on the alto saxophone was immature and unattractive. Ramey heard it as a "combination of a man talking and drinking wine at the same time." Ramey called it a "Sweet Lucy" sound. Sweet Lucy was the name for California muscatel and white port, available for a dollar a gallon, and the favorite beverage of local winos.

Gene Ramey was a worrier, and there was in his young friend a good deal to worry about. Charlie was no longer the "happy-go-lucky" kid who had clowned around with the Deans of Swing and willingly submitted to being the butt of their jokes. Ramey found him antisocial and belligerent, and thought this was because Charlie was an only child, sheltered and coddled by his mother, always told that he was right and supported by her in everything that he did. Most of his time had been spent with adults. Along the way his personality had developed strange facets. Charlie's adjustment to the chaffing and verbal sparring that marked life on the streets was a line of wise patter that could easily be ill-taken.

Charlie had created an enemy in Dave Dexter, Jr., a young newspaperman with the Kansas City *Journal-Post*. Dexter was an ardent jazz fan and local correspondent for several musical publications, including *Down Beat, Metronome,* and *Orchestra World*. Not that Charlie was ready for press attention, but it was always well to think of the future. Dexter was a tireless propagandist for Kansas City jazz and an admirer of Charlie's very idols. Charlie didn't like Dexter and singled the newspaperman out as a target for his practical jokes. The hot foot was then making the rounds. A match was secretly slipped into the seam of the victim's shoe, between the sole and upper part, then lighted. The pranks resulted in much hilarity and, on occasion, burned shoes and feet. The newspaperman did not find the joke amusing or enjoy the laughter at his expense. Charlie would divert Dexter and lift his wallet. "If you caught him in the act, he would laugh it off and return the wallet," Dexter wrote later. "For all of his surliness and bad habits he could charm the leaves from a tree. When he wanted something he got it." The bad relations were to continue throughout their careers, after Dexter became editor of *Down Beat,* and later artists-and-repertoire director of jazz recording at Capitol Records. In Dexter's opinion Charlie was a "spoiled brat."

Another practical joke was played on Old Man Virgil. Charlie dissolved several benzedrine tablets in the junk dealer's wine. For the next forty-eight hours the old man wheeled his barrow non-stop up and down the alleys like a man possessed.

Charlie and a teen-age drummer called L'il Phil went on a nutmeg high that lasted two days. Nutmeg could be bought for a few cents in any grocery store. Taken with a cup of coffee or floated on top of an orange soda, it produced spectacular results, but it was hard on stomach linings. After the two-day high Charlie and L'il Phil could eat nothing but soup. They had no idea of where they had been or what clubs they had visited. Marijuana was also cheap and easily obtained. A woman known as the Old Lady, who lived in a shack on the north side, hand-rolled and sold "sticks of shit," a dozen for a dollar. Once L'il Phil had gotten hold of a packet of cocaine, which Charlie and the drummer sniffed. There was no end of adventure for a young man growing up in the district.

The summer of 1936 Charlie's steady girl friend, Rebecca Ruffing, graduated from Lincoln High. She was a handsome, light-skinned girl with soft wavy hair and a mature figure. She and Charlie had been on an intimate basis since his second year in school. Rebecca was nineteen, four years older than Charlie. Since she had completed her education and Charlie had a regular job, they decided to get married. There was opposition when Charlie broached the idea to his mother. Addie Parker argued that he was too young, the difference in their ages too great, and that his work as a musician offered little security for a lasting union. "Mama, I'm in love," Charlie told his mother. "And I'm old enough to get married." One day the couple went to city hall and were married by a justice of the peace. Charlie brought his bride to live in the Olive Street house. Within a few months Mrs. Ruffing and Rebecca's brothers and sisters moved in as well. These arrangements did nothing to interfere with Charlie's activities. After the first few weeks he spent no more time at home than usual.

Charlie's hope that Rebecca would spend some of her time in night clubs, listening to him play and waiting at a ringside table, was soon dispelled. Rebecca had no interest in Kansas City night life or its characters. She was a homebody. She soon showed herself to be a young lady with a strong will and domineering personality. Charlie Parker now had two maternal figures at the same address. They nagged him and urged him to moderate his ways and assume his responsibilities as a husband; but they cooked his meals, mended his clothes, and gave him the feeling of being the man of the house. Nothing they said had the least effect on his lifestyle.

The marriage brought the year 1935 full circle. At an age when good all-around American boys win their Eagle Scout badges, build up wind for the track season, or plan a dream date for the annual junior prom, Charlie could count his achievements with a certain measure of worldly pride. He was a high-school dropout, professional musician, dabbler in drugs, student of strange modes, a member of Local 627 of the AFM, married, and, as Rebecca soon told him, the father of a child-to-be. That August he celebrated his fifteenth birthday. Once it had passed, he pointed out that he was actually going on sixteen. Meanwhile Charlie stuck doggedly to his practice regimen. He completed the cycle of twelve major scales, running the gamut from C through B natural, and back to his starting point. That done he proceeded to learn the blues in each of the twelve keys. Discoveries of new modal and tonal relationships were exciting. He was into sounds he had heard coming from unlettered blues singers who had worked their way up from the cotton plantations of the Mississippi delta and sang for coins on Kansas City streets. Charlie spent a long time with the blues. It was his favorite bag. He got to where he could play the blues in every key. He was beginning to discover ways to move from one key to another. When he felt that he was completely at home in the blues, he next subjected *I Got Rhythm* to the same treatment. It was a favorite jam vehicle for Kansas City jazzmen. He taught himself to move from one chord to the next in every one of the twelve keys. When he had at last finished with *I Got Rhythm* he began work on the long, difficult number called *Cherokee*. He felt that he was almost ready.

The Making of a Jazzman

Until the spring of 1936 Kansas City had been content to pursue its parochial ways. It was the cool, dark cellar described by Art Tatum. Now the vintage wines were about to be discovered, sampled, and merchandised. Short-wave broadcasts from the Reno Club over local station W9XBY brought artists-and-repertoire man John Hammond out from New York in June. Hammond wanted to see if the Basie band was as good as it sounded. It was even better. As Hammond wrote later in *Down Beat*, "It seemed to have all the virtues of a small combo, with the inspired soloists, complete relaxation, plus the drive and dynamics of a disciplined orchestra." Hammond had been instrumental in launching Benny Goodman as the King of Swing.

Swing bands were in demand. Hammond immediately got in touch with Willard Alexander at Music Corporation of America, the largest booking agency in the country, suggesting that Basie be signed without delay. He also brought the band to the attention of the Vocalion Record Company, with which he was associated, recommending an exclusive recording contract.

Meanwhile others had picked up the trail. The word had leaked out that Kansas City jazz was "different." Joe Glaser, who managed Louis Armstrong, arrived, booked a suite at the Muehlebach Hotel, and began making the rounds of the night clubs. The Count Basie story unfolded with bewildering rapidity. Willard Alexander flew in from New York, was impressed, and went home to persuade his partners that MCA should accept Hammond's recommendation and add Count Basie to its talent stable. There were objections. The Count Basie band played without written music, and that was unheard of in 1936. The band had no book, no uniforms, no bus, and needed new instruments. "Colored bands" were still a problem. They could not be booked in certain locations. While these matters were being discussed at top level, Joe Glaser slipped into the Reno Club and signed Oran Lips Page to an exclusive personal contract. "In two years I'll have your name in the bright lights. I'll make you bigger than Louis Armstrong," Glaser told the trumpet star of the Basie orchestra. Glaser thought Page the most commercial attraction in the band. Page was hustled off to Chicago to start recruiting an orchestra of his own under Glaser's aegis. The Basie band was minus one of its solo talents. The infighting typical of the entertainment business had begun.

While Vocalion was weighing Hammond's recommendations, Jack Kapp, the free-wheeling president of the newly launched and talent-hungry Decca Record Company, dispatched his brother Dave to bag Basie. Kapp, a smooth talker, found Basie as naive as the rest of the Kansas City musicians accustomed to salaries of a few dollars a week. Kapp offered the bandleader an exclusive contract, a guarantee of twenty-four record sides, immediate nation-wide exposure on Decca's new thirty-five-cent popular label, and seven hundred fifty dollars cash, more money than Basie had seen in his life.

Without bothering to consult Hammond or telephone Willard Alexander at MCA for advice, Basie signed. According to the chagrined Hammond, who had set everything in motion, it was "the most expensive blunder of Basie's life." When examined closely, the contract was seen to call for the band's exclusive services for three years. The seven hundred fifty dollars was full payment for the twenty-four sides by the entire band. The customary 5-percent royalty Basie would have received from Vocalion was conspicuously missing from the Decca contract. It was typical of the deals imposed on unsuspecting country, blues, and black artists. The arrangement with MCA materialized in September. Outfitted with uniforms, a bus, and new instruments, the Count Basie Orchestra left for Chicago and the first leg of its successful breakthrough to national fame. The band that was to change the course of jazz was on its way. The Kansas City cellar had been broached for the first time.

Charlie Parker looked on from the sidelines. Old timers told him that more had happened in Kaycee that summer than in the past twenty years. The "big break" and the "big money" were on the lips of those who stayed behind. The best jobs in town were up for the taking. The district was a hotbed of rumors. The Clouds of Joy were being groomed for Eastern ballroom and theater appearances. Big Joe Turner and Pete Johnson were waiting for Hammond to telephone with news that a suitable spot for them had been found in a New York night club. Charlie Christian, the young guitarist from Oklahoma City, was being scouted by an undercover man for a name bandleader. One night at the Roseland Ballroom on Troost Avenue, Charlie heard Christian outplay Efferge Ware, Eddie Durham, and Jim Daddy Walker, the three best and most experienced guitarists in town. Christian had really eaten them up that night, and Christian was barely a year older than Charlie. If Christian could do it, so could he. His most pressing need was a new saxophone, but that was not so easily come by, even at Depression price levels. A new one by a top manufacturer cost between two and three hundred dollars. The sum seemed beyond his grasp. Then an odd stroke of fate intervened.

Charlie had been recruited for a casual job over the

Thanksgiving holidays in Eldon, Missouri, at a roadhouse owned by a Mr. Musser. Eldon was a hundred and fifty miles from Kansas City, in the Ozark lake and resort country. The musicians left in the middle of the afternoon, traveling in two cars, a Buick driven by Musser and an old Chevrolet, carrying Charlie and bassist George Wilkerson, and driven by drummer Ernest Daniels. Charlie rode in the back seat with the string bass and drum equipment.

The weather had turned cold, and they could see patches of snow under the trees and in shaded spots in the woods. The Ozarks looked bare and gloomy. As it grew dark Daniels had trouble keeping up with the faster Buick over the mountain roads. About eight miles from Eldon, Daniels entered a curve at high speed. No one had noticed the ice sheeted over the surface of the road, water that had seeped down from a thawed embankment and frozen. The Buick crossed the patch without difficulty. The Chevrolet went into a dizzying skid. Daniels fought with the wheel, but the Chevrolet was out of control. It struck a ditch and overturned, ejecting musicians and instruments as it rolled.

The bass violin and bass drum cushioned the force of Charlie's ejection. He staggered to his feet as the Buick returned to the scene of the accident. He was cut and bruised, and there were intense pains in his chest, but he could walk and move his arms. The Chevrolet was demolished. Wilkerson lay unconscious in the ditch. Ernest Daniels, his friend on many a midnight excursion, was suffering from a punctured lung. Wilkerson died before he could receive medical attention. Charlie returned to Kansas City with Daniels, who was hospitalized. Charlie refused medical attention. He went home and let Addie and Rebecca nurse him back to health. A few days later Mr. Musser telephoned to say that he felt partly to blame and had instructed his attorney to work out an insurance settlement.

The legal affair moved slowly, but when Charlie was up and about and ready to play again, a check for several hundred dollars arrived in the mail. Charlie at once took a cab downtown to the Jenkins Music Company, where he bought himself the best saxophone in the house, complete with a handsome reinforced leather case, a new neckstrap, and an assortment of reeds. The old horn that his mother had bought, with its leaky pads, twine, and rubber bands, was given in trade.

The new saxophone was an E-flat alto bearing the scroll and crest of the French firm of H. and A. Selmer. A booklet that came with the instrument told Charlie a lot of things he had not known about saxophones. It had been invented and patented by a Belgian named Adolphe Sax in 1840. He had a contract to supply instruments of various types to the French military bands. In designing the saxophone he had combined a clarinet mouthpiece with an old keyed brass instrument called the serpent. The saxophone was actually a combination of brass and reed instruments. It had the power of the brass and the facility of the reeds. The first saxophone had been made by hand by Mr. Sax's father. All that had taken place a hundred years ago. The Selmer firm was the "successor to Messrs. Sax," according to the booklet. Selmer had bought out the plans and patents and taken over the original plant and its corps of workmen. Their descendants, now in the fourth or fifth generation, still worked for Selmer. The bells of their saxophones were still shaped by a master craftsman, who used a wooden mallet a hundred years old and a huge tree stump behind the factory for an anvil. Without directly saying so, the booklet told you that you were now the owner of the best saxophone money could buy.

When Charlie hefted the new Selmer and stood in front of the mirror in his room, he felt like Lester Young in front of the Count Basie Orchestra, mowing everybody down with big soft notes. It was easy to believe. The light caught the curved surfaces of polished brass, gleamed and threw off beams to the corners of the room. The reflections were so bright they dazzled. The keys seemed to lie right under his fingers, as if the people in the Selmer factory had made them exactly for Charlie. The keys had a quick, sure action, like the spring of a mousetrap, yet the action was smooth and quiet. The way the mouthpiece slipped onto the neck was easy and sure. Charlie played a scale and marked the pitch point on the cork, the way the clerk had showed him. The pearl buttons and edges of the key rings were silky. The new saxophone smelled of clean new metal, jeweler's rouge, and the new velvet lining of the carrying case. The sound was different, too. It was hard and pure. Equipped for the first time in his life with a reliable instrument, Charlie went to work at Paseo Hall with the Tommy Douglas Orchestra, one of the emerging bands in the realignment of the Kansas City music scene in the post-Basie period.

Tommy Douglas was an enigmatic figure in the Kansas City jazz community. He was the best-trained man in town, and, for that matter, the entire Southwest. There wasn't much argument about that. As a young man of Charlie's age, Douglas had received a scholarship to the Boston Conservatory of Music, whether through talent or the largesse of a sponsor, Charlie never learned; the band leader no longer talked much about that period of his life. Douglas attended the famous music school for four years, spending the summers working with dance orchestras led by Jelly Roll Morton, Duke Ellington, and George E. Lee. Then he had graduated, and there was a rumor that he had auditioned successfully for a chair in a leading symphony orchestra but was not hired because of his color. As every musician in Kansas City knew, there was not a single Negro musician in any of the symphony orchestras in the country. In 1929 Douglas came back to Kansas City and went to work as an arranger and musical director for other bandleaders. Then he went out with bands of his own.

Douglas bands were known for their musicianship. The bands played Douglas's arrangements and were musically advanced. But none of them was very successful. From 1929 to 1936 Tommy Douglas was constantly in hot water with radio station managers, booking agents, and dance hall operators, both at home and on the road. Local 627 fined him three hundred dollars for using non-union men on a job at El Torreon Ballroom.

Some said that Tommy had no luck, others that his personality was against him—he was "dicty" and put on airs. He had never quite gotten over the Boston Conservatory. No one denied that he was an extraordinary musician.

Tommy Douglas was the kind of man who could play anything written and write down anything played. He could play all of the saxophones. He knew his harmony inside and out. He was a master of the Boehm clarinet, which no one else in Kansas City could play; it was the one used in symphony and classical work. Tommy was just as good on the Albert system clarinet, the favorite of the old New Orleans jazzmen.

Tommy Douglas was a middle-sized man with sloping shoulders and a large soft jaw and fleshy face, rather like a football that sagged at one end. He made you show up on time and sit in a certain place on the bandstand, and was strict about time out for intermissions. Charlie took his place in the small band at Paseo Hall, doing exactly what he was told, watching the leader's fingers, listening to his improvisations, trying to follow the difficult but beautiful modulations, asking questions, calling him Mr. Douglas. This was the professional relationship Charlie had been seeking ever since he took to roaming the district. Tommy Douglas, not a man he could idolize, or even like very much, but one whom he could respect, was the first professional musician to take a serious interest in him.

If Douglas was taken in by the pseudo-humble manner, he was not deceived by other qualities in his new saxophonist, ones that were readily apparent to a trained man. Charlie was serious. That counted for a lot. He had an infinite capacity for practice, and that could take even an untalented man a considerable distance. The chunky boy had an excellent natural ear, and something close to perfect pitch. These qualities, which Tommy Douglas recognized as natural ones, were offset by the acquired ones. Charlie had the merest smattering of harmony, most of it wrong. Self-taught methods of handling the saxophone had resulted in serious errors of technique. The fingering was incorrect, as was the embouchure. Charlie was using a soft reed that would never produce a good tone, even in an imported Selmer.

One thing Tommy Douglas could do was teach. The bandleader set out to deal with the defects in Charlie's musicianship. He suggested a stronger reed, and showed Charlie how to whittle it to the right shape for his lips and teeth, explaining the principles of proper embouchure.* Douglas changed Charlie's method of fingering. He told Charlie that, whether he liked it or not, the foundation of good reed style was mastery of the clarinet. Douglas demonstrated the speed with which the instrument could be played. Charlie saw at once that the clarinet could do what he had attempted at the High Hat jam session, the double-time passages, and do them very easily. Charlie still didn't like the soft, buzzing sound of the clarinet in its chalumeau register, or the thin, piercing one of its upper range. Could the clarinet's agility be transferred to the saxophone? Mr. Douglas didn't know. He had never considered it. He thought it might, but with some years of practice. There was a far larger column of air to be manipulated. Lester Young was about the fastest player so far. Douglas lent Charlie a spare Albert system clarinet, and Charlie took it home and practiced.

During the winter of 1936 Charlie sat next to the bandleader who had never had any luck, playing dances at the Paseo Ballroom, parties and balls for the social clubs in town, and the odd night in a nearby city, Topeka or St. Joseph, furnishing music for a college prom or fraternity dance. When Douglas took a solo Charlie would listen carefully, taking it all in. Douglas didn't swing as much as Lester Young or Ben Webster. Douglas used "passing tones," and "added chords." That came from the conservatory training. Douglas wrote out simple clarinet parts for Charlie. At last he was serving a real apprenticeship, the kind that had made Lester Young into a great saxophonist.

In the spring of 1937 the Tommy Douglas Orchestra disbanded, and Charlie joined the pool of Kansas City jazzmen working casuals.

One night he and Gene Ramey went to the Reno Club for the spook breakfast. It was a gala occasion. Jo Jones, who had replaced Jesse Price in the Count Basie Orchestra, was in town

* Embouchure: the relationship of a reed musician's lips, tongue, teeth, and facial muscles to the mouthpiece and reed of his instrument. A good embouchure is essential for control of pitch, dynamics, and flow of wind. One's embouchure is complex and personal. Its perfection requires thousands of hours of study and practice and makes possible the virtuosity heard in such saxophonists as Lester Young and Coleman Hawkins.

for the weekend, sitting in on drums, and there were more than
fifty Kansas City jazzmen waiting their turn to take part. Jo
Jones was a big man now. His drumming on a chase chorus
with Basie and Walter Page on *Swinging at the Daisy Chain*
had been noted by record reviewers, who called attention to his
smooth, effortless beat, his mastery of the high-hat cymbal, and
his skill in playing behind soloists.

"Fast company," Ramey remarked. "Maybe you'd better
sit this one out."

"I'm as ready as I'll ever be," Charlie told him. The new
saxophone gave him confidence.

When his turn came he mounted the bandstand below the
balcony where he had sat so many nights. It was the first time
he had jammed at the Reno. He could hear Jo Jones marking
time behind him, playing accents on the high-hat cymbal. It
was a beautiful sound, of paper-thin metal deftly struck. It
made you want to go. *I Got Rhythm* was being played, and that
suited Charlie. He knew the changes. He waited for Jo's pickup cue and launched into his solo. Practically every jazz musician in Kansas City was in the house. They had come to hear
and be heard, and they were a tough audience. If you couldn't
make it, you could go back and start over again, the way everyone else had done it, or give up and try for a job in the post
office.

Behind him Charlie had a drummer who would be able to
follow anything. He played his line on the first thirty-two bars
of *I Got Rhythm*. It was acceptable. He could tell that from the
drumming and the audience response. But Charlie wanted to
put a "this is mine" stamp on what he was playing. He was
afraid to try the double-time stuff. He wasn't that fast yet, or
sure. He used one of the passing chords that he had learned
from Tommy Douglas. It took him out of the key. He fell back
on one of the scales he had mastered at home and the change
went off brilliantly. People were startled. There was real sus-
pense now. They were wondering how he was going to come
out of it. Charlie was into another key now and beginning to
realize that he didn't know the chords. For C-minor seventh
you substituted what———? He didn't know. It was part of an

art that Tommy Douglas called transposition, that Douglas had learned at the Boston Conservatory. There was a system for it. Tommy Douglas could have called out the proper chords in an instant. Charlie was lost. He didn't know where to go. He missed a phrase. Then he lost his grip on the time, the worst sin of all. The beat and the line went surging ahead. Jo Jones rode the cymbals like an angry demon. The same terrible thing that had happened at the High Hat was happening all over again, but in worse circumstances. Jo Jones stopped drumming. The smooth, effortless, buoyant song of the drums stopped. Charlie stood there, rigid, frightened, holding the saxophone. The new Selmer. And a cymbal came sailing through the air. Jo Jones had snatched it from the cymbal ring and thrown it at Charlie's feet. The cymbal landed with a shattering crash. In the silence that gripped the crowd at the Reno Club the crash of the cymbal seemed to bounce off every wall and ricochet back to the band shell. Then, as had happened that night a year before at the High Hat Club, came the chorus of laughter, guffaws, and cat-calls. He had flopped in the big time, had been "gonged off."

"Who's next up there?" someone called out.

Charlie flushed and ground his teeth. He climbed down from the bandstand. This time he didn't burst into tears. Ramey was waiting for him at the table. Ramey's kind, worried face was warm and sympathetic. He didn't say, "I told you to wait." Instead he told Charlie, "That was a great change into the new key. You almost had it together." Ramey looked at Charlie and said, "Don't let it get under your skin. You got a lot of time yet."

"They're laughing at me now," Charlie said. "I'll be back."

Charlie slipped the Selmer back into its velvet-lined case. As he walked out of the club they were still laughing. "I'll be back," he told himself. "I'll fix these cats."

PART II

Woodshedding in the Ozarks

A touring car carried Charlie back over the winding road to Eldon in the Ozarks. It was early summer, 1937. A few weeks had passed since the debacle at the Reno Club. Charlie was wedged in the back seat with his possessions, a suitcase, a blue band jacket, a wind-up portable phonograph, and a carrying case with all of Lester Young's records. Solos by Lester were featured on the records by the Count Basie Orchestra that had begun to appear at the rate of about one every month since the beginning of the Decca contract. The new company with its blue and gold thirty-five-cent label was moving aggressively into the national market.

Charlie had picked up each new release as it appeared in

the stores: *Swinging at the Daisy Chain* coupled with *Pennies from Heaven, Honeysuckle Rose, Boo Hoo, Exactly Like You—* eight Basie performances and eight Lester Young solos in all. Just before he left Kansas City, a review in *Down Beat* had called Charlie's attention to four additional and highly desirable Lester Young solos, recorded under a pseudonym, Jones-Smith, Inc. The session was a bootleg date for Vocalion engineered by John Hammond. The five-piece band included Jo Jones, Walter Page, Basie, Lester, and a trumpeter, Tatti Smith. In this intimate setting, Lester's talents were afforded extensive exposure. Lester had been able to stretch out, the way he had on the good nights at the Reno. The twelve Lester Young solos contained in the record collection became Charlie's case book. The records were already well played, *Lady Be Good* so often that the grooves were beginning to break down from the pressure of the steel needle and heavy pickup head. Grooves containing the saxophone solos betrayed themselves by bands of gray that gave off a fine dust with each playing, blurring a little the saxophone tones and adding crackling effects to Count Basie's piano arabesques, even coarsening the sound of Jo Jones's cymbals. Charlie would never forget the cymbals. They had sent him off to the Ozarks.

The job was at Lake Taneycomo, in the heart of the Ozarks, a few miles south of Eldon and the scene of the Thanksgiving Day accident. The leader was Charlie's old benefactor, George Ewing Lee, who had secured the resort contract for the summer months when steaming heat would drive affluent Kansas City folk to the countryside. The band played for dancing each night in an old wooden pavilion overlooking the lake. The hours, nine to two, were comfortable by town standards; the musicians could look forward to a relaxed schedule with free time for fishing and boating. None of these pleasures held any allure for Charlie. He had signed on with George Lee for a purpose.

The pianist in the Lee unit was Carrie Powell, one of the sound chord men in Kansas City; the guitarist, Efferge Ware, hosted the free jazz clinics in Paseo Park. Powell and Ware had recommended Charlie for the job, and had volunteered to give him daily instruction in harmony. Charlie's lessons began in the late morning and were given in the deserted pavilion. Carrie Powell would spell out the notes of the major triads; Charlie would play along, and they would proceed through the circle of fifths. It was a tedious business, seemingly with little relationship to the playing of jazz, but after a week Charlie saw how it might fit into his own scheme of harmony. "This is the way music is written," the pianist told him. "If you want to work in dance bands, you have to have this down cold."

The records were Charlie's most important subject for study. His portable phonograph had a set screw that could be tightened to lower the speed of the turntable. This adjustment made it easier for him to analyze the solos and study the nuances of tone that made Lester sound as if he were singing, shouting, and talking through the saxophone. Charlie learned each solo by heart, replaying the powdery grooves, listening for the notes through the increasing hiss of surface noise. Charlie broke down Lester's method. The bag of tricks. The way Lester worked an odd triplet into a run of dotted eights (for greater rhythmic tension). The way Lester shaped held notes to make them "swing." The long, brusque honking notes set off boldly against a series of phantom puffs of sound, and the way Lester outlined some of his notes with air space. The entire duct through which air flowed, from the bottom of the lungs to the bell of the horn, was involved in the production of saxophone sounds. Charlie learned that the most subtle controls of all came from how he used his throat and cheek muscles. He was losing his "Sweet Lucy" sound. Charlie experimented with the "false fingering" he had seen Lester use, and discovered that the same note could often be produced by different, unorthodox finger positions. The pitch was the same, but the weight and quality of the note were different. He slowly committed each of the Lester Young solos to memory. He hummed and sang them to himself. Then he learned to play each in turn, note for note, experimenting with the fingering and shaping of the oral cavity until he imagined that he sounded just like Lester. Nobody was that good. Perhaps no one would ever be that good. But he thought he sounded like Lester Young. That was the main thing.

At night the big, silky voice of George Lee filled the resort ballroom. People out in boats and canoes said that they could hear it across the lake. Lee's favorite numbers were *What Is This Thing Called Love*, *St. James Infirmary*, and *If I Could Be with You One Hour Tonight*. Charlie took note of Lee's phrasing and patterns of breath control. Charlie learned ways to work saxophone phrases into the air space between the words of the lyrics. One night Lee told him, "Nice little things you're doing back there."

At Lake Taneycomo Charlie lost all track of the passage of time. Hot summer days faded into dusk. There was just time to wolf down a quick meal at a back table where the musicians ate, and then the evening job began. After Labor Day the crowds thinned. Only a few guests, waiting for the onset of Indian summer, remained at the resort. Early in October Lee paid off the men, and they went back to the city brimming with health, relaxed and full of tales about the summer job and Lake Taneycomo, where "living was easy." Everyone except Charlie. He had grown an inch in his seventeenth year; he looked drawn, tense, and determined.

Charlie's first appearance back in Kansas City was at a jam session at the Reno Club. There was no Jo Jones on hand. His friend, Jesse Price, sat behind the drums. The rhythm section included Gene Ramey. Ramey was now established as the town's best bassist. The leading jazzmen in Kansas City had gathered to do battle. The jammers were working over *I Got Rhythm* at a fast bounce tempo when Charlie's turn came. He checked his reed and played three choruses of the number. There were no bleeps, no honks, and no breakdowns. Gingerly he tried the eight-bar bridge at double time, and made it. Jesse Price followed him readily. Charlie could hear Jesse's little flams closing off sentences, saying, "Steady! Good! Go on!" When Charlie finished up there was a moment of silence. Then, instead of whistles and guffaws, the murmurs of approval that went with an acceptable performance at a Kansas City jam session.

Jazzmen in Kansas City the fall of 1937 recall the astonishing change in the young musician. "From a laughingstock Charlie had made himself into a saxophonist worth listening to," said Gene Ramey. "He'd gotten rid of his 'Sweet Lucy' sound. He had one of his own. Clean and without much vibrato. He hadn't given up the strange ideas, stuff like double timing and weird modulations in and out of key, but they made a little sense now. He knew every one of Lester Young's solos by heart. He sounded almost exactly like Lester Young, Lester playing alto, but with something else of his own that was beginning to come through. The difference was unbelievable."

Another Kansas City jazzman who recalls the change is Jay McShann, who became Charlie's employer two years later. From Muskegon, Oklahoma, a veteran of territorial bands, McShann had arrived in Kansas City that fall seeking to further his career. He was twenty-two, five years older than Charlie. McShann played a powerful blues and boogie-woogie piano, in the style of Pete Johnson. Versatile, personable, blessed with a sanguine disposition and excellent health, McShann caught on quickly. According to the pianist, now a successful attraction in midwestern lounges and cabarets:

"I first ran into Charlie in November or December of 1937 at one of those famous Kansas City jam sessions. Charlie seemed to live for them. I was in a rhythm section one night when this cocky kid pushed his way on stage. He was a teenager, barely seventeen, and looked like a high school kid. He had a tone that cut. Knew his changes. He'd get off on a line of his own and I would think he was headed for trouble, but he was like a cat landing on all four feet. A lot of people couldn't understand what he was trying to do, but it made sense harmonically and it always swung.

"Musical ideas, that is what jam sessions were really about. Charlie was able to hold his own against older men, some of them with years of big-band experience. He was a strange kid, very aggressive and wise. He liked to play practical jokes. And he was always borrowing money, a couple of dollars that you'd never get back. He was trying to act like a grown man. It was hard to believe those stories about what a poor musician he'd been. That fall when he came back from the Ozarks he was ready.

"I joined a band headed up by Jesse Price and Prof Smith for à job at Lucille's Band Box. It was the old Subway Club, at Eighteenth and Woodland, and Lucille took over after Piney Brown died. The band was a mixture of old pros, from the Prince Stewart Orchestra, and young musicians, like myself and Charlie. Prof needed a second alto player and Jesse pulled Prof's coat about Charlie. For the audition Charlie showed up late, and in a taxi, even though the Band Box wasn't but a ten-minute walk from his house. He paid the driver to follow him into the club carrying the saxophone case. Prof dug it all but didn't say anything. After he heard Bird play he told him he could have the job. He was that promising."

The rhythm section was built around Price's drums. Price had the knack of being felt rather than heard. He was a perfect big-band drummer, smooth and fast. With McShann on piano and young Billy Hadnott on bass, the band, like all good Kansas City bands, swung from the rhythm section. There were three trumpets, a brilliant young trombonist, Fred Beckett, Odel West and Jimmy Keith on tenor, Prof Smith and Charlie on alto. (Most of the men were in their middle or late twenties. Smith was thirty-four. As usual, Charlie was the young person in the group.) For his first real band job he was surrounded by the good Kansas City sounds, supported by a swinging Kansas City rhythm section, seated alongside one of the finest alto saxophonists in jazz.

Prof Smith came from the same school of hard-playing, barnstorming musicians that had produced Lester Young. Originally from Dallas, Prof Smith had taught himself to play clarinet without formal instruction, by hanging around the honky-tonks and listening to clarinet players, in much the same way that Charlie had taught himself saxophone. At the age of twenty Prof Smith had been recruited by the legendary Oklahoma City Blue Devils. Prof played the alto saxophone with something of Lester Young's pure, light sound.

He showed Charlie some of the secrets of preparing mouthpieces and sandpapering reeds as Charlie sat at his side night after night. The odd, chameleon-like side of Charlie's nature appeared once more, as it had during the job with Tommy Douglas. Prof Smith had fired his imagination. The wise, aggressive, would-be hustler became the sedulous disciple. Charlie began a new phase of his learning period.

"He'd listen to you," Smith said later. "He used to call me his dad. I called him my boy. I couldn't get rid of him. He was always up under me. In my band we'd split solos. If I took two, he'd take two. If I'd take three, he'd take three, and so forth. He always wanted me to take the first solo. I guess he thought he'd learn something that way. He did play like me quite a bit, I guess. But, after a while, anything I could make on my horn, he could make, too, and make something better out of it."

When the Band Box job ended, the Price-Smith band played the College Inn, at Twelfth and Wyandotte, near the Muehlebach Hotel. Working conditions in Kansas City were deteriorating. Everyone in the district was worried about the political situation. The Kansas City *Star* had begun a series of articles exposing voting frauds perpetrated by the Pendergast machine. A front-page photograph showed a two-story dwelling on the North Side—its address had been used to register over two hundred fraudulent voters. Anti-Pendergast forces had closed ranks, forming the Citizens-Fusion committee, and were pushing hard for sweeping reforms. Tom Pendergast was said to be under investigation by the Department of Internal Revenue for income tax evasion, the crime that had jailed Al Capone. There was talk of shutting down the more unsavory night clubs, ones in which jazzmen often found employment. The College Inn job ran out. Prof Smith cut the band to seven pieces and accepted a job at the Antlers Club in the West Bottoms, across the street from the Armour packing house. It lasted a few weeks. Charlie then worked at the Hey Hay Club with George E. Lee, bassist Winston Williams, and white drummer Richard Dickert. When that job wound up, he joined the growing ranks of unemployed Kansas City musicians.

One afternoon Charlie was standing on his lucky corner,

Twelfth and Paseo, a hang-out for musicians, hustlers, and night people, when he ran into Joe Barone, proprietor of the nearby Boulevard Lounge. Barone needed a saxophone player. The pay was two dollars a night. Charlie accepted.

Barone had to advance him fourteen dollars to get his horn out of pawn. Later that week Charlie won the money back in a bet with the night club owner. During intermission a white couple walked into the club. The man was a jazz buff whom Charlie recognized from the Reno Club. The girl was tall, blonde, beautiful, and elegantly dressed. As the couple waited to be seated Charlie, watching from the bandstand, could see the girl survey the little honky-tonk and its patrons, then stiffen and hold back, as if she wished to leave. In her well-bred, finishing-school voice, loud enough for everyone in the club to hear, she told her escort, "Why, they're all *colored* in here!" Reluctantly the girl let herself be persuaded to sit down and listen to a set. The couple took one of the back tables, well away from the rest.

The Boulevard Room was primarily a beer joint. Each table was supplied with a bowl of pretzels. Charlie at once called one of the waiters and sent the man to remove the pretzels from the table. Then he gave the waiter a dollar bill and sent him around the corner to a grocery with instructions to bring back two boxes of cookies, one chocolate, the other vanilla. He had the waiter mix the black and white cookies in a clean bowl and place the bowl back on the table. Then he called Joe Barone and bet him fourteen dollars that the girl would eat only the vanilla wafers. "Okay," Barone said. "You're on." As the next set was played Charlie and the club owner watched while the blonde sipped at an Alexander and nibbled cookies taken from the jar, absent-mindedly sorting the white from the black, eating only the vanilla wafers.

"Okay, Charlie, you win," Barone told his saxophonist after the set. "The pawn ticket is on me."

The Apple

It was August again. Kansas City sweltered in humid heat. Jobs were scarce. Prof Smith had gone to New York, hopefully to attract national interest in booking a band that hardly existed. At home the family situation had deteriorated seriously. The presence of the numerous Ruffing family under one roof had led to continual friction. A son, Leon, born to Charlie and Rebecca in 1936, had done little to cement the marriage. Rebecca never wanted to go out or to hear Charlie play in a night club; now, she had turned into a stay-at-home and a complainer. Rebecca was four years older than Charlie, and the oldest of her own family, with a big-sister mentality. She wanted to mother Charlie and boss him. He wouldn't tolerate that, and there were fights, occasionally violent. "This house isn't big enough for two nasty people, Charles," his mother told him, and suggested he leave town for a while. Charlie pawned his saxophone at Hurst's loan office and, with a few dollars from his mother's last paycheck, set out on his first trip away from Kansas City, to Chicago.

Charlie's musical debut there was heard by Billy Eckstine, then a young vocalist breaking into show business with the Earl Hines Orchestra. According to Eckstine, he had gone to the 65 Club on the south side for the weekly breakfast dance. It began at six-thirty and was hosted by the King Kolax band with Goon Gardner on alto saxophone. "A guy comes up that looks like he just got off a freight car, the raggedest guy you'd ever want to see . . . and he asks Goon, 'Say, man, can I come up and blow your horn?' Now Goon was a kind of lazy guy . . . just as long as Goon could go to the bar and talk to the chicks, it was all right with him. So he said, 'Yes, man, go ahead.' And this cat gets up there and I'm telling you he blew the bell off that thing! . . . Bird was . . . playing like you never heard—wailing on alto then. . . . He blew so much he upset everybody in the joint." *

Kansas City ideas were thrusting themselves forward: long melody lines, persuasive swing, the self-reliance that came from constant jamming—notes often bizarre and disturbing, but logical and right. At eighteen Charlie was striking out resolutely toward the musical no-man's-land. At eighteen he had come to live for nothing else except his music. He believed he was the world's best saxophone player. He was tough and confident, already on the way to becoming the charismatic egomaniac of mature years.

Goon Gardner took Charlie home, gave him clothing, found him a few casual jobs, and lent him a clarinet. Charlie stayed in Chicago a few weeks. Then he pawned Gardner's clarinet and hitched a ride in a band bus to New York, where he went to Prof Smith's apartment.

---

* Billy Eckstine, with Nat Shapiro and Nat Hentoff: *Hear Me Talkin' to Ya*, New York: Dover Publications, 1966, pp. 352–3.

"He sure did look awful when he got in," Prof Smith re-called. "He'd worn his shoes so long that his legs were all swol-len up. He stayed up there with me for a good while. . . . Dur-ing the day, my wife worked, and I was always out looking around, and I let him stay at my place and sleep in my bed. He'd go out and blow all night somewhere and then come in and go to sleep in my bed. I'd make him leave in the afternoon before my wife came home. She didn't like him sleeping in our bed, because he wouldn't pull his clothes off before he went to bed. He would go down to Monroe's and play all night. The boys were beginning to listen to him." *

Sometimes Charlie would pay his way into the Savoy Ball-room and make his way through the Lindy Hoppers so that he could stand in front of the bandstand. The bandstand at the Savoy was large enough to accommodate two orchestras. The band in residence was the Chick Webb Orchestra. Charlie watched the hunchbacked little drummer with his grinning death's head as he paced the powerful, hard-swinging band. It had the reputation of defeating most opponents at the nation's most famous ballroom. Sometimes the opposition would be Fletcher Henderson or Duke Ellington. The two bands would play alternate sets. The incoming band would pick up the riff and for a few minutes both bands would be playing at the same time. Sidemen in these bands could be compared to stars on major league baseball teams. They had arrived after years of struggling in the minor leagues. None of them could suggest where Charlie might find work. "Try the after-hours spots," he was advised. "Always the chance a bandleader will fall in and listen." He'd already done that. Few had listened.

After a few weeks of cadging meals from the Smiths, Charlie got himself a job at Jimmy's Chicken Shack in lower Harlem. It was the first time in his life that he worked at a non-music job for pay. Besides running the automatic dish-washer, Charlie was the pot walloper, responsible for cleaning pots and pans. It was unpleasant work. His hands were con-

* Don Gazzaway, "Buster & Bird: Conversations with Buster Smith," *Jazz Review*, February 1960.

stantly soiled with food. Steam from the sinks left a film of grease on his hair, his hands, and his face.

To add to his discomfort, he could see the glamorous goings-on in the main room as the swinging doors opened and closed to admit hurrying waiters. The Chicken Shack was a popular restaurant that attracted musicians and the Harlem sporting crowd. It was owned by John Williams, former first altoist of the Clouds of Joy. The clientele included such celebrities as Joe Louis, Ethel Waters, racketeer Dickie Wells, columnist Dan Burley of the New York *Amsterdam News*, and other well-known figures of the Afro-American world. The job had one saving feature: the Chicken Shack served up its soul food with music, often of high quality. During Charlie's tenure as dishwasher, the featured artist out front was pianist Art Tatum.

Tatum would start out on a tune like *Begin the Beguine.* One chord would lead to another until the pattern had run through the entire cycle of fifths. Charlie had heard Coleman Hawkins blowing on good nights, running chords, but not with Tatum's finesse. Tatum was the master harmonist. All of the changes were right—smooth, ingenuous, laced together with effortless transitions, and exciting little surprises. All Tatum had to do was sit down at the piano, and the flow of musical ideas began, continuing without interruption for a thirty-minute set. It was like turning on the spigot. Tatum had a little trick that Charlie liked: he would work quotations from popular melodies into the changes, bits from *Them There Eyes* into the middle of *Beguine, Goodbye Forever* into *The Man I Love.* Time would suddenly be doubled. All of the modulations and rhythmic patterns stayed under control. Every note was accurately struck. The touch was light and feathery. Tatum handled arpeggios like a concert pianist, only everything Tatum played was deeply rooted in jazz.

Charlie wondered if the saxophone could be played with the speed and accuracy of Tatum's piano. If that could be done, it would be a major breakthrough. The saxophone was the more versatile instrument. More expressive. Once the piano note was struck, it was finished. You couldn't bend it or color it.

Not even Tatum could do that. A pianist had to get his coloring from big chords and the way the chords were shaded and what texture could be coaxed from the keyboard itself. With the saxophone it was different. There was a column of air—a plastic thing. You could shape notes, bend notes, take away from and add to pitch. The piano had flash, grace, elegance, and as Tatum handled it, dazzling speed. To be able to move that fast on the saxophone would be something important. That would be something.

Between sets, Tatum, who had been nearly blind from birth, would grope his way slowly back to the kitchen. The pianist didn't like to be led or assisted, and the waiters would stand out of his path. He was supposed to be able to see light and shadow with one good eye, to make out forms, doorways, people, perhaps to distinguish between black and white keys on the piano. The pianist kept a quart of good bonded whiskey in one of the glassware cupboards. The bottle was consumed, slowly and in regular doses, each night, replaced with a fresh bottle of the identical brand the next day. Whiskey was as necessary to the pianist as his meals or his sleep. Tatum lived only for the piano. The whiskey sealed him off. Everything else was a mere accessory to his life. He was a self-contained, nocturnal man. When Tatum came into the kitchen and made his way to the cupboard where the whiskey was kept, Charlie found himself too shy to speak. Anyway, there was nothing to say. Tatum was saying everything on the keyboard. Tatum would have his taste of whiskey and go back through the swinging doors to the main room. Charlie could see the soft, chunky body at the piano, Tatum's head hanging over the keyboard like a drooping flower, not really looking at the keys, even with the good eye, running those breath-taking arpeggios.

Pay at the Chicken Shack was nine dollars a week. The hours were long, midnight to eight, the same shift that his mother still worked at Western Union in Kansas City. They were confining hours that tied him down when the rest of the musicians were working, or jamming. When Tatum's contract ran out and the pianist left to fill an engagement in Hollywood, Charlie quit. He had stayed as long as Tatum stayed, almost three months. He never wanted to wash dishes again. He didn't want to leave New York either. There was a special tempo there. It was getting into his blood. He had the feeling that everything of importance happened in New York, and that Harlem was the center of Afro-American life.

The money Charlie saved lasted a week. Then a trumpeter named Jerry Hurwitz, who had taken Charlie to a few jam sessions in Greenwich Village, told him about a job at the Parisien Ballroom, on Broadway near Forty-eighth Street. Charlie took the subway downtown with rising hopes. The address was in the Times Square area, in the heart of the theater district, only a few blocks south of the famous Roseland Ballroom, where the name bands played. But the Parisien was no glamorous ballroom. It was a taxi-dance hall.

Charlie walked up two narrow flights of stairs, past battered signs saying, "YOUR PICK—FIFTY BEAUTIFUL HOSTESSES. TEN CENTS A DANCE." It was early, and he found a score of girls, heavily made-up, in satin evening gowns, waiting for the first customers. He was hired without discussion.

The seven-piece band of middle-aged hacks sat on a dimly lighted bandstand at one end of the hall. The band's repertory consisted of every tune that any musician or customer could remember from the past forty years. There was no band book, no written music, not even stock arrangements. Everything was played by ear.

Musicians at the Parisien worked to one inflexible rule: No number lasted longer than a minute. Sixty seconds. Behind the dingy drapes of the bandstand, mounted on the wall, was a special clock that made a loud "click-click" at the end of each minute. That was the cue for the bandleader to segue into the next tune. There was no change of key, or of tempo. *You Stepped Out of a Dream* dissolved into *You're an Old Smoothie; Nice Work if You Can Get It* into *Bye Bye Blackbird*. An in-chorus, a middle part (with room for a few short, desultory solos), followed by an out-chorus. *When Buddha Smiles* into *Chinatown My Chinatown*. Sixty seconds used up, the "click-click," a nod from the leader, and the next tune. The dancers continued without breaking. The leader was a dispirited man of fifty who played a watered-down Louis Armstrong style and spent the ten-minute intermissions studying horse-tip sheets. Like the others in the band, he had long since lost any real interest in music.

When Charlie Parker left Kansas City, where popular music was so much a part of life itself, he had imagined his own repertory of tunes fairly complete. It was a drop in the bucket compared to the requirements of musicians at the Parisien. As the minutes drifted by and the band segued from tune to tune, he acquired an extensive vocabulary of the popular song in America for the past forty years. *Blue Skies, Cheerful Little Earful, The Shiek (of Araby), Jeepers Creepers, Carolina in the Morning, Carolina Moon, Cryin' for the Carolines, When Dixie Stars Are Playing Peek-a-Boo, Tell Me Little Gypsy, When Irish Eyes Are Smiling, If I Were a Bee and You Were a Red Red Rose, Love Is Where You Find It*—at the Parisien. Charlie remembered the days in Kansas City when he would go into the music store, memorize new tunes from sheet music, and leave without buying, the musical intelligence in his head. There were a lot of tunes they hadn't stocked. There were oldies like *My Merry Oldsmobile* and *Over There*. A Cole Porter medley: *Don't Fence Me In, It's De-Lovely, Miss Otis Regrets*. The honeysuckle music filled the taxi dance hall with its ooze and flabby beat.

Miss Brown to You. Victor Herbert's *Kiss Me Again* to wind up the fifty-minute set and put customers in the mood for soft drinks served at tables set out in the back under green trelliswork twined with faded artificial flowers.

Each dance cost the customer a ten-cent ticket, which was given to one of the satin-sheathed hostesses. Each dance lasted sixty seconds. An hour spent on the floor, or at the tables, came to six dollars, and that seemed like a lot of money in 1938. The girls received 40 percent of the face value of the tickets. Those with two years' seniority received 45 percent. The Parisien was a staging area for hustlers on the move from one town to another, for call girls fresh out of telephone numbers, for starstruck, disorganized young girls who had run away from homes in small Midwestern towns and the South.

Customers at the Parisien Ballroom were visiting firemen, middle-aged business men from Brooklyn and The Bronx out for a night on the town, hard city mashers training for pimpdom. The hostesses referred amiably to their employment as "vertical prostitution." There was no open vice in New York. The gap was filled by the taxi-dance halls. The Parisien and several rivals all had their reputations and steady followings. Successful hostesses went on Caribbean holidays, supported families, retired and opened beauty salons, wore mink coats. They were past mistresses of the little sexual drama that began with flirtations across a barrier in the lobby. Most of the hard action took place in front of the bandstand, away from the main part of the dance hall and prying eyes. There the girls did their bumps, grinds, and bellyrubs, their faces vacant, both arms clamped around their partners' necks, parlaying orange tickets in skeins to be cashed at the close of business each night. The Parisien smelled of musty broadcloth, of armpits and unclean bottoms, of sweat laced with "White Shoulders," the perfume in vogue with taxi-dance queens that year.

The most lucrative concession at the Parisien was the sale of rubbers in the men's room by an elderly attendant who bore a startling resemblance to the Negro leader Marcus Garvey. This man made more than the musicians. "Got me the best shit house in the whole goddam city," the old man would boast to Charlie in his coarse country accent. "Always tellin' my own boy, never mind 'bout schoolin'—just git yo'seff a shit house and"—he paused for effect—"stay in yo' hole!" The last words would be underscored, a new slant on "place keeping." Charlie had seen almost as much of it in New York as in Kansas City. The eighteen-year-old who thought himself the world's best saxophone player listened and said nothing, and continued to grind fifty-minute sets at the Parisien Ballroom.

To while away the time on the bandstand, Charlie began to use Tatum's little trick of working quotations from odd tunes into the melody being played. *Blue Turning Gray Over You* seemed appropriate for an aging jewelry salesman struggling with a hostess young enough to be his granddaughter. A few bars of Jimmy Noone's old number, *Apex Blues*, often played in

Kansas City burlesque houses, applauded bumps and grinds. *I Found a Million Dollar Baby in a Five and Ten Cent Store* roused an occasional smile. These and other bits of musical intelligence woven into the mindless potpourri were admired by the hostesses. Charlie became their favorite musician.

On the Parisien job Charlie's horizons expanded in another way. Kansas City had been a Jim Crow town, as rigidly structured as any city in the Deep South. Young men of Charlie's generation did not take liberties with white women. Those who dared were taken for rides to Swope Park, and their bodies were fished out of the Missouri River. New York City was a little more liberal in that respect. Charlie's first white girlfriend was a Parisien hostess. She responded to his saxophone language.

A peroxide blonde from Georgia, she lived with a sister, supported a daughter of seven, did not accept dates after work. Charlie would take her uptown to his room at the Woodside Hotel and they would turn on with a stick of cannabis and spend an hour in bed. Later Charlie would take her to Monroe's Uptown House, where he could sit in with the band.

One morning at Dan Wall's Chili House, an all-night restaurant at Seventh Avenue and 139th Street, Charlie was jamming with a rhythm section led by guitarist Biddy Fleet. They were working *Cherokee*. Charlie had been over the changes countless times, and the tune was beginning to sound stale. Charlie got to thinking, "There's got to be something more, some new way to go." Then an idea struck him: if he played the top notes of the chords instead of the middle or lower notes, he would have a new line. It was worth trying. Asking Biddy Fleet to continue, Charlie played through another chorus. The notes sounded strange, but it worked. He was using the upper intervals, ninths, elevenths, thirteenths, skimming along on the very tops of the chords. Nobody knew where he was getting the new line. It had never been done in jazz before. He could find no one to collaborate on these experiments. The rest of the musicians were sleeping on him. He felt he had stumbled on to something. Hawkins, Lester Young, none of those players had ever used a similar line. It was his.

When he could stand the Parisien no longer, he accepted a summer job in Kew Gardens, a subway ride from Harlem. It was as dull as the taxi dance, except that you didn't have to change the tune every sixty seconds. Customers requested *Bei Mir Bist Du Schon, Mahzel,* and numbers made popular by Al Jolson and Fanny Brice a decade before. Charlie worked a few weeks and went back to Clark Monroe's Uptown House for a non-salaried job with drummer Ebenezer Paul and trumpeter Dave Riddick. The musicians divided the kitty. One evening a veteran named Banjo Burney dropped in to recruit Charlie for an out-of-town job at Annapolis, Maryland. The job was at a pleasant little club catering to Naval Academy cadets. There was no hotel for Negroes, and the musicians boarded in a private home in the local ghetto. The patrons were elegant young men in uniform with their dates. While Charlie was at Annapolis a telegram arrived from his mother telling him that Charles, Sr., had died. She sent him fare for a train ticket back to Kansas City. He returned to his hometown.

The funeral was a searing experience for which Charlie found himself unprepared. His father had been slashed by a prostitute. Medical attention had been slow in coming and Charles, Sr., had bled to death. Charlie had not seen his father since the last ephemeral visit to the house on Olive Street, shortly after the family moved into town from the suburbs and Charles, Sr., began working as a cook on the Santa Fe Chief. The body was so shriveled from hard living and loss of blood as to be barely recognizable. Charlie could hardly believe that this was the worldly-wise song-and-dance man who had been the romantic figure of his childhood. The embalming job, the best his mother could afford, had been badly done. The pale, emaciated, face with its lines of bitterness and defeat lay cushioned on the quilted white satin of the cheap coffin and would haunt Charlie for the rest of his life. He began to realize how deeply he had come to depend upon substitute figures—88 Keyes, George E. Lee, Jesse Price, Prof Smith, Old Man Virgil. But he would never forget the face in the coffin.

Charlie made the rounds of the night clubs. No one was hiring musicians.

Tootie Clarkin had sold out and moved across the county line, in preparation for the worst. Pendergast had been indicted for income tax fraud. A federal attorney named Maurice Milligan produced evidence to show that Pendergast had gambled away as much as a hundred thousand dollars in a single day of wagering at the tracks and had defrauded the government of more than a half million dollars in undeclared taxes. Milligan had unmasked the interlocking corporations set up around Pendergast's Ready Mixed Concrete Company, which had the monopoly of supplying concrete for all paving, public works, and civic buildings in Kansas City. He had then traced the intricate lines of privilege, influence, and graft through the Kansas City body politic. The man who had controlled Kansas City for thirteen years was convicted and sentenced to the federal penitentiary at Leavenworth. Not even intervention by Senator Harry S. Truman had been able to save Pendergast.

As the boss fell, down came a whole gallery of Kansas City bigwigs: Judge Henry McElroy, former city manager; W. W. Graves, district attorney of Jackson County; Police Chief Otto Higgins; and Big Charley Carollo, the ex-Lazia bodyguard, who had become the collector of the "lug" for the Pendergast machine after Lazia was machine-gunned to death. The good old days of unstamped liquor, needled beer, loaded dice, open prostitution, street-corner traffic in narcotics, of corrupt police and gangsters in bullet-proof limousines, were over. And so were the days when the police winked at closing ordinances and cabarets rocked and blasted their way through the night. As its new mayor Kansas City elected Bryce Smith, a short, puffy little bakery owner who had headed the reform movement. As soon as the city hall had been swept clean, a massive campaign was begun to whitewash Kansas City. Along with the gambling places, "horse rooms," and brothels the new administration closed the gangster-run clubs where jazz had been played in Kansas City for the past thirteen years. It was the end of an era.

Charlie was ready to beat his way back to New York City when he received an offer to join the Harlan Leonard Rockets, a new Kansas City band that had just signed a recording contract with RCA Victor. Leonard was an alumnus of Lincoln High School. In 1922 he had received his diploma, with special honors in music, and joined the Bennie Moten Kansas City Orchestra. A well-set, handsome, dark man with strong, regular features, Leonard was exactly the kind of musician Charlie was not—legitimately trained, a fast sight-reader, a man known for his perfect intonation and ability to lead sections. He had served in that capacity with Moten and Thamon Hayes before taking over the Rockets. Leonard was a man Charlie respected but did not like very much. The band had Jessie Price on drums and a good rhythm section. The brass and reeds were competent, but a bit stiff. Except for tenor saxophonist Henry Bridges, Jr., and Fred Beckett, who played trombone in a fluid style using only the closed three positions, nobody was saying very much. It was a good, solid, old-fashioned Kansas City band, closer to Moten than Basie.

As usual, Charlie was much younger than anyone else. Leonard was thirty-five, an old man in Charlie's eyes. Leonard was also a strict disciplinarian. Charlie lasted less than five weeks. Half of the time he was late to work, so that Leonard was obliged to leave the podium and return to the section in order to have the reeds sound right. Before the fifth week had elapsed Leonard tactfully suggested that Charlie resign in the interest of the general good. Charlie left owing a week's pay, drawn, as usual, in advance. His career had reached a crossroads.

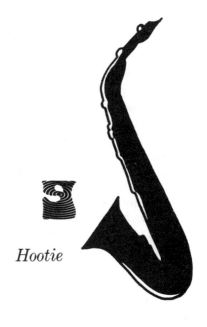

Hootie

The Prof Smith Orchestra completed Charlie's apprenticeship as a jazz and dance band musician, Kansas City style. He had pursued his independent experiments, acquired the skills of the professional, and made himself into a formidable competitor at jam sessions. As the spring of 1939 approached, his talents were in readiness for their full exposure, lacking only the proper setting. Once again Charlie was to be in the right place at the right time. Despite the hard times besetting the music community in Kansas City, a band was then being organized to open a new ballroom in the downtown area. Backed by Walter Bales, the businessman who had sponsored Basie, it was being formed under the leadership of Charlie's old comrade-in-arms from Lucille's Band Box, blues and boogie-woogie pianist Jay McShann. Unlike the Rockets, this was a youth band, full of enthusiasm and inclined to experiment. It would be the last of the great Kansas City bands.

Its recruitment involved a series of raids, financed by Bales, on three Omaha orchestras, those of Lloyd Hunter, Red Perkins, and Nat Towles. In many ways the band was reminiscent of Count Basie. The raids paralleled those Bennie Moten had made on the Oklahoma City Blue Devils that led to the Basie nucleus. Like Basie, the Jay McShann Orchestra was strongly oriented toward the blues, and toward that hallmark of Kansas City style, the riff, a rhythmic figure providing the framework for extended band improvisations and the unfolding of solos. Vocalist Walter Brown, discovered in a Vine Street honky-tonk, sang the blues in a latter-day Jimmy Rushing style, with a keening voice of unusual carrying power and the poignant edge peculiar to Kansas City bluesmen.

The band swung from the rhythm section. To the leader's piano were added Gene Ramey's bass and Gus Johnson's drums. Ramey played with a flat, broad tone, learned from Walter Page; like Page, he was a steady, unobtrusive, behind-the-beat section man, felt more often than heard, the pivot man around whom the band pulse centered. Johnson, a barnstorming drummer who had migrated to Kansas City from Tyler, Texas, played aggressively, with an almost metallic sonority. Ramey and Johnson were complements, like the Walter Page–Jo Jones team with Basie. There was a similar fusing of fat and thin sounds. McShann, Ramey, and Johnson had been working together for about eighteen months, ever since McShann left Lucille's to launch his trio at Martin's 210 Club, a share of which was owned by the jazz-minded Mr. Bales. McShann had worked up a repertory of fast blues and boogie woogie numbers—*So You Won't Jump, Hold 'em Hootie* and *Vine Street Boogie*—enthusiastically performed in his rampant, highly percussive manner. He was a pianist with fast, supple wrists, who did not use his thumbs very much. The rhythm section was fleshed out to orchestral proportions by the addition of Kansas City guitarist Leonard "Lucky" Enois and compared not unfavorably with that of the Count Basie Orchestra, in 1939 the best in jazz.

The band was neither as easy nor as smooth. It was brash, eager, and aggressive, not without its rough spots, but it swung hard. As with all Kansas City bands, its soloists had the feeling of the rhythm rising under them. Their solos emerged from the rich, percussive foundation of the rhythm section.

Solo trumpet work was divided between Orville "Piggy" Minor, who played a Lips Page style, broad-toned and gusty, and a frail young man from Oklahoma City named Bernard "Buddy" Anderson, who after Charlie was the most innovative musician in the band. Bud Gould was the single trombonist. The reeds, four strong, used Bob Mabane, a convincing tenor saxophonist cast in the Kansas City mold; William J. Scott, lead tenor; and John Jackson and Charlie Parker, alto saxophones.

As a final similarity between the Count Basie Orchestra of 1936 and the Jay McShann Orchestra of 1939, old Kaycee hands noted the parallel roles played by Lester Young and Charlie Parker. In both instances, it was saxophonists, not brassmen, who were the moving forces of the orchestral machinery, quite the opposite of the situation with Northern and Eastern bands.

After several weeks of rehearsals, the band moved into John "Tums" Tumino's Century Ballroom, at 36th and Broadway, alternating with the Rockets, and also worked at the Casa Fiesta, College Inn, and Tootie's Mayfair. That summer there was a long engagement at suburban Fairyland Park. Then the band left Kansas City for its first road trip, through Missouri, Kansas, and Oklahoma, with a holdover stay at the Casa Dell in Tulsa. In the fall of 1940 the band found itself at liberty one weekend in Wichita, where McShann had often appeared with the Al Denny and Eddie Hill bands. There he was engaged by an old friend, Fred Higginson, manager of radio KFBI, to record a series of transcriptions. In 1940 this was something of a novelty. Few bands, certainly none in the unknown or territorial category, had made radio transcriptions. On November 30, 1940, a Saturday, a group from the band recorded *I Found a New Baby* and *Body and Soul*, using Buddy Anderson and Orville Minor, trumpets; Bud Gould, trombone, doubling violin;

William Scott, tenor saxophone; Charlie Parker, alto saxophone; Jay McShann, piano; Gene Ramey, bass; and Gus Johnson, drums. On December 2, the following Monday, with Bob Mabane replacing Scott on tenor, the small band recorded *Honeysuckle Rose, Lady Be Good, Coquette, Moten Swing*, and an untitled blues.

That Charlie Parker was the inspiration of the Jay McShann Orchestra and its best soloist is made clear on the KFBI transcriptions. On *Honeysuckle Rose* the tempo is close to metronome 300. Driven relentlessly by Johnson and Ramey, the meter is too fast for any of the wind players except Charlie. Unison parts are rough, and the solos precipitous.

Charlie's entrance, after Minor's erratic trumpet solo, is dashing and self-assured. Playing in perfect time, he constructs a line from a series of meticulously dotted eighth and sixteenth notes, throwing in an occasional *grupetto*, à la Lester Young. In 1940, only a handful of jazz musicians were able to make statements so incisive under like time demands. There is more than a suggestion of Art Tatum in the crisp attack and flowing cadences. There are new things, too—turns of his own, use of major seconds and sevenths, and diminished chords. Finally, already faintly in evidence on these post-teen performances, there is that salient characteristic of what would become the most innovative instrumental style in jazz, the feeling throughout the whole solo that the improviser was actually playing in two different meters at once, the implication of double-time.

Charlie was already able to play a full thirty-two-bar chorus without breath-control problems. His solo is a jet stream of notes, propelled by a comfortable reserve of air, with control well in hand. Charlie was ready to close the gap between himself and the leading jazzmen: Young, Tatum, Benny Goodman, Roy Eldridge.

There is still more to be heard on the Wichita transcriptions. The ballads constitute a kind of casebook study of saxophone style as it existed in 1940. *Coquette* is played very nearly straight in the popular style heard nightly in ballrooms throughout America, at that point in the evening when the electrician turned his muted blue spotlights on the slowly revolving chandeliers and couples danced cheek-to-cheek across the polished floors. The tune is played as it might have been by Carmen Lombardo or even Rudy Wiedoeft. From it Charlie drains the last drop of sentiment instilled by the Tin Pan Alley tunesmiths. "This is a very bad piece of music and worse use of the instrument," Charlie seems to be telling us, "but it requires technique, and this too I can do." The temptation to inflect the long, mannerly procession of quarter notes is irresistible, so that Charlie's *Coquette* is ever on the verge of blossoming forth into a genuine swing tune.

Having paid his respects to the Wiedoeft school, Charlie proceeds to *Body and Soul* for a rundown of establishment saxophone style as practiced by Coleman Hawkins. The phrasing is on the beat and predictable, the line carefully adjusted to the chord sequence. Charlie does not have Hawkins's mastery of changes or opulent sound, but the performance is a notable exercise.

Lady Be Good had been a standard vehicle for Lester Young. It was one of the recordings Charlie had taken with him to the Ozarks, worn to the bottom of the grooves and memorized note for note. As one listens to the Wichita *Lady Be Good* it is clear that Charlie was hatched from the Lestorian egg. This *Lady Be Good is* Lester, Lester in the disguise of a sedulous imitator, and on alto saxophone. When the tape is played at half speed, so that the register of the alto is lowered to that of the tenor, it is impossible to distinguish master from disciple. One hears the whole inventory of Lestorian devices: offsets of long notes against short, contrasts of tone achieved by false fingering, the shaping of sounds, decaying upper register gasps, the rise and fall of the melodic line, and the effortless swing. The startling employment of the alto saxophone heard by Billy Eckstine at the 65 Club in Chicago is all here on tape for the historian and musicologist to study. The transcriptions are perhaps the most revealing record left by a jazz musician of his origin, inspiration, models, and apprenticeship.

The transcriptions are also valuable for the light they throw on changes to come in trumpet style. The solos by Piggy Minor are furious rides adding little to brass tradition. That had already been done better by Lips Page. But Minor's opposite number in the McShann trumpet section was already into a new concept. Buddy Anderson has an important solo on *Moten Swing*. His vibrato is light, phrasing relaxed, tone suave and masked. He is able to blend legato and staccato passages in a way that had not been done before. Anderson's work foreshadows developments to follow in the bebop period and the playing of Fats Navarro and Dizzy Gillespie.

The Wichita transcriptions establish Charlie's point of development in the period before his revolutionary statements. He was not, as later many were to believe, a maverick genius. His roots lay deep in a rich, unspoiled folk culture. He had learned at first hand from the masters of his art, had listened to every important soloist in jazz, either on record, or by catching them as the name bands passed through Kansas City. He was determined, dedicated, tireless, and ambitious. Jazz had become a way of life, jealous of his entire time, energy, and being. He had taken the pains to prepare himself, and he was precocious. Taking into account his association with George E. Lee, Jesse Price, Prof Smith, Harlan Leonard, and Jay McShann, the various jobs in New York, to say nothing of the time devoted to jamming and to practice, Charlie, by any conservative estimate, had devoted not less than fifteen thousand hours to the alto saxophone.

That was the kind of preparation virtuoso performers brought to the recital hall, although no one thought of musical apprenticeship for jazzmen in comparable terms. But there was just as much preparation. There was as much virtuosity, and a greater amount of interpretation involved, because the jazzman is composer as well as performer. Innovations to follow would rest on this solid foundation; 1940 ended with the Jay McShann Orchestra headed back to Kansas City. The band had yet to play a major engagement or make a commercial phonograph record. Charlie Parker was an unknown saxophonist in the reed section of an obscure territorial band knocking about the Southwest. He was twenty years old.

The band returned to Kansas City for a rest and a refit. Its

excellent morale is attested to by the lack of turnover in the
ranks. There were only two changes in personnel when the
band opened at John Tumino's Century Room. The easy-going
ways of the Jay McShann Orchestra are reflected in the lyrics
of a novelty number then a part of the repertoire and later recorded for Decca (Decca 8559, April 30, 1941). Titled *Hootie's
Ignorant Oil*, it was composed by McShann and sung by Walter
Brown:

> *When you get drunk, why do you do the things you do?*
> *When you get drunk, why do you do the things you do?*
> *You talk loud and long and don't care what you say or do.*
>
> *Last night do you remember standing on Eighteenth*
>   *and Vine? (2)*
> *If I'd of been your pappy, you wouldn't have been called*
>   *no son of mine.*
>
> *Now, don't drink, Hootie! Hootie, Hootie, it won't spoil, (2)*
> *Now I know why folks all call it ignorant oil.*
>
> *So hold it, Hootie! Hootie, don't drink that stuff! (2)*
> *'cause you don't know just when you've had enough!*

"Ignorant oil" was Kansas City argot for booze, and the
reference was to McShann, whose occasional sprees had earned
him the nickname "Hootie." The joke was over the heads of
most listeners, and was carried off nightly without the slightest
damage to band morale. No one seemed to enjoy it more than
the leader.

According to McShann, "Charlie was one of the reasons we
had such a happy-go-lucky band. We spent almost as much time
rehearsing and working up ideas as we did playing jobs. I gave
Charlie a lot of room. Once I had to remonstrate with him
about his careless attire—he was easily the worst-dressed man
in the band. He told me, 'Hootie, would you like it if I came to
the bandstand looking like a doctor and played like a doctor?' I
had no answer to that. Another of his sayings was, 'If you come
in loose, you'll get ideas and play good notes. If you act just a
little bit foolish, good ideas will come to you.' He lived his music

twenty-four hours a day. He never played the same way two nights running. His head was full of ideas and melodies. He'd take his horn out and start playing in hotels and dressing rooms. He couldn't wait for the job to start so that he could play solos and get his ideas out."

"Bird was a most receptive being," Gene Ramey said of Charlie in this period. "He got into his music all the sounds right around him—the swish of a car speeding down a highway, the hum of wind as it goes through the leaves . . . Everything had a musical message for him. If he heard a dog bark, he would say the dog was speaking. . . . Sometimes on the dance floor, while he was playing, women would perform in front of him. Their attitudes, their gestures, their faces would awaken in him an emotional shock that he would express musically in his solos. As soon as his tones became piercing, we understood at once what he meant.

"Bird had his own way of starting from a chord in B-natural and B-flat. Then he would run a cycle against that; and, probably, it would only be two or three bars before we got to the channel that he would come back to the basic changes. In those days we called it 'running out of key.' Bird used to sit and try to tell us what he was doing. I am sure at that time nobody else in the band could play, for example, even the channel to *Cherokee*. So Bird used to play a series of *Tea for Two* phrases against the channel, and since this was a melody that could easily be remembered, it gave the guys something to play during those bars. When I look back, it seems to me that Bird was at that time so advanced in jazz that I do not think we realized to what degree his ideas had become perfected." *

* Interview with Gene Ramey, *Jazz Review*, Vol. 3, No. 9 (November 1960), p. 8.

The Band That Played
the Blues

By the early spring of 1941 things were looking up for the new band. Tums Tumino, operator of the Continental Room, had volunteered to act as pro tem booker for the band and had lined up an extensive road trip, and Dave Dexter, the jazz writer who had first brought the attention of *Down Beat* readers to McShann's talents, was trying to interest a major label in a record contract. The road trip began in March and took the band to the Atlantic seaboard, then southward. Few if any of the musicians had been into the old South; most came from states bordering on or north of the Mason-Dixon line. In Martinsville, Virginia, while the band was playing the last set of the engagement, the promoter made off with the box-office receipts. McShann was arrested for being in default of deposit on the hall, and the trip interrupted until the monies were made good. Although the defaulting promoter was well-known in town no attempt was made to locate him, and the incident was treated as a capital joke played at the expense of the barnstormers.

Pressures were stringent in the Deep South. When the band reached Jackson, Mississippi, the musicians were admonished to conduct themselves with the utmost discretion. Ground rules in Jackson called for black people to be off the streets no later than eleven P.M. It was therefore necessary to begin the dance at seven-thirty and finish promptly at ten-thirty so that musicians and dancers alike could hurry home to outleg the curfew. Bandmen were billeted in private homes and rooming houses, there being no proper hotel in Jackson. Charlie and Walter Brown were assigned to cots on the front screened porch of a house. Not being sleepy, and assuming that all was well, they left on the porch light and continued to talk, mostly about attractive girls in Jackson, until midnight, when a police car arrived bearing four lawmen, holstered and rednecked. Walter and Charlie were placed under arrest; the burning light constituted an infraction of the curfew. Charlie and the band's principal vocalist were not able to rejoin the band for several days, and when they arrived were considerably worse for wear. They bore lumps on the head where they had been beaten with nightsticks by members of the Jackson constabulary. As a memento of the occasion, Charlie composed a tune temporarily titled *What Price Love?*, later to surface as *Yardbird Suite*.

The trip through the deep South was Charlie's first hard look at naked racism. He had visited several parts of the United States and found segregation everywhere. In New York it was implied and indirect; in Kansas City, implied and covertly enforced. In the Deep South it was overt, rigidly structured, and tirelessly enforced by a tough, ruthless police force, armed to the teeth with .45-caliber revolvers and sawed off 12-gauge shotguns. The trip afforded him time to do some serious thinking about social problems. The obvious and only possible escape was to resign from the band; but six years of his life had gone into achieving a place in that band. In looking back over his own experience and those of his musical heroes, Charlie realized that black attitudes had undergone certain changes in two generations of jazzmen. Many of Louis Armstrong's generation had become minstrel men, putting on a show, and irreverent young Negroes were calling them Uncle Toms. Jazzmen of Lester Young's generation were more sophisticated and discerning, but they were not ready to fight back; they sidestepped difficult situations and buried themselves in an elaborately Bohemian way of life. As name bands attained prominence, it became possible for their leaders to turn down bookings in certain states and notorious cities, like Jackson. The McShann Orchestra had not reached such a status; for bands of its caliber a tour of the South was a matter of economic survival.

In working out his own solutions to social problems, Charlie fell back on the training he had received on the street corners of Kansas City, and on the adjustments he had made as a teenager constantly associated with older people, especially the sporting-life types found in the district, those who "had all the hypes scored." His ability to act out roles dictated by unequal encounters with older people now proved to be of the greatest value—as he saw it, it was the key to survival. An accomplished mimic, Charlie began to study the regional speech and manners of Negroes trapped in the cotton-and-turpentine economies of Alabama, Mississippi, and Texas. A narrow line separated "acting out" from "copping out." It was possible to allay hostility and soften confrontations by improvising the necessary roles, just as one might improvise a successful jazz solo. With skill and experience it was even possible to act out parts and convert such situations into charades played at the expense of the oppressor. The McShann road trips took place five years before the appearance, in New York, of the first hipster. In 1941 Charlie was already into his role of the cool, wiggy cat with everything under control. The mother wit of the Kansas City street corner and the tactics of the jam session were being applied to life on a broader front. Charlie was learning to score all the situations and to have, at ready, the right lines and postures. Never to be at a loss, or disadvantage—that was his objective.

After a few nasty incidents like those in Martinsville and Jackson, Charlie was given, at his own request and with the general approval of the musicians, the added job of driving the truck carrying uniforms and band instruments. His companion was a second vocalist picked up by the band in San Antonio, a young man named Al Hibbler. A balladeer in the tradition of George E. Lee and Pha Terrell (Terrell was vocal star of Andy Kirk's Clouds of Joy), Hibbler gave the band an extra box-office appeal. Hibbler's favorite numbers were *Blue Champagne, T'is Autumn, Old Folks,* and *Skylark.* Charlie liked them, too. The exercises in saxophone accompaniments to ballads begun behind George E. Lee at Lake Taneycomo were continued and the Hibbler-Parker collaborations were among the evening's highlights wherever the Jay McShann Orchestra appeared.

Blind from birth, the big, easygoing singer had developed his own special set of perceptions; he and Charlie soon became very tight. Both had developed intuition to a point approaching clairvoyance. Parker and Hibbler shared an ability to size up strangers quickly on the basis of voice qualities. Guile, larceny, enmity, or the genocidal hatred masked by the beefy faces of Southern lawmen were made transparent by the speaker's vibrato, dynamics, and voice timbre. A single word, *"Boy,"* the one most often heard from white lips, could sum up the speaker's character and intentions.

Al Hibbler still recalls those road trips with amusement. A blind man was, after all, ostensibly harmless, as was the stuttering truck driver impersonated by Charlie. Charlie would stall the vehicle in the main street of a town and, by a mixture of bumbling ineptitude and guileful con, manage to obtain, instead of a traffic citation, a police escort to the dance hall where the band was scheduled to appear. Arriving there, Charlie would grin, assist Hibbler from the cab, and, producing a sack of tobacco and cigarette papers, proceed to roll, one-handed, a cigarette with deft, lightning movements of his fingers. Then he would light up, thank the escorting policemen for their courtesy, and go inside. It was a trick he had picked up on the streets of Kansas City, only Charlie had gone the hustlers one better. He had practiced until he could do it with one hand. The cigarette trick became part of his bag.

One-nighters in the South had their pleasant aspects as well. There was a certain advantage in the lack of hotels. Charlie, who had acquired the reputation of the band's leading trencherman, liked boarding out in private homes. That meant good home-cooked meals with grits, greens, homemade biscuits, molasses, chickory-flavored coffee, and female companionship. The trip proved to be a liberal education in how the "other half" lived, and survived, below the line. Brothers and sisters down there put on their masks every time they ventured out of their own neighborhoods. As for the white people, few of them had any inkling of what went on behind the masks, or in the homes, any more than they knew what was going on in American music. It was a life apart, a different culture, a different language.

When the band wound up a short engagement in New Orleans, word came that negotiations by Dexter and Tumino had resulted in a contract for McShann to cut six sides for Decca in Dallas, the most westerly point on the road trip and the site of the label's regional recording facility. The first official session of the Jay McShann Orchestra for a commercial label took place there April 30, 1941. The full band recorded *Swingmatism*, a riff original; *Hootie Blues*, co-authored and arranged by Charlie; and a blues instrumental, *Dexter Blues*, named for Dave Dexter. McShann then made two fast-blues piano solos (*Hold 'em Hootie* and *Vine Street Boogie*). As an afterthought, Walter Brown, already featured on *Hootie*, sang *Confessin' the Blues*, accompanied by the rhythm section (McShann, Ramey, Gus Johnson). Unfortunately Hibbler was not given a chance to record.

The session was supervised by Dave Kapp, who had come out from New York for the assignment. He was the same artists-and-repertoire man who had filched the Count Basie Orchestra from John Hammond. Kapp had supervised all of the Basie sessions, as well as those of the Clouds of Joy; he was known in the industry as a specialist in handling "colored" orchestras. Kapp was also believed to have the formula for producing juke box hits; it had been established by his selection of *Until the Real Thing Comes Along* as a vehicle for Pha Terrell. It is worth noting that Decca had just lost the services of Count Basie, and that Kapp was undoubtedly keen on restocking the Decca shelves with more good Kansas City music.

Of the six sides recorded at Dallas, *Confessin' the Blues* proved to be the sleeper. It would be the pivotal performance, affecting the image and future of the Jay McShann Orchestra. Perhaps because it was recorded at the end of the afternoon, when everyone was loose, and because the performance was impromptu, with no instrumental distractions for the juke box listener, *Confessin' the Blues* came off with a relaxed, uningenuous quality. Manly, pleading, and breathless, Walter Brown sings a variant of the standard urban blues:

> *Baby, here I telephone you with my heart in my hand,*
> *I want you to read it, mama, hoping that you'll understand.*
> *Well, baby! —Mama, please don't dog me 'round,*
> *I'd rather love you, baby, than anyone else I know in town.*

And, as McShann's insinuating piano tinkles on, Walter Brown concludes with the irresistible:

> *When my days are long and dreary and the sun refuse to shine,*
> *I would never be blue and lonely if I knew that you were mine,*
> *Well, baby—will you make everything all right?*
> *Can I have you today, babe? Or will it be tomorrow night?*

As Decca 8559, bearing the familiar blue and gold label, retailing at thirty-five cents, the 78 rpm shellac record appeared on the market a few weeks after the Dallas session and quickly made its way toward the top of the rhythm-and-blues hit list. The eventual sales of *Confessin' the Blues* exceeded 500,000 or nearly $200,000 at retail, substantial figures for an item of this kind in 1941.

Jack Kapp needed no further convincing. From then on the Jay McShann Orchestra was the band that played the blues, and its prime attraction was Walter Brown. No matter that the McShann book contained about 50 percent riff originals in the Kansas City tradition (*Swingmatism*, *Sepian Bounce*); 25 percent ballads, beautifully handled by Hibbler and Parker; and 25 percent blues, Walter Brown's bag—a product mix that, if properly presented, would have made McShann a worthy rival to Kirk and Basie. McShann was blues merchandise, typed and now packaged by Decca. All McShann releases appeared on the Decca "Sepia Series," with eight thousand numbers assigned to the Decca "race" catalogue, and intended for sale exclusively to black people. Back to back with *Confessin' the Blues* but never played on the juke boxes, and scarcely listened to by the general public, was *Hootie Blues*, a throwaway on Decca's part, one of the important jazz records of the decade.

If *Confessin' the Blues* created a stir on the nation's juke boxes, the effect of *Hootie Blues* sent a shock wave through those musicians who stumbled onto the B side. To all intents and purposes *Hootie* was another Walter Brown vehicle. Sandwiched in between the opening orchestral chorus and the lyric are twelve bars of alto saxophone, occupying an interval of about thirty seconds (metronome $\sJ = 100$). Those twelve bars were heard as a sermon from the mount. The sinuous line and the stark, pristine architecture of sound revealed a totally new jazz concept. There are seven cadences, a line of buoyant updrafts and tumbling descents, with the rests not on odd or unusual intervals of the scale but on the very common ones for jazzmen, the third, the fifth and the tonic, arrived at in a new way. Each note is shaped, and the plastic quality of the sound is unique. True pitches are more often suggested, or just touched upon, than played. The loud/soft dynamics are manipulated against the carefully controlled variations of pitch. And, as a final stroke, Charlie brings the line to rest at precisely the point required to cue the vocalist into the first line of the lyric. *Hootie* is a miniature, yet a performance so rounded, assured, and musically right, that it constitutes a landmark among the literature of jazz. It is a Pandora's box of things to come.

A future star saxophonist, Sonny Criss, studying alto in Los Angeles, recalls buying the record in a Central Avenue music store. "The saxophonist was not identified on the label or in any of the reviews that appeared in trade magazines. I only knew that some musician I might never meet or hear again had discovered a new way through the blues progression. That solo on *Hootie Blues* started me in a completely new direction." Like many important breakthroughs, the meaning of *Hootie Blues* was shared by a select few. Nor was its meaning immediately clear. *Hootie Blues* was an enigmatic road sign beckoning toward a very distant and as yet unknown destination.

Once *Confessin' the Blues* was spinning merrily on the juke boxes, Dave Kapp took a more active hand in the affairs of the band. John Tumino was persuaded to step down in favor of the powerful General Amusement Corporation. After a holdover engagement at Jubilee Junction in Jefferson City, Missouri, the band came into Chicago for a followup session in mid-November at Decca's midwestern studios, where seven sides were recorded. All featured Walter Brown. Charlie's only chance to be heard was by way of a short series of obbligato passages behind the singer on *One Woman's Blues*. Using its expertise and leverage, General Amusement soon arranged the booking that was the goal of every orchestra in America, an engagement at New York's Savoy Ballroom. After one-week stands at the Regal Theater in Chicago and the Paradise Theater in Detroit, the Jay McShann Orchestra, still traveling in passenger cars, with Charlie Parker and Al Hibbler riding in the instrument truck, arrived in New York. Hibbler remembers their excitement and a friendly encounter with a New York mounted policeman when they lost their way and were circling aimlessly around Central Park. Charlie was back in his adopted city.

On the second Friday of January, 1942, the band opened at the Savoy, "Home of Happy Feet," the world's most famous ballroom, a huge upstairs pavilion on 140th Street. It did not matter that the debut was overshadowed by America's entry into World War II, or that Harlem had been ruled off-limits for white folk. On opening night the band shared the stand with the Lucky Millinder Orchestra, then enjoying such talents as pianist Clyde Hart, trumpeter Freddie Webster, altoman Tab Smith, trumpeter Dizzy Gillespie, and vocalist Sister Rosetta Tharpe. *Clap Hands Here Comes Charlie* featured Parker on a "walk-on-playing" solo. He was starred on *Cherokee*, played at a furious tempo. As far as the dancers were concerned, *Cherokee* was a tour de force of saxophone acrobatics. For musicians the tune, with its involved harmony and lightning changes, represented the other side of the *Hootie* coin. *Hootie* was quiet, introspective, and blue; *Cherokee*, brash, aggressive, and dazzling.

Charlie received his first attention from the music press. Barry Ulanov, covering the band's debut for *Metronome* magazine, wrote, "The jazz set forth by Parker on alto is superb. Parker's tone tends to rubberiness, and he has a tendency to play too many notes, but his continual search for wild ideas, and the consistency with which he finds them compensate for the weakness that should easily be overcome."

Avant garde trumpeter Howard McGhee heard Charlie for the first time over a radio in a dressing room at the Adams Theatre in Newark, where he was working with the Charlie Barnett Orchestra. McGhee was chatting with Oscar Pettiford, Al Killian, Peanuts Holland, and Ralph Burns when bassist Chubby Jackson tuned in the regular Sunday afternoon broadcast from the Savoy Ballroom. A spectacular alto saxophonist was heard playing *Cherokee*. Ten choruses followed. Nobody knew the name of the musician. When the Barnett band finished the last show that night, the sidemen went to the Savoy. The Jay McShann Orchestra was featured. McGhee asked McShann to play *Cherokee*, and the identity of the unknown saxophonist was revealed. The Barnett sidemen had never heard such spectacular improvisation on the instrument. They talked to Charlie, found out that he came from Kansas City, and invited him out to dinner when the Savoy closed.

Twenty-five hundred miles away in Albuquerque, New Mexico, the broadcasts from the Savoy were picked up on short-wave radio by John Lewis, then studying music and anthropology at the University of New Mexico, and later to become pianist and musical director of the Modern Jazz Quartet.

"The alto solos on those broadcasts opened up a whole new world of music for me. I'd known Jay McShann from the time he used to barnstorm in the Southwest and about his band, but the alto saxophone was new and years ahead of anybody in jazz. He was into a whole new system of sound and time. The emcee didn't even announce his name on the broadcasts. I didn't learn that it was Charlie Parker until after the war. It took me all that time to solve the mystery."

Jazz musicians in other bands were drawn to the Savoy, much in the same way as they had gathered to hear Lester Young and Count Basie in 1937. That had been roughly five years before. It was time for a new generation of jazzmen and new ideas. Drummer Big Sid Catlett, bassist Chubby Jackson, trumpeters Howard McGhee and Dizzy Gillespie began sitting in with the band during closing sets. After the job the musicians would jam at one of the after-hours clubs in Harlem.

The band was a hit with dancers as well. It had the same solid beat and bluesy sound that they had admired in Basie and the Clouds of Joy. During its repeat stands at the Savoy the McShann Orchestra faced off against such well-known organizations as the Savoy Sultans, Cecil Scott, Erskine Hawkins, and the Chick Webb Orchestra, all of them with first-rate soloists. Between bookings at the Savoy and the Apollo Theater the band played one-nighters in New England and south along the Atlantic seaboard.

That spring of 1942, jazz musicians were inclined to write World War II off as a bad joke. Walter Brown sang *You Say Forward, I'll March*, composed by McShann and himself, but he didn't really mean it. Jazzmen did not know it yet, but swing had run its course, and the days of the big bands were numbered. As Pearl Harbor led swiftly to a shooting war and global involvement, one regulation after another, emanating from Washington, made deeper and deeper inroads into the entertainment industry; first, blackouts along the Atlantic coast because of submarine warfare; then gas rationing and the conversion of band instrument factories to war plants; and after that, stringent travel priorities and the National Conscription Act. Jazzmen were required to register with their draft boards, and before long the draft was sucking at the ranks of the dance orchestras.

That summer the underpinning of the record industry was shaken by irreconcilable differences between the major labels and the American Federation of Musicians. All recording came to a stop. Faced with competition from mechanical media, and failing to obtain an acceptable royalty agreement with the manufacturers, the union called a recording ban effective August 1, 1942. The timing was unfortunate. Manufacturers were in no mood to bargain. Shipments of Indian shellac, an essential ingredient in the manufacture of 78-rpm discs, had been cut off by the war. Manufacturers could readily project the volume of production for the foreseeable future by referring to their shellac reserves, in no case sufficient for more than eighteen months. Therefore, they had no great desire to add to their backlogs, and refused to sign with the union. A final flurry of recording as the deadline approached found the Jay McShann Orchestra cutting four last sides for Decca on July 2.

Charlie played two eight bar solos on *Sepian Bounce*, one of the band's riff originals. He took twelve bars on *Jumpin' Blues*, a tune he had worked up and orchestrated on short notice. In its opening measures his solo revealed the germ idea that appeared later as *Ornithology*. Al Hibbler sang *Get Me on Your Mind*, the vocalist's only chance to record with McShann (Hibbler would soon attain stardom with the Duke Ellington Orchestra). On *Lonely Boy Blues* Charlie overblew F-sharp, half a step above the natural register of the saxophone, with striking results. It was another first. The solo was as intense as *Hootie*, though less elaborate in structure. Soon after the final Decca session McShann announced that the band was headed out on a long road trip that would take the musicians back home to Kansas City. The announcement was greeted by cheers from everyone except Charlie. Kansas City no longer held any allure for him.

Charlie told McShann that he would stay in New York. In the summer of 1942, Charlie left organized music and went underground, disappearing into the backwaters of Harlem, the city within a city that would be his base of operations for the rest of his career. For three years he had served out the final leg of his apprenticeship in the saxophone section of the last of the great Kansas City bands, saturated by the swirl of its bluesy and buoyant rhythms. Now he was ready to strike out on his own.

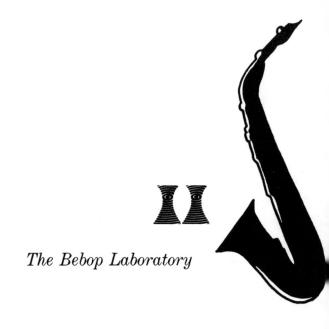

II

The Bebop Laboratory

In New York jazz musicians looking for the action found it in half a dozen after-hours clubs uptown. The most famous of these was Minton's Playhouse, the laboratory in which musical experiments about to emerge as the bebop revolution began around 1941. In spite of its exotic name, Minton's was a drab sort of a place. A marquee extending from the entrance to the curbstone, the latter painted white and zoned as a passenger-loading area, gave the club a faint aura of prestige on otherwise dingy 118th Street. Inside there was the usual checkroom with its divided door and coatracks, a long bar, tables, a wall with mirrors, somewhat the worse for the wear, and a band-stand like those in many of the old Kansas City clubs of Pendergast days—cramped, large enough for a baby grand piano and a drum outfit, and, at a stretch, standing room for five or six musicians. There was no decor of note. Minton's Playhouse was poorly lit, reasonably clean, attractively priced, and out of the way—the kind of place jazz musicians liked. As the word began to get around, taxicabs pulled up to the faded green awning with a frequency enjoyed only by the in-places of those years, taxis that discharged musicians easily identified by the trumpet and saxophone cases they carried. Had the management at Minton's thought to provide a guest book, it would have contained the name of every important jazz figure of the transition years.

The club was named after its owner, Henry Minton, a middle-aged man who enjoyed the slight distinction of having been the first Negro ("colored" was then the official expression) delegate to Local 802, the New York chapter of the American Federation of Musicians. Until late 1940 Minton ran the club by himself. It drew trade from the Hotel Cecil, whose lobby could be reached by a connecting door. In better days the premises had been the hotel dining room. Minton's Playhouse became a hangout for old-timers drifting in and out of the dance band business. There was no real music policy. The baby grand piano often went untouched for days. Business declined steadily until the owner bestirred himself to hire a new manager. His choice was Teddy Hill.

With great reliability and faint distinction, the soberfaced, dependable Hill had played the various saxophones in bands led by the immortal King Oliver and Louis Armstrong. He had written his share of arrangements, composed a few songs (but no hits), and learned the ins and outs of the dance band business. Finally, in mature years, Teddy Hill had become a bandleader in his own right.

Teddy Hill had never quite succeeded in any capacity, but he had been around and he knew a lot of people in the entertainment world and had ideas. "Why not," he told Henry Minton, "hire a house band and build up the jam session business? And," adjusting the dark gray felt hat that he wore in all seasons, indoors and out, to conceal the encircling bald spot on his head, "throw a Monday night feed for artists in the stage shows up at the Apollo? We could put a notice on the call board and invite everybody in the cast." Monday night was show business Sunday. At-liberty night. To Henry Minton the plan sounded worth a try.

"Celebrity Night" at Minton's Playhouse, its dinners hosted by Teddy Hill, quiet and hatted, soon became famous coast to coast. Wherever show folk or jazzmen might be working—at the Howard in Philadelphia or the Regal in Chicago or way out on the Coast at the Lincoln Theater in Los Angeles—the word was passed. Buffet-style dinners at Minton's mustered up all of the succulent dishes that artists had known from childhood, and could so seldom find on the road: barbecued ribs with real Creole sauce, panfried chicken, collard greens simmered with a hambone, sweet potato pie, candied yams, red beans and rice. Once in a while Hill gilded the lily and flew in a shipment of crawdads from Kansas City or Mississippi River catfish from St. Louis. He raised the price of mixed drinks from twenty-five cents to thirty cents. In 1941 Teddy Hill and Henry Minton were well into the soul-food business. The Playhouse had a new lease on life. Minton's became the place to go on Mondays in the early Forties. It was also the scene of the palace revolution that overturned jazz.

As architect of the music policy at Minton's Playhouse, Teddy Hill took a page from the book of the Kansas City club operators, hiring himself a rhythm section dressed up with a single horn, an open invitation to the jam-minded. Hill could see the ominous ripples troubling the surface of popular music. The old "jazz" of the Twenties, played by the men with whom he had worked, Oliver and Armstrong and the rest, was dead. Swing itself faced serious difficulties. There were new ideas afloat, new voices, a new generation of jazzmen who knew their instruments and could play. Those were the people Teddy Hill wanted to attract to the Playhouse, along with established stars.

To lead the house band at Minton's Teddy Hill hired the very man he had fired less than a year before, Kenny "Klook" Clarke, the drummer whose percussion work had disrupted the last Teddy Hill Orchestra. A year before he had lectured Clarke about "dropping bombs," telling the intransigent young drummer, "Keep your beat down on the bass drum where it belongs. People don't want to hear that kind of stuff. They want music they can dance to." The young drummer had merely glared at him. "Klook," Clarke's nickname, had arisen from the onomatopoetic *klook-a-mop*, a kind of double bomb, one of Clarke's favorite percussion figures. Now, months after he had fired Kenny Clarke, Teddy Hill thought about the bombs, the jagged, zigzaggy rhythms that somehow worked, and got in touch with the drummer and offered him the contract for the house band at Minton's.

"I was a little surprised when he sounded me," Clarke said later. "After we talked a while I knew what he wanted. In 1937 I'd gotten tired of playing like Jo Jones. It was time for jazz drummers to move ahead. I took the main beat away from the bass drum and up to the top cymbal. I found out I could get pitch and timbre variations up there, according to the way the stick struck the cymbal, and a pretty sound. The beat had a better flow. It was lighter and tastier. That left me free to use the bass drum, the tom-toms and snare for accents. I was trying to lay new rhythmic patterns over the regular beat. Solo lines were getting longer. Soloists needed more help from the drummer—kicks, accents, cues, all kind of little things like that."

Who else?

Klook suggested a pianist named Thelonious Sphere Monk, a heavy, bearlike, bemused young man who never appeared in public without his "shades" and was one of the first jazzmen to cultivate a goatee. Monk had begun his career as a piano player with a gospel group that worked the church circuit, had seen the Spartan interiors of hundreds of white frame Baptist churches in the South and Midwest, beat upon their tuneless pianos, listened to the hand-clapping, hosanna-shouting congregations as they joined in with the gospel lights he accompanied. Monk was soaked not so much in the brine of the ancient blues as the equally ancient Afro-American gospel song. To maintain his musical integrity during those endless road trips through the heartland of straight-laced Afro-America Monk jammed where and when he could. Mary Lou Williams reported hearing him one night in a Kansas City after-hours club. Thelonious Monk wanted to get out of the gospel business and to play jazz, but on his own rather demanding terms.

When not on the road Thelonious Monk lived at home with a devoted, doting, permissive, widowed mother, that recurrent tragic heroine in the biographies of so many jazzmen. Mother and son, later a wife and alter-mother named Nellie, lived in a fourth-floor walk-up flat on San Juan Hill, in Manhattan's West Sixties. There was a small Steinway grand piano, acquired by the most exacting household economies, so that Thelonious would have a proper instrument upon which to compose and practice. He had already created several striking new compositions, *Blue Monk, Epistrophy,* and *'Round About Midnight,* with its strange excursions into unlikely signatures. A large mirror attached to the ceiling reflected the keyboard and its action, and that of the strings and hammers.

Thelonious was self-taught from the age of six. Beyond the simplicities of the Baptist hymn book, he did not bother to read music. He played in what appeared to be an awkward style, fingers flat, splayed out on the keys. With Monk one had the feeling of music being crushed out of the instrument, like wine from grapes. Sometimes he hit all twelve keys at once, using the odd thumb to catch two at the same time. Monk held his head at an angle when he played, chin raised, eyes lost behind the dark shades, seemingly listening for the chords and their reverberations. In the privacy of his home he spent hour upon hour at the Steinway, practicing at any time of the day or night, unchallenged by neighbors, testing possible and improbable combinations of sound, peering up through the dark glasses at the mirror of the ceiling, locked into the architecture of the sounds that he roused and the narcissistic image projected by the mirror.

Monk's keyboard texture was thick, but he left a lot of air space between the chords, and the big chords fell at unexpected intervals. The rhythm seemed jagged, like a child hopping squares on the sidewalk, but it swung in the same way that Klook's off-center drumming swung. The chords were churchy and gospel-rooted, with a strong blues tinge, stretched into queer intervals and upper extensions. Monk's harmonic schema seemed to evolve from the midriff of the modes, the flatted fifths, leading him afield into whole-tone scales, a method akin to Charlie Parker's modular attack but with different results. When Monk and Klook worked together the music was disturbing and different, but it cooked. The bass drum coughed out its cannon shots. Sticks danced on the taut drum heads. The sizzle of cymbals insinuated pungent vibrations into every corner of the after-hours club. Caught up in this heady flux were the dissonant, chunky chords from the piano.

Minton's began as a dueling field for encounters between jazzmen of different persuasions. It ended as a bloody battleground where no quarter was asked or given, on which established reputations were demolished and new culture heroes elevated. At the first sessions, in the spring of 1941, when Charlie Parker was still on the road with Jay McShann, the old guard held the balance of power. The old guard could count on the services of a formidable array of improvisers, all famous as soloists with major orchestras: saxophonists Coleman Hawkins, Ben Webster, Chu Berry, Johnny Hodges, Benny Carter, and Willie Smith; trumpeters Lips Page, Cootie Williams, Charlie Shavers, Harry James, and Roy Eldridge; pianists Fats Waller, Teddy Wilson, Jess Stacy, and Mary Lou Williams. Nor were name bandleaders averse to taking a hand when the brawling got nasty. Duke Ellington, Andy Kirk, Count Basie, Artie Shaw, Lionel Hampton, and Benny Goodman all appeared on the bandstand at Minton's, lending their prestige and efforts to the mounting hue and cry of battle.

Occupying a middle ground between the musical left and right were figures of the transition, pianists Clyde Hart and Tadd Dameron, trombonists Fred Beckett and Dickie Wells, trumpeter Peanuts Holland, tenormen Dick Wilson and Henry Bridges, Jr., and three major figures respected by everyone in the jazz community, Art Tatum, Lester Young, and Charlie Christian.

The brilliant array of jazzmen from the past, the middle period, and the future did not all appear at Minton's Playhouse on a given night. Sessions were informal and personnel unpredictable. Outside of the men in the house band, nobody got paid. On certain nights there might be a surfeit of saxophonists. On another, all of the trumpet men in the business seemed to be in town and would arrive at the same time; then the walls would shudder with lip trills and double B's.

There were so many names at Minton's that reputations didn't mean anything. Coleman Hawkins and Roy Eldridge had to put up or shut up like everyone else. Once a man had played through his bag and been topped, heard his best lines turned inside out, like the sleeves of an old garment, or used as a starting point for a better solo, there was nothing left except to bottle up and go. It was how you stood up to the challenge, how you responded under pressure, the musical ideas you created then that counted. The rest was mere chord-running, cliché-making, or empty virtuosity. In this witch's broth, sometime between 1941 and 1944, swing dissolved into the new jazz style, bebop.*

The winds of change sweeping the jazz community blew their hardest during the time of the AFM recording ban. Instead of a record-by-record documentation of the changes in jazz style—the result of the close supervision given by the major labels to the bands under contract—only a handful of imperfect artifacts survive. In May, 1941, amateur engineer Jerry Newman, using a portable turntable, glass-based acetate discs, and a bulky amplifier, recorded at Minton's and Monroe's. Although the originals were badly worn by private playings before their historic worth was realized, they nevertheless afford a dim, scratchy record of those stirring nights. *Down on Teddy's Hill* with its exhortations of *"Go!"* and *"Blow!"* give us some idea of the prevailing excitement and audience participation. There are several choruses, funky and wry, by Thelonious Monk that gave jazz piano a new dimension. The chief soloist is Charlie Christian, playing out the last weeks of his professional

---

* The word *bebop* was thought to be onomatopoetic in origin, like *klook-a-mop*, and in fact may have been derived from the latter. Others said it had been invented by the jivey, irrepressible Fats Waller. Nobody liked it much, least of all the new jazzmen. But it stuck.

life, still in the superlative form that made him a star with
Benny Goodman. (Christian succumbed to tuberculosis in
March 1942.) The co-star is Kenny Clarke. That Clarke was indeed the founder of the new percussion style is evident. One
hears a forcing beat, a delicious complexity of polyrhythms,
and an unusual awareness of the needs of the soloist. There is
also a bit of John Birks Gillespie, then twenty-three and trying
his wings, not yet quite sure of himself or his style. Apart from
Clarke's masterful drumming, there is nothing here up to the
standard of the Wichita transcriptions or *Hootie Blues*, with
their clear, positive declaration that something new had been
added. As good as it was, the music of Clarke and Monk needed
a horn.

Charlie Parker was on the bandstand at Monroe's on this
and other nights that Jerry Newman recorded. Unfortunately,
Newman's tastes in saxophonists ran to orthodox men, Benny
Carter and Herbie Fields. Newman did not like Parker's jazz,
an opinion in which he was not alone. It didn't seem to swing.
The tone was too cutting. The flow of ideas was too rapid for
the layman to follow. Newman didn't think of it as jazz at all,
but rather as some kind of "Chinese music," as Cab Calloway
scornfully called the new style. Newman's equipment, so laboriously lugged to the after-hours clubs, was switched off when it
came Charlie's turn to solo. The most assiduous of amateur engineers, Dean Benedetti—whose method was the reverse, to
switch off everyone but Parker—would not appear for another
year or so.*

Charlie Parker was not much in evidence at Minton's during its opening months. After leaving McShann, Charlie had established his base at Monroe's Uptown House, 133rd Street and
Seventh Avenue, his old hang-out from Parisien Ballroom days.
Monroe's was a cabaret with a floor show policy, but after the
last show the stage was cleared and a small band led by Vic
Coulsen took over. Jamming was encouraged and participating
jazzmen had a kitty to split for their night's work. The kitty

* After Jerry Newman's death, his effects would reveal a paper disc on whose
faded sound track could be heard the unmistakable sound of Charlie Parker's alto
playing *Cherokee*.

was a big inducement for Charlie. On a dull night his share amounted to eighty or ninety cents, barely enough to buy a meal. On a good night, when Harlem numbers men dropped into Monroe's, his share might run as high as eight or nine dollars.

In the fall of 1941 the key men in the brewing bebop revolution began to discover one another. One night the musicians in the house band at Minton's were tipped off that a new saxophonist had arrived in town, a fellow called Bird, or Yardbird, that he was from Kansas City and played like Lester Young, only twice as fast, and on alto saxophone. Nobody believed this. Lester was the top man on saxophone. There had been no new statement on the alto since Johnny Hodges appeared with Duke Ellington ten years before. Still, the story had to be checked out. One night Kenny Clarke and Thelonious Monk decided to see for themselves. On the bandstand at Monroe's they found a man younger than themselves, wearing sunglasses in sport frames, an unpressed suit and rumpled shirt, playing one chorus after another as if his life depended on it. The mordant tone, the precise articulation of the notes, the vehemence with which each was played, the breath-taking speed with which the horn was gotten over, these were all new to the idiom.

"Bird was playing stuff we'd never heard before," recalls Clarke, now an elder statesman of jazz and living in Paris. "He was into figures I thought I'd invented for drums. He was twice as fast as Lester Young and into harmony Lester hadn't touched. Bird was running the same way we were, but he was way out ahead of us. I don't think he was aware of the changes he had created. It was his way of playing jazz, part of his own experience. Bird didn't talk much. He was quiet and reserved, in fact rather meek. We laid a few dollars on him and got him to move from Monroe's down to Minton's. Teddy Hill refused to put another man on the payroll, so we decided to pool our money and give him an allowance. I invited him to the pad I shared with Doc West, another drummer and a good cook. We set him up to meals. He could really eat. He was thin and half starved. He was trying to live off the kitty at Monroe's.

"Pretty soon Minton's got to be a bad place for older cats. Dizzy began coming up regularly and that gave us the four key instruments—trumpet, alto, piano, and drums. That, plus a good bass, was the band of the future. One night, after weeks of trying, Dizzy cut Roy Eldridge. It was one night out of many, but it meant a great deal. Roy had been top dog for years. We closed our ranks after that.

"To make things tough for outsiders, we invented difficult riffs. Some of our tunes used the 'A' part of one tune, like *I Got Rhythm*, but the channel came from something else, say *Honeysuckle Rose*. The swing guys would be completely hung up in the channel. They'd have to stop playing. After we closed Minton's we'd eat and play until the next morning at Monroe's. There wasn't any prospect that the music would ever come to anything. It was a way of letting off steam and having fun."

During this period of high creativity Charlie Parker was living a hopelessly disorganized life. He lived from hand to mouth, on cadged and proffered meals, in strange beds, and changed his address often. His clothing frequently gave the impression it had been slept in. More often than not, that was the case. Sometimes his horn was in hock, so that he was obliged to play on a borrowed instrument. For this reason he always kept his reed and mouthpiece detached from the saxophone and carried them in his pocket. Despite his lack of funds, Charlie had begun to experiment with hard drugs. They were as easily obtained in New York as they had been in Kansas City. Every Harlem block had its insinuating pusher, eager to encourage new habits and nurse them through their incubating period, on credit if necessary, especially if the user showed promise of success in the music business. Caps of heroin or morphine could be bought for prices ranging from fifty cents to three dollars, depending upon one's state of affluence. A cap of white powder, heated in an old teaspoon, converted into a colorless liquid, and injected into a vein, would produce a state of euphoria lasting twelve hours or more. That was enough to carry one through the essential part of the day. It was more important than food, or a decent room. And what a euphoria it was! Compared to heroin, the kicks derived from marijuana, from nutmeg floated on top of a soft drink, from benzedrine inhalers soaked in sweet wine were kid stuff.

Narcotics had always been as much a part of the jazzman's culture as gangsters, pimps, prostitutes, gamblers, and drunken customers who requested *Sweet Adeline*. Many jazzmen had given heroin a try and backed off, frightened by its powerful effects and the admonitions of those who had become hooked. Charlie had seen his share of junkies in Kansas City. He had first tried the drug there. It had been included in the various experiments undertaken with his teenage friend, drummer "L'il Phil," who had become a drug peddler and heroin addict. Returning to Kansas City from a road trip with McShann, Charlie heard the story of L'il Phil's tragedy. His friend had gone out with a territorial band for a tour of the Deep South. Ill with withdrawal symptoms, wandering about in a state of confusion, the drummer had become separated from his fellow musicians and left behind in a small Mississippi town, where he was arrested, hauled before a local court, judged insane, and remanded to an asylum. After months of useless treatment the sick man had been released—literally turned into the street. Ragged, penniless, suffering from amnesia, L'il Phil had wandered and begged his way through the South before turning up by chance many months later in Kansas City.

The deeply disturbing example of his old comrade did nothing to curb Charlie's persistent dabbling with drugs. Charlie's attitude was conditioned by the discovery that his physiology, uniquely resilient in so many ways, could tolerate heroin far better than most. Junkies were usually detached and on the nod. They had no appetite for food, and less for sex. They shunned alcohol as if it were poison. Charlie experienced none of these reactions. His appetites went unchecked. He could drink and he could eat like a horse and run after all of the women that interested him. At Monroe's, where the management stood drinks, he would start the night with two double whiskeys, and continue to down shots between sets. Nor was there ever a time when he could not play.

Drugs allayed the pressure he suffered from the lack of

steady work, the public indifference to his music, his contradictory, indeed ridiculous role—a creative artist composing and improvising in a night club. Drugs screened off the greasy spoon restaurants and cheap rooming houses with their unswept stairs and malodorous hall toilets. Drugs kept him out of the military draft: an army psychiatrist had taken one look at the needle marks on his arm and immediately classified him as 4-F. Heroin became his staff of life. The monkey on his back kept the outside world off it. Like all who meddled with drugs, Charlie believed that he could kick the habit at his own convenience. He experimented with goof balls (phenobarbital) to decelerate his highs and alleviate withdrawal symptoms. The score became the most urgent task of each day. He learned the trick of borrowing small amounts of money, a dollar or two, sums too small to be remembered. His lifestyle was hardening into a mold he would never succeed in breaking. Except for a single factor, there was nothing to distinguish Charlie from hundreds of other Negro youths who had been drawn to New York City and were drifting aimlessly about the streets of Harlem, in imminent danger of being swallowed by the underworld. That factor was the saxophone.

Charlie had turned twenty-one. However precariously, he had established himself in the underground of the city of his dreams. He was dug in on the front line. He was learning to live from one day to the next, without a five-cent piece in his pocket, without the slightest concern of the morrow. A place to sleep, alcohol, drugs, sexual outlets, food—these were his material needs. These and a place to play amounted to the total fulfillment of his life. The prescored hype, the act, con, guile, the small loan and, above all, the mania to play harder and longer than anyone else were all the currency he needed. He had no welfare check, no unemployment insurance, no job, no money, but he was making out. And he was into fresh musical discoveries every night.

He was fast becoming a legend in the jazz underground. Musicians from traveling bands were steered uptown to hear him perform. They were amazed by his ability to improvise from any tune or sort of musical material. One night three notes were struck at random on the piano. Charlie immediately resolved them into a melody, clothed them in a harmonic pattern, and played several choruses ad lib. Another night a key on his saxophone broke. He sent the waiter to the kitchen for a teaspoon, and with the bent spoon and a rubber band from his pocket soon had the horn back in playing condition. Listeners went away shaking their heads. On the road they spread the word about the fabulous unknown alto saxophonist, a young Mozart spouting forth melodies by the yard at an obscure club in upper Harlem. The legend began to proliferate.

On bitter winter nights Charlie would drop into the Braddock Bar, a musicians' hangout next to the Apollo Theater. The bar operated on a two-for-one policy, and Charlie had discovered a way to cadge free drinks. If a customer ordered a whiskey, he would be poured two shots and a chaser. The second glass would sit on the bar and sometimes be overlooked in the general confusion of a busy night. Charlie would cruise up and down the bar, his pockets empty, downing "sleepers." The gambit was acceptable to those who knew him, but was not well taken by strangers. One night he was caught in the theft and called to account by a group of Harlem toughs. Either he would stand them all a round of drinks, or they would take him out the back entrance of Braddock's onto 126th Street and teach him a lesson. Charlie talked fast. He was getting nowhere until he remembered that the current attraction at the Apollo was the Jay McShann Orchestra. "Give me ten minutes," Charlie told the toughs. "You'll have your round of drinks." Then he went to the stage door and sent a note in to Gene Ramey.

Luckily, the band was between stage shows and his old friend was available. Ramey appeared, shocked at what he saw. "Bird was thin and drawn. He looked like an unmade bed. It was six degrees below zero and Bird was wearing a T-shirt, no socks, and an expensive black overcoat. He was in a serious jam at the Braddock and needed two dollars to bail himself out of trouble." * Ramey advanced the money and Charlie made good the round of drinks. Later that night he was on the bandstand

* Interview in *Jazz Review*, November 1960.

at Minton's, playing his solos with the black overcoat still on his back to conceal the fact that his only suit was in pawn. It was a beautiful coat, fleece-lined, with a fur collar. A lucky match for his size, 44-short, it had been purchased for a few dollars from an acquaintance who made a living as a shoplifter.

Despite his insecure way of life, perhaps because of it, Charlie married for the second time. He had been divorced two years after the birth of Leon by his first wife, Rebecca Ruffing, who had been awarded a weekly alimony of five dollars, a sum that Charlie paid reluctantly, intermittently, and then not at all. Charlie's second marriage was to Geraldine Marguerite Scott of Washington, D.C. A stunning girl, Geraldine loved the glamour of clubs and night life. The marriage survived on very uncertain terms. The Parkers had no real home other than hotel rooms and boarding houses. Geraldine was an indifferent housekeeper, and most meals were taken out. The liaison dissolved itself within the first year and Charlie went back to the old, irresponsible, nomadic way of life that he had been following since his middle teens. Charlie's future liaisons notwithstanding, no record was ever produced of his having divorced wife number two.

By mid-December Charlie's condition was cause for alarm. Fellow musicians realized that something practical would have to be done. Trumpeter Benny Harris undertook to get Charlie on the payroll of the Earl Hines Orchestra; tenor saxophonist Budd Johnson had given notice, and the leader was looking for a replacement. Harris began "preaching Bird" to Hines. One night, after closing at the Savoy, the trumpeter talked Hines into making a trip uptown and acted as a guide for a party that included Hines, Harris, Johnson, vocalist Billy Eckstine, saxophonist Scoops Carry, and Count Basie. They found Charlie at Monroe's Uptown House. He was in superlative form. Chorus followed upon chorus. If Charlie was high it didn't show, or at least Hines wasn't aware of it. The band leader was impressed. "He's fine," Hines told Harris, "but that's not going to help us much. This fellow plays alto saxophone. What I need is a tenor man."

After the set Harris brought Charlie to the table and

Hines asked if he could play tenor. Charlie said that he could. Did he own a tenor saxophone? He did not. In fact, the alto he had that night was borrowed.

"All right," Hines said. "I'll buy you a tenor saxophone. You can join us tomorrow." Hines stripped a ten-dollar bill off the impressive roll carried by bandleaders on their talent scouting trips, told Charlie to buy himself a clean shirt, and wrote down the address of the studio in midtown Manhattan where the band was rehearsing for its next engagement.

12

The Last of the
Big Bands

Cigar-smoking, personable, aggressive, possessed of a serene self-confidence, Earl Hines was a healthy extrovert who sat front and center of his bands and ran the show from the piano bench. When Charlie joined the band Hines was thirty-seven, a veteran of twenty years in the music business, at the peak of his powers, and firmly fixed in jazz history. One of the young Turks who had gathered around Louis Armstrong in the Twenties, Hines took part in the historical Armstrong Hot Five recordings of 1928 (*A Monday Date, West End Blues*). To make himself heard through the clamor of large bands in those pre-amplifier days, Hines played octaves instead of single-note runs, chipping out rock-hard lines with incisive strokes of the wrist. Hines was the *paterfamilias* of modern jazz piano, and the main inspiration of Art Tatum.

Blessed with one of the largest pairs of hands in jazz, and one of the most beautiful, Hines could stretch tenths with ease, and bridge twelfths. There was a rumor, never confirmed, that early in his career, when the necessity of playing octaves was much on his mind, he had submitted to the surgeon's knife and had the webbing between the fingers cut. Hines sat at the piano as befitted a member of jazz royalty, tall, broad of shoulder, immaculately dressed in formal black, unshakable in his self-confidence, cigar tucked in one corner of his mouth, cueing his all-star bands with pianistic signals, tossing off sparkling runs and tremolos that rippled through the texture of the bands.

The 1942 edition of the Earl Hines Orchestra was a far cry from the muscular bands that established the leader during his long stay at the gangster-controlled Grand Terrace Club on the south side of Chicago. Those bands had backed floor shows featuring Ethel Waters and Bojangles Robinson; their ranks included many fine soloists, Jabbo Smith, Omer Simeon, Ray Nance, Trummy Young, vocalist Herb Jeffries. The curtain still rose to reveal the pianist under a spotlight as the musicians chanted "Faw-tha Hines! Faw-tha Hines!" But that chant, a trademark familiar to radio audiences for years, now emerged as something very close to a private joke on the part of irreverent young sidemen recruited from the bop-oriented clubs of Harlem. The Earl Hines Orchestra of 1942 had been infiltrated by the jazz revolutionaries. Each section had its cell of insurgents. The band's sonority bristled with flatted fifths, odd triplets, and other material of the new sound scheme. Fellow bandleaders of a more conservative bent warned Hines that he had recruited much too well and was sitting on a powder keg.

Bereted and goateed, Dizzy Gillespie starred in a trumpet section with fellow rebels Benny Harris, Shorty McConnell, and Gail Brockman; with trombonist Benny Green the section came close to being an all-star bebop brass team. The reeds offered the unlikely combination of traditionalist John Williams, whose career stretched back to black vaudeville and tent shows; Goon

Gardner, Charlie's collaborator at the 65 Club in Chicago; Scoops Carry, a very fine altoist, later to become a Chicago attorney and official of the American Federation of Musicians; and Charlie. Shadow Wilson, a Klook Clarke disciple, handled the drums. In Billy Eckstine the band had the most promising singer since Herb Jeffries and Pha Terrell. Hines's recordings made the year before—*X Y Z*, *Yellow Fire*, *Jersey Bounce*, and *Water Boy* and *Jelly Jelly*, the latter two sides featuring Eckstine—reflected the trend toward progressive ideas, a drift that Hines saw as timely and commercial, and with increasing difficulty sought to keep under control.

His confidence restored by a steady job, Charlie very soon collided with the leader in a typically oblique confrontation. The band was rehearsing a complicated new Jimmy Mundy score. After twenty minutes and two choppy runs through, with rough spots still to be ironed out, Hines went on to the next number. A few days later the same piece of music was called for again. Sidemen dutifully rummaged through fiberboard cases, hauled out the chart, and placed it on the racks. Parker was the exception. His rack remained empty, although the saxophone stood on his lap at ready.

Hines leaned over the piano and asked, "Well, Charlie, aren't you going to get your music out for us?"

Charlie stared back and said, "I already know it."

"The new Mundy chart. That's what I'm talking about."

"I know it," Charlie told the leader.

Hines was incredulous, but soon discovered Charlie was not bluffing. He had committed the saxophone part to memory during the short run-through a few days before. Charlie played the part without a mistake. "Knew it backwards and forwards," Hines said later. "Note perfect! Charlie had a photographic memory."

Privately Charlie found the new Mundy arrangement, for which Hines had paid a fancy price, dull, not to mention lacking in solo opportunities. Charlie's attitude toward scores was prejudiced by the Kansas City jazzman's free approach to improvisation. He thought of arrangers as parasites and brain-pickers, industriously bottling other people's ideas with all of the inspiration of an old lady canning apricots. For him the real fun of being with Hines lay in the companionship with Benny Harris, Billy Eckstine, and the effervescent Dizzy Gillespie. Charlie and Dizzy spent a good deal of time woodshedding backstage, sight-reading parts from trumpet and saxophone exercise books, building up speed so that they could whiz through tricky passages at double the recommended time. It was a great conditioner for chops and fingers. When they had mastered an exercise they would exchange books, so that the saxophone played the trumpet part and vice versa. Useful phrases, as well as random quotations from the method books, would pop up in cadenzas at the next stage show, often to the consternation of theater audiences and the dismay of the veteran bandleader. The speed with which Bird and Diz could get over their horns became legendary. Notes spurted from their instruments like pips of light from a fireworks display. Nobody in jazz played with such speed and precision. In virtuosity alone they were without equals in the band business, true *enfants terribles*.

During this period Charlie was disgorging musical ideas at a constant and rapid rate. He never bothered to write anything down—ideas simply came too fast. Many were lost in the musty dressing rooms backstage; other bits and pieces floated around in a private inner Sargasso, to be salvaged in later years as parts of a bridge in *Klactoveesedstene*, or the theme for *Dexterity*. Dizzy began inserting some of their ideas into fresh tunes, *A Night in Tunisia*, its title inspired by the campaign in supposedly exotic North Africa, and a strange abracadabra called *Salt Peanuts*, with unexpected changes and trampoline leaps from octave to octave.

The Earl Hines Orchestra opened at the Apollo Theater January 15, 1943, then leapfrogged across the theater circuit with stands at the Howard, Royal, Regal, and Paradise. Charlie created a stir at a jam session in the El Grotto Room of Chicago's southside Pershing Hotel, the first of many performances he would give there. An impromptu session was laid on one night in Charlie's room at the Ritz Hotel in Chicago. Contrabassist Oscar Pettiford, hearing that "Bird and Diz" were at the hotel, and lacking cab fare, had carried his bass three miles across town on a cold, windy night so that he could join the visitors in a three-man session that carried on until dawn. Wherever they went Charlie and Dizzy were hailed as visiting celebrities. Young jazzmen invited them to jam sessions and paid their way into theaters and dance halls wherever the band appeared.

At the stage shows, on which the band backed up several vaudeville acts and closed the program with its own presentation, audiences heard a curious mélange of styles. It was almost as if the public were being treated to a mixture of Palestrina, Mozart, and Alban Berg, all played by the same orchestra as a medley. John Williams played a quaint, old-fashioned round-toned alto saxophone with a strong vibrato, just as he had with the Clouds of Joy. Scoops Carry's clear, cool delivery lay in the middle ground between swing and bop. Dizzy's puckish sorties spoke for the new generation, complementing Charlie's tenor saxophone. Dizzy sat downstage, at the extreme left, and Charlie sat at the opposite end of the stage, so that their solos seemed to erupt irreverently from two poles, framing in the band and its sound. Dead center sat Hines, resplendent, a little pompous, playing the on-the-beat piano that had made his reputation back in 1928. The Earl Hines Orchestra of 1942–44, in which old and new ideas struggled so intensely for recognition, left no legacy of records. The AFM recording ban continued without respite.

Theater jobs required that musicians be on the band cart, properly attired and ready to play, as Hines gave the downbeat for *Rosetta*, the band's theme, and the curtain rose. According to Eckstine, "Charlie must have missed as many shows as he made." Matinees in particular were a problem. To solve it, Charlie worked out a method of sleeping on the job. Saxophone firmly in his jaw, cheeks puffed out, fingers on the keys, eyes closed but inscrutable behind dark glasses, Charlie would doze in his chair until his turn came to solo; then Scoops Carry or Goon Gardner would jab him in the ribs and he would bob up like a jack-in-the-box, improvising on pure reflexes, depending upon his unfailing ear and musical prescience to set him on course within a bar or two.

Fined by Hines for missing shows, Charlie took to sleeping under the band cart, explaining to Eckstine that the idea was to save Father hotel bills and to ensure his own presence on-stage when it came time for the next day's matinee. The following day the matinee was played without Charlie, whose chair remained conspicuously empty. At the end of the show, when the curtain fell and the musicians were packing up, a scuttling sound was heard from under the band cart. It was Charlie. He was red-eyed and puffy with an unaccustomed surfeit of sleep. He had slept the entire night under the band cart, and straight through the matinee as well, vaudeville acts and chants of "Faw-tha Hines" notwithstanding. On another occasion, having removed his shoes so that he could enjoy a catnap between evening shows, Charlie came running onstage in stocking feet at the cue for his spectacular solo in *A Night in Tunisia.*

One day Benny Harris told Charlie, "The Man is going to fire you if you goof any more. Besides, the reed parts are written for five saxophones, and four don't sound right." Musicians gathered in a ring around Charlie, backing him to the wall, punching him on the shoulders until, cornered and bruised, he cried out, "I'm mad enough to kill one of you guys!" "Okay," said Harris, a small, intense man who had boxed professionally. "If you can whip fourteen of us, go ahead. If you really want to fight, Bird, try me and get your ass kicked in." The therapy worked, but only for a while. As Harris said, "We all loved Bird so much that we spoiled him."

A female singer named Sarah Vaughn (then spelled without the final "a") joined the band for its return engagement at the Apollo Theater the week of April 23, 1943. Miss Vaughan was then nineteen, the daughter of a working-class Newark family. Like so many fine Afro-American singers, she had been trained in a church choir, at the Newark Zion Baptist Church. She also played piano and organ, and appeared with the band on the latter instrument. Sarah sang in a clear, controlled voice, limpid rather than bluesy. She was gifted with perfect pitch. The men in the sections found great satisfaction in playing behind her. The slight, subtle liberties she took with pitch created exhilarating results. Sarah was that rarity, a jazzman's vocalist. Charlie loved to play obbligattos behind Sarah, wishing only that he had one of the alto chairs; his real instrument would have been a natural counter voice to her own. Sarah was featured on *Body and Soul* and two new ballads, *East of the Sun* and *You Are My First Love*. Vaughan-Parker collaborations on *You Are My First Love* regularly stopped the show at big theaters in the East and Midwest.

The return engagement at the Apollo afforded a few extra days in New York, a chance to unwind and revisit the uptown clubs. Klook still led the house band at Minton's, and jam sessions at Monroe's continued into the late hours of morning. A few of the boppers were filtering downtown, into paying jobs on Fifty-second Street, where several small clubs had opened to attract the G.I. business. Oscar Pettiford had arrived from Chicago and was working with Roy Eldridge at the Onyx Club. The next Hines road trip was a packaged tour called the Blue Ribbon Salute, sponsored by the Pabst brewing firm as its contribution to the war effort. Hosted by comedian Ralph Cooper, who specialized in imitations of zoot suiters and other Harlem street-corner types, the show carried several acts and was booked out on a fast tour of army camps in the South and Midwest.

One night in Pine Bluff, Arkansas, the band played a public dance. Between sets Dizzy was sitting at the piano, picking out chords. A rednecked farm worker came up, tossed a quarter on the piano, pointed at Dizzy, and said, "Boy, play me some of that old *Darktown Strutters' Ball!*" Apart from its racist implications, the Shelton Brooks tune had never, by any stretch of the imagination, passed for jazz. Dizzy did not react or look up. He continued to sit at the piano bench, quietly trying chords. The request was ignored, and the quarter lay where it had fallen, on the piano top. But the Southerner was not so easily fobbed off. After the dance, when Dizzy entered the men's room, he was struck savagely on the side of the head with a beer bottle. Ready to do battle, the trumpeter was restrained by fellow bandsmen, who smelled riot in the air. At this moment Charlie intervened. Wagging a finger portentously at the assailant, Charlie said in a cultivated accent that he took to be English as spoken at Oxford University: "You took advantage of my friend." Confused, the assailant left the scene. Dizzy required stitches at the Pine Bluff hospital, and the trip continued as before.

Schedules were tight and accommodations poor. Jim Crow prevailed in many of the military camps in spite of efforts to integrate the armed forces. Rapidly rising prices had eroded salaries, pegged at what once would have been attractive figures, to mere subsistence wages. The rift between the boppers and the leader widened during the Blue Ribbon tour. When Eckstine's personal manager, Billy Shaw, demanded a raise in salary, Hines turned down the request. Shaw pulled Eckstine out of the band and booked him into the Onyx Club on Fifty-second Street. When Sarah Vaughan left, also to work a single on The Street, Earl Hines no longer had names to place alongside his own in the marquee lights. The boppers began to fight the traditionalists, and the brass and reed sections were turned into musical barricades. "Bird, it's still the best band in show business," Scoops Carry told Charlie in a mediative tone. "And the most modern."

"It's a jail," Charlie told the other saxophonist.

Soon other defections followed. Dizzy Gillespie left to join Oscar Pettiford. Charlie was supposed to join the group—it would have been the first real bebop small band—but could not accept the offer because he had failed to clear his union card with the New York Local 802. He hung on for a week, then went to Washington to work with his old comrade-in-arms from Kansas City, pianist Sir Charles Thompson. In a matter of weeks the Earl Hines Orchestra was a shambles, torn apart by internal explosions, exactly as Fatha's fellow bandleaders had feared. Frustrated and bitter, Hines fired the remnants of his reed section and hired a twelve-piece all-girl string group. The new band lasted less than two months, and was described in *Variety* as a twenty-thousand-dollar flop. The girls hadn't drawn flies, couldn't play, and proved to be as much trouble as the boppers. Hines wisely went back to playing the style of piano he had made his own, in the appropriate setting of a small band with compatible older-school jazzmen. His romance with the avant garde had ended, and the tradition of Earl Hines Orchestras, extending back into the Twenties, came to a close. Jazz, as he came to see, was apt to be a young man's game.

When the Washington job wound up Charlie returned to Kansas City, where he found his mother knocking around alone in the two-story house on Olive Street with its great outside staircase and unpainted balcony. Addie Parker was continuing to nibble away at the mortgage. In the foreseeable future the house would be hers, and, as she reminded Charlie, his own home as well, a permanent base between road trips and bookings, with a telephone on the entrance wall handy to receive his calls. She had gone to the expense of putting in a one-party line so that the calls might come through without interference. There was a small nest egg in the savings account for any emergency that might arise. His son, Leon, was no longer in Kansas City. According to Addie he had been taken off by Rebecca to Baltimore. The big house seemed empty.

Charlie was overwhelmed with sadness and love for his mother. What a life she had led! She had rolled with the punches and survived, kept the home together, raised him, spoiled him, supported his ambitions, catered to his desires, bought his first saxophone, shared every success, the first out-of-town job at Lake Taneycomo, his selection by Jay McShann to lead the reed section of an important band, his employment with Earl Hines. She had tolerated Rebecca and Rebecca's family. She had raised Leon as if he were her own child, supporting herself at menial jobs, saving money, buying the house. It was the black women who survived and kept his race solvent. The men were either failures, doomed from the start, like his father, or hustlers. The men were expendable, as Charlie felt that his own vital force and talent would in the end prove expendable.

The heavenly city Charlie had known as a youth no longer existed. Old Man Virgil had died and been buried in a pauper's grave. The armless man at the corner of Twelfth and Paseo had dropped from sight. The Reno Club was shuttered. So was the Sunset, where Charlie had listened to Pete Johnson and Big Joe Turner; the High Hat, where he had first tried to jam; and the Band Box, where he had broken in with Prof Smith. The electric streets of the district where the good Kansas City sounds had once coursed from every door were silent and dark. A succession of reform administrations had brought unemployment and desolation to the district. The last of the great Kansas City bands were busy most of the year filling out-of-town engagements. Charlie and Buddy Anderson organized a six-piece band for a job at Tootie Clarkin's new Mayfair Club, located across the Jackson County Line and beyond the reach of police interference. One day Charlie was out driving with Clifford Scott, one of his oldest friends in Kansas City. They ended up on Cliff Drive, overlooking the city. Suddenly Charlie said, "Scotty, pull over to the side. There's something I want to tell you." When the car stopped he turned and looked his friend squarely in the eye, saying slowly and menacingly, "Scotty, if I ever hear of you using hard, I'm going to come back and kill you!" But he did not or could not stop using hard stuff himself.

Loose and far from unhappy, but disturbingly nostalgic for New York, Charlie kept in touch with his friends by telephone, running up bills that soon exceeded the modest contributions he was making toward Addie Parker's household expenses. Billy Eckstine was working on Fifty-second Street at the Yacht Club, and the trade press was beginning to take notice of his talents. One writer had called Eckstine "the Sepia Sinatra." Eckstine, Dizzy, and some others were pulling Billy Shaw's coat about organizing a contemporary big band, not a compromise à la Father Hines, but a band using the talents of young jazzmen. The idea was not so far-fetched as it seemed. It was easier for an unknown band to break in than ever before. Wartime pressures had created a terrific flux in the entertainment business. Such a venture required financing and the right front man. Shaw thought Eckstine carried enough drawing power to bring it off. Eckstine was sounding people he had in mind for the key jobs in the dream band. Did Charlie have eyes?

Charlie's answer was "yes." Eckstine promised to keep him posted.

The man who held the key to the band project combined a set of qualities so unlikely in the vanity-ridden world of show business that some people thought him unreal. Eckstine was then twenty-nine. He came from a middle-class family in Pittsburgh, and had attended Howard University. He was called "B.E." or "Mr. B" or just "B" by his intimates; the nickname lent itself to pleasing variations enjoyed by those minded toward improvisation. B wore size 38-regular three-button suits like a haberdasher's model, and was outrageously good-looking in a slim, smooth, svelte way. He could have passed for one of the sleek panderers who cruised 125th Street in late-model Cadillacs custom-painted chartreuse or lavender, or succeeded as a pop singer without really trying. B had first kicked around obscure clubs in Buffalo and Detroit before latching onto a billing at Chicago's Club de Lisa on south State Street. There he was spotted by Budd Johnson and set up to be "discovered" by Father Hines, then casting about for someone to replace Herb Jeffries. Eckstine joined Hines in 1939 and soon produced a hit record for Bluebird (the RCA Victor race label), the suggestively lubricious *Jelly Jelly*, a contemporary version of the double-entendre blues. *Jelly Jelly* picked up a lot of mileage on the juke boxes and brought a new talent to the attention of the public. B's voice was a natural baritone of good range and without the trouble spots encountered by so many untrained voices. His voice had a round, rich, sensuous, softly masculine quality. It was called velvety by writers in the trade papers who reviewed his records, sexy by female listeners, who were the principal buyers of the records. But Mr. B was more than a dreamboat vehicle for the latest popular ballad. He was a genuine jazz singer with Sarah Vaughan's same rare brand of musicianship, so ungrudgingly admired by jazzmen.

Sought after by women, Mr. B repeatedly turned down invitations to parties so that he could "hang out with the guys" and, as often as possible, take part in their jam sessions. Eckstine played trumpet and valve trombone, with nowhere the brilliance of Dizzy or Benny Green, but acceptably enough. B saw himself as a frustrated jazzman, and would gladly have exchanged his vast vocal gifts for the ability to improvise like the men behind him.

Eckstine was even-tempered, straightforward in his personal relationships, and thoroughly reliable. The grand design for the dream band boiled down to the one suitable and available personality and a final denominator, money. Billy Shaw found it at the William Morris agency, at least the assurance of backing provided Shaw could show booking interest in the band. Shaw attained his objective in the classic way: he sold Eckstine, and the imaginary band, to De Luxe Records, an independent label that had jumped the gun on the AFM ban by signing with Petrillo early in 1944, months before the major labels got around to working out an agreement with the union boss.

On April 13, while Charlie was still in Kansas City, Eckstine recorded three sides for De Luxe in New York. *Good Jelly* paraphrased and upstaged the Bluebird hit. It was backed by *I Stay in the Mood for You* and followed by *I Got a Date with Rhythm*, both well suited to Eckstine's delivery. Retail store counters and juke box operators, starved for fresh material for two years because of the AFM recording ban, received the records with enthusiasm. The ban had created an unprecedented seller's market; while the majors continued to drag their feet, new labels were springing up by the score in New York and Los Angeles, with products tailored to the consumers of blues, gospel, and jazz.

As soon as the records reached the market, the fast-talking, persuasive Shaw was on the telephone, squeezing booking commitments from ballroom operators. In a matter of days Shaw had enough to convince the brass at the William Morris office, and the needed backing was forthcoming. Eckstine then left on a trip to Detroit and Chicago to round up his key men. By this time Charlie's job at Tootie's Mayfair had ended, and he had gone to Chicago to work in the Noble Sissle Orchestra, an old-fashioned band that backed floor shows at the gaudy new Rumboogie Club. Eckstine told Charlie that Dizzy Gillespie had been hired as musical director, the job Charlie would have liked for himself; Charlie would head up the reed section. Despite his disappointment Charlie accepted, and began getting the reeds together. He hired John Jackson, his alter ego from the McShann band, and Gene "Jug" Ammons, son of famed old-time Chicago boogie-woogie pianist Albert Ammons and a "bad man" on tenor, whom Charlie had encountered at a Chicago jam session. Charlie also persuaded Eckstine to hire Buddy Anderson for the brass section.

Men converged on New York from Chicago, Detroit, Kansas City, Boston, Philadelphia, and Washington. Rehearsals began at the Nola Studios in midtown Manhattan the first week of May. Agency money provided uniforms and drawing accounts. As director of the reed section, Charlie's first problem was to find or develop a baritone saxophonist capable of handling the big instrument in the style demanded. Unable to find one, Charlie converted Leo Parker, a six-foot altoist from Washington. Charlie soon had his namesake playing the heavy saxophone faster than it had ever been played before. The reeds then shaped up with Jug Ammons and Tom Crump on tenors, Charlie and John Jackson on altos, and Leo Parker on baritone. Within a few days Charlie had the section blended and blowing powerfully against the brass in the way that made big bands of that era so exciting to hear.

Dizzy Gillespie led the trumpet section, backed by Buddy Anderson, Gail Brockman, and Shorty McConnell. The trombone section had Benny Green, Rudy Morrison, and Howard Scott. For his rhythm section Eckstine used the Yacht Club trio (John Malachi, Connie Wainwright, and Tommy Potter), augmented by ex-Hines percussionist Shadow Wilson. As an added bonus Sarah Vaughan came in as the "girl singer." The band that carried the hopes of the avant garde, and included almost every one of its key figures, consisted of nine veterans from the ill-fated Earl Hines Orchestra (Eckstine, Vaughan, Parker, Crump, Gillespie, Brockman, McConnell, Green, and Harris) and three Kansas City jazzmen, veterans of the Jay McShann Orchestra (Parker, Anderson, Jackson). This nucleus of seasoned players gave the band its essential inner tension and tone. But at once there was a discouraging setback—in the space of two weeks three sidemen were served with induction notices and hustled off to boot camps: saxophonist Tom Crump, replaced by Junior Williams (ex-McShann), trombonist Benny Green, and drummer Shadow Wilson, the latter two major losses.

The most pressing problem for the band was the lack of a book, a property acquired by successful leaders at considerable expense and over a period of time. There were more "blowing" than "writing" musicians in the Eckstine ranks. Dizzy burned midnight oil creating several charts, a revised version of *A Night in Tunisia,* and new backgrounds for Eckstine vocals. Jerry Valentine contributed *Second Balcony Jump.*

Still, the Eckstine cupboard was dangerously bare at the last minute. When it became obvious that, despite its individual talents, a modernized band of seven brass and five reeds could not operate on the old free-blowing Kansas City principle, Billy Shaw advanced money to buy arrangements from Count Basie and Boyd Raeburn. The idea of a commonwealth venture was discarded; the Morris agency had too heavy a cash investment in the band. At last, with the blessings of many people in the music business, including Count Basie, the dream band took to the road, playing its first one-nighter in Wilmington, Delaware.

"So started the frantic odyssey of one of the most musically advanced jazz bands ever organized," *Down Beat* reported. Another trade journal predicted that the "band was so far ahead of its day that it was doomed to failure."

The breaking-in period was desperately trying, Benny Green was sorely missed, and percussionist Shadow Wilson more so. Eckstine made numerous telephone calls trying to obtain a suitable drummer. Klook Clarke had been drafted. Finally Art Blakey, contacted at the Tic Toc Club in Boston, agreed to join as soon as his contract expired, in another thirty days. The band carried on without an adequate drummer. So long as the music was danceable and the crowds had Mr. B and Sarah to enjoy, rough spots in the ensemble playing went unnoticed, or at least uncomplained about by the unsophisticated audiences in the hinterlands. The itinerary took the band down the Atlantic seaboard to Florida.

As the band moved west, through the Deep South and into Texas, morale remained high and things began to fall into place. In Kansas City the barnstormers were joined by Tadd Dameron, formerly pianist with Harlan Leonard and Andy Kirk. Dameron came not as a piano player but a full-time arranger, and promptly began overhauling the patchwork book. With him Dameron brought scores of two beautiful originals, *Cool Breeze* and *Ladybird*, representing new standards in charting. Additional arrangements by Budd Johnson and Gil Fuller arrived by registered mail. Art Blakey caught up with the band in St. Louis, and immediately the rhythm section began to go. St. Louis proved a memorable stop. There Buddy Anderson's ailment was diagnosed as tuberculosis, and the wispy trumpeter went home to Oklahoma City for a long convalescence that would lead to his permanent retirement from brass work. As a temporary substitute for Anderson the band used the son of an East St. Louis dentist, an eighteen-year-old high school senior named Miles Davis. Hearing that "Bird and Diz" were in town, the future star had showed up at the band's first rehearsal, trumpet in hand, wistfully hoping to be allowed to sit in.

The band was scheduled for two weeks at the Plantation Club, a "black and tan" cabaret modeled after Chicago's Grand Terrace, using all-Negro talent and catering to the white trade. When the musicians attempted to use the front entrance, the management objected; jazz and (it was implied) black musicians were expected to use the rear entrance. Charlie wanted to make an issue of the ruling; Dizzy, still mindful of the stitches taken at Pine Bluff, thought it "not worth the hassle." The politic Eckstine, with a hundred details on his mind, agreed; they would soon be in Chicago, more civilized territory. Charlie felt differently. He went around to the back tables where the musicians were relaxing after a rehearsal, asking each man if he had drunk from the glass in front of him. Receiving an affirmative answer, Charlie carefully broke each glass, explaining that the management would of course not expect any of its regular customers to use the same glass. After a number of glasses had been destroyed, the club's owner, a well-known St. Louis gangster, arrived. The engagement was cancelled forthwith, and violence only narrowly averted. Eckstine got on the telephone to the William Morris agency, and the resourceful Billy Shaw was able to turn the near-disaster to account, rebooking the band at the Club Riviera, a black cabaret on the other side of town.

As the band moved north, the sections began to jell. Then the sections took on that magic of the old Kansas City bands, in which each section swung as a single instrument, and the sections swung against sections, until the dance hall or theater vibrated. Only then did a band discover a life of its own, greater than the sum total of its book and assembled talents. The nature of that mystique, profound, spiritual, and vitalizing, had been the secret of Count Basie, Duke Ellington, and a few others. Usually it came after a lengthy search. The Billy Eckstine Orchestra seemed to have stumbled upon it in unseemly haste. This was not really the case. The Eckstine mystique was a sudden blooming, after years of maturation, like the flower of a century plant. It had been developing for years and represented the aspirations of a generation of musicians, beautifully trained in the old swing bands, speaking the same language, brought together in a common cause. The road trip became not so much a tour as a crusade.

The band bussed into Chicago the last week of August 1944, for a two-week stand at the Regal Theater. In spite of sweltering heat, there were lines of people waiting for seats. Howard McGhee, working across town with Charlie Barnett, came over to fill in for Buddy Anderson. Reviewing the Regal show in *Down Beat*'s "Caught in the Act" column, John Sipple noted the band's bite, precision, and overwhelming swing. "The driving force behind the reeds," Sipple wrote, "is Charlie Parker. After hearing the band do six shows at the Regal, your reviewer did not hear a single repeated idea in the many choruses he took." Sipple observed that Parker had stopped the show on all six occasions with a sixteen-bar improvisation between verses on Sarah Vaughan's *I'll Wait and Pray*.

The Sipple piece was Charlie's first significant press notice. Charlie clipped it out of the paper and sent it along to his mother, alerting her first by telephone to call her attention, somewhat prematurely, to his rapid advancement in the jazz world. From Chicago the band went to Detroit for a week at the Paradise Theater, then drove on to New York. In six months the band had grossed over a hundred thousand dollars. The William Morris office was enthusiastic. De Luxe Records picked up its option. Billy Shaw was the boy wonder of the booking industry. The band was established as a major attraction, commanding fees of five thousand dollars a week and more, the same fees asked for Basie and Ellington.

It was August, a month that figured prominently in the tides of Charlie Parker's life. His birthday, the Lake Taneycomo interlude, his departure from the Jay McShann Orchestra, and the parting of the ways with Father Hines all bore August datelines. Also, the band was back in New York, that switchyard of sidemen and band routes. Now another cycle had come full turn for Charlie. He told Eckstine he wanted to quit. He had waited out his union card. He had been offered a job on Fifty-second Street. It paid scale, substantially less than his salary with Eckstine, and Eckstine offered a raise. Charlie wasn't interested. He had no complaint against the leader. He liked the gang. He'd simply had it with big bands. Charlie was sorry. That was what he wanted to do. He wanted the freedom of the small combo and the excitement of working in New York. When the bus left for Baltimore that day, Charlie was not aboard. That night he hailed a cruising cab for the ride downtown and his first paying job on Fifty-second Street.

13

The Street

The Street was a collection of buildings, four stories high and constructed of the durable, stodgy brownstone favored by architects at the turn of the century. The brownstone buildings stood shoulder to shoulder, one wall wedged against the next, facing one another along Fifty-second Street in the block between Fifth and Sixth Avenues. Once each had housed a single, affluent New York family. Now, with corroded plumbing and wiring systems that gave cause for concern to the fire department, they provided studios for sign painters and silkscreen operators, mail-order drops, and import-export concerns run out of a hat, offices for private detectives and teachers of the piano and saxophone, and darkrooms shared by photographers who prowled Broadway night clubs with Speed Graphics and baggy pockets stuffed with flash bulbs.

By day The Street was dingier than most, a dispiriting block that lay between chic Fifth Avenue and the glitter of Broadway two blocks west. The clubs that sprang up there during the war years occupied unused basements or abandoned ground floors of the brownstone buildings. They were clustered at the west end of the block, seven in all: Jimmy Ryan's, the Onyx, Famous Door, Samoa, Downbeat, Spotlight, and Three Deuces. In front of each club the inevitable badge of the period cabaret, a marquee—its green canvas bleached by sun, stained by rain, supported by two iron poles—extended from the brownstone front to the curbstone. Some of the clubs were nothing more than damp converted basements, thirty feet wide and not much deeper, low of ceiling, with tiny checkrooms and miniature bars, furnished with a clutter of tables and chairs most likely picked up at an auction sale. The Famous Door was described by bandleader Woody Herman as "a ratty, overcrowded little basement joint." Prices ran high for those days, seventy-five cents for a bottle of beer or a dilute, insipid whiskey highball.

Customers sat at tables large enough to cover with a pocket handkerchief, and paid a cover charge of three dollars. The Street was a hustler's operation, geared to a high rate of turnover. After every thirty-minute set the clubs were cleared and the customers prodded along to the next place of entertainment. Each club displayed on its wall a printed card saying "MAXIMUM OCCUPANCY PERMITTED ON THESE PREMISES IS 60" or whatever total had been assigned by the New York Fire Department. The limits were flagrantly violated on busy nights when the bar stood four or five deep with stags and buffs. Most of the operators were New York editions of the Black Hand, the same breed that had flourished in Kansas City under boss Tom Pendergast.

By means of a transformation similar to the one that had turned the shabby district of Kansas City into a tarnished fairyland, The Street after dark became a place of glamour and promise. Neon lights brightened the sooty façades of the

brownstones. Banners bearing the names of the featured artists inside fluttered against the awnings of the marquees, and if
one were interested in the wonderful world of jazz, he might
find there its principal stars in an improbable concentration.

Arriving on The Street by taxi on a warm night just after
Labor Day, September, 1944, Charlie could see in a single
sweeping glance the names on the banners. It was as if he had
before him a chart showing, by means of its leading figures, the
entire course of jazz history from the beginnings at the turn of
the century in New Orleans to the present moment. At Jimmy
Ryan's, the club nearest to Fifth Avenue, the legendary Sidney
Bechet, the last of the master Creole clarinetists, those founding fathers of jazz reed style, headed a five-piece New Orleans
band that included Zutty Singleton, a drummer who had played
with the mythical Buddy Bolden, and a rhythm section of au-
thentic New Orleans jazzmen, or "musicianers," as Bechet
called them in his gruff patois. The old man, with his squashed
face, seemingly chipped from a very hard wood, played clarinet
and soprano saxophone, a curved, bell-less orphan of the reed
family, blowing with a skirling vibrato that carried to the sidewalk and could be heard above the swish of taxicab tires.

At the Onyx the public was invited to hear the grand master of jazz tenor saxophone, Coleman Hawkins himself, now
forty, old as jazzmen went, veteran of famous bands from 1922
to the present, still firmly in command of his improvisational
powers and the earth-shaking tone that was his trademark.
Like Father Hines, the Hawk was feeling his way toward the
new sounds, although with greater circumspection. The Coleman Hawkins Quintet employed two first-rate young sidemen,
Howard McGhee and Max Roach, another Klook Clarke protégé, on drums. The infusion of new blood had given Coleman
Hawkins a new lease on life. He was playing smoothly and
well.

Across the way, at the Famous Door, the matchless Art
Tatum held forth, no longer as a single, but with a trio includ-
ing guitarist Tiny Grimes and fleet bassist Slam Stewart.
Mildred Bailey, accompanied by her husband, vibraphonist Red
Norvo, and a mellow gathering of white musicians, was the at-

traction at the Club Downbeat. Fats Waller and a five-piece band topped the bill at the Spotlight. Advertised as "Fifty Thousand Killer-Watts of Jive," Leo Watson and his Spirits of Rhythm led the show at the Samoa, leavening the solid musical content of the instrumental combos with maniacal scat singing and such originals as *Sweet Marihuana Brown* (set to the tune of *Sweet Georgia Brown*) and *She Ain't No Saint*, a ballad about the neighborhood call girl.

Unadorned by signs, in the midst of this hive of activity stood the White Rose Bar, where musicians and their cronies repaired between sets. At the White Rose you could rub elbows with any of the distinguished jazzmen or ladies appearing at the clubs on The Street, or members of their supporting bands. Prices at the White Rose were scaled to the working man, ten cents for draft beer and twenty-five for whiskey shots. The White Rose was a clearing house for gossip. There one might find personal managers, agents, promotion men for music publishing houses, writers for the music trades, wives and girl-friends of musicians, and artists-and-repertoire men for the independent record labels. Also Mayor Pincus (self-appointed), a short, scarlet-faced character who resembled a burlesque comedian and hustled tips as a door-opener for cab drivers.

Fats Waller, Art Tatum, Coleman Hawkins, Sidney Bechet and the other top attractions at the clubs along The Street played the set beginning at nine P.M. and continuing on the hour until half past three the next morning. The odd sets were played by second-billed attractions and these were of as much interest to jazz fans as those featured. Sidney Bechet was spelled by Eddie Condon's Chicagoans—Bobby Hackett, Bud Freeman, Pee Wee Russell, Dave Bowman and George Wettling. At the Onyx Club saxophone buffs were surfeited with tenor sounds; Don Byas, lately starred in the Count Basie Orchestra, led a quintet of his own. The rambunctious Fats Waller was spelled by the John Kirby Sextet, playing a kind of jazz chamber music. Relieving Mildred Bailey and Red Norvo at the Downbeat was the "Black Angel of Jazz Violin," Hezekiah Stuff Smith. At the Famous Door the Art Tatum Trio was platooned by the Ben Webster Quartet.

The only name missing from a true cavalcade of jazz history was Lester Young. Lester had been out of circulation for a while, doing time in the detention barracks of a Georgia military camp, allegedly for boiling dental cocaine with muscatel wine. As for big bands, the warrenlike clubs of The Street were too small to handle them, and in any case, as people were beginning to realize, big bands were on the way out. That was the whole point of The Street. The big entertainment package was being superseded by the budget pack. The reason lay in the economics of cabaret operation (Marxian dialectics applied to show biz). The combo made a comfortable nut for the operator, who had been harassed by wartime liquor shortages and was now saddled with the latest imposition of the war, a 10 percent cabaret tax. That tax would lead to an epidemic of overnight bankruptcies. The probability was foreseen by the shrewder operators, who simply let tax liabilities ride on until the government intervened, then sold the key to someone else and dropped out of sight. The change in ownership of the jazz clubs on The Street was rapid; seasoned jazzmen took care to stay current on their wages. But such considerations were secondary to the playing of jazz. In 1944 musicians working The Street thought themselves fortunate and found working conditions favorably comparable to the great days in New Orleans before World War I, or Kansas City during the halcyon days of the Pendergast regime. The freedom from the demands of the big bands was welcome as well. In 1944 the jazz combo was in to stay. It would dominate jazz from that year onward.

Charlie's gig was at the seventh club on The Street, the last one on the south side, nearest Sixth Avenue. That was the Three Deuces, its coat of arms three cards spread in the lucky hand, a saxophone rampant. The Three Deuces was operated by one Sammy Kaye, a native of Brooklyn, young, Jewish, unaffiliated with the Mafia, and a jazz buff. Unlike rival operators, Kaye was turned on to the new sounds. He had made the scene at Minton's and knew something of emergent reputations in the bebop underground. When Kaye learned that Charlie Parker had quit the Billy Eckstine Orchestra, he at once negotiated to bring him to the Deuces. The club was enjoying a spell of economic health, due to Kaye's foresight in signing an un-known young pianist from Pittsburgh, a fellow named Erroll Garner, who played a full, melodious keyboard style that trans-formed outworn show tunes into moments of magic. At the time Charlie was hired, the band spelling Garner, who worked as a single, was a mere trio: drummer Stan Levey, pianist Joe Albany, and bassist Curly Russell. It badly needed a horn. What it really needed to conform to Klook Clarke's band of the future was two horns. Charlie was hired for sixty-five dollars a week, somewhat less than his salary with Eckstine. Charlie pointed out that the instrumentation was too thin and obtained a commitment from Kaye to add a trumpet. Dizzy Gillespie, contacted in Washington, said that he would give the matter consideration, promising a decision as soon as Eckstine re-turned to New York. Meanwhile, Howard McGhee came over between sets to sit in.

Charlie had been on The Street less than a week when he was invited to make his first record date for an independent label, a Newark concern named Savoy. Tatum's guitarist, Tiny Grimes, had promoted the contract. Once a member of a vocal group known as the Cats and the Fiddle, Grimes had somehow convinced Savoy that he was destined for fame as a ballad singer. In 1944 anything round, ten inches in diameter, with a hole in the center, had no trouble in finding a ready market. Savoy agreed, but played the situation as cagily as possible; its budget (less than two hundred dollars) called for a grand total of five musicians. Pianist Clyde Hart, bassist Jimmy Butts, and drummer Doc West had already been hired. Grimes, doubling on electric guitar, would be the fourth. A single horn was needed. The date would pay union scale, thirty dollars for three hours of work. Charlie accepted without giving the matter much thought. The session did not sound very promising to him. Five instruments would make for a painfully shallow backing for any vocalist. Eckstine had used sixteen men for the De Luxe date. When Sinatra recorded for Columbia, a small symphony of thirty-odd provided the background music. Still, the thirty dollars would come in handy.

On the afternoon of September 15, Charlie, Grimes, Hart,

Butts, and West met at the Nola Studios, down Fifty-second Street at Broadway. The session was supervised by Teddy Reig, the young A&R man for Savoy. After warming up with an ad-lib blues called *Tiny's Tempo*, the musicians got down to the business of the day. The first vocal was one that Grimes had composed for himself. Titled *I'll Always Love You Just the Same*, it was as wordy (and dull) as its title suggests. Grimes was not really a professional singer. He simply wanted to be. He did not know how to phrase, how to breathe, or how to pace himself. By the time *I'll Always Love You Just the Same* had been laboriously rehearsed, run down, and thrice recorded, well over an hour of the allotted three had passed. Not one of the takes was really acceptable, to the singer, to Reig, or to anyone else. The only thing notable about them were the obbligattos played by alto saxophone—jewels reminiscent of the show-stopping performance behind Sarah Vaughan on *I'll Wait and Pray*.

The next tune tackled was a sad little bebop ballad titled *Romance without Finance*, also penned by Grimes. It sparkled with such lines as:

> *Romance without finance is a nu-sance (oh, but it is!),*
> *Oh baby, mama, mama, give up that gold!*

and:

> *You so great, and you so fine,*
> *You ain't got no money, you can't be mine.*
> *It ain't no joke, to be stone broke,*
> *Baby, you know I ain't lyin'*
> *When I say, romance without finance. . . .*

No amount of enthusiasm by the accompanying musicians was able to save it. After several false starts and three hobbling takes, another of the precious hours had been used. At this point Tiny Grimes's "pipes," strained by the unaccustomed exertions, were in such shape that he found it impossible to sing another line. Now the Savoy A&R director, an ambling obese man with a squeaky voice and irascible manner, found himself in a tight spot. Faced with material that he privately considered worthless, Reig proposed that the musicians throw something together to round out the four sides. Perhaps another instrumental to go along with *Tiny's Tempo*. The instrumentals could be used as B sides to the vocals, should Savoy see fit to release them. It would be better than going back empty-handed to his boss, a short-fused man named Herman Lubinski, who had parlayed a hole-in-the-wall "race record" store into an independent label. Less than twenty minutes of studio time remained. No one had thought to bring along any original material that might serve their purpose. Could someone suggest anything to record?

Charlie could. From his bag of melodies he played a figure based on *I Got Rhythm*. He had dozens of them. The others worked for a few moments to master the line. It was run down and timed, and a trial recording was made. The tempo seemed a shade slow. Hal West forced the pace a bit, and the musicians tried it again. The second playback was entered into the studio log as acceptable. Charlie offered the title *Red Cross*, not in memory of the samaritan organization but after a man named Cross who traveled with Billy Eckstine as a personal valet. The final take of *Red Cross* was completed as the third hour ended.* Reig did not have to pay out overtime. The Savoy budget stayed nicely within its two-hundred-dollar limit. Such were the circumstances of the first fortuitous, imperfect recording session of bebop discography.

Red Cross begins with a unison chorus of five instruments. The expertise of The Street professionals is manifest in the rich sonority and smooth blend achieved by the skeletal band, and by its easy, limber swing. But *Red Cross* is really a vehicle for the alto saxophone. At the channel, or bridge—that eight-bar section where Tin Pan Alley tunes shift to their counter melody (bars 17 through 24)—the alto appears alone, heightening the

---

* The *Red Cross* motif soon gained wide currency as *Mop Mop*. Although invented by Charlie Parker, it was picked up, recorded, and copyrighted by Coleman Hawkins, who collected substantial royalties from its many recorded versions and playings on the air.

tension for a solo to follow. At the end of the unison chorus it is the alto that takes over. And here, for the first time, faithfully recorded and fully dimensional, as the amateur recordings of Newman and Benedetti were not, is the new sound of the alto saxophone, Charlie Parker as insiders heard him in the after-hours clubs of Harlem.

The qualities that made audio prisoners of Charlie's camp followers are here. The saxophone sound is strong and virile. The hard reed has been mastered and made articulate. The sound is richer in the middle register than the boyish and lyric Wichita transcriptions or *Hootie Blues*. It is a grown man who addresses us now. Blues inflections continue to float on the surface of the notes, like an oil film on pond water. The phrasing goes in such a way that the line generates its powerful rhythmic implications. Statements are made without hesitation, although each line is freshly improvised, as can be heard on the separate takes of *Red Cross*, cut consecutively in the short span of fifteen minutes, and still available as Savoy reissues. These are pure improvisations, played off the top, and against the clock at that, played with the precision of a symphony musician performing a Mozart work many times rehearsed and made note perfect. Each of the solos on *Red Cross* is shaped to provide its own design, with a beginning, a middle, and an end. Each is a work of art in miniature to the extent that jazz performances can be lasting and valuable works of art, characterized by the strengths and weaknesses of such creations, in which the player is at once performer and composer, his fragile art captured on the medium of the phonograph recording.

Tiny's Tempo lacks the urgent musical dialectic of *Red Cross*. It is mellow and funky. Not the blues of despair but a jolly, bubbling, genital blues. How richly the notes ride over the flux of rhythm. With what skill are they modeled to the contours of the longer line.

Some weeks after the session, Savoy released *I'll Always Love You Just the Same*, coupled with *Tiny's Tempo* (Savoy 526) and *Romance without Finance*, coupled with *Red Cross* (Savoy 532). Heard on juke boxes alongside tunes by Eckstine, Vaughan, Jeffries, Sinatra, Como, and Crosby, they sounded more forlorn than they had at Nola Studios. It remained for the B sides to be dug out by collectors, like finds from the rubble of an archeological dig. *Tiny's Tempo* and *Red Cross* became the foundation stones of every modern jazz record collection. When Savoy at last understood the value of the B sides, the two instrumentals were coupled and made available to the trade as Savoy 541.

Within a few weeks Dizzy Gillespie arrived, and the combo at the Three Deuces began to shape up. After the usual shuffling process the rhythm section settled on Stan Levey, drums, Curly Russell, bass, and Al Haig, piano. This was Clarke's streamlined band of the future. It no longer operated in the uncertain setting of an after-hours spot, but was presented as a bona-fide attraction in a downtown night club. Its music was spare and functional. The rhythm section furnished support for the horns. The basic 4/4 beat was plucked out by the string bass. Picked up by the drummer on top cymbal, this became the band's pulse. Snare, bass, and tom-toms were used to build counter rhythms. The bassist was the band's time keeper, the pivot around which all else moved. Haig threw out chords like bursts of musical confetti. The rhythmic product, complex and urgent, gave the foundation essential to the front line.

Up front trumpet and saxophone reduced the instrumentation of the big band (seven brass and five reeds) to the lowest common denominator—one brass and one reed. Each horn was a section in itself. The horns played the unison parts. They also exchanged leads, invented counter themes, and, of course, took solos. In the hands of young jazzmen like Charlie Parker and Dizzy Gillespie, everything that the big bands had been able to do was implied by the two horns, and a great deal more besides. The playing was a constant and creative process. There was no band book. No customer at the Deuces ever glimpsed so much as an arrangement or sheet of music paper. The tunes had no names, or numbers. They were simply tunes, heard and carried in the heads of the musicians. The names came later. The repertoire of the Parker-Gillespie combo—*A Night in Tunisia, Salt Peanuts, Epistrophy, 'Round About Midnight, Swingmatism*—

had been assembled from jam sessions and road trips. To these were added tunes worked up for the job at the Deuces: *A Dizzy Atmosphere, Blue 'n Boogie, Groovin' High, Anthropology,* and *Shaw Nuff,* the latter in honor of Billy Shaw, the bopper's good friend on agency row. The tunes were riffs based on the harmonic structure of popular songs. *I Got Rhythm* furnished the scaffolding for *A Dizzy Atmosphere, Red Cross, Anthropology,* and *Fifty-second Street Theme. Groovin' High* was *Whispering*; *What Is This Thing Called Love?* became *Hot House*; *Fine and Dandy* became *Keen and Peachy*; *S'Wonderful* became *Stupendous. Byas a Drink* was rooted in *Stompin' at the Savoy,* and *Ice Freezes Red* in *Indiana.*

Chi Chi was the fast-stepping lady friend of a well-known disc jockey named Symphony Sid, the first on the air with the new sounds. *Scrapple from the Apple* was *I Got Rhythm* with a *Honeysuckle Rose* bridge. Tin Pan Alley was being scrambled like data fed into a military coding machine to emerge as a new musical intelligence. The Parker-Gillespie sets were explosions of pure musical energy. Listeners were rocked back on their heels and numbed by its force. The entire body of American jazz, from Bolden to Basie, was being subjected to an exhaustive re-examination. Beret at a rakish angle, goatee bobbing, Dizzy would center the horn against his lips and spurt forth festoons of notes. The saxophone would support his escalations, comment on his statements, underline, paraphrase, punctuate, and countervoice. The saxophone solos were still more brilliant. They seemed to begin where the trumpet had stopped. The saxophone was played with an accuracy and at a speed that made the listener's hair stand on end. There had been nothing like this band since the King Oliver Creole Jazz band, fresh up from New Orleans, with young Louis Armstrong on second cornet, opened at the Lincoln Gardens in Chicago in 1922.

A visit to the Three Deuces came as a rude shock to most. Not one writer for the metropolitan press or the trades liked the music. Most hated and blasted it. A few critics made honest efforts to write meaningful reviews and thus explain the bebop phenomenon to their readers, but without much success.

Chord alterations were difficult to follow, and everything was played outrageously fast. The only point of agreement was that the boppers did know how to play their instruments. Why in heaven's name couldn't they play them properly? Jazz critics of long standing, who should have known better, missed the important points. The music they took to calling "non-jazz" or "anti-jazz" conformed to all of the rules by which jazz always had been measured. It was collectively improvised and intensely personal in intonation (though now *cool* instead of coarsely *hot*). The same critics complained that the new music "didn't swing." Actually, it swung more than ever, but old arteries were too stiff to react. Nor did the boppers go out of their way to explain their art. They looked upon the music press with the same contempt they felt for the show business establishment. One prominent critic wrote, "Parker's version of bebop varies from Dizzy's in so much as he plays chromatic scales up and down all the keys." Charlie was to quote this gem for years, often admonishing his sidemen to "watch out for those chromatics."

"Name" bandleaders, feeling themselves threatened and anxious to deal bebop a death blow, made vitriolic and foolish statements. Interviewed by a staffer for *Down Beat*, Tommy Dorsey stated: "Bebop has set music back twenty years." Louis Armstrong, great innovator of another era, said the boppers were playing wrong chords. John Hammond, patron saint of the swingman, still highly placed in A&R ranks, unwisely went on record as saying that "To me, bebop is a collection of nauseating cliches, repeated *ad infinitum*." The Latin phrase dredged up from his two years at Yale put an official seal of disapproval on bop. Sigmund Spaeth, the widely read writer on popular music, pontificated: "The gradual development (or decadence) of the distortion of jazz . . . to the artificial absurdities of the so-called 'Bebop' style must be fairly obvious even to the casual listener." New York columnist Jimmy Cannon, back from an unnerving descent into the basement club where Charlie and Dizzy were joyously in performance, reported to his estimated one million readers, "Bebop sounds to me like a hardware store in an earthquake." As the very hip observer Louis

Gottlieb remarked, the impression of most people exposed to bebop for the first time was that it was painful, and that their leg was being pulled.

Boppers found the knocks predictable and hilarious. They took delight in quoting the latest put-down. The two names of the swing tradition who did not issue such statements, because they knew better, were Duke Ellington and Count Basie, men who had made their own contributions to jazz history and valued good music in whatever form.

Meanwhile the stepchild of jazz had its foot wedged stubbornly in the Fifty-second Street door. By the winter of 1944–45 the Parker-Gillespie band was The Street's most controversial attraction, and the most exciting. Nightly performances from the Deuces set off shock waves that were felt from coast to coast. Arriving in New York on buses carrying various big bands, young musicians made the Deuces their first stop, pilgrims converging on a new Mecca. Many of them quit their jobs so that they could hang out on The Street and hear Bird and Diz every night and, if their luck were in, jam with the men they idolized. The new music, now fully implemented in the first real bebop small band, and played by its chief innovators, was heard as a revelation, and its practitioners as prophets.

During Charlie Parker's first year on The Street he met the two women destined to play major roles in his life, Doris Sydnor and Chan Richardson. He could not have picked women more unalike. Doris was tall, reserved, and shy. From a working-class background in Chicago she came to New York in the mid-Forties and found employment as a cocktail waitress and hat-check girl in Harlem and on The Street. Although she had been around night clubs a great part of her life, Doris knew little about jazz. It was a commodity dispensed in the places where she worked. In New York she began meeting the men who played jazz and who were part of the bebop movement. In this way she met and fell in love with Charlie Parker. When she could, she carried his instrument case, and at an after-hours club held down a back table where he could rest, drink, and talk to friends between sets. Painfully thin, so much so that she stooped to conceal her height, she was a maternal figure, a follower-around, a picker-up, a putter-to-bed. Doris remained at the edge of the scene, frequently looking rather out of it, more tolerated than accepted, a hopeless square, patient and tenacious.

Chan Richardson was everything Doris was not. Chan was hip and beautiful. A dancer and ex-model, Chan had literally grown up on Fifty-second Street, where her mother, an ex-Ziegfeld Follies girl, had come during the Depression, following the death and financial ruin of her husband, a successful night club operator of the speakeasy era. Once mistress of a multi-roomed house set on a walled estate in Westchester, Mrs. Richardson had salvaged enough from the family wreckage to acquire the hat-check concession at the chic Cotton Club. Mother and daughter lived close by, in a fading, old, but still substantial three-story brownstone house at 7 West 52nd Street. There Mrs. Richardson raised the only child of the ill-starred marriage.

The Cotton Club concession was a lucrative one. Occasionally Chan helped her mother there, or filled in at the checkstand at the Three Deuces. But this sort of work did not appeal to Chan. After graduating from a midtown high school, she took professional dancing lessons and went into chorus work. At the age of nineteen Chan was one of Manhattan's night people. A generation before, bobby soxers had grown up on *In the Mood* and Glenn Miller; Chan grew up on *Ornithology* and *Groovin' High*. The prickly tunes the boppers played, to the confoundment of the squares, were as familiar to her as nursery rhymes. She could tell you who composed them and when. And if they had yet been recorded. Jive was a second language. Chan spoke the cryptic argot of the boppers in a chimelike voice, fluently and with charm. Her culture heroes were the figures of the bop revolution. She worked diligently to know every one of them personally. When her mother warned of dangerous personal involvements, Chan angrily replied, "Mother, you're so square. I don't have to sleep with these cats. They're my buddies."

Chan was a striking girl. She had straight shoulders, free-wheeling hips, and spectacular legs—a dancer's body that caused juices to flow as she spiked her way along the battered old sidewalks of Fifty-second Street. Chan had good, high, rose-ate Irish-American coloring. Handsome black hair was worn in a sleek pageboy. Merry dark eyes and dimples completed the picture of every jazzman's sweetheart, an implausible Miss Hip, a swinging, jive-talking cover girl, cued to the action, picking up on all of the riffs. When Chan Richardson zoomed into the Three Deuces from the wintry street, skin aglow, beaver coat furled back from the high shoulders, the faces of table-sitters swung like those in a tennis gallery.

Chan gave more than lip service to the bebop movement. She was imbued with the same zealot energy that drove Dean Benedetti to ever more improbable feats of amateur engineering. Chan pulled coats. She press-agented the new music with writers, managers, and artists-and-repertoire men. She was responsible for more than one of the early independent record sessions. If a bass player was needed on an out-of-town gig, or in a recording studio on short notice, Chan could find the right man. Her black book had all the telephone numbers, listed in a slanting hand, each *i* dotted with a tiny circle.

Chan redecorated the old brownstone at the end of the block. Seven West 52 became a combination salon, hotel, short-order restaurant, baggage checkroom, and *poste restante* for jazzmen. The front door, reached after unlatching a heavy, knee-high black iron gate and crossing a small stone courtyard, was never locked. Open house for in-people prevailed at 7 West 52 twenty-four hours a day. A jazzman with the right credentials, even a stranger from out of town with a correct referral, might check in at 7 West 52 without advance notice and there find temporary bed and board, listen to records, use the telephone, store a trunk, catch up on the gossip of the dance-band world. In a short time he could fill himself in on any detail having to do with bandleaders, band routes, changes of personnel (actual or pending), hirings, firings, openings, closings, and busts. Seven West 52 was the East Coast clearing house for intelligence of vital concern to the working musician. The old brownstone was also a handy place where men working in the clubs on The Street could fall in between sets. Chan became a very important person on The Street. She was its Pearl Mesta, with a touch of Madame de Stael.

Charlie became a frequent caller at 7 West 52 and, as the most important new musician, a favored one. He and Chan began dating, and were often seen at Minton's and Monroe's Uptown House after the Deuces closed its doors. It was Charlie's first serious interest in a girl who knew so much about jazz and appreciated the conditions under which it was played. In 1946 neither Charlie nor Chan was ready for anything more than a pleasant, passing romance. Both were too popular, and too busy. A more serious and mature relationship would have to wait for a later period in their lives.

A Dizzy Atmosphere

The new underground required a new linguistics. To "broom" meant to travel by air; the hipster figure of speech referred to the witch's favored conveyance. Money was *gold*. *Eyes* meant willingness or enthusiasm. A *pad* was a bed, therefore someone's room or apartment. Old jazzmen's expressions, once in, were now out, and hopelessly dated the speaker. As root ideas they gave way to verbal improvisations, in the same way that old tunes served as armatures for bop compositions (*A Dizzy Atmosphere* from *I Got Rhythm*). Etymology remained reasonably straightforward. The intent was always the same: to exclude the uninitiated, to confound the square, to strengthen the inner community. *Out of the world* became *gone*, shorter and more allusive. *Blow your top* became *flip your wig*, leading to *flipped, flipped out, wigged, wig*, and *wiggy*. *Knocked out* yielded *gassed*, as in an old-fashioned dentist's chair. The verb *gas* gave the noun *gas*, a delightful experience (an evening at the Deuces, or uptown at Minton's). *Cool* and *dig* served as verbs, adverbs, adjectives, and nouns. Hipsters invented such portmanteau words as *chinchy* (cheap plus stingy). *Like*, already done to death in the mother tongue as adjective, adverb, verb, preposition, and conjunction, now appeared in every other sentence. Sometimes it stood alone, a sentence in itself, followed by an implied exclamation point or question mark, or merely a dash and a raised eyebrow. If you were *hip*, you *dug* (or used your imagination). The *put down* became the *put on*, a highly developed art, often so subtle that the victim was unaware that he was being put.

Dan Burley, the with-it columnist for the New York *Amsterdam News*, New York's leading Negro newspaper, compiled and published *The Original Handbook of Harlem Jive*, a slightly fanciful lexicon of the new argot. It contained parodies of John Greenleaf Whittier's "Barefoot Boy" and the soliloquy from *Hamlet*, in jive ("to dig, or not to dig, Jack, that is the question . . ."). Slim Gaillard began recording his musical versions of jive, liberally mixed with nonsense syllables, such hits as *Cement Mixer* (*Puttie-puttie*) and *A-Reet-a-Voutee*. *Pod*, more commonly *pot*, first appeared to describe cannabis, standard drug since jazz began in New Orleans, heir to a lengthy list of names: hay, golden leaf, cool green, gage, muggles, mezzirolls (after Chicago jazzman Milton Mezzrow), and shit.

Like the new music, the new linguistics revolved around fixed points and established ideas. Like the music, it was a language in motion, subtly changing from day to day, with ever fresh coinages and connotations, subject to common concepts and needs. Spoken quickly, inflected, it was a nearly incomprehensible dialect. Linguistically as well as musically the boppers had closed the door. The idea was to be on the inside looking out. That was the reason for all those heavily smoked glasses, defiantly worn in the darkest night club.

With the new sounds and language came new mores.

If the new language was exotic, by contrast behavior had become curiously circumspect. Loud voices were frowned down, as were hurried, headlong (frantic) actions. (This detail of mores was explored at length by Harry the Hipster Gibson in his recording *Frantic Ferdinand the 4-F Freak*.) Dress tended to become neater and more conservative. The handshake gave way to the palm-and-finger brush. "Yes, Daddy . . . I'm hip . . . Wot happening?"

The life jazzmen lived, the hours they worked, the large amount of time spent in rootless transit all set them apart from the workaday world. Jazz had always been anti-establishment, and jazzmen painfully beholden to their equivocal place in the entertainment world. Now came the hipsters, in revolt against the very jazz establishment. To hedonistic concepts of life prevalent among swingmen, the new lifestyle added a social awareness. The two-party system of government with its Humpty-Dumpty candidates was a *hype*. Its courts of law were an elaborate farce. The system was seen as a complex mechanism designed to oppress. World War II was a grotesque show staged by sick old men who had succeeded in turning America into a huge prison camp.

After The Street closed, musicians used to gather at the Stage Door Delicatessen, an all-night place on Sixth Avenue around the corner from Fifty-second, where they sat at marble-topped tables eating their multi-layered sandwiches. There they would listen to a drummer named Mouse as he invented an imaginary dialogue in which Churchill, Stalin, Hitler, Franklin D. Roosevelt, Haile Selassie, and Mussolini took part. The heads of government had been turned into real heads by the Mouse. Liberally supplied with pot, he summoned them to an imaginary summit conference, there to moderate their differences. Relaxed, cooled-out, the statesmen were described as they chummily discussed ways and means of ending the war.

Of the leading practitioners of the new music, the in-people chose Charlie Parker over Dizzy Gillespie as their object of reverence. Without question Dizzy was a wonderful improviser and trumpeter. But he was less a prime mover than Charlie. Dizzy had won his nickname by throwing spitballs at the first row of a theater audience; once, after an altercation with his bandleader, he slashed Cab Calloway's coattails with a razor blade. Dizzy was verbal, witty, extroverted, sunny of disposition—everything Charlie was not. Dizzy was accessible to everyone. You did not elevate such a man to a hierarchy.

Blowing musicians, who were in the position to know, all agreed that Parker was the fountainhead of the new music. The flow of musical ideas suggested mysterious, primal forces. Given a little improvisation, Charlie's nickname lent itself to the contemporary folklore. *Yardbird* was homely, if not demeaning. Shortened to *Bird*, it suggested airy flight, light, limitless horizons, otherworldliness. Unlike his collaborator, Charlie was inaccessible. He was cryptic, oblique, unpredictable, intuitive rather than rational, unmistakably "heavy." Like any disfranchised group, the in-people hungered for a mythic hero, and proceeded to make one.

What had begun as a fan club and grown into a ragged coterie of camp followers had by late 1944 become a cult. Its clairvoyant and exorcist was Dean Benedetti, who arrived in New York that fall. A native of Susanville, California, a mountain town on the Nevada border with a small Italian colony, Benedetti had begun his musical studies on piano at an early age in a home turned on to Verdi. By the time Dean was eighteen he had achieved a high degree of competence on the reed instruments, especially the alto saxophone. Benedetti had played in regional bands in San Francisco and Los Angeles before joining the orchestra that carried him east and deposited him, like a piece of driftwood, in New York. Once there, he was informed, as were all young saxophonists from the provinces, of Charlie Parker's virtuosity. Upon hearing Charlie perform on the instrument he assumed himself to have mastered, Dean underwent the series of reactions common to saxophonists exposed to Parker for the first time: disbelief, shock, impotent anger, and despair. And, at last, enlightenment: here, obviously, was the way the instrument was meant to be played. That was quite clear to Dean. He then began to study Charlie's methods: fingering, embouchure, breath control, patterns of phrasing, favorite turns, most-used progressions. Dean aped personal mannerisms and angles of holding the horn, experimented with reeds, mouthpieces, makes of instruments—in short, exhausted all avenues of inquiry open to the experienced professional in an effort to emulate his model. The results were insignificant. There was more than sheer virtuosity involved. Or method. Bird's saxophone playing was not just a style. It was the man himself. So Dean came at last to the inescapable conclusion that no alternative remained except to abandon playing the alto saxophone. It was then that he decided to devote himself to his life's work, following Parker about, recording Bird's solos. To Dean the solos were priceless. They were being expended upon thin air, sermons shouted into a desert. No one wrote them down. No two were alike. Charlie often quoted but never repeated himself. Every solo was unique, as the consecutive takes of *Red Cross* were unique. Listeners marveled and later recounted the exploits of the night before, building the legend of the Bird, but no one did anything. Dean, in his austere, priestly fashion, was the first to remedy the situation.

Through his connections with the demimonde of The Street, Dean was able to arrange a purchase through a fence who handled loot burglarized from Manhattan apartments. The fence had picked up a pre-war portable recording machine of German manufacture (a great rarity in 1944), a prototype of the tape machines that would appear in abundance in the Fifties. It used wire spools instead of tapes. Its fidelity was not very high, but that did not matter. The trained ear could fill in what was missing: tonal color, dimension, and the timbre of the notes. The professional could supply all those. With his German machine and a supply of wire spools, Dean became a familiar figure on The Street. He followed Charlie to the Deuces, to other clubs where Charlie sat in between sets, to Minton's, to Monroe's, to sessions in hotel rooms, to occasional one-night stands out of town in Philadelphia, Toronto, and Chicago, inscribing his musical notes on the portable apparatus.

Once Charlie went to Chicago to play a one-nighter at the El Grotto, a dance hall located in the basement of the southside Pershing Hotel. Dean preceded Charlie by twenty-four hours, and by Greyhound bus. Arriving early, Dean tried to set up his microphone in the El Grotto, only to be ejected by the management, acting on instructions from the Chicago local, musician boss Petrillo's bailiwick. Unauthorized recordings were no longer permitted there. Dean then rented a room directly above the bandstand and, working with a keyhole saw, pocket knife, and old tablespoon, cut a hole through to the night club and dropped his microphone and slender wire lead until it swung like a tiny, gray, unobtrusive spider above the piano. Secure in the privacy of his room, Dean recorded the entire performance, the Parker parts. It was an outstanding evening, as he had felt sure it would be; musicians always played better when the scene was changed, and before fresh audiences.

Dean carried a kit of essential tools when he traveled to strange clubs: electrician's pliers, fasteners, a spare microphone. The keyhole saw purchased in Chicago was replaced by an improved model, one that could be assembled from collapsible parts by means of a thumb screw. To deal with the varying color schemes in various clubs, Dean carried rolls of thin lead wire in colors to match walls and ceilings. Good camouflage was very important if his setup was to avoid the prying eyes of club managers and union business agents. Sleazy drapes in small clubs were good. They had not been cleaned for years and were stiff with dirt, ideal for concealing and holding a small microphone. He hung microphones on them, in potted palms, under the lee of the piano, from plaques and picture frames. Sometimes Dean boldly cut into the club's public address system. Then the impulses fed into the German machine were richer and stronger, and needed careful monitoring.

The wire collection grew, an endless sequence of saxophone solos, miles and miles of saxophone solos on the wire spools, with only blurted shreds of starts and finishes by other instruments, trumpet, piano or vibraphone. Dean knew where each solo belonged, with what tune, to what chord change. The spools were marked and dated: "Deuces, 11–18–44; Minton's, 1–18–45." Dean picked up a carrying case designed to hold 78-rpm shellac records. It made a good file for his collection of spools. They were always ready for auditioning, as available to those interested as tracts handed out by a splinter church: the tapes gave Dean the inside track with Bird. It was assumed that Dean was very close to Bird. It was Dean who could tell you what reed Charlie used, where he was living, with whom, his whereabouts between sets at the Deuces, his schedule for the evening after the club shut. If Bird was hung up for money, if a contact had to be made, it was Dean who handled the matter. Dean was Mr. Knows-where-it's-at. Mr. Fixit, social secretary, the score cat.

A typical Parker day began toward dusk, if one could actually say that the last had ended; sleep was never allowed to interfere with fascinating adventures. Assuming that Charlie had slept—in someone's pad, or his own, in a bed, alone or with a female companion, on a floor, on occasion in a bathtub—it would be necessary to get him up and about for the opening set at the Deuces. Usually this happened when dusk brought an agreeable obscurity to the ugly, noisy streets. Then Bird would drop on his shades and consider the first business of the day. If he was on the needle, he would prepare a shot and give himself an injection, tying off the veins of his left arm with a necktie, a habit that accounted for the hard-used appearance of his ties and their formidable knots. Charlie was running a ten-dollar-a-day habit when he used. The outlay was using up all of his wages. He knew he could drop the habit any time he chose, to show that he wasn't dependent on it, but that was becoming more and more difficult. If Bird were merely on pills, he would work out a promising combination, one that he imagined would allay any gathering narcotic malaise. He would dissolve the pills (red lights, blue lights, nembutals) in a Dixie cup and drink off the contents. Then it would be time to think about a good meal. His appetite had never been better.

Charlie had many favorite foods. Chinese dinners, barbecued ribs with all the fixings, or the immense sandwiches with their outlandish kosher ingredients (*kicks*) that one could order at the Stage Delicatessen. Charlie liked to have his custom-built, three kinds of smoked fish layered with Chicago corned beef and imported Swiss, served with cole slaw and kosher pickles and green tomatoes. He liked the new cafeterias, as large as department stores, in the neighborhood of Broadway and Fiftieth, where the dishes were laid out in a mosaic of pastel hues on a checkerboard of stainless steel. He would stack his tray with soup, roast beef, mashed potatoes, two vegetables, a fruit salad, Bismarck rolls, butter, jello, chocolate cream pie, an extra dessert, and coffee. Charlie liked to have a whole table to himself when he ate. He did not talk then. If addressed he would answer in grunts or monosyllables: "Yeah!" "Gone!" "Cool!"

After Charlie had stuffed himself with food, he would walk to the Deuces with brisk, purposeful strides. It was only a few blocks, but he called it his constitutional. The club would be filled for the opening set. There would be introductions, new faces, musicians from out of town. He reacted to the growing attention with ambivalence. It was unaccustomed, now overdone, and a little embarrassing. But he knew very well that he could outplay anybody in jazz.

The cool manners and conservative dress of the hipsters were foreign to his Kansas City background. He dressed like an Eighteenth Street hustler lately arrived in New York and steered to the first Broadway suitery. Pin stripes, chalk stripes, dark material with bold patterns, big lapels with deeply cut notches—whatever the salesman urged on him. He had no taste in clothes, and no sense of style. He exercised his own choice only in the fabrics. There he was his own man. Hard materials, twills and twists, hard to touch, guaranteed to "wear like iron," stuff that would stand up, take a beating. Jackets were dropped on a chair as he entered a room. Pants were removed while sitting, or lying in bed, balled and lobbed like a basketball to the nearest dresser, or into the hoop of a floor lamp. Charlie didn't want to be bothered with clothes all that much. They were something you wore, to keep you warm, something to put on and take off. The same went for ties, hard, durable material that sprang back in your hands when you tested it in the store, that would stand up under his sailor's knots.

His character structure was undergoing the last of its changes. Its armature was wrapped with dense, successive layers. The shabby-genteel kid too good to hustle the Kansas

City Star. The mini-man of the back alleys and Kansas City streets. The personable, promising freshman who attended Lincoln High School for three years and never advanced a grade. The intransigent, obnoxious bad boy of the big bands, bane of their image conscious leaders. The demon-driven bad axe of a thousand evaporated jam sessions. Pied Piper of a humorless, glassed-in hipster rabble. The armoring of the ego was nearly complete. He was sure of himself. He was hardened, durable, and undentable. The approval of the hipster community confirmed the correctness of his code. His lifestyle was veering toward its final goal, to live freely, as he pleased, without hang-ups of any kind, to be cool and wiggy, and in control. His life had become an unending series of kicks: food, alcohol, drugs, sex, and, as always and above all, the music. The music was the big game, supported by and supporting the little games. Charlie was learning to play his way through life. He began to live on the level of total spontaneity.

The new language of the hipsters came to him naturally. It was what the jazz musician had always spoken, though constantly updated, like his own musical ideas. *Cool, dig, solid, gone, gold, drag* were new and useful words. They expressed much quickly. Charlie was shy of hipster elaborations. He added nothing to the vocabulary, as did Lester Young, one of the great hip verbalists.

What mattered now was that he was playing on his own terms, in the right setting, with a five-piece combo, in an intimate club run by an understanding boss. He liked to work with Dizzy because Diz responded to the challenge and could get over the horn so fast. Between sets Charlie would drop into the White Rose bar for a double. If the mood moved him he would carry his horn to the Onyx, or Dean would bring it, and he would sit in. Coleman Hawkins was glad to have him these days. Charlie was "Little Yard from Kaycee," now grown into the bad boy of jazz and a man to be reckoned with. When the Deuces closed Dean would be waiting for him. Dean kept people off his back, eased the way, lined up chicks, the way Red Cross had done for Eckstine. Dean would organize a group and commandeer cabs, and they would roll uptown. Charlie would take advantage of the cab ride to grab a few winks of sleep. He suffered from insomnia. Dean always saw to it that the party included someone to pay cab fares and "flip the bills" at a restaurant. After a big meal Charlie might jam, or be set for a date with one or two of the chicks. The strong-blowing musician had his pick. Models, dancers, cigarette girls, hat-check girls, camera girls, call girls, night people, all willing and skilled. Sex was their recreation. White girls he suspected of making it with him because he was black, and a stud.

Dean on the sidelines, but never far off. Dean running errands, going back to the cafeteria counter to pick up a second order of cabinet pudding, a third cup of coffee. Dean commandeering taxis, controlling the inner circle, fetching Charlie's instrument case, lining up pussy, laying a dinner check on the mark. Bird with his gregarious, armed, compulsive personality, hard-pressed to keep up with some mysterious schedule of his own making. Dean in his tailored camel's hair band jacket with the brass buttons just like the ones Woody Herman wore, unfigured sports shirts with hand stitching on the seams and skillfully rolled collars. Needlework *DB* on the breast pocket. Tall and erect, thick, glossy, raven-black Italian-American hair sprayed and set in three ascending and equal waves; pale classic Mediterranean ivory face without humor; severe, composed, mindful of tasks, a parvenu priest burdened with very heavy responsibilities. Dean taking time off to hustle his daily bread by discreet sales of homemade marijuana cigarettes in cafeterias and night-club men's rooms. Dean prodding the faithful to pony up when Bird was without funds (chronic), needed a pill, a fix, cab fare. Dean checking out tapes like a hip librarian, screening supplicants, instructing the uninitiated, arranging audiences with the Presence, offsteering squares. Dean summoned to the pay telephone on the graffiti-scarred wall at the Three Deuces, its number miraculously known to someone calling from Terre Haute or Fresno, checking on Bird, his health and whereabouts, increments to the legend, news of recording sessions planned (the new discography was woefully thin—the faithful were still trying to find *their* copies of *Hootie Blues* on the discontinued blue Decca label). "What's happening back there, man?" the cut-off-from-everything voice, disembowelled and faraway, would importune Dean, and hang on for some desperately needed revelation of vital events taking place nightly back in the Apple. "No, man, two weeks of one-nighters straight through to Seattle. Then Woody's gonna break it up. Dig that kinda shit. Only———what's happening back there, man?" came the anxious murmur. "Like———what's Bird putting down now?" There was a rumor that the Parker-Gillespie All-Stars might be booked into a club in Hollywood and the new music heard for the first time on the West Coast. Dean didn't know. He stood at the pay phone, staring at the graffiti, and told them in his hieratic tone that the action was back in New York; to know what was happening you had to broom back to the Apple.

PART III

15

The Independent Record
Derby

I want to tell you lovin' things . . .
When the lights are low . . .
Ah wants all yo' lovin', or none at all,
Ah wants all yo' kisses,
Yo' big fat juicy kisses,
Or none at all . . .*

Once again the new sounds were being smothered in cant and corn. In the studio, behind the singer, a ragged patchwork of solos was being played by eight of the better jazzmen on The

---

* *I Want Every Bit of It*, Rubberlegs Williams, Continental 6020. Composed by Clarence and Spencer Williams, copyright MCA Music.

Street, among them Charlie Parker, Dizzy Gillespie, Don Byas, and Clyde Hart. The singer was Rubberlegs Williams, veteran of thirty years in show business—carnivals, minstrel shows, a pickaninny troupe, a female impersonator act, eccentric dancer as well as bluesman. Now he was making a record date for Continental, a rival to Savoy in the race field, and the mistakes of the *Red Cross* date were being compounded. Such a singer needed bottleneck guitars, a washboard, and a gin bottle. When two sides had been completed the artists took a ten-minute break. While Dizzy diverted the singer, Charlie dropped three benzedrine tablets into his coffee. The rest of the session was a crazy affair, with Rubberlegs belting out the lyrics in a foghorn voice while the jazzmen played wry bits behind.

The same musicians, unencumbered by Rubberlegs, returned to the Continental studios and again the results were trifling. By mixing swing and bop jazzmen, the director of A&R had cancelled out the efforts of both. One of the sides was titled *Ooh Ooh My My* and had a ridiculous vocal by Trummy Young. A third try with Charlie, Dizzy, and Sarah Vaughan produced another disappointment, and incredibly Continental failed to record *I'll Wait and Pray*, the show-stopper of the theater circuit. Another independent, Apollo, teamed old-fashioned trumpeter Buck Clayton with Charlie and Dexter Gordon (*The Street Beat, &c.*). Individually and collectively, Charlie and Dizzy fulfilled fourteen contracts between the time the union signed its first agreement with the independents and the end of 1945, appearing under their own names and various pseudonyms. Of these fourteen sessions, only four produced jazz of permanent value.

This state of affairs could be blamed on bad A&R work and the chaotic state of the record industry. As major labels and the union continued their stalemate, independents began pushing their way into the industry. The union licensed anyone willing to sign the royalty agreement, the sticking point so far as the majors were concerned. By the end of 1945 the union recklessly had licensed over three-hundred and fifty independent entrepreneurs. Any hustler with a few hundred bucks to gamble could get into the business. Encouraged by the overnight success of such lucky, once-in-a-blue-moon juke box hits as *Open the Door Richard*, *The Honeydripper*, and *Cement Mixer*, newcomers were obsessed with the idea of making a fast dollar. An unemployed song writer named Jack Riley produced *Cement Mixer* on his Cadet label with less than five hundred dollars. In four months the record grossed three hundred thousand dollars, of which about a quarter was profit. Almost none of the entrepreneurs had any experience in producing or manufacturing records, or even qualifications as business men. A few visits to a night club quickly convinced the newcomer that he had long harbored a unique talent for artists-and-repertoire work. He was impressed with the glamor of his new vocation. Whim, guesswork, and irrational personal preference determined the choice of artists. Third- and fourth-rate talent was signed to exclusive contracts and hustled into the recording studio. Jazz musicians working in New York, the center of the recording industry, participated in scores of hastily organized sessions as back-up men and accompanists, mainly because they were on the spot and were competent.

A Guild date early in 1945 brought about the first bebop breakthrough. Charlie and Dizzy cut *Groovin' High*, *All the Things You Are*, and *A Dizzy Atmosphere* for this short-lived entrant in the independent recording derby. Only a compromise on the drummer, swing veteran Cozy Cole for Stan Levey, the result of sloppy A&R work, prevented the session from being a definitive one, but the results were still spectacular. On a later date the band cut *Salt Peanuts*, *Shaw Nuff*, *Hot House*, and *Lover Man*. The music seems to explode from the grooves into the listener's ear. Good pressings, expert engineering, and a live "room sound" add to the natural brilliance of the performances. Trumpet-saxophone interchanges are like computer dialogues, ideas compressed into the shortest possible span. The simple structures and hard polished timbre are reminiscent of Varese. Rapidly moving lines open up areas that jazz explored for the next twenty years. The listener is deluged with a flight of melodies, rhythms, and sounds. *Shaw Nuff*, and *A Dizzy Atmosphere* are typical of the rapid tempi played by the boppers. Against these are set off slow pieces like Tadd Dameron's *Hot*

House, with its finely wrought line. The lone Sarah Vaughan vocal (*Lover Man*) is less a sung ballad than a collaboration between three sensitive improvisers. As small band records, the Guilds rank with the best in discography, alongside those made by the Benny Goodman Sextet, picked Ellington groups, the Kansas City Six, the Holiday Vocalions and the Hot Fives and Hot Sevens of Louis Armstrong.* Like the Bartok Quartets, their art appealed to an elite—to hipsters, to jazz musicians. They appeared in every contemporary collection. When worn out, they were replaced with fresh copies. In the Twenties the same thing had happened with Louis Armstrong's records. Now the compliment was being paid by working musicians to Charlie Parker.

A few weeks after the Guild sessions Charlie and Dizzy were back in another studio for yet another label, Comet, and under a more favorable set of conditions. The shots were called by Red Norvo, director of A&R for the occasion. A veteran leader of big and small bands, Norvo was a familiar figure on The Street and one of its respected transitional figures. On paper his team of swing stars—pianist Teddy Wilson, tenorman Flip Phillips, bassist Slam Stewart, and drummer J. C. Heard—seemed bad choices for a meaningful collaboration with the *enfants terribles* of jazz. The imperturbable and musicianly Norvo acted as a kind of musical moderator. He did not attempt to plan complicated ensembles, but left the jazzmen free to improvise around a series of simple themes, a slow blues, a fast blues, *Get Happy*, *Hallelujah*. The Comet tracks are a series of rounds. *Slam Slam Blues* opens with Slam Stewart's mellow-as-a-cello bowed solo and is followed by one of Charlie's important statements, a twelve-bar architecture of quivering densities. On *Get Happy* Charlie seems to sprint onstage, like a runner in a modern marathon, bringing an awaited musical intelligence. *Congo Blues*, taken fast, is sheer musical energy, its materials raked out of an atomic oven. Dizzy's crackling muted trumpet solo set new standards for the instrument.

---

* Due to mismanagement Guild retired from the field after a few months. The masters were sold to Musicraft and, several years later, by Musicraft to Savoy. They are now issued from time to time on that label. See *Running Discography*.

There are fine solos by Norvo, by Slam and by Teddy Wilson, but they belong very clearly to a bygone era. Old and new are neatly juxtaposed. The Comet session is remarkable in that it was made at nine in the morning, that most desolate of hours for jazz folk. Charlie and Dizzy had jammed straight through until studio time, with only a brief pause for breakfast; two of the sidemen had arrived in town that morning from a road trip. Everyone was tired, but loose. That, Norvo believes, had a great deal to do with the success of the session. The Comet tracks ran long by as much as five minutes, and had to be issued on twelve-inch shellacs. Fragile and easily broken, they nevertheless appeared in contemporary collections, along with the Guilds.

The definitive session, toward which bop had been striving, was realized November 26, 1945, by Savoy. The element missing from the previous flawed sessions was present at last in the person of percussionist Max Roach. Few sessions have begun with less promise. Thelonious Monk was the intended pianist, but failed to show. Argonne Thorton, located in Hector's Cafeteria, was pressed into service as a substitute. Dizzy had just signed an exclusive contract with Musicraft and appeared incognito. The trumpet player of record was nineteen-year-old Miles Davis, then a day student at Juilliard School of Music and sitter-in on The Street by night. Charlie was late as usual. During the warm-up his reed developed an unmanageable squeak and a messenger had to be sent to midtown band-instrument stores in search of Rico number fives.

Hipsters and fellow musicians trouped in and out of the studio as if it were a bus depot. Once recording got under way there were breaks to send out for soft drinks, ice, food, liquor, narcotics, and girlfriends. Miles Davis took a thirty-minute nap on the floor of the studio. Savoy A&R director Teddy Reig half dozed through it all like an Oriental deity, directing with a minimum of effort. The three-hour union time limit was ignored. Despite distractions enough to have wrecked an ordinary date, the results were such that Savoy would refer to the occasion as "The Greatest Recording Session in Modern Jazz History."

Billie's Bounce (Shaw saluted again, though his name was

misspelled) is medium tempo and in the style of *Red Cross*, but much superior. The percussion work is right and the rhythm section sounds like those heard in the bop dens. Unison passages have a funky edge. This is the twelve-bar blues again, the blues with its three indispensible chords. Within their exterior discipline Charlie created by means of his own. As Howard McGhee said, "Bird could make more tunes out of the blues than any musician who ever lived." *Now's the Time* is catchy and unforgettable, yet difficult to repeat. It has that extra-dimensional quality that distinguishes master works, however small. It is timeless. Its three minutes seem much longer. It is perfectly balanced, perfectly logical, haunting, eerie, the finest achievement of the boppers to that point.

Koko is taken at a headlong pace, close to 300 on the metronome. *Koko* is *Cherokee*, arrived in discography from the green curtain on Olive Street, by way of Minton's, the Savoy, the Apollo Theater, band routes. Twin sides of a medal, *Koko* and *Now's the Time* remind us of the duality found in all of Parker's work. *Now's the Time* is cool, nocturnal, bluesy. *Koko* is tense and aggressive, very sure, a piece of astonishing and reckless virtuosity: sixty-four bars of difficult changes, saxophone playing to end saxophone playing—to castrate all other saxophonists. But *Koko* is not the kind of music one wishes to hear often. It is disturbing, in the way that some of Schoenberg is disturbing. One can listen to *Now's the Time*, over and over again, always with pleasure.

The rights to *Now's the Time* were sold, outright and in perpetuity, in exchange for fifty dollars laid on Charlie at the studio. Although it became one of the key tunes of the Forties, it brought Charlie no further return. Pirated by Slim Moore, a honking rhythm-and-blues saxophonist, it appeared on juke boxes retitled *The Hucklebuck*, grotesque and profitable. This came as no great surprise to anyone used to the morals of the song-publishing and record-making industry—"a world that has never regarded jazz as anything much more than an undefended treasurehouse to be pillaged at leisure, with vast sums of money to be made out of sickly, bowdlerized versions," as jazz columnist Benny Green wrote in the *London Observer*.*

The trade reviews of *Now's the Time* were uniformly bad and served only to confirm the boppers' distrust of the music press. Reviewing *Now's the Time* in tandem with *Billie's Bounce*, *Down Beat* of April 22, 1946, said: "These two sides are excellent examples of the other side of the Gillespie craze—the bad taste and ill-advised fanaticism of Dizzy's uninhibited style. Only Charlie Parker, who is a better musician and who deserves more credit than Dizzy for the style anyway, saves these from a bad fate. At that he's far off form—a bad reed and inexcusable fluffs do not add up to good jazz. The trumpet man, whoever the misled kid is [it was Miles Davis], plays Gillespie in the same manner as a majority of the kids who copy their idol do—with most of the faults, lack of order and meaning, the complete adherence to technical acrobatics. Drummer Max Roach, who was with Gillespie's ill-fated big band, fails to help as much as he easily could have. Good, bad or indifferent, the mass of Gillespie's followers will love these sides, for even bad music is great if it's Diz. This is the sort of stuff that has thrown innumerable impressionable young musicians out of stride, that has harmed many of them irreparably. This can be as harmful to jazz as Sammy Kaye." *Down Beat* customarily rated records on a descending scale of four-quarter notes (excellent) to one-quarter note (poor). The reviewer refused to rate *Now's the Time*, one of the great records and great compositions of the decade.

The difference between improvisation and composition may be confusing to the layman. Jazzmen are basically improvisers, but they are also composers. As improvisers they must have something to improvise on. In Charlie Parker's day two sources of material were commonly used: the twelve-bar blues and the thirty-two-bar ballad. These materials supplied the chord scheme for improvisations. The source was implied, and only the rankest beginner would play the copyrighted line of a standard tune. He would create his own line. The bopper's rep-

* Reprinted in Benny Green: *The Reluctant Art* (London; MacGibbon and Kee; 1962), p. 124.

ertoire was stocked with newly minted instrumental standards based on the source material. Thus Gershwin's *I Got Rhythm*, because of its attractive sequence of chords, served as the framework for dozens of bop standards, including *Red Cross, Shaw Nuff, Anthropology, 52nd Street Theme, A Dizzy Atmosphere* and others. When these tunes came to be recorded the question of copyright arose, and since the tune bore little resemblance to the Tin Pan Alley original (although it was transparent to a good jazzman because of the run of chords), there seemed no reason not to apply for a new copyright. Thus Charlie Parker came to be a composer of sorts, though a very careless one so far as his copyrights were concerned. He was a portable fountain of musical ideas and usually too busy thinking up new ones to bother about the legal niceties of the old. Most bop originals used the idea of the Kansas City riff to establish a strong rhythmic-melodic pattern that was repeated in the second and fourth eight bars, with a counter theme in the third eight bars (AABA).

The *Now's the Time* session ended another era. November brought hard times to The Street. The war was winding down. Prodded by military authorities, teams of vice detectives and narcos descended in a locust horde on The Street, rounding up "vicious elements" along with peaceful and innocent souls. Some clubs were padlocked, others declared off-limits for servicemen. Charlie and Dizzy found themselves out of work and took their troubles to Billy Shaw, who was as enthusiastic about the new music as ever. The dedications had done nothing to dampen that enthusiasm. Long-distance telephone calls to Billy Berg, the leading importer of jazz talent to the hinterlands of California, and Shaw's fast, hard sell immediately produced an interesting engagement, eight weeks at Berg's jazz bistro in Hollywood. Shaw gave Billy Berg a package loaded with talent. Besides Bird and Diz the band included Stan Levey, Al Haig, bassist Ray Brown, and bebop's first vibraphonist, Milt "Bags" Jackson. Early in December 1945, The Street rebels left for the West Coast. It was the first time any of them had ever been as far west as California, and the first time bop had ventured so far afield.

"... he was the most affectionate
child you ever saw.
He'd call in from the next room,
'Mama, are you there?
Mama, I love you!'"
Kansas City, Kansas, 1922,
fourteen months.

Charlie would never
be allowed to carry papers
like other little boys.
A clean little Bird,
blissfully unaware of cabarets,
night life, band routes,
fast women, heroin—
and apartheid, American style.
Before the move from the
suburbs to Kansas City, Missouri.

1

2

Charlie strung out on a "burn"—bad heroin picked up
on Central Avenue, Los Angeles, just after the
band's arrival for its historical West Coast debut.
Barely able to stand or hold the horn,
Charlie has relinquished his duties as co-leader to
the cool, professional Dizzy Gillespie.
Billy Berg's, Hollywood, Christmas week, 1945.

Same year, same man. The dashing avant-garde combo
leader as idealized by a showbusiness
photographer. Used widely by Charlie Parker's
booking agency for publicity purposes. The dedication
is to saxophonist Don Lanphere.

With Bird (in dark glasses) at one end and Dizzy at the other, the Earl Fatha' Hines Orchestra of 1943 was teetering precariously on the brink of collapse. Front row, left to right: *Dizzy Gillespie, Little Benny Harris, Shorts McConnell,* Fatha', *Sarah Vaughan,* A. Crump, *Goon Gardner,* Scoops Carey, John Williams, *Charlie Parker.* The bebop insurgents who were to bring about the destruction of the famous band are shown in italics.

3

4 5

Doris saw to his fresh linen and was one of the few women of hundreds in his life who loved Charlie for himself. Square as a box, embarrassingly thin, Doris was the last of three "legal" wives. Birdland, spring, 1950.

6

7

The Richard Wagner and Cosima Liszt of our time. Chan Richardson was beautiful and hip, thoroughly conditioned to night life, and a tireless publicist for Charlie Parker and his music. The perfect marriage, only slightly burdened by its common law status. Birdland, fall, 1950.

Right on! Dried out after seven months at Camarillo State Hospital, glowing with health and vitality, charged with fresh ideas, Charlie returned to professional life for one of his finest sessions, the *Cool Blues* date for Dial. Seven improvisations on record in less than thirty minutes, all without preparation. C. P. MacGregor Studios, Hollywood, 1947.

9
10

The Quintet—easily the
leading jazz combo of its day.
In the front line: Bird and
twenty-one-year-old Miles Davis,
making his debut as a small
band sideman. In the rhythm
section: Tommy Potter, bass;
Duke Jordan, piano; and (hidden)
master percussionist
Max Roach. The Three Deuces,
Fifty-second Street, 1947.

The jazzman's perennial desire
for music status, fronting
a string group, brought Charlie
a temporary satisfaction.
Uninspired arrangements, played
note for note behind him,
set after set, severely limited
his ability to swing and
improvise. What had begun as
a glorification ended as a drag.
At Birdland, the club named
after Charlie, spring, 1950.

Charlie liked to perform sleight-of-hand tricks.
He could roll a cigarette with one hand.
He sometimes surprised friends with displays of his skill
as an amateur pickpocket. The plump, smooth, tapering fingers
of the saxophone's greatest virtuoso, ready for the downbeat.

TOP: The Jazzman as visiting celebrity. In a taxi
with Roy Eldridge on the triumphant, whirlwind tour of Sweden.
Fall, 1950, the last good season.

BOTTOM: Following two back-to-back concerts at the Stockholm
Konserthuset, Charlie jammed until dawn at the headquarters
of the affiliated Swedish Jazz Clubs, surrounded by framed
photographs of musical celebrities and crowds of admirers.

Unrecorded but still remembered. One of the all-star Sunday
afternoon jam sessions at Bob Reisner's Open Door: Charles Mingus,
bass; Roy Haynes, drums; Thelonious Monk, piano; Charlie Parker,
alto saxophone. Greenwich Village, *ca.* 1953.

15

Bird in flight—
New York, Paris, Kansas City,
Chicago, Stockholm,
Hollywood.

16

17

18

19

21

ABOVE, LEFT: Lester Young. "The President," tribal hero of Kansas City saxophonists.

ABOVE, RIGHT: On the road with Bird and Chood. Charlie, left, and Red Rodney, far right, following a jam session in Kansas City, 1951.

BELOW, LEFT: Billy Eckstine and Bird. Mr. B, who pledged his vocal talents and good looks as collateral to underwrite the most revolutionary band in jazz history.

BELOW, RIGHT: Jay McShann, the ambitious percussive young pianist from Muskogee, Oklahoma, shortly after his arrival in Kansas City.

23

25

26

TOP: Erroll Garner, coolest and most durable of
Parker's contemporaries. The Haig Club, Hollywood, 1947.

BOTTOM: Howard McGhee, brilliant trumpet player
and stable combo leader, who carried Charlie through
the worst of the Lotus Land period.

BELOW, LEFT: Max Roach, an innovator of modern polyrhythmic drum
style and leading percussionist of the new music. Chicago, *ca.* 1948.

BELOW, RIGHT: Dizzy Gillespie, who, with Charlie, was
co-leader of the first bop band. Billy Berg's, December, 1945.

28

"Had he been untalented
and white, he might
have lived out his life as a
happy square."
Candid shot
of Charlie, probably Fifty-
second Street, *ca.* 1947.

Every act—eating,
playing, balling,
shooting up—was done
with compulsive intensity.
"Scoffing up a storm"
at a Hollywood
garden party, 1951.

Tired, fat, disenchanted,
and looking ten or
fifteen years older than
his actual age of thirty-two,
a very played out Bird.
Charlie resting on
an upturned instrument case
after the all-star Verve
recording session
with fellow saxophone greats
Johnny Hodges, Benny Carte
and Ben Webster.
Hollywood, summer, 1952.

On stage for the last time. Charlie Parker in his bronze coffin,
before the ridiculous funeral oration by Reverend Licorice,
a sentimental organ playing of *The Lost Chord*, the coffin juggling
by honorary pallbearers drafted from booking agencies
and trade journals, and other incidents of the final act in
the theatre of the absurd at
the Abyssinian Baptist Church, Harlem, 1955.

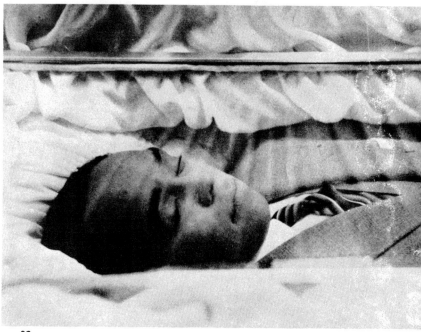

32

33 SINCERELY,
YOUR FRIEND,

15

Yardbird in Lotus

Land

The trip to the West Coast was made by rail. During a stopover to change trains in Chicago the musicians interrupted their itinerary to jam on the Southside, causing them to lose their reservations on the limited Sante Fe Chief. As the result, they were obliged to take a slower train, its equipment much abused during the war. The trip, originally scheduled for three days and two nights, dragged on for the better part a week. Somewhere in New Mexico or Arizona, no one was quite sure where, the train made one of its many unscheduled stops, clanking to a halt in the middle of the desert. Charlie had been in a drugged sleep since Chicago. Startled by the hiss of air brakes and other strange noises, Charlie awoke to stare out of the window at a flat expanse of sage and chaparral blazing under a cloudless sky and winter sun. He promptly panicked. Gathering up his valise and instrument case, Charlie climbed down to the right of way and, stumbling over crushed rock and cinders, struck out across the desert. As others called for him to stop, he kept walking doggedly toward the horizon. Stan Levey, the most practical man in the party, overtook Charlie near a barbed wire fence. Charlie was in a state of panic. Heroin withdrawal symptoms had set in. He was out of drugs. "Got to find me a doctor!" he said to Levey. Sweating and shivering, he was persuaded to return to the train, and was strapped into a bunk with a belt.

The men in the band were shaken. Dizzy told Levey that Milt Jackson had been added to the band so that there would be an extra voice if Charlie goofed. That had been decided back in New York. Dizzy had been watching his friend deteriorate for the past six months. The random experiments with drugs had grown into a full-sized habit. Twenty hours later the slow train pulled into Union Station at Los Angeles. Charlie was a sick man. The band was scheduled to open at Billy Berg's that night.

Dean Benedetti met the train. Benedetti had come ahead by Greyhound bus for the opening. He brought bad news of the drug scene in Los Angeles. The town was uptight. Drugs sold for double and triple the New York prices, when you could get them at all. Marijuana was available, but no heroin. There was a discussion among the musicians. Dizzy proposed hiring a standby saxophonist, and Charlie immediately grew angry. "I'll score and everything will be cool," he told the others. "Dean, call us a cab." Charlie asked the driver to take them to the nearest doctor. They found a general practitioner in the Wilshire District. Charlie invented a story that he was suffering from painful kidney stones. For the doctor's benefit, he enlarged on the ordeal of the long cross-country trip and the need to be ready for the opening. When the doctor began talking about laboratory tests and X-rays, Charlie dropped a twenty-dollar bill on the desk. The doctor wrote out a prescription for three days' supply of morphine and asked Charlie not to come back. The prescription was filled at the nearest pharmacy. When Charlie scored from legitimate sources morphine was the drug obtained. He used it in the same way that he used heroin, by injection into a vein in the arm, or mainlining. Sometimes he combined the two drugs for a shot of "H and M."

Opening night at Billy Berg's proved to be a red-letter event, its attendance *de rigueur* for everyone with any claim to status in the West Coast jazz community. People came for the opening from points as far away as San Diego, Phoenix, and Seattle. The band played the first two sets without Charlie. He remained in the dressing room, eating the two Conquistador dinners, slowly pulling himself together. The fix had set him right again. Drug-store stuff, obtained only by means of a doctor's prescription, was always pure. Charlie's circus entrance, blowing, climaxed the evening, and the debut was hailed by jazz fans as a respectable counterpart to the historic first performance of Stravinsky's *Rites of Spring* in Paris. After the very successful opening, attendance at Bill Berg's dropped off rapidly, and within a week the band was playing to half-filled houses. The public stayed away. Berg's clientele was reduced to a hard core of hipsters and jazz musicians. Bar receipts were unaccountably low. Customers would remain at a table for hours, catching set after set, ordering an occasional bottle of beer or an iced coffee. Between sets they would adjourn to the men's room, there to light up and turn on, remaining pleasantly high for the evening, but not on Berg's poured drinks.

On his good nights Charlie was genial and relaxed. His face was smoothed out, and he looked his twenty-five years. He would welcome young local jazzmen to his dressing room and, when Berg's closed, let them carry him off in their noisy old prewar jalopies to jam at one of the spots along Central Avenue: the Brown Bomber, Lovejoys, the Club Alabam, or the Bird in the Basket. On other nights Charlie was withdrawn and morose. He was as irascible as a petty tyrant. His followers stood their distance then. He sweated a lot, and his breath was bad. His playing became aggressive. Slow tunes had an eerie, other-worldly quality. His eyes were ringed, dull, distant, bloodshot. He looked the part of a dissolute middle-aged musician too long in the jazz business. No one could believe he was twenty-five. He looked forty. Then the next night he would be himself again. When he had scored he was Dr. Jekyll. When he had not, he was Hyde. It all depended on whether he had taken his fix. For the first time in his life, heroin had caught up with him. A vital and telling alteration had taken place in his physiology. There was a new alignment of bodily functions, perhaps of metabolism or enzyme balance. His body had adjusted to the imperious need for heroin in daily doses. His tolerance for the drug remained high, as it had in the early stages. He retained his great appetite for food, for pills, for alcohol, for sex, and his insatiable lust to play and improvise, and to compete against all musical comers. But now, except for those periods when an excessive and disastrous intake of alcohol shorted out his craving for drugs, there would never again arise the possibility of putting aside the habit at will, or considering it as a mere dabbling or experimentation. He was hooked. And he would be dependent on drugs, and those who supplied drugs to the jazz trade, for the rest of his life.

It took Dean Benedetti to solve the problem of a reliable drug source. Charlie's new contact was one of the bizarre characters to be found in the ghetto during those years. His real name was Emry Byrd. He was better known as "Moose the Mooch." A personable, sanguine man, the Moose once had been an athletic star and honor student at Jefferson High, a black school in the southwestern part of the city. Now the lower limbs were paralyzed by poliomyelitis. The Moose moved about slowly and cheerfully on crutches. He was the proprietor of a shoeshine stand on Central Avenue in the middle Thirties, where the action was. Jazz and blues records were displayed in racks facing the customer, so that the shine stand doubled as a music store. But its real business was the drug traffic. The Moose always had a supply of good Mexican green cannabis on hand. His main line was heroin. The shine stand was a contact and pickup point for users in music and show business. The Moose was an avid jazz fan and, like most urban black people of his generation, had instantly recognized bebop as the contemporary style. He was pleased to have its leading exponent as one of his customers. Charlie became one of the Moose's regulars, enjoying extensions of credit and serving as a reference for other musicians. Once Charlie was safely "connected" in Los Angeles, all began to go well.

Midway through the Berg engagement, on December 29, Charlie and Dizzy took part in a slapdash record date organized by Slim Gaillard, the man responsible for *Cement Mixer*. A tall, raffish, hard-jiving entertainer who doubled on several instruments, Gaillard had been in show business for a decade. Once he had teamed with Slam Stewart. As Slim and Slam they made a smash hit for Decca in 1938, *Flat Foot Floogie with a Floy-Floy*. Now the sponsoring label was Beltone, run out of somebody's hat, and the idea was to re-do the old hit.

After an untidy remake of *Flat Foot Floogie*, the musicians recorded *Dizzy Boogie*, an eight-bar novelty; then a remarkable oddity titled *Poppity Pop Goes the Motor-sickle*, mainly nonsense syllables by Gaillard; and, as the requisite fourth side, a delightfully informal *Slim's Jam*, a miniature jam session. Acting as interlocutor, Slim introduced each musician and solo. When Charlie finished a twelve-bar chorus Slim said, "What's the matter? You got to cut out? Got to make a Jubilee? Well, all reet, let's set a riff on this last chorus."

Jubilee was the Armed Forces Radio Services (AFRS) show broadcast weekly to military personnel overseas. Charlie and Dizzy were due to meet the rest of the men in the Billy Berg band for a Jubilee broadcast later that day. The program was produced by Jimmy Lyons, now director of the Monterey Jazz Festival, and emceed by Bubbles Whitman, "The Stomach that Walks like a Man." The conservative AFRS had opted to grant the new music a brief hearing. "And heah's that ole perfessor of rebop [sic] himself," cried The Stomach as he introduced the musicians, and the band played *A Dizzy Atmosphere*. That track and *Salt Peanuts*, recently discovered in the AFRS files at Munich by British collector Tony Williams, are the only recordings made by the Parker-Gillespie All-Stars before they disbanded.

Charlie and Dizzy were featured in a jazz concert staged January 29 by local impressario Norman Granz. It was held at the Los Angeles Philharmonic Auditorium, ugly, vaultlike, and hallowed, where long-hair music had been presented to Southern California audiences for the past thirty years. Granz's idea was to recreate the excitements of the jam session for a mass audience. The Philharmonic seated twenty-eight hundred persons and was sold out. Horn men stood in a line abreast under the glare of spots. The cast included several distinguished jazzmen: high-note trumpeter Al Killian (ex-Basie, Barnett, and Hampton); Willie Smith, former alto sax star with the Jimmy Lunceford Orchestra; and, as featured tenor saxophonist, no less a figure than Lester Young, lately returned to the jazz life after the horrors of the detention barracks at a Georgia army camp.

It was Charlie's first major concert, and the first time that he had appeared on the same stage with Lester Young. Lester did not recognize him. Lester seemed dazed and detached. Other musicians said he was drinking a lot. Charlie waited nervously for Lester to take the first solo. Charlie listened with awe, then with growing sadness as Lester continued. The hero of the Reno Club was no longer playing with the same fire. Something had gone out of him. He had aged. The army experience had taken something away. Lester played *The Man I Love*. The notes were soft and lush. Charlie followed Lester on *Sweet Georgia Brown* and took a good solo. The concert was so successful that Granz immediately began making plans for a second, more ambitious program. Thus was born the idea of Jazz at the Philharmonic, which would identify Norman Granz productions and take jazz concerts around the world.

Charlie also appeared on the second Jazz at the Philharmonic concert. The evening began with the awarding of *Down Beat* plaques for best of instrument to Willie Smith (alto saxophone) and Charlie Ventura (tenor saxophone). Charlie was passed by (he had finished fifth), as was Lester Young. Both sulked majestically in the background, fingering their horns, waiting for the action to begin. Tension mounted as the concert got under way, and the sell-out crowd at the Philharmonic Auditorium soon heard the real thing. Lester demolished Charlie Ventura. Then Charlie Parker, following the man who had been his idol, topped the whole performance. His solo on *Lady Be Good* is one of his greatest improvisations. Of the improvisation John Lewis, musicologist and director of the latter-day MJQ, said, "Bird made a blues out of *Lady Be Good*. That solo made old men out of everyone onstage that night." The concert had an interesting sequel. It was actually too successful. Because of audience enthusiasm and dancing in the aisles Granz was denied further use of the Philharmonic Auditorium. Thereafter he went elsewhere, in Los Angeles, and eventually the world, but the original name stuck.

The Parker-Gillespie Sextet closed at Billy Berg's the first Monday in February. The following night Charlie, Dizzy, Levey, and Ray Brown joined George Handy, pianist and arranger for the Boyd Raeburn Orchestra, to rehearse what was to be the first record session for a new Hollywood label, Dial— launched by me. Handy had contracted to lead the session and produce the musicians. His plan called for Lester Young to complete the front line, and had the makings of a supersession. It proved to be too good to be true. Lester could not be found that evening. The rest of the musicians arrived at Electro Broadcast Studios in Glendale with a small army of hipsters and their women in tow, and the rehearsal took place in monumental confusion. The studios, part of a broadcasting station owned by a local splinter religious organization, were located in an elegiac little park adjoining Forest Lawn Cemetery, the world's most lavishly appointed burying ground. As the task force overflowed from the studio onto the park, bringing pot smoking and free love in a public place to prim suburban Glendale, recording arrangements became hopelessly confused. While all of this was amusing, it was not conducive to the making of records. A test playback of *Lover*, with a short Parker solo, was completed but nothing else. Undaunted, Handy declared himself well pleased with the evening's work, assured the Dial management that all would be well, and instructed his musicians to be on hand promptly at eight the following night for the actual session. At seven-thirty Handy reported in that he could not produce Charlie, let alone Lester. Handy had bird-dogged Charlie for the whole night. Sometime around dawn

Charlie had given him the slip. Thus was missed the chance to record one of the outstanding small bands of jazz.

Their contracts fulfilled, it was time for the jazzmen to return to New York. They were fed up with Southern California, its great distances, bland climate, lackadaisical ways, and indefensible Jim Crow policies. They were homesick for The Apple. Marvin Freeman, Los Angeles attorney and silent partner in Dial, pulled strings to secure reservations for a flight on United Airlines. Dizzy picked up the tickets and issued one to each man. That proved a mistake. When it came time to leave, Charlie could not be found. Stan Levey ran up twenty dollars on a taxicab meter in a fruitless search, and the musicians left Los Angeles without Charlie. That night they were back on The Street. Charlie had turned in his ticket for cash. The money, over one hundred dollars, was gone in a single day, and Charlie found himself stranded in California without funds or a job.

Charlie made no attempt to return to New York. He found himself a job at a newly opened bottle club, the Finale, at 115 South San Pedro Street. It was in Little Tokyo, once the Japanese quarter and now, its original inhabitants in internment camps, an appendage of the Negro city. The club was run by vaudevillian Foster Johnson and operated without a liquor license. Customers purchased "membership" cards for two dollars, brought liquor in paper bags, and were served glasses, ice, and mixers. In the lobby of the old and deserted building, a poster announced "CHARLIE PARKER—New Star, Alto Saxophone, 1945 Esquire Jazz Poll—AND HIS ORCHESTRA." The award was a minor one, but a talking point.

Past doors of darkened offices occupied by obscure business firms, one came to a long room with a ceiling so low that a tall man could reach up and touch the metal sheating overhead. Once the hall had been a meeting place for a Japanese cultural society. At one end was a small stage. An old upright piano sat on the floor. There were odd tables and chairs, and the usual hastily improvised decor of the marginal cabaret. The Finale soon became a West Coast Minton's. The low ceiling made for excellent acoustics, and Charlie's presence acted as a magnet for resident and visiting jazzmen, among them Stan Getz, Zoot

Sims, Miles Davis, Gerry Mulligan, Red Rodney, Hampton Hawes, Serge Chaloff, Shorty Rogers, Ralph Burns, Johnny Bothwell, Gerald Wilson, Sonny Criss, and Charlie Ventura. Sessions at the Finale Club were probably the finest in the country in 1946, Minton's and The Street notwithstanding. When music at the Finale had settled into its three-o'clock groove, Foster Johnson, a slender man of effortless movement, would spring lightly onstage and improvise steps to *A Dizzy Atmosphere* or *Now's the Time*. It was at the humble little bottle club located in Little Tokyo that I heard a great deal of Charlie Parker in the spring of 1946 and was able to work out arrangements to record him.

My own involvement with the contemporary jazz scene had begun the summer before, when the merchant marine discharged me after three years of service as a radio officer and I opened Tempo Music Shop at 5946 Hollywood Boulevard, a few blocks east of Vine and across the street from the Florentine Gardens. The capital came from wages earned on a fourteen-month trip to New Guinea. I built the store fixtures with the help of an unemployed studio carpenter and used my own home phonograph as the store playback. My own record collection went into an inventory of collector's items. The original idea at Tempo was to sell classic jazz to collectors, as was done at a rival establishment called Jazzman. Hipsters and boppers soon invaded Tempo and drove our customers across town to the other store. Tempo became a headquarters for followers of the new music. Louis Gottlieb, then studying composition at UCLA with Arnold Schoenberg, was one of our strongest supporters. Gottlieb loved to discuss the merits of the two greatest musical minds of the century: Schoenberg and Charlie Parker. When Dean Benedetti arrived in California he came directly to Tempo and set up a command post in the beaverboard listening booth, playing his wire spools for all who wanted to hear and hipping people to the coming engagement at Billy Berg's. The event was first announced in our monthly newsletter, "Jazz Tempo", under a headline that read "BEBOP INVADES THE WEST." The beaverboard wall of the booth was used to collect signatures. Before Tempo was a year old the wall had a lot of good ones: Lester Young, Nat King Cole, Miles Davis, Andre Previn, Burl Ives, Earl Robinson, Cisco Houston, Moe Asch, Gerry Mulligan, Howard McGhee, Stan Getz, Dave Dexter, George Avakian, Boyd Raeburn, Kid Ory, Norman Granz, Leadbelly, Red Rodney, and Charlie Parker. The turntable, concealed in a well behind a counter faced with split bamboo, spun throughout the day and into the night with records ordered direct from independent manufacturers in the East and stocked to satisfy the demands of the bop customers: *Congo Blues, Shaw Nuff, Billie's Bounce, Street Beat, Lover Man, Koko, Red Cross.* It took hundreds of playings of those records to wean me away from classical jazz. The boppers were about to give up on me when the band opened at Berg's. I went along and shared a table with several customers. The live performance, complete with Charlie's dramatic entrance, convinced me that bop was in the main line of the jazz tradition.

Dial Records was a natural outgrowth of Tempo. The world's first jazz record store, Commodore Music Shop in New York, had established the precedent for store-based labels with Commodore Records. My partner, Marvin Freeman, a Los Angeles attorney, had been one of the pioneer jazz collectors in Los Angeles when I began searching for rare records in local junk shops. He agreed to furnish part of the capital. The idea sounded like fun. When we realized that no other firm was actively recording the boppers, we decided to concentrate on that phase of jazz.

One evening about nine o'clock a downy-cheeked young man named Woody Isbell, one of Tempo's most loyal customers, came in to say, "I've got somebody outside in the short [car] who wants to talk to you." The passenger was Charlie Parker, and this was one of his good nights. Charlie looked fresh and rested. His face was boyish, and the smile disarming. The eyes didn't match the rest of the face. They lay behind a mask, cautious and watchful, the wise eyes of a mature man of the world.

Charlie apologized for the costly Glendale fiasco; he had not wanted to record with George Handy. Nor did he want to record any more with Dizzy; the Guild sides had completed their collaborations. It was time for new modes. The trumpet

player of his choice would not be a virtuoso capable of fireworks, but a different sort of musician, someone who played a
relaxed legato style, with a warm tone, in the lower and middle
registers, someone like Miles Davis, who would be arriving in
Los Angeles within a week or two. Charlie spoke of his future
and frustrated ambitions. He had been told that Igor Stravinsky and Arnold Schoenberg had made their permanent home in
Southern California, and he now saw the area in a new light.
He wanted a home of his own, with books, paintings, and a
piano, a splendid library of records, and perhaps a swimming
pool, so that he might regain his health. He wanted to listen to
everything by Stravinsky and Schoenberg, and Hindemith,
Bartok, Varese, and Alban Berg as well. He planned to compose seriously. He would write a beautiful mood piece, similar
to his *Confirmation*, for the first Dial record date. Names of
musicians that Charlie would like to use, and who were available on the Coast, were discussed, as were social and political
ideas. On the subject of segregation Charlie said, "That's un-
cool, but you and I don't have to talk about that!" He spoke of
his experiences with record companies in the East, their obsession with the juke box hit and their ingenuous methods of
cheating jazzmen out of their compositions. He hadn't forgotten *Now's the Time*. He said nothing about his problem with
narcotics. I was afraid to mention it. The discussion lasted for
an hour, and before Charlie left we had drawn up a hand-written agreement.

From cash on hand in the Tempo register, Charlie was
given a hundred-dollar advance to bind the contract. A few
days later a formal contract with terms and an option for one
year's renewal was drawn up by Marvin and filed with the
union, and a tentative date was chosen for the first session.
Plans were completed, the band personnel agreed to, and rehearsals staged at the Finale Club.

On a gray, dripping Thurday afternoon at the end of
March, Charlie assembled his men at Radio Recorders on Santa
Monica Boulevard in Hollywood: Miles Davis, trumpet, Lucky
Thompson, tenor, Dodo Marmarosa, piano, Arv Garrison, gui-
tar, Vic McMillan, bass, and Roy Porter, drums. Miles had ar-

This contract made the 26th day of February 1946 at Hollywood California between Charley Parker and DIAL RECORD COMPANY 5946 Hollywood Blvd Hollywood California provides the following covenants:

1. That the undersigned Charley Parker agrees to record exclusively under his own name only for DIAL RECORDS for a period of one year from date

2. That DIAL RECORDS agrees to make at least twelve ten-inch sides with Charley Parker as featured artist or band leader during the above period of one year.

FOR
DIAL RECORDS   Charlie Parker
Ross Russell

·ived in Los Angeles with the Benny Carter Orchestra. The ›thers were hand-picked from the pool at the Finale Club. Scheduled for one o'clock, the session did not begin until two. There had been a rehearsal the night before at the Finale, but ›ractically nothing had been accomplished; in fact, there had ›een altercations and a reshuffling of the original personnel. Nor had Charlie written the promised original compositions.

Once inside the studio, with its austere setting and functional furniture—microphones, booms, wires, a few metal chairs—Charlie became all business. He rolled up his sleeves, unlimbered the saxophone, blazed through a few scales, and went to work. The very playing of these casual notes seemed to create an atmosphere.

Sturdy and barrel-chested, speaking in a deep, steady voice, Charlie began rehearsing his men, first playing the line at the tempo he wanted, then drilling the others in their parts. Occasionally a chord or note was named, but usually it was just played. After twenty minutes the band was ready to make the first master. A red warning light alerted the musicians. Marvin and I stood by in the control booth with the engineers. At a nod from Charlie the turntables began rolling. The first tune was a Parker original, titled *Moose the Mooche*, dedicated to Mr. Byrd, a bright and jolly number. After that came *Yardbird Suite*, quiet and reserved, but very beautiful, based on the old *What Price Love?* motif inspired many years before by the police encounter in Jackson, Mississippi. Next Charlie recorded *Ornithology*, which also had its roots in the past. It was an extension of a motif first used by Charlie in one of his solos on the McShann Deccas.

The punch behind the rhythm section came from Roy Porter, who sat over his drums with a pork-pie hat on his head. Arv Garrison, the slender guitarist, had set up shop slightly out of the line of fire with his electric equipment. It was evident he was happy to be on the date. From the piano came pleasing chords and runs. That was Dodo Marmarosa, with his short, strong figure and excellent position at the piano. An enormous head dwarfed the body and was responsible for his nickname,

Dodobird. He was a jazz pianist who warmed up for the ses
sions at the Finale Club by playing through the Bach two-par
inventions at high speed, and his keyboard texture had a Bach
like quality. Unruffled, eyes heavy, Lucky Thompson was tak
ing the session in stride, as was Miles Davis, wooden and dead
panned, not playing much on his solos but warming the
ensemble parts with his broad tone.

After each of the takes Charlie would ask to have the mas
ter played back. Mistakes would be noted and corrected and an
other version recorded, until he was satisfied. The mistakes
were in all cases the fault of the sidemen, especially Miles
Davis, who was slow to learn new material. Often Charlie's
most original solo was played on the first and rejected take, al
though these were saved and later issued as alternates by Dial
Charlie's playing in the studio was more tempered and conserv
ative than one heard in a night club. He restricted himself to a
single solo chorus on each tune, either because he wanted to
give the others a chance or because he was reluctant to give too
much of himself.

The last side of the session was *A Night in Tunisia*. The
first time around Charlie played a stunning break. When the
master was played back, it was obvious this version could not
be used. It was full of mistakes made by others. "I'll never
make that break again," Charlie said. Nor was he quite able to
duplicate the suspenseful line of the first effort. After many
false starts and five complete versions of *Tunisia*, the session
ended at nine in the evening. Except for time out for coffee and
Danish pastry, Charlie had worked at an all-out pace for seven
hours. It was an impressive display of disciplined musicianship.
I had been listening to jazz for ten years and had heard most of
the great players, but apart from Louis Armstrong I had never
known a musician so committed or so wholly absorbed in the
creative role.

The session that had begun with so many hitches yielded a
considerable variety: the lyrical *Yardbird Suite*, the tough,
hearty *Moose the Mooche*, the welcome remake of *A Night in
Tunisia*, previously available only in the Boyd Raeburn ver-

sion, and, easily the best side of the date, *Ornithology*, which became a bebop standard. Three of the sidemen on the session —Dodo Marmarosa, Miles Davis, and Lucky Thompson—went on to win awards as *Down Beat*'s New Stars of 1946.

To settle the matter of composer credits, Dial proposed to set up a publishing company to copyright and publish Charlie's originals. The legal work was done, a trademark was applied for, and applications were prepared to register *Ornithology*, *Yardbird Suite*, and *Moose the Mooche* for copyright. They lacked only Charlie's signature and his lead sheets. This agreement was never returned by Charlie, and for that reason the tunes were not copyrighted. They remained in a limbo of known, often-performed works, very close to the public domain, and were frequently pirated. Dial also offered Charlie a contract under which he would be paid two cents per side, the maximum rate, for all records sold using his original compositions. This agreement was signed and witnessed, and became effective. There seemed good reason to believe that royalties would come in for many years.

Dial 1002, *Ornithology*, backed by *A Night in Tunisia*, was mastered, electroplated, and rushed into production at a custom-pressing plant in Inglewood. It was placed on the market early in April and I left town on a sales and promotional trip. Three weeks later I returned to find my partner discouraged and upset. Without comment Marvin handed me two pieces of mail received during my absence. As I read them through I began to understand the rationale of Eastern record companies that saved themselves the bother and expense of paying out artists' royalties by the expedient of buying jazz compositions outright for a few dollars. In spite of the advances that we had given Charlie, and in spite of the long term income we were trying to set up for him from record royalties, he had entered into an astonishing agreement.

The printed characters were in Charlie's hand. A second document implemented the first. Typed, witnessed by both parties, countersigned and stamped by a notary public, it spelled out the hand-written agreement in more formal terms.

4121 McKinley
April 3, 1946

I, Charlie Parker
do here by sign
one half, (½), of
royalties concerning
all contracts with
Dial Record company,
over to the undersigne
Imery Byrd

Charles Parker
(C)
Emry Byrd

San Quentin, California

June 30, 1946

Mr. Marvin Freeman
5225 Wilshire Blvd.
Los Angeles, California

Dear Mr. Freeman:

May I introduce myself as Emery Byrd. Sometime
ago I was assigned by Charley Parker, to one half
of all royalties from contracts with Dial Record
Company. This understanding was put into writing
and notarized on the third day of May, 1946.

I wish to announce, due to misfortune, my change
of address from 1135 East 45th Street, Los Angeles
to Box A-3892, San Quentin, California. If there
is anything which I might do to make this contract
a benefit to me, will you kindly let me know.

Thanking you for any consideration you may have to
offer concerning this matter.

Respectfully,

Emery Byrd
#A-3892 Emery Byrd.

Los Angeles, California,

May 3, 1946.

Mr. Marvin Freeman
5225 Wilshire Blvd.,
Los Angeles, California.

Dear Sir:

      This is to advise that I, Charlie Parker, do hereby assign one half (1/2) of royalties from all contracts with Dial Record Company to Emery Byrd, 1135 E. 45th Street, Los Angeles 11, California.

Charlie Parker
Charles Parker

Emery Byrd

3rd May 46
Willis M. Taylor

Dec April 1, 1948

Marvin smiled ruefully. "Well, at least we gave ourselves the satisfaction of playing the young idealists. Doing our good deeds. Seeing to the artist's need in his declining years. That sort of thing."

"But will this stand up in a court test?" I asked.

"The first won't. The second, that's the one he had notarized, will. It's a valid legal document. Of course, it means that Charlie has signed over one half of everything he receives from Dial for the rest of his life. For a few packs of cocaine or whatever it is he uses."

"I think it's heroin," I told my partner.

Marvin dropped the two documents into the Parker file and handed it to his secretary. Then we went over the recording company accounts. Our original agreement was that I would put up five hundred dollars and do all of the work and Marvin would supply the capital. He had already advanced seven thousand dollars, a sum in excess of our estimates. We had paid for two record dates, manufactured four 78-rpm records, bought labels, stationery, a little advertising, and incurred some accounts receivable. It was clear that we weren't about to produce a *Cement Mixer* or an *Open the Door Richard*. Marvin told me that his own finances would not permit him to advance any further capital. He suggested that we postpone all further recording indefinitely and begin recouping money. What had started out as fun now had the look of becoming complicated, burdensome, and risky.

Then the morning's mail at Marvin's law office brought another letter from the co-beneficiary of the Dial royalty contract. Concise and formal, it reflected the honors supposedly won in English at Jefferson High School by Moose the Mooche. It added the final twist to the bizarre financial arrangements between Charlie and his source of supply, now obviously out of circulation for a spell.

17

Sparrow's Last Jump

Panic had struck Central Avenue. Drugs were unobtainable at any price. Junkies were sweating it out in cheap hotels. And in the same week of bad vibrations, the gentlemen of the Los Angeles vice squad, cruising Little Tokyo in one of their unmarked Buicks, had noted the increased business at the Finale Club. Foster Johnson had been instructed to have ready a cash sum as his weekly contribution to the bagman for the squad. The club was run as a fun thing by a man who loved the music and enjoyed dancing to it. As the result of the police visit, the dancer-proprietor had decided to return to his regular profession, working for someone better equipped to handle the realities of night club operation. There was no notice given to the

218

members of the band. The musicians arrived one night to find the doors locked and themselves out of a job. Charlie Parker then dropped completely out of sight. For some days even his closest associates could not find him.

Tracked down after a patient search by Howard McGhee, Charlie was found living in a garage on McKinley Avenue, one of the shabbier streets of the ghetto. The garage was furnished with a metal cot, two odd chairs, and an old chest of drawers, its paint scaling off in ribbons. There was a single, uncurtained window, and a small rug on the concrete floor. The walls had no weather-proofing, nor was there any kind of heating. In spring-time California days are sunny and mild, but the nights are apt to be cold, with temperatures dropping below forty degrees. Charlie was using his overcoat as a blanket. He had not eaten in several days, and was subsisting on a diet of California port wine, available then for one dollar a gallon. The wine was Charlie's food, drink—and medicine. He had prescribed it for himself. This, he told Howard, had seemed like a good time to kick the habit. Howard packed Charlie's few belongings and moved him into the stucco bungalow the McGhees were renting on West Forty-first Street.

The McGhees themselves were up to their ears in problems. A mixed couple (ex-model Dorothy McGhee was tall and very blonde), they were subject to continual harrassment by the Los Angeles police, recruited during the war years from mal-educated migrants from the Southwest who brought their racism with them. Racism put a healthy punch into Los Angeles law enforcement. Recently the McGhees had been arrested for sitting together in the downtown Million Dollar Theater watching a James Cagney movie. Vice officers had kicked in the front door of the Forty-first Street bungalow and arrested Howard for possession of drugs, the evidence being planted by one of the officers while the raid was in progress. A mixed couple was enough to make any self-respecting L.A. cop blind with fury. Meanwhile the McGhees made arrangements to take over operation of the defunct Finale Club, and reopened it in May with Dorothy collecting one-dollar admissions at the door. The take was divided among the house band, composed of

Howard, Charlie, Dodo Marmarosa, Red Callender, and Roy Porter. With the reopening of the club, Charlie once again had a job, however precarious, a place to live, and loyal friends.

Charlie had not used heroin since Emry Byrd's arrest. He was trying very hard to kick the habit. But it seemed impossible for him to get along without alcohol. Port wine had been replaced by whiskey, and he was drinking large amounts of it, a quart or more daily. In all honesty one had to say that Charlie tolerated drugs better than alcohol.

Charlie had developed odd behavior patterns and strange tics. His limbs twitched. Occasionally, while he was playing, the saxophone would shoot up into the air, carrying his arms with it, as if jerked by a cord. One night he turned his back on the audience and played an entire set facing the wall. His playing was no longer the spontaneous act it had been. Sometimes he would not play at all but sat holding the saxophone on his lap. Physically and emotionally he was a sick man that spring. This was a serious crisis in his life. Relationships between Dial and its principal artist became distressingly difficult. Each visit to the Finale brought forth demands for money, for advances against earnings months into the future. Charlie kept insisting that the Dial contract be implemented, and that he was ready to make another record session. He would use the Finale band and bring Miles back for the occasion. He would write half a dozen beautiful new tunes, and so on. I tried to talk the usual common sense supposedly applicable in the situation of a man who is wasting his health and talent, but his armored personality was impervious to any argument and he resented the intrusion. It was impossible to discuss much of anything with Charlie. Perhaps if I had been black, a junkie, or a jazz musician the barriers would have come down, but even that was doubtful. He had a way of keeping everyone at arm's length. Intimates were in awe of him. As John Lewis put it: "Bird was like *fire!* You couldn't get too close!" The only thing Charlie liked to hear from me was my opinion of his musicianship. I told him he was certainly one of the giants of Afro-American music, among the handful of all-time greats with Armstrong, Ellington, and Lester Young. He liked that and smiled.

"Do you really mean that?" he wanted to know.

"Certainly." I added a few similar opinions given by Gottlieb and others.

"Yeah!" he exclaimed. "Now what about our record date?"

"I'll see."

Marvin agreed to raise the money. A bond was posted with the union, a studio selected and a time set. It was impossible to keep him from drinking. There were nights at the Finale when he couldn't play at all. Howard McGhee had serious doubts about what would happen in the studio. In an atmosphere painful to recall, the second Charlie Parker session took place Tuesday, July 29, at the C. P. MacGregor Transcription Studios, on Western Avenue south of Wilshire Boulevard, where Dial had recently recorded a Woody Herman group with surpassing results. The musicians were hastily assembled: Charlie, Howard (a bastion of strength and hope), pianist Jimmy Bunn, drummer Roy Porter, and bassist Bob Dingbod Kesterson, who arrived with his instrument on an Italian motor scooter. The calendar date itself was a carefully kept secret. No outsiders attended. With me in the control booth were Marvin, Marvin's younger brother, Richard Freeman, M.D., a psychiatrist, engineer Ben Jordan, Bobby Dukoff, a well-known studio musician, saxophonist, and manufacturer of saxophone mouthpieces, and Elliott Grennard, Hollywood correspondent for *Billboard* magazine. There were no other musicians, and no hipsters. A man named Slim, the custodian at the Finale Club, had come along to help with the instruments.

As Marvin and I waited for the session to begin, we anxiously asked ourselves the obvious questions. Had everything possible been done? The right sidemen picked for so delicate a situation? Would the new pianist find the right chords? Should the session be made at all? Would it be a complete waste of money? Everything obviously depended on the star of the production, the condition of his reflexes, his willingness, health, mood, the alcoholic content of his bloodstream. Would he come to life and take charge, as on the *Ornithology* session? Would he last through four takes, and three hours? Or even be able to play? The contracts were signed, the bond posted, and the studio reserved for five hours at a hundred dollars an hour. "Ridiculous way to run a business," Marvin commented, and I could sense his disenchantment. "Everything hinging on one man."

The five musicians were dwarfed by the immensity of the transcription studio with its high, vaulted ceiling. Seventy-piece orchestras had recorded there. Charlie sat slumped in a metal chair. He was wearing the trousers to his current good suit, suspenders over a clean white shirt, and no tie. The saxophone lay in its open case on the floor. He seemed to have lost interest in the session. Nothing had been prepared. What did he want to play? There was a grunted, noncommital response. Quietly Howard McGhee took over, suggesting that Charlie warm up his horn. Charlie played a scale. The playing was mechanical, and the tone cold. Someone suggested *Max Is Making Wax*, a Fifty-second Street favorite. Dull-eyed, with clumsy fingers, Charlie hooked the saxophone to the neckstrap and took his place at the microphone. The red warning light flashed. Ben Jordan started the twin turntables, leading the cutting styluses into the run-in grooves on sixteen-inch acetate blanks. The band began recording *Max Is Making Wax*. Much too fast.

The rhythm section was shaky, the men in it unnerved by the tension. The alto wobbled into the ensemble line, uneven and out of focus. The decibel needles on Ben Jordan's instrument panel jiggled. The alto was drifting on and off mike. Jordan rode the gain knobs to keep the dynamics at a constant level. Saxophone phrases came in short bursts, like gunfire. The take ran a bare two and a half minutes, and was obviously worthless. Marvin sent his brother out to see what could be done. After a talk with Charlie, Richard came back to the control booth.

"What seems to be wrong?" Marvin asked his brother.

"I'd guess that Charlie is suffering from malnutrition and acute alcoholism. It's impossible to say without taking him to a hospital. He won't go." Richard picked up his medical bag. "I'll give him something."

"Drugs?"

"No, phenobarbital. He claims his dosage is ten tablets. I'm going to take a chance with six, but there's no guarantee what will happen."

Bobby Dukoff, the manufacturer of saxophone mouthpieces, said, "I couldn't blow one blessed bar in that condition." The *Billboard* man sat quietly in the corner, taking notes that would furnish the raw material for a prize winning short story titled *Sparrow's Last Jump.** Richard dropped six yellow tablets into a paper cup and filled the cup from the water cooler. Charlie drank it down. With forced enthusiasm Marvin said, "Charlie that last number was wonderful—just wonderful!" Charlie nodded vacantly and said that he would like to try *Lover Man*. The rhythm section began running down the chord changes, and Howard cleared the valves of his trumpet. I told Ben Jordan to forget about our customary procedures, just to record everything, false starts, missed notes, bloopers, breakdowns, conversation, not to interrupt the musicians, just to keep the turntables rolling and the mikes open and ride the gain the best way he could. I sat down and listened to the opening of *Lover Man*.

There was a long, seemingly endless piano introduction as Jimmy Bunn marked time, waiting for the saxophone. Charlie had missed the cue. The alto came in at last, several bars late. Charlie's tone had steadied. It was strident and anguished. It had a heartbreak quality. The phrases were choked with the bitterness and frustration of the months in California. The notes passed in a sad, stately grandeur. Charlie seemed to be performing on pure reflexes, no longer a thinking musician. These were the raw notes of a nightmare, coming from a deep subterranean level. There was a last, eerie, suspended, unfinished phrase, then silence. Those in the control booth were slightly embarrassed, disturbed and deeply affected.

We did not waste time with a playback. There was a short wait, then Charlie did *The Gypsy*. His reflexes were getting rubbery. Phrases came in swoops and gasps, with a lot of air space between. Too much space. Roy Porter yelled, "Blow, man,

---

* Elliott Grennard: *Sparrow's Last Jump*, published in *Harper's Magazine*, May 1947.

blow, Bird!" Charlie faltered. The trumpet stormed in. Howard McGhee tried to pull the music together. The take ended in a fumbled coda. Then came a last effort, a fourth side, ill-chosen and disastrously fast, *Be-bop*. The saxophone shot into the air. Ben Jordan's needles dropped. Charlie was now spinning around in front of the mike, and Howard waved me outside to steady him. *Be-bop* came to an end, and Charlie slumped in his chair.

Richard Freeman said, "I'd give him a morphine injection, but it's too risky. Charlie should be put to bed as soon as possible."

Charlie was then living in a room at the Civic Hotel, around the corner from the Finale Club. A taxi was called, and he was sent home in Slim's care, with instructions that he be put to bed at once. Howard McGhee wanted to salvage something from the session, which he felt was a dead loss. After a break for refreshments, the four remaining musicians returned to the studio and Howard recorded two trumpet solos with the rhythm section. He had never played better. The trumpet crackled. He sounded like Roy Eldridge on a good night. Lacking another horn, the instrumentation was painfully thin, and the masters were of little value. The session looked like a complete washout. Marvin wrote out a check for studio time. Richard had to return to duty at the Veterans' Administration Hospital. I agreed to drive downtown alone and see if all was well at the Civic Hotel.

The Civic occupied the three upper floors of a four-story brick building at the corner of First and San Pedro Streets. It was a third-rate hotel, but comfortable and clean. The lobby was on the second floor and reached by stairs leading up from the street. As I drove up I noticed water on the pavement and a fire department salvage truck parked at the curb, its red light swinging in an arc and a fireman on standby. Then four firemen came down the hotel stairs carrying a mattress, which they threw onto the street and began spraying with portable chemical units. The mattress was charred and smoking. Charlie's room was on the top floor. When I got there firemen were removing tarpaulins and a damaged bed was being pushed out into the hall. The manager, a Chinese, told me what happened in singsong English. Charlie had arrived by cab and Slim had seen him to bed, then left. Sometime later Charlie had appeared in the lobby, wanting to make a call on the pay phone. There were no telephones in the rooms at the Civic. Except for a pair of socks, he was stark naked. Charlie was carrying a quarter and wanted the manager to make change. He didn't seem to realize that he was naked, and became angry when other guests began to protest. There had been a disagreeable scene and a great deal of bad language. With difficulty the manager persuaded Charlie to return to his room. The police were not called.

Soon the same events were repeated. This time, the manager got Charlie back into the room and locked the door. Another thirty minutes passed, then an excited guest came running to the lobby to report smoke pouring from under the door of Charlie's room. The manager called the fire department, hurried upstairs, and unlocked the door. The mattress was on fire. Flames were starting to burn the wooden bedstead and the room was rapidly filling with smoke. The manager dragged Charlie, angry and naked, into the hall. Panicky guests came running from nearby rooms.

Soon sirens could be heard converging on the Civic Hotel as the Los Angeles Fire Department sent out its crack units to cover a priority fire in a downtown hotel. The neighborhood became a confusion of sirens, engines, and red lights. In the wake of the fire engines came police cars. Uniformed men carrying hoses, axes, portable spray units, and evacuation fans rushed into Charlie's room. He struggled to throw off the effects of the phenobarbital tablets and became abusive over what seemed to him a gross invasion of privacy. The firemen ignored Charlie. The police did not. He was promptly pacified with a blackjack ("sapped down cold," in department parlance), prodded onto his back, his arm twisted behind him, and manacled. Then he was rolled into a blanket, carried downstairs, and heaved into a squad car. It was all over in two or three minutes. The police had no time to waste on a disturbance in a "jigaboo hotel" with a naked, raving black man who had caused all that equipment to roll. That was the last anyone saw of Charlie for ten days.

While the hip community buzzed with rumors, including one that Charlie was dead, the search began. I promptly lost the trail at the Lincoln Heights division of the city jail, where Charlie had first been taken and booked. The booking record was incomplete, and Charlie was no longer there. Through professional channels Richard learned that Charlie had been transferred to the Psychopathic Ward of the county jail, located in an old building on the east side of Los Angeles. Howard and I drove down and were admitted to an enormous circular room. Its sunken floor was furnished with tables and benches, at which sat forty or fifty inmates in institutional gray pajamas, men in various states of dementia, elation, and depression. There were pajamaed orators, mimes, statues—Napoleons, Lenins, Barrymores. But no Charles Parker, Jr.

Finally an attendant appeared. We were guided up the steps to a circular system of cells, enclosing the entire room, each with a steel door and each door with a small, barred window. A door stood ajar. Inside was a small cell, large enough for an iron cot, a white wooden night stand, and a white wooden chair. The far wall had a single window, fitted with iron bars and, inside the bars, chain-link grating. Charlie Parker lay on the iron cot. He was wearing gray pajamas and a gray straitjacket. The leather restraining straps and sleeves of the strait jacket had been left loose, and his arms lay on the bed at his side. One wrist was chained to the iron cot with a pair of police handcuffs. He was staring at the ceiling. The attendant told us we could visit for five minutes.

Charlie was fully conscious. He looked subdued and angry. He sat up in bed. He leaned forward as far as his manacled wrist would allow and shouted, "For God's sake, man, get me out of this joint!" Then he launched into a tirade against the jail, the police, and California in general. He told Howard to find the attendant and get his clothes, and directed me to make reservations on the first plane leaving for the Apple. He was still going when the attendant returned to say that the five minutes were up.

"You're not going to leave me in this joint?" Charlie demanded as we were ushered out.

"We'll get you out," Howard told him. "Some kind of way."

I had a feeling that wasn't going to be so easy.

18

Relaxin' at Camarillo

Hearings for the human debris dumped by the Los Angeles police department into the Psychopathic Ward of the county jail were held every two weeks, on the premises—an arrangement that avoided the inconvenience and expense of conveying prisoners to and from regular courts. A simulated judge's bench, made of plywood nailed to a frame of two-by-fours, stained to resemble oak and mounted on rubber-tired wheels, was trundled along the upper level upon which the cell doors faced. The bench was brought to a stop in front of the cell housing the prisoner whose hearing was scheduled. A bailiff declared the court in session. A judge, his black robe thrown over a business suit, stood behind the bench. The prisoner was not normally represented by counsel. A summons, the report of the arresting officer, record examinations, and recommendations by psychiatrists, if any, were read. A court order was then handed down and the prisoner remanded to one of three local mental institutions, Norwalk, Patton, or Camarillo.

Charlie was charged with indecent exposure, resisting arrest, and suspected arson. Marvin was certain the arson charge could be defeated. Convictions on one or both of the first two counts might result in a jail sentence of three to six months. But the authorities had gone further; Charlie was now suspected of being insane. There was no mention of drug addiction, although the needle marks on his arm should have been evidence to any examining physician. And Norwalk and Patton, we learned, were old line maximum-security institutions intended for psychotics and the criminally insane. Once inside their walls, the business of getting out would be difficult. The only workable solution was to maneuver things so that Charlie could be sent to the third facility, Camarillo State Hospital. Camarillo was known as the "country club" of mental institutions. It was staffed by doctors, psychiatrists, and social workers. It offered a rehabilitation program for chronic alcoholics and addicts.

Marvin asked for a continuance and prepared the necessary papers to transfer Charlie's case to the superior court docket of Stanley Mosk, a young judge known for his liberal views. At the hearing, conducted *in absentia*, Marvin, Richard, Howard, and I appeared as character witnesses and *amici curiae*. The court was briefed on Charlie's career and his contributions to American music. Judge Mosk (he later became state attorney general and a member of the California Supreme Court) agreed that there was no evidence of psychosis or reason that Charlie should not be given benefit of the facilities at Camarillo. He ordered Charlie confined to Camarillo State Hospital for a minimum period of six months, the case to be reviewed at the end of that time in the light of later medical findings. The criminal charges were held in continuance. Charlie had expected to walk into the street a free man, but everyone else was elated. The following day Charlie was removed from the Psychopathic Ward and sent in a van to Camarillo.

Camarillo State Hospital was located seventy miles north of the city, near the small town of the same name. Low buildings of white stucco, with red tile roofs and arched porches, in the California Mission style, lay at the crest of rolling hills, overlooking vegetable gardens, lawns and the sea. The surrounding countryside was a checkerboard of truck farms and lima bean fields screened by stately windbreaks of eucalyptus trees. The climate was the same as that enjoyed by the millionaire colony at nearby Santa Barbara. For the first six weeks Charlie lived quietly at Camarillo, adjusting himself to the new life. He was uncomplaining and unresponsive, and showed little interest in outside events, even the news of the opening of Dizzy's new big band at the Spotlight. "Convalescing," Richard said, after our first visit to Camarillo. In the next month we could see changes for the better. Charlie was eating well and had gained eight pounds. His breath had cleared and his eyes brightened. With a shy touch of pride he told us that he had volunteered to work in a vegetable garden. He had never done anything like this. Tending lettuce was a "gas," he said. It was good to work with the soil and growing things. Saturday nights he played in the hospital band on a C-melody saxophone. The band was a ten-piecer, recruited from doctors, nurses, and inmates. Charlie told of the pleasure of playing for the patients, some of them with very "loose wigs." He was the best player in the group, and this pleased him. The night club pallor he had acquired over the years was being replaced by a glowing tan that gave his dark chocolate skin a healthy patina. His muscles had firmed. He was beginning to look like a healthy man.

Dean Benedetti returned from a visit to Camarillo with a report that Charlie was learning to lay bricks. Charlie was seriously considering giving up music and becoming a mason, Benedetti said. The word went around Hollywood that Bird was on a big health kick, and a few diets were changed. Members of the California hip community made weekly shuttle trips between Hollywood and Camarillo to see Charlie during visiting hours.

Doris Sydnor arrived from New York, rented a room, took a job as a waitress, gathered up various personal effects of Charlie's that were scattered over Southern California, and announced that she would wait for his release. Meanwhile Chan Richardson, who had also followed Charlie to California, had returned to New York. The maneuvering of the key women in Charlie's life had taken a new turn.

Richard and I made monthly trips to Camarillo to discuss his case. Charlie's file had been assigned to a psychiatrist named Hammond, a European refugee, whose reported conferences with the patient, available for Richard's inspection, seemed to have made little progress. Richard read, "Mr. Parker admits to having smoked 'Mary Anna' cigarettes." It was doubtful if Charlie had smoked marijuana in years. Charlie was pulling the doctor's leg. The psychiatrist evidently understood little about America, black people, music, or drugs. Another report, by a staff committee, noted "superior intelligence, auditory hallucinations, sexual fantasies, paranoid tendencies, and a highly evasive personality." There was as yet no general diagnosis, but the committee was working hard to fit Charlie into some kind of a pigeonhole. Meanwhile, the advisability of electric shock therapy was being weighed, a cause for great concern on Richard's part.

"It's a mild form of electrocution, and drastic as hell," Richard said. "The patient is knocked senseless with a non-lethal shock and then placed on a litter of beds so that he can slowly reorganize the shattered bits and pieces of his personality. It could permanently impair Charlie's reflexes, reduce him to a manageable personality, but a very average musician. They like to play around with exotic treatments at these places—free frontal lobotomies, that sort of thing." Richard got onto the committee, and the idea was dropped.

The young doctor had become fascinated with Charlie's case. Richard had studied the piano many years in the hope of becoming a great concert pianist. "I'd give anything for a tenth of Charlie's talent," he said. "Or a twentieth! To me, as an ordinary man, with barely average talent, his life seems like a tragic, willful waste, but, as a doctor, I know this isn't so."

Richard admitted his feelings were ambivalent. He conceded that such ability was accompanied by unusual responsibilities and unusual stresses, to say nothing of the pressure that came from life in Negro America. Despite the staff's suspicion of schizophrenia, Richard did not think Charlie a psychotic. Richard believed Charlie a psychopathic personality; a classic psychopathic, Richard thought: "A man living from moment to moment. A man living for the pleasure principle, music, food, sex, drugs, kicks, his personality arrested at an infantile level. A man with almost no feeling of guilt and only the smallest, most atrophied nub of conscience. One of the army of psychopaths supplying the populations of prisons and mental institutions. Except for his music, a potential member of that population. But with Charlie Parker it is the music factor that makes all the difference. That's really the only reason we're interested in him. The only reason his followers are interested in him. The reason we're willing to stop our own lives and clean up his messes. People like Charlie require somebody like that, to follow them through life and clean up the shit."

As Charlie's health improved, he began to make noises about getting out of Camarillo. As he saw things, it was up to us to do something. He wanted to know what was going on outside down to the most minute detail. He was ready to play again. The mason's gig had been forgotten. "If something doesn't start shaking pretty quick," he told us, "I'm going over the wall." Hipsters were hatching a plot to expedite his escape. Charlie's status had been complicated by a ruling classifying him as a non-resident. Once every six months California unburdened itself of its non-resident patients by shipping them in a sealed train back to their place of origin. In this case Charlie would be returned to New York, and the whole game of institutional chairs would begin again. If, as he threatened, he went "over the wall," he would soon be picked up by the police. Richard dug through the state mental hygiene code and found an alternative: upon recommendation of a board in Sacramento, it was possible for an inmate to be released into the custody of an approved California resident who would then become legally responsible for him. Richard could not accept the responsibility. Marvin refused. Doris was willing but could not qualify. Did I want the job?

I didn't. I had seen enough to realize that no one could exert the slightest control over Charlie Parker. Again feelings were ambivalent. There was Dial to consider. That fall I had sold Tempo Music Shop and become the sole owner of Dial Records. Its operation was now my sole activity. Marvin had generously offered me ownership of the company, provided I paid back the original investment, and this was possible by means of the store sale, curtailment of plans for new record dates, and improving sales of the records. The Dial catalogue offered six releases, enough to interest distributors in San Francisco, Chicago, and New York, four sides of the *Ornithology* session plus the fruits of the Woody Herman and Dizzy Gillespie dates. After weighing the risks I decided to apply for Charlie's release in my custody, and with Marvin's help filled out a four-page form with questions about place of birth, citizenship, health, police record, war service record, years of residency in California, and income. The forms were forwarded to Camarillo with a request for Charlie's release in my custody.

A committee was formed to stage a Charlie Parker benefit concert in Hollywood. Besides me it included Charlie Emge, West Coast editor for *Down Beat*, Eddie Laguna of Sunset Records, and Maynard Sloate and June Orr, partners in Sloate-Orr Associates, an up-and-coming booking agency. Local and visiting musicians were contacted and asked to donate their services. Application was made to the musicians' union to permit free services at a bona-fide benefit. The money would be used to rehabilitate Charlie as soon as he was released. Nobody had any extra money at the time. Doris was earning a living wage as a waitress, Marvin was out of funds, and Dial had yet to show a profit. Charlie had lost all of his clothing in the Civic Hotel fiasco. While plans for the benefit were being completed, I received a letter on plain stationery, printed in Charlie's own hand, saying that he was about to "blow his top" and demanding "come right down here and get me out of this joint." "There isn't much to write about," Charlie said, "except the hope for a quick release." There was no mention of the Camarillo lettuce fields, the Saturday night dances, or his passing thoughts of following the mason's trade. He was clearly ready to return to the music business and resume his recording and performing activities. The letter closed with "Until you come down and get me," as if I had the power to manipulate the state institutional system.

A letter dated December 24 from Thomas W. Haggerty, M.D., superintendent of Camarillo State Hospital, was noncommital. According to Dr. Haggerty, "Charles Parker was brought before the staff December 12, for consideration of parole and the staff felt that a release from the hospital at this time was not considered best for Mr. Parker. On the other hand, he is a non-resident of California, and unless we could discharge him as recovered, it will be necessary for us to obtain permission from the Department of Mental Hygiene, Deportation Division, for his release."

Richard again visited the hospital, and learned that Dr. Hammond had left the institution and Charlie's case had been transferred to a new reviewing board. Richard continued to press the authorities for Charlie's release before the next deportation of inmates to the East Coast. At the end of January the Department of Mental Hygiene in Sacramento handed down its decision, and the hospital announced that it was ready to release Charlie Parker to my custody. I drove up to Camarillo in my new 1946 Chevrolet. Charlie was waiting in the visitor's room, beaming and healthy. If the psychiatrists had not gotten very far with their therapy, at least Camarillo had done a good job in recharging his batteries. To protect Dial, I suggested that since the original contract had been only partially fulfilled, it seemed right to allow us to renew our option for another year. Charlie agreed. This matter would be the source of later bad feeling, Charlie contending that I "wouldn't let him out until he signed the paper." We drove back to Los Angeles for a celebration at Tempo Music Shop hosted by its new owner, Lee Wilder. The first order of business was to replenish

Charlie's wardrobe. A committee of sharp dressers, headed by Dean, went off to see to this at Zeidler and Zeidler, the hip clothing store on Hollywood Boulevard. Charlie chose two suits, Hollywood versions of the sharp Broadway models he preferred, and the necessary accessories, shirts, ties, underwear, socks, and shoes.

Charlie and Doris began housekeeping in a furnished room downtown. Charlie spent the first week or two relaxing and renewing old friendships. He was gay, boyish, and gregarious. He won a pizza-eating contest. He finished third in the 1946 *Down Beat* alto saxophone poll, behind Johnny Hodges and Willie Smith. One evening he accompanied a group of hipsters for a party on the beach at Santa Monica. A dip was proposed and several daring souls stripped to their shorts and went in the water. Charlie followed, laughing, having the time of his life, fully dressed, wearing one of the new suits. Afterwards the hipsters said that he had walked on the water, like Jesus. Subsequent attentions by a good cleaner were unable to restore the suit to its original condition. The shoes were a total loss. "That's my Charlie!" Doris said. "He was just being playful." The benefit committee wrote off one Zeidler and Zeidler suit.

Early in February Charlie joined Howard McGhee for a gig at the Club Hi De Ho on south Western Avenue. It was Howard's job, but Howard made him the co-leader with a salary of two hundred dollars a week. Charlie's playing was more relaxed and lyrical than before. He had never played better or looked better.

Unfortunately, he was back in the night club environment. Pushers followed him to the Hi De Ho and tried to turn him on. He chased them out of the club. He couldn't let booze alone, though, and began running up large bar bills. One night he polished off eight double whiskey shots before the opening set. Charlie and Doris planned to return to New York as soon as the worst of the winter weather was over. The Street was jumping again, and he felt left out of things. Dizzy was getting all of the attention. Charlie promised to make a single farewell record session for me before his departure. I began planning well in advance, determined to make it a good one. Meanwhile I began negotiations with night club operators in Chicago and New York in hope of finding a steady job for Charlie in one of the night clubs. I also got in touch with Chan Richardson, who had returned to New York and was again living at 7 West 52nd Street. I explained the situation to Chan and asked her help in sounding night club operators since none of the established booking agencies showed any interest in handling Charlie. In two weeks a very helpful (and revealing) letter arrived. It discussed her past relations with Charlie, her feelings for him as a man and musician, her pregnancy (from a previous marriage), the other woman (Doris), and reported two business-like discussions about Charlie's possible employment with Sammy Kaye, owner of the Three Deuces.

February 7, 1947

Dear Ross,

It sure knocked me out to get your letter. I had a rough idea what happened to Bird, but I didn't know any of the details.

I love Bird for I know how capable his mind is, and I'm certain that Bird is a genius. I've known him for about three years. And I've been close enough to him to see the various drags that have indirectly led to this breakdown. Because I'd give anything to see Bird get straight I'd like to tell you some of them.

This—from Bird:

He's had a habit since he was fifteen.

He was in an asylum in Kansas City years ago.

This—from knowing him:

Around New York, the last few years he had a habit but he kept himself pretty straight. There was a girl who gave him the money to keep straight in N.Y. I was trying to get him to kick, and I didn't know about her at the time. I hear she's out there with him now. . . . Doris Parker . . . She really loves Bird and would do anything for him, but I doubt that she'd deny him anything he wanted.

Bird and I had a scuffle and I guess his faith in me was pretty shaken. He went to California with Diz. I came out in February last year. I was pregnant and Bird was drug about that. He wanted me to have an abortion. I wanted the baby (Which I had in August incidentally) so Bird dug that it meant more to me than he did. I'm hip that the coast did him no good, cause I sure couldn't understand the way he was thinking. I know the time he was working at the Finale he was trying to be real straight. He practically carried a brief case. When that fell through I dug how much it hurt him. Bird is probably the most sensitive cat I know. Then at one of Granz's gigs, Bird was juiced and they asked him to get off stage. That was another blow.

I couldn't make it any more on the coast and I wanted to have my baby in N.Y. so I cut out in May. I knew what was happening to Bird. But I didn't see any way to avoid it. He refused to have anything to do with me at all; wouldn't even see me. I've written several letters but never had an answer. I'll do anything within my power to see Bird on his feet again. But I really think N.Y. is the best place for him. People are funny on the coast.

I know if you'll stick by him it will help a lot. You can't expect any gratitude from Bird, cause anything he gets, he feels as if it was coming to him. But basically it will help. McGhee is good for him too, cause Howard is a real cool and settled cat.

If you could see that he doesn't get a lot of gold in a lump sum, cause he'll only shoot it up. Bird is not to be trusted with money. I doubt if he'll resist the temptation of getting on just once or twice with the cats, and soon he'll have another habit. He's easily influenced if it's something he wants to do but shouldn't. What Bird needs is a nursemaid. I would take the job, but I have my baby to think about. Also I'm leaving Wednesday to dance at the Chanticleer in Baltimore. You can always reach me at the N.Y. address that you have. My mother stays there.

Don't hesitate to ask me for anything that might help Bird. I'll do anything I possible can to help this truly unfortunate situation.

I'm sure that if Bird were given the opportunity that Diz was, he could straighten himself out. He knows how much he blows and he's hurt cause Diz is making all that gold.

Sammy Kaye knows Bird, and Bird will have a bad reputation to work down. But I'll take your letter in tonight and talk with him. I know he'll give Bird an opportunity.

By the way, the Spotlite has closed and the Deuces and Downbeat are the only clubs left on the street. (musically) The job situation here is terrible. The cats are even renting studios just to blow.

I'll enclose a P.S. after I talk to Mr. Kaye. I wish you'd keep me posted on Bird. And thanks a million for the records. As for

Bird's hurting you, he'll hurt anyone that he's close to. But it's worth knowing him and realizing his greatness. He showed me, or rather told me about the Dial contract and I've never seen him so proud. Bird has a seven year old son in K.C. It might be good for him to see him. This letter probably sounds very distracted, but I'm just writing things as I think of them.

Bird is a great actor and a lot of things he does are for effect.

It will kill me to see him straight again, and to meet you. I know what you are doing for him. Please tell him he has all my best thoughts, and I hope he will forgive and forget as I have done. Tell him my little girl is beautiful and the first word she will say is Bird. Tell him I'm bringing her up to love him.

Until I see Sammy, I'll close. Thanks again for everything.

> *Sincerely,*
> S/ CHAN RICHARDSON

QUOTE BIRD: *They can get it out of your blood, but they can't get it out of your mind.*

[THE ABOVE TYPED; THE FOLLOWING BY HAND:]
Just spoke to Sammy. He offered $700 for the band. He said to let him know two weeks ahead and he can put them in any date. I'd advise you to ask for a two month guarantee at least, when you talk business. Sammy is a good guy. All you have to do is B. S. a little.

I don't know how good $700, but if you talk a little maybe you can raise it a little. $66 a man is scale here—and $90.75 for a leader. Hal West has always worked scale for Sammy. So I figured if you pay as follows it might work out all right.

Hal West	70	But you can work that
Red	75	out—you know the
Wardell	75	earning capacity of
Errol	100	these men better than I
Howard	190	do.
Bird*	190	Hoping to hear
—		from you soon.
	$700	Please keep this letter in confidence.

* The first name references in the proposed band were: Red Callender, bass; Wardell Gray, tenor saxophone; Erroll Garner, piano; Howard McGhee, trumpet; Bird (Charlie Parker), alto saxophone and leader.

The final Dial record session ended up as two, thanks to a strange set of circumstances. For the final session I had rounded up the best jazzmen available in Southern California: Howard McGhee, trumpet; Wardell Gray, the exciting new tenorman from the Eckstine Orchestra; Dodo Marmarosa, piano; Barney Kessel, former Charlie Barnet guitarist; Red Callender, formerly bassist with Lester Young and the King Cole Trio; and Don Lamond, Woody Herman's new drummer. Nothing had been overlooked to produce a true all-star session. Then, at the last moment, Charlie told me that he wanted to use an unknown singer he had discovered working in a club on Central Avenue. The singer's name was Earl Coleman, and he sang like Eckstine. Earl Coleman's merits aside, I had no interest in singers. Dial was not set up to compete in the jukebox derby. I also knew that any singer would ruin the instrumental date, just as it had in all those abortive sessions in New York. I offered Charlie an alternative. The blowing musicians would interfere with the singer and spoil the man's record debut. Why not do a separate date, featuring Coleman with a small, intimate group? Charlie swallowed the bait. I immediately made a deal with Erroll Garner to provide a rhythm section. His very fine trio, with Callender and drummer Doc West, was then unemployed. February 17 the Garner Trio, Charlie, and Earl Coleman met at the C. P. MacGregor studios for the session. The tight budget was reminiscent of the Tiny Grimes *Red Cross* date for Savoy. In fact, two of the musicians were the same.

Earl Coleman struggled for two hours to complete acceptable takes on two vocals, *Dark Shadows* and *This Is Always*. I didn't like them, although they were better than I realized. After the last take of *Dark Shadows* Earl was unable to sing another note and retired to the sidelines. Then, in an incredible half hour, without preparation of any kind, Charlie invented two new tunes, *Bird's Nest*, based on *I Got Rhythm*, and *Cool Blues*, and reeled off seven takes in thirty minutes. They were two of his best records ever. The collaboration between Charlie and Erroll contributed a unique page in Charlie's discography. The music was mellow, relaxed, and lyrical. When *Cool Blues* was released in France a year later, it won the Grand Prix du Disque. In America it was a *success d'estime* and sold well.

The farewell session followed a week later in the same studio. At the rehearsal held the day before, Charlie appeared badly hung over, sullen, short-tempered, and looking less than well. He arrived an hour late with a single scrap of music paper instead of the four originals he had promised. On the music paper he had scribbled, during the taxi ride to the club, the line of a new, untitled twelve-bar blues.

No one could read Charlie's notation. When Howard tactfully pointed out mistakes in the musical spelling, Charlie crumpled the music paper, threw it on the floor, picked up the horn, and played out the theme. It was beautiful, strange, and difficult. The rest of the hour was spent struggling to master its insinuating line.

The farewell session at C. P. MacGregor's was delayed over two hours while Howard looked for Charlie. Howard found him, fully clothed, asleep in a bathtub. He had passed out and slept the whole night there. Charlie arrived stiff, groggy and disheveled. Quantities of black coffee were sent for and Charlie pulled himself together, grunted, mumbled, and blued the studio air with many a "Shee-it!" and "Motherfucker!" while Howard went about rehearsing the others on three originals of his own, brought along to save the session. Charlie warmed up with a blast of scales and became the take-charge bandleader of the *Ornithology* date. The order of solos was set and the beat laid down. His twelve-bar blues, later titled *Relaxin' at Camarillo*, was recorded first. Charlie had it note perfect. The others required five takes. Charlie played vigorous and original solos on all five. The three McGhee originals (*Cheers, Stupendous,* and *Carvin' the Bird*) yielded solid ensembles and outstanding solos by Howard, Dodo, Kessel, and the brilliant new tenorman, Wardell Gray. The date ended early in the evening with four more Parker sides in the can for Dial. "That's all she wrote," Charlie said as he packed up his horn. "When I lay my hair down next it's going to be in the Apple."

A few days later, supplied with first-class air travel tickets purchased from the last of the benefit funds, Charlie and Doris left for New York. I had agreed to drive them to the airport, and arranged a one-o'clock rendezvous at Tempo Music Shop, which would allow time for the twenty-mile drive across town. They arrived at one-thirty, in a cab and needing the fare. By taking back roads, hopefully thus avoiding traffic, and driving fast it would be just possible to make the plane. Halfway to the airport Charlie ordered me to stop at the next bar so that he could go inside and "buy a pack of cigarettes." I refused to stop and threw him my own pack. He brooded the rest of the way in silence. We arrived at Los Angeles International with two or three minutes to spare. There was the usual brinkmanship at the ticket and baggage check. I went with them as far as the field gate and stood there as they boarded the plane, Charlie wearing his last Z and Z suit, Doris walking in his shadow, carrying the saxophone case, suddenly too precious to trust to the luggage department. The plane door closed, the boarding steps were rolled away, and the flight took off for points east. I did not see Charlie again until that fall. To record him further, and for other reasons, it was necessary to move the Dial offices to New York.

Klactoveesedstene

During Charlie's sixteen months in California a great deal had happened to change the jazz scene. Bebop had achieved a sudden, dramatic breakthrough. The new music with its cool sounds and galvanic rhythms had been taken up by the under-thirty generation of the urban ghettos. Large Eastern cities now boasted smart jazz clubs, patterned after those of Fifty-second Street, but larger and more comfortable: the Argyle Lounge in Chicago, El Sino in Detroit, others in Boston, Philadelphia, Washington, Cleveland, St. Louis, Kansas City, and Milwaukee. Patrons went to listen, not to dance. The jazz musician—significantly, the saxophone player—had surfaced as the culture hero of the new generation. Small combos and bands led by veterans of the bebop wars were being booked out over the lounge circuit for real money. After years of scuffling, Lester Young suddenly found himself in the fifty-thousand-dollar tax bracket and in need of expert accounting advice. Dizzy Gillespie was the most-talked-of new jazzman. Bereted and goateed, interviewed and photographed, ever smiling and clowning, Diz had become Mister Bebop. According to the press he was the man who had invented it all. Dizzy was more familiar to record buyers than Duke Ellington or Louis Armstrong. Dizzy had cashed in while Charlie was in California. Charlie Parker remained a mysterious, prophetic figure, hardly known to the public.

Charlie moved into the Dewey Square hotel on 117th Street, where he and Doris Syndor would live for the next year. He was offered a contract at eight hundred dollars a week, four weeks, with options, for a five-piece band at the Three Deuces. After the months of hand-to-mouth existence in California, that sounded pretty good. Charlie at once began picking his sidemen. Miles Davis, back in New York, studying at Juilliard, was Charlie's first and only choice on trumpet. Charlie built the rhythm section around Max Roach, in the opinion of many now the best drummer in jazz. Max had gone beyond Kenny Clarke in the development of cross rhythms, the complex figures that made bebop so compelling. Unlike many technically expert drummers, Max had taste, an uncanny sense of playing behind a soloist, and the ability to improvise constantly. Supporting Max were two comparative unknowns, pianist Duke Jordan and Tommy Potter, former bassist with the Eckstine Orchestra, both sound, dependable musicians.

All of Charlie's sidemen could have worked for higher wages elsewhere, but the inducement of being with Bird outweighed any other considerations. Jordan and Potter received a hundred twenty-five dollars a week, Max and Miles a hundred thirty-five. Charlie had the difference of two hundred eighty dollars clear. It was the best wage he had received in his twelve years in the music business. He did not know yet that jazzmen with a fraction of his ability were earning a thousand dollars weekly or better. Charlie concluded his new arrangements by signing a personal management contract with Billy Shaw, who had moved up to executive assistant at the powerful Moe Gale Agency. Shaw told him, "Show me you're straight and I'll double your earnings in six months."

The Quintet opened at the Deuces in April, opposite the Lennie Tristano Trio, a booking that brought the jazz community out in large numbers. The blind pianist had become the leading jazz pedagogue and had developed interesting methods of instruction. Tristano first taught embryo jazzmen to transcribe Lester Young solos from records. Next they learned to sing the solos, finally to play the solos on their own instruments. After Tristano's pupils had mastered Lester Young, they were advanced to similar studies of Charlie Parker. Tristano played a very personal style of piano, cool and cerebral.

With the Charlie Parker Quintet installed at the Three Deuces the club once more became a hipster rallying point. The engagement that began as two weeks with options was extended indefinitely. The new rhythm section was the best Charlie had used. Max Roach brought jazz drumming to a new level of artistry. The stick was a blur in his hand as he attacked the huge ride cymbal, filling the club with waves of airy sound. Max would add little percussion figures, muffled thuds on the bass, pistol shots on the snares, jungly throbs on the tom-toms, puffs of air caught between the surfaces of the high-hat cymbals, pickups and press rolls, a dazzling mosaic of subtle sounds. Tommy Potter's bass pumped out its light, strong tone and Duke Jordan interpolated his chords. Then Charlie and Miles Davis would spell out the ensemble line of a bebop classic, or the newer pattern of one of the California tunes. Sometimes the erratic, brilliant trumpeter, Fats Navarro, would sit in and some thought that Fats should be the trumpet player in the Quintet; the more responsible counseled that two unpredictable musicians in the same band would be a disaster and Miles stayed. Charlie raced through *Koko* at impossible tempi. From up tunes he went to cool ones, *Now's the Time* and *Yardbird Suite*. He played long improvisations on slow ballads. He never played anything the same way twice. There were typical openings and closings, favorite turns, but no clichés. His playing came from such an excess of creativity and emotion that an ex-. tended improvisation of ten minutes seemed too short for his run of ideas.

Meanwhile he was living life to the hilt. He still consumed enormous quantities of food. He used heroin in increasing amounts. He downed double whiskey shots like a Western bad-man. He balled the alluring and willing women to be found in Fifty-second Street clubs in those days. He drove his stocky body to the limit. The hipster community, disorganized and scattered during the eighteen months of his exile in California, rallied to his leadership. His music spelled out the subculture of the hipster movement. His lifestyle became its beau ideal. He was the cool cat who could do anything. The Sepia Superman with all the plays and all the answers. He lived straight off the top. He was the Pied Piper who led his followers on raids on the steam table at Hector's Cafeteria or hansom carriage rides through Central Park. He liked to organize a gang for a ride on the A train, boarding the subway for the long, high-speed express trip from Times Square to 125th Street in Harlem, and back again. Charlie would stand in the vestibule of the front car, staring at the twisting rails and swerving red lights, mes-merized by the roaring tunnel of sound as the express gathered speed and hurtled through the night.

As a cocksman Charlie was much in demand. His sexual energy seemed to flow from the same spring as his music and with a comparable force. Years of saxophone playing and the demands on tongue and lips had given him a tremendous oral effect. One night at the Three Deuces he spotted a beautiful model that excited him and that he wanted. Finishing the set, he went directly to her table and, ignoring the party there, pulled up a chair at her side. Without preamble or introduction, he asked in an eager, charged voice, "Are you going to let me suck your pussy tonight?" The girl blushed deeply; but when the club closed she left with Charlie, not her own escort. Such uninhibited approaches, delivered for maximum shock effect, worked with certain types of women. *You Go to My Head* (". . . like the bubbles in a glass of champagne"), the unofficial theme song of oral eroticists, became a favored ballad and a

vehicle for coded messages played across tables of the Three
Deuces to women with whom he was having affairs.

Charlie's libido was not diminished by his use of narcotics,
but like many heroin users he gradually found a greater time
and effort required to bring himself to climax. His companions
did not complain. They liked him all the better. Sometimes he
dated two girls at once. When he was interested in a woman he
was very direct in his manner. He gave her his undivided attention. His reputation, experience and skill at verbal games made
conquests easy. Now that he was established as a figure in show
business he no longer found it necessary to resort to such gambits as offering girls fake wedding rings, as he had done when
he was married to Geraldine. The women Charlie dated were
varied as to type, color and personality, as widely varied as
those with whom he found lasting and meaningful relationships, Rebecca, Geraldine, Doris, and Chan.

Charlie's direct, sex-as-function attitude was derived from
his class and ethnic background and conditioned by years of living among night people. It was scarcely an innovation, although his hipster followers considered it so. Contrasted with
the young white hipsters, who were seeking emancipation from
the multiple hangups of a post-Victorian background, and, in
many cases, desperately striving to become "white Negroes,"
Charlie was a sexual revolutionary. He was not above making
sexual conquests for the sake of scoring, or, in the case of white
targets, asserting his mastery and black male force. He entered
into hundreds of affairs, most of them short-lasting. He met
very few women who were interested in him as a creative artist.

The Charlie Parker Quintet recorded for the first time in a
session for Savoy, cutting four sides (*Donna Lee*, *Chasing the
Bird*, *Cheryl*, *Buzzy*) that revealed the superb instrument
Charlie had assembled. The rhythm section was smooth and
light, even on the fastest tempi, and infinitely flexible. Miles,
improved over his *Ornithology* outing, continued to play the ensemble parts elegantly and contributed meaningful solos. *Chasing the Bird* had innovative contrapuntal lines. Soon after the
first Savoy date Charlie made a second, cutting an additional

four tracks (*Milestones, Little Willie Leaps, Half Nelson,* and *Sippin' at Bells*). The Savoy recordings achieved the unities lacking in sessions on the West Coast, where the best drummers were never available. The very stiff reeds that Charlie had used in the past had been discarded in favor of reeds in the middle ranges of hardness (2–2½). He had found ways to get results with the softer reed. There was a new smoothness in his playing, and a delicacy of sound, without any loss of brilliance.

The ambivalent feelings Charlie had developed toward Dizzy Gillespie were displayed at a concert in Carnegie Hall the night of September 29. The Gillespie big band was the featured attraction on a program designed to expose bebop to a larger public. Charlie might have received better billing had the sponsors been more confident of his reliability. He was programmed to appear only briefly, in a short set alone with Dizzy and a rhythm section drawn from the big band. A large claque of hipsters and musicians had taken over a front section at Carnegie Hall for what they expected to be a classic confrontation—the publicized Mister Bebop versus the real genius of the movement. It would be the first time Bird and Diz had played together since the Billy Berg engagement. Charlie did not appear until after the intermission. He walked onstage casually, almost indifferently, his eyes heavy-lidded, a sly smile on his face, badly dressed in an unpressed suit, his necktie twisted into one of its hard knots.

The Parker-Gillespie set at once exploded into a duel, the weapons being trumpet and saxophone, and the common ground such established bop classics as *A Night in Tunisia* and *Dizzy Atmosphere.* Sparks flew immediately. On the ensemble part of *Tunisia* Charlie played a fantastic counterpoint to the theme that would have routed a lesser musician than Gillespie. Off and running, Charlie plunged recklessly and breathtakingly into the alto break while Dizzy, no longer in his jolly mood, retired to gather his forces. After the break the saxophone chorus was played with a fierce, hard, professional brilliance. Dizzy came back with a chorus of equal quality, lustrous, chiseled, accurately articulated. The duel waxed its hottest on *Dizzy Atmosphere,* taken at an incredible tempo that left drummer Joe

Harris and pianist John Lewis scrambling frantically. There were feints, sorties, lines paraphrased half a tone off pitch, tricky gambits, musical shorthand, stopped time, lightning excursions into strange scales and keys. Parker was the aggressor, Dizzy the counter puncher. The hipster claque reacted noisily as the spirit of Minton's came to Carnegie Hall. The public was bewildered. Despite the bristling hostility that surrounded the performers, Parker's solos retained that continuity and completeness of form that marked his best work. No matter what chances he took, how fragmentary or allusive the improvisation, he was always able to resolve the line. It was one of his fire-eating nights, a display of astonishing musical powers.

The music played that night was recorded by a sound studio in an upper floor of the auditorium. From the master acetates dubs were made, then pirated, to be released as a set of three 78-rpm records on a label whimsically called Black Deuce. Titled, *A Night at Carnegie Hall—Bird and Diz in Concert*, the Black Deuce 78s were sold under counters of large record stores. Black Deuce had no address, office, or tangible management. Sales were made to stores for cash, and no records were kept of transactions. The sales were eventually stopped when an injunction was obtained against several leading jazz retailers. Eventually the masters were bought, made legal, and issued on Savoy.

Meanwhile Dial Records, a mere babe in the woods in this jungle of larceny, viewed with alarm the availability of its exclusive artist on competing labels and Charlie's willingness to record for rival concerns. After the second Savoy violation I turned the matter over to New York attorney Alan J. Berlan. When contacted, Savoy produced a contract signed November 19, 1945, a week before the *Now's the Time* session, in which Charlie guaranteed Savoy an option on his services for eight additional sides. Charlie had been silent on the matter. Savoy claimed no prior knowledge of the exclusive Parker-Dial contract and was legally blameless. The musicians' union refused to intervene. The Moe Gale agency took a dim view of Charlie's recording for either label. In Billy Shaw's view neither independent had satisfactory promotional or distribution facilities, or the clout to benefit a major artist. Shaw instructed Charlie to make no further recordings for Savoy. As to the existing, union-approved Dial contract, Shaw advised Charlie to sit that one out. The contract would expire the following spring. By then Shaw would have Charlie signed with a major label.

It appeared that Charlie had made his last record for Dial. Then Shaw's grand strategy was suddenly abandoned when another impasse between the American Federation of Musicians and the major labels led to a new recording ban. Fearing that it might drag on for several years, like the 1942 ban, Shaw reversed his tactics. It was essential that Charlie Parker have record releases to keep his name before the public. A small label would be better than none. Shaw was on the pipe to me at once. The inevitable lunch at Lindy's followed. He was a hard bargainer. There were to be no more low-budget sessions. He would let me record his artist again. Charlie was ready to record again at considerably higher fees. The Savoy breach of contract was forgotten. Plans were made to record as many sides as possible before the expiration of the AFM deadline December 30. In this manner were the final three Dial recording sessions made. They produced some of his finest performances.

The first session was made October 25 at WOR Studios, Forty-eighth and Broadway. Benefiting from experience in California, I reserved the studio from eight P.M. on and instructed the musicians to be on hand at seven. Again Charlie crossed me up. When I arrived at six-thirty he was already there. He was uptight and said he needed fifty dollars. He had instructed his contact to meet him at WOR. This made the current rumors official. "So you're back on," I said as I handed him the money. He said nothing and went into the men's room to prepare his fix. Twenty minutes later he was all smoothed out, in a "mad, blowing mood," as the Dial studio log shows. Microphones were set up to capture the sound of the Quintet as one heard it at the Three Deuces. Special care was taken to install a tiny high-frequency microphone to catch the hiss of Max Roach's cymbal, so essential a part of the new rhythm section. As the session began, the advantage of recording with a real working band was apparent. The material came from the repertoire of tunes performed nightly, their difficult ensemble parts made note perfect by constant playing. Charlie began with *Dexterity*, rhythmic and Lestorian, reminiscent of his Kansas City roots. *Bongobop* had intriguing Afro-Cuban overlays and predated by many years the Bossa Nova vogue. *The Hymn* was a tour de force, metronome 310, after the manner of his famous *Koko*, introduced by a theme played at half-time, followed by a diamond-hard alto solo. The session concluded with two elegant ballads, *All the Things You Are* and *Embraceable You*.

From the pretty, sentimental original melody of *Embraceable You* Charlie created a new and finer melody. The first three measures tell us a good deal about his musicianship. There are two phrases, connected by a typical Parker turn. The progression, in G major, is from the tonic chord to the diminished to the D-seventh chord. In the third measure the fifteenth (the root doubled) is implied, yet the phrase comes to rest on the significant note, a marvelous B-natural (the thirteenth). With that essential B, Charlie invests *Embraceable You* with his own magic. The improvisation is a good example of his use of higher intervals, the phantom notes he heard in 1938 at Wall's Chili Parlor.

Embraceable You is one of the famous ballad improvisations in fifty years of jazz discography. Was it inspired by the fix he had obtained in the washroom of the recording studio two hours earlier? On the contrary, with Charlie Parker drugs had become a necessary, indeed, functional element on his lifestyle, as vital to his existence as to the psychological freedom he needed to excite his creative force.

The session required only fifteen takes for six sides. The *Ornithology* session had required sixteen to complete four. This one had run four hours against six, a new high in efficiency. Again the studio was the scene of undistracted and concentrated creativity. Charlie's intense demands on his sidemen were accepted without a murmur. And after a performance of this kind, one was ready to forgive almost anything.

To beat the recording ban it was necessary to schedule the sessions at close intervals. The second was planned for Novem-

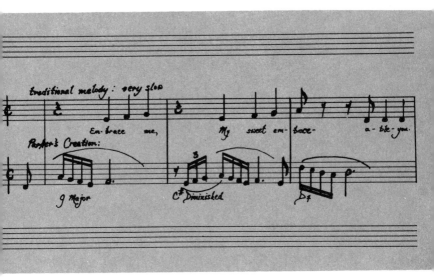

ber 4. The afternoon of that day Charlie appeared at the Dial office, 520 West 50th Street, saying that he needed one hundred and fifty dollars to pay a hotel bill. He looked ill and strung out. A check would not do, and again cash had to be raised. Charlie was an hour late for the session that night. He was in superlative form, recording three originals (*Bird Feathers*, *Scrapple From the Apple*, and *Klactoveesedstene*) and three ballads (*My Old Flame*, *Out of Nowhere*, and *Don't Blame Me*). Everything went so well that he approved the first tries on *My Old Flame* and *Don't Blame Me*. *Scrapple From the Apple* was another muscular performance like *Dexterity*. *Klactoveesedstene* opened with marchlike figures leading to the main theme. Then came fragments, bursts of notes fired into space, cryptic, disjointed, Webern-esque, but arriving by some miracle at a perfect synthesis in the final bars.

The *Klactoveesedstene* title was his own. He wrote it out one night at the Deuces on the back of a minimum charge card, offering no explanation of its meaning. When I asked, he gave me a stony stare and walked off. Was it a person, a place, an abstract idea, or a new entry in the jive lexicon? After consulting the large desk model of Webster's and after that Skeat's Etymological Dictionary, both without result, I asked a psychiatrist if she could help. She could not. I then consulted Dean Benedetti, who pointed out at once what to him was quite obvious: "Klactoveesedstene? Why, man, it's just a sound." As a rule Charlie did not bother to title his compositions. Often they were known to members of the Quintet by numbers. The Dial studio log listed them by means of a different series of master numbers, with a new set assigned each session. Until it was titled, *Klactoveesedstene* was simply Dial D–1112. Usually I dreamed up some kind of a title when it was time to release the record.

After the *Klactoveesedstene* session the Quintet left town for two weeks at El Sino in Detroit. There, sickened by a dose of bad heroin, Charlie quarreled with the lounge owner, walked out on the job, and capped the evening by throwing his saxophone out of the fourth-floor window of a hotel. The instrument was smashed beyond repair. A trouble shooter for the Gale Agency was immediately sent to Detroit and Charlie was flown back to New York. After a stormy session with Billy Shaw, Charlie promised to "straighten up and fly right." For the last time, Shaw asserted, he was forgiven. The agency advanced money to buy a new horn, the latest model from Selmer et Cie., Paris.

The new horn was truly a masterpiece of the instrument maker's craft. In the middle and lower registers there was a new richness and roundness of sound. Trombonist J. J. Johnson was added for the December 17 session. Charlie recorded five originals (*Drifting on a Reed*, *Charlie's Wig*, *Bird Feathers*, *Crazeology*, and *Quasimodo*) and one ballad (*How Deep Is the Ocean*). The performances represented a new level of virtuosity. That night there was none of the joy of discovery that had made previous sessions memorable. The playing was smooth, fast, and a little perfunctory. The six sides were reeled off in two hours and forty minutes.

The *How Deep Is the Ocean* session ended Charlie's relations with Dial. The contract had produced seven sessions and thirty-four sides—and had been breached four times, not counting the bootleg Black Deuce issues. For the last three Dial sessions he had received a total of twenty-seven hundred dollars for nine hours work, plus mechanical and composer royalties. The last Dial session was the only one I did not personally supervise. December 17 found me bedridden with the flu. Two days before, I had supervised the rehearsal, required because J. J. Johnson had been added to the Quintet. The actual session was nominally supervised by my wife, Dorothy. That the playing was polished and, for Charlie, perfunctory, seemed to have little to do with my own absence or the presence of J. J. Johnson, easily the best trombonist of the new music. Charlie's mood had simply undergone a passing alteration. That evening virtuosity lay at a high point on his curve, and the creative force at a lower one.

Many jazz critics and collectors feel that Parker's finest recording in commercial studios was completed as the year 1947 came to a close. Most of these performances were for Dial and Savoy. In both instances the directors of artists and repertoire, Teddy Reig and myself, had similar ideas as to how jazz talent should be handled. We rejected the notion then popular, and still more popular today (Don Schlitten of RCA and Onyx Records is a notable exception), of attempting to act as musical directors of events in the studio. Neither of us believed in forcing upon the artist musical material chosen for commercial or personal reasons, or fellow musicians not of his own choosing. Perhaps we were singularly blessed in not being able to read music. In our experience good record sessions were put together well before the first musician arrived at the studio. There we endeavored to provide an emotional climate conducive to the creative process. This seemed to me the only logical way to record music so wholly dependent upon improvisation, and I am sure that Teddy Reig would agree, even though he sought similar objectives by different means, as he did at the famous *Now's the Time* session. Both of us believed so strongly in Charlie's talent, and heard that talent at full cry so often in the sterile confines of the cabaret that we were able to bend a great deal of effort toward containing it on the medium of the phonograph record (in 1947 tape had not yet arrived). At the end of a successful session we both had the feeling that by foresight and luck we had preserved for posterity a little of that prodigal excess of musicality. Unfortunately those who had contractual and commercial control of Charlie's talent in subsequent years had their own and altogether different ideas of the director's function.

Despite Billy Shaw's warnings, Charlie could not resist the temptation to sneak in an unofficial session for an independent label on the afternoon of Christmas Day in Detroit, where he was filling a return engagement at El Sino. Four sides were made with the Quintet at United Sound studios that afternoon, when most Americans were sitting down to a Christmas dinner. Charlie also recorded two long tracks, *The Bird* and *Repetition*, for Norman Granz with the twenty-five piece Neal Hefti Orchestra. Then Charlie left on a cross-country tour with Jazz at the Philharmonic.

It was a hectic trip of one-nighters, flights at odd hours, and tight schedules. Charlie did not miss any of the concerts until the tour reached the West Coast, but he was frequently late. In Los Angeles Charlie disappeared completely. While Sarah Vaughan extended her set to cover the deficiency and Norman Granz underwent the first of many frights to come at finding his featured saxophonist missing, Charlie and Doris took themselves a brief Mexican holiday. They returned to Los Angeles in time to importune Granz for an advance and rejoin the barnstormers for the next leg of the itinerary, and duly reported that they had been married by a Mexican justice in Tijuana, Baja California. There was no thought given to one significant loose end in Charlie's life, the marriage to Geraldine, and whether or not he had taken the trouble to divorce his second wife. Perhaps he had forgotten himself.

Bird at Work

The year 1948 began with the announcement that Charlie had won his first poll, in *Metronome*. Miles Davis and Max Roach were climbing to the top of the trumpet and drum divisions. The Quintet had more class than any other group in jazz. Momentum built up over the years was making itself felt. The Moe Gale office booked the Quintet out over the lounge circuit at ever-increasing fees. To dig Bird was *in*. People were intrigued by his sabbatical in California. The stay at Camarillo was seen as a self-imposed sanctuary. Here he was, in their neighborhood club, articulating imperious messages over the saxophone. Listening required real concentration. Nothing glib came out of the horn. Every solo was played with high seriousness. The saxophone cried of love, rage, and black power. The elements heard in black music since the first rural bluesman had drifted to the urban ghettos had been contained and contemporized. There was nothing of Louis Armstrong's archaic minstrelry. Nor of Lester's bittersweet romanticism. This was the real grit that Bird put down. An evening with Charlie Parker was not an entertainment. Listening to Charlie was a demanding, moving, often chilling experience—like an evening with Lenny Bruce.

The world's hippest musician still dressed like a Vine Street hustler. When Doris saw to it, the suits were pressed and the linen fresh. When Doris did not see to it, the suits and shirts appeared to have been slept in. Although Charlie could be charming offstage, he seldom smiled while on it. There he was deadly serious, a bundle of purposeful energy. Requests were ignored unless they happened to call for a tune he liked or had recorded. Even then it was scarcely recognizable, for it was played with new variations. Psychologically Charlie seemed incapable of repeating himself. One improvisation simply led to another. Each set was played as if he were trying to shake down the walls of a modern Jericho. After he had gone for several weeks at this killing pace, he would be exhausted, become difficult, unreliable, or revert to his bad-boy style.

As a master of ceremonies, a chore which as a bandleader he could not very well avoid, although he hated it, Charlie traffiicked in his own kind of Biercean humor. His arch rival, Dizzy, had an easy way with the public and a ready wit. Once, when Dizzy played a college date at an Ivy League school, an extra chair was needed on the crowded bandstand and a crewcut undergraduate had hastened to hand one up from the floor. Dizzy smiled graciously and said, "Mighty white of you, old man." Charlie couldn't do that. Nor was he developing into the amiable bandleader the Gale Agency had expected. Charlie worked from a set of stock remarks considered hilarious by the cognoscenti, but less well understood by the public and sometimes resented by them, not to mention night club operators. These were delivered in a George Arliss voice and couched in stilted, stiff-collar phrases. As the set opened the crowd would be told: "Ladies and gentlemen, the management of —— Club has gone to *enormous* expense to bring you the Charlie Parker Quintet." The weighting of the word made the management sound like pikers. Patrons would take a second look at their watered-down one-dollar drinks and wonder if they were being taken. Sets began without further ado, usually without bothering to introduce sidemen or numbers. One night Charlie was approached by a campaign worker for a national cancer drive and took it upon himself to announce that the management would start things off by making a contribution. Having already made one, the management was silent. "All right, folks, skip it," Charlie said brusquely. "The house is cheap!" When enthusiastic applause followed a good performance he would tell the audience, "Thank you, ladies and gentlemen, ordinary applause will suffice." The groundwork for later patronization of the public, to be made a fine art by Miles Davis, was being laid.

The Argyle Lounge in Chicago, the liveliest club on the lounge circuit, and one of the best paying, was the scene of the jazz scandal of 1948. Charlie finished a set and placed his horn on the top of the piano. Then he stepped off the bandstand, walked past the tables on the main floor, into the foyer, entered the pay telephone booth, closed the door, and proceeded to urinate on the floor. The yellow stream gushed forth as from a stallion, its pool dark and foaming as it spread under the door of the telephone booth and into the foyer. He came from the booth laughing. There was no explanation or apology. Was he mindlessly relieving himself? Was he urinating on the public, on Billy Shaw, Dizzy Gillespie, or the operator of the Argyle Lounge, or was he too impatient to wait his turn at the woefully inadequate, one-at-a-time toilet at the Argyle? Perhaps he didn't know himself.

For urban black people of his generation, Charlie was a genuine culture hero. The revolutionary nature of his music was explicit. He had rephrased Negro music without altering its essential truth and purity. Implicit in his lifestyle was defiance of the white establishment. Iconoclast, breaker of rules, master of the put-on, Bird was the first jazz musician who carried the battle to the enemy. The telephone booth incident, the act of throwing his saxophone out of a hotel window, walking into the sea wearing a new suit, standing up the promoter of a Paris jazz concert, drinking sixteen double whiskies in two hours, eating twenty hamburgers at a sitting, riding a policeman's horse into Charlie's Tavern in New York, the put-on of a prominent British music journalist, the patronizing way he took his pleasure with any white girl who offered herself—every episode in the cumulative legend of the Bird, however ineffectual and childish, was seen as a blow struck against the forces of oppression. In the mid-Forties there was no Martin Luther King, Jr., no Malcolm X, Eldridge Cleaver, Angela Davis, or Shirley Chisholm. In a sense Charlie was a forerunner of those militant figures of the political arena. He was completely non-political, in fact never in his lifetime so much as cast a ballot. To do so would have been camp. If Lester Young was the first hipster, Charlie Parker was the first angry black man in music. Because he was ahead of his time, he bore the burdens of loneliness and frustration. The futility of the blows he directed at the establishment did much to encourage his dependence upon heroin and alcohol, adding to his loneliness and accelerating an inner drive toward self-destruction. In a mechanistic, militaristic society anyone, black or white, who has real talent and new ideas is in trouble. If he is black, he is in still greater trouble. And, if he is ahead of his time, he lives in peril. This sense of peril was always with Charlie. He kept it under control by his skillful mix of play-acting, stance-taking, and the magic of his playing. In his day he was almost alone among the leading figures of jazz who, in their social and political orientation, looked to him for leadership. In the post-Parker generation would come the declared and alienated militants, men like Miles Davis, John Coltrane, Albert Ayler, and Archie Shepp—the children of Bird.

The telephone booth incident necessitated another emergency trip for the Gale trouble shooter. The management of the Argyle Lounge was mollified; a new attraction was booked in at a bargain rate and the Quintet closed out. Back in New York there was another stormy scene at the agency office. Billy

Shaw worked himself into a towering rage, accused Charlie of ingratitude, and threatened him with an industry-wide black-listing. (An accumulation of such stormy scenes with the temperamental artists in whom Shaw specialized would result in his death from a heart attack before he was fifty.) Didn't Charlie want to drive a Cadillac like others in the music business, see his name in footlights, own income property on Long Island? Why did Charlie think Billy Shaw had tried so long and patiently to build him as a major attraction, using all of his skills and cunning, all of the resources of the prestigious Moe Gale office? Billy Shaw was fighting for Charlie's commercial soul. The Napoleonlike figure of the booking business paced the floor, waved arms, wrung hands, pounded the desk. Once again, Charlie was forgiven for the last time. But there was a penalty. His out-of-town bookings were cancelled and the Quintet sent to the Siberia of decaying Fifty-second Street for a stand at the Onyx Club. Charlie found Lawrence 88 Keyes, the one-time leader of the Deans of Swing, working as an intermission pianist down the block. He would leave the job between sets to "hear my hometown play again."

Just why alcoholism and narcotic addiction have been the classic occupational hazards of the jazz business, and cirrhosis of the liver its most common occupational disease, has always intrigued the outsider. From 1900, when jazz began in New Orleans, until 1950, when jazz began to break out of the night club and into the concert hall and festival grounds, the conditions under which it was played varied little. Barrelhouses, honky-tonks, joints, lounges—these were mere passing names for cabarets, the locale where jazzmen worked. They were operated by gangsters who offered music or flesh to bring in the business, and profited from the sale of liquor. If one adds to such cheap, overstimulating places of employment the other significant factors—long hours, the reversed hours of work and sleep, the insecurity of the musician's trade, and the pressure of competition, not to mention the frustration of essaying the role of creative artist in such an environment—the appetite for toxicants becomes understandable.

In the good old New Orleans days marijuana was as common as Bull Durham tobacco, and cocaine could be bought across the counter of any corner drug store. Alcohol in its various forms remained the most accessible and usually the cheapest of intoxicants from the beginnings in New Orleans until 1940. Heroin did not come into vogue until the war years. That Lester Young was an alcoholic and Charlie Parker a drug addict was simply a matter of the generation gap. Heroin packed a powerful wallop. It was a trip on a jet airplane instead of one on a plane with piston engines. Ironically, heroin was easier to manage on the bandstand than alcohol. It didn't make a musician sloppy, the way alcohol did. Heroin was better and had greater staying power. Charlie said many times that he played better off the stuff (*Cool Blues*) than on it (*Klactoveesedstene*). In theory this was fine. In practice it didn't work for him. When Charlie was strung out he was sick, therefore unable to play. When he was high he played well, often brilliantly.

Booze and dope were the jazzman's escape hatches. Heroin was a hip, expensive substitute for alcohol. The high incidence of heroin users during the Forties can be explained in terms of a vogue—heroin as the "new thing." Its popularity in the bebop period was enhanced by Charlie's example. No other musician challenged his record as a sustained user, though many tried. Many jazzmen, then and now prominent, were one-time addicts. Those still on the scene have long since dispensed with the habit. Of those who tried to run with Charlie Parker, most succumbed to their addiction. For starters there are the tragic cases of Fats Navarro, Serge Chaloff, and Sonny Berman, the brilliant young trumpeter who starred in the Woody Herman Orchestra, and whose death from an overdose at the age of twenty-three robbed the jazz world of a most promising talent. "To play like Bird, you have to do like Bird!"—such was the false counsel offered by the folklore of jazz in the turbulent Forties. But no one played like Bird, and few could stand the pace. Bird, with his strong, thick-boned, deep-chested body, raced and reeled his way through life at a pace that would have killed a lesser man before reaching his majority, embracing every new kick and experience as if there were no tomorrow. It

was evident to anyone who knew Charlie that a man as gifted
with insight could not fail to observe the ominous signs of personal malaise induced by his steady consumption of heroin
which, by 1948, had reached epic proportions. That Charlie was
never able to make a meaningful break with his addiction was
a matter of lifestyle, and despair. In spite of his successes and
growing prestige Charlie saw no future for the music he
played, or for his race in America. To live once, and to the limit
—that was his game plan.

Early in April I arranged a party at the Onyx Club for
Marshall Stearns and Sidney Finkelstein. Stearns was then associate professor of English at Cornell University, a Chaucer
scholar, authority on English poets Robert Henryson and Dylan
Thomas, and America's leading jazz historian. Stearns had
founded the first jazz club in America, at Yale, where John
Hammond had been a protégé. Finkelstein was the principal
Marxist jazz critic, and author of the recently published *Jazz:
A People's Music*. The time seemed auspicious to expose these
eminences to an intimate hearing of the new music. Both had
worldwide prestige and contacts. After months of urging,
Stearns had made the trip from Ithaca to hear Charlie live for
the first time. Finkelstein, something of a recluse, seldom visited night clubs. Both were eager to meet Charlie.

I found Charlie chastened but hardly crushed. He had
pulled a respectable audience to The Street that night. In the
house were Georgie Auld, Milt Jackson, Chubby Jackson, Barry
Ulanov, Leonard Feather, and Billie Holiday, just released
after a six-month sentence for narcotics, looking tragic and
lovely in a striking white fur wrap. The Quintet was playing
opposite the pleasing Margie Hyams Quartet. After the first
set Charlie came to the table "to meet the wiggy cats" who
wrote books about jazz. Charlie very shrewdly and quickly
sized up both men. Finkelstein he ignored. The Marxist critic
was tough and hardboiled and, as Charlie could see, came from
a proletarian background like his own. Charlie figured that
Finkelstein, like himself, was a man on the make, but with a
new hype. Charlie concentrated on the patrician Stearns, born

to wealth, educated at Harvard and Yale. Much to Stearns's discomfort, Charlie insisted on calling him Professor. When Stearns went to the men's room, Charlie followed. As Stearns stood at the urinal, Charlie stood immediately behind, and said: "Look in the mirror, Professor."

When Stearns looked up, their eyes met. "Here we are, Professor," Charlie said philosophically. "You and me. Two human beings. You started at the top and I started at the bottom . . ." Then he explained that he was urgently in the need of money and asked for a loan of fifty dollars, a sum that Stearns would never have dreamed of bringing to a night club. As Stearns fumbled to rearrange his clothing, wash his hands, and extricate himself from this strange and embarrassing situation, Charlie began to lower the amount of the requested loan. Down it went—fifty, forty, twenty-five, fifteen, ten dollars. When it reached five dollars, Stearns came across. Later I took Charlie to task for his actions, pointing out that Dr. Stearns was in a position to advance his career, and that his own earnings were probably in excess of an associate English professor's salary at Cornell University. Charlie grinned at me.

"Coming on like Billy Shaw now," Charlie told me. "I only hit him for a nickle note, man!" Then he tried me for two hundred dollars. I refused. He fished a five-cent piece from his pocket and held it up. "That's my hype," he said. He put the coin back in his pocket and clipped the new saxophone to his neckpiece. Then, with the evening's squares put in their place, he whisked through a brilliant set. After the set he walked past us into Fifty-second Street as if the table were empty.

Practical jokes were part of the mosiac of his lifestyle. At six A.M. one morning he appeared at Tadd Dameron's apartment and began ringing the bell persistently. Dead with sleep, Dameron came to the door and opened the peephole. "Open up, man!" Charlie told the pianist. Dameron fumbled with the burglar-proof bar, standard equipment on Harlem apartments even in those days, and opened the door. "Got a match?" Charlie asked casually. Dameron rummaged in the dark hallway and found one. Charlie lit a cigarette, nodded his thanks, and walked downstairs to a waiting cab.

Charlie was passed over when invitations were issued to American jazzmen for the annual Paris Jazz Fair, the most important European festival. The *New Yorker* magazine published a lengthy profile of Dizzy Gillespie, an indication that Dizzy had arrived as a figure of interest to the American white middle class. Dizzy was depicted as a whimsical sprite, but really crazy like a fox, actually an astute business man. On the advice of his tax accountant, Dizzy was buying an apartment house in Queens. *Life* magazine carried a photo essay on the bebop movement. Dizzy was described as the chief architect of the new sounds. Incredibly, Charlie Parker was not mentioned. The two magazine pieces added to his bitterness and the hostility he felt toward his former collaborator. The architect of the new music was himself, as everyone in the jazz business knew. But Dizzy was attractive copy and he was not.

Shortly after the Stearns party, the Dewey Square Hotel was raided by the local narks. Charlie escaped arrest, narrowly preserving his record of never having been busted. When he returned several days later to pick up his personal effects, he was detained and questioned. Charlie was warned by the police that they were waiting for his next slip. There were veiled hints that his cabaret card—a police license without which no performer could work in New York City—might be in jeopardy. Charlie and Doris moved from the questionable environs of Dewey Square into the Marden, a third-rate hotel in the Times Square area. Restaurants, amusements, places of employment, the Moe Gale office were all within easy walking distance.

Charlie went on what he described as a "health kick." Regular meals were taken at the Automat or Toffinetti's. No stimulants stronger than beer or benzedrine inhalers were used. Charlie spent a great deal of time in his room, bored, playing with the cat and arguing with Doris. He attended endless movies, gangster, western, and horror films featured in double and triple bills at the old theaters on Forty-second Street. His health improved, and soon he was again playing at his best. As a reward Billy Shaw pulled the Quintet out of Fifty-second Street and booked it into the Royal Roost.

The Roost was the first of the Broadway jazz palaces that

would bring about the eclipse of Fifty-second Street. Originally a cellar restaurant specializing in fried chicken, it had been taken over by Ralph Watkins, former operator of Kelly's Stables, and converted into a new kind of jazz club. Among its innovations were a seventy-five-cent door charge, the first in New York, a milk bar for those too young to drink alcoholic beverages, and a bullpen or bleachers, where customers could sit and listen as long as they liked without having to pay a cover charge. The Royal Roost was large, comfortable, and attractively lighted. Artists had decent dressing rooms. A long bar running the length of one side encouraged fraternization of musicians and jazz fans. Watkins's venture was an immediate success and established a precedent for more lavish clubs to follow—the Aquarium, Basin Street, Bop City, and Birdland.

When Charlie arrived opening night he found Babs Gonzales, a jivey singer associated with the Three Bips and a Bop, waiting for him. A volatile man with a reputation for occasional violence, Babs had a bone to pick. During the Dewey Square raids Charlie had stayed several nights in Babs' pad and left unannounced, with two of Babs' suits, which he had pawned. Charlie greeted his colleague affably. The pawn tickets were in his wallet. He produced them and said, "Babs, my man, the threads are in for ten apiece. Here's a twenty to bail them out and a dime note for your trouble." Then they went to the bar for a drink. Babs got on Charlie about the dope habit, saying that anyone with Charlie's musical ability and prestige ought to have the will power to stop using heroin. Charlie stared back at the singer and said quietly, "Wait until everybody gets rich off your style and you don't have any bread, then lecture me about drugs."

Charlie was playing so well at the Roost that it seemed a shame not to record him. Teddy Reig suggested two dates, clandestine of course, since the ban was still in effect. They were held at Nola Studios with two substitutes in the rhythm section, bassist Curly Russell and pianist John Lewis. Charlie cut eight sides, his last for Savoy, *Barbados*, *Ah-Leu-Cha*, *Constellation*, and *Parker's Mood*; and *Perhaps*, *Marmaduke*, *Klaunstance*, and *Bird Gets the Worm*. *Ah-Leu-Cha* was a fur-

ther exploration of the contrapuntal methods used on *Chasin'
the Bird*. *Parker's Mood*, the saxophone alone with the rhythm
section, was a triumph. *Parker's Mood* ranks with Charlie's
blues classics, *Hootie Blues*, *Slam Slam Blues*, *Now's the Time*,
Cool Blues, and *Relaxin' at Camarillo*. The saxophone line
crosses all of the classic blues intersections. There are headlong
plunges and airborne ascents. Slides, slurs, notes intensified by
means of false fingerings, sixteenth and thirty-second notes,
clusters of triplets and quintuplets, grace notes, and quivering
commas make up its attractive topography.

With *Parker's Mood* Charlie had made his last record for
an independent. When the differences between the AFM and
the manufacturers were settled in November, Billy Shaw
signed Charlie Parker to a one year's contract with Mercury, a
subsidiary of Metro-Goldwyn-Mayer, for whom Norman Granz
was in charge of jazz recording. For the Mercury date Charlie
was surrounded by musical directors, arrangers, spare engineers, and assistant recording supervisors, with Granz calling
the shots. It had been decided to record Charlie in a new and
more commercial context. Since Afro-Cuban music was in
vogue at the moment, Granz had hired the Machito Orchestra,
the reigning favorite at the Palladium Ballroom, the Savoy of
the rumba addict. Standing in front of its noisy sections Charlie
recorded two long solos, *No Noise* and *Mango Mangue*. Publicized as "Charlie Parker Plays South of the Border," the records were rushed onto the market. They made interesting listening but to many of Charlie's fans seemed musical stunts.
Gone were the days when Charlie acted as his own conductor,
contractor, composer, bandleader, and chief soloist. As soon as
the first records were on the market Norman Granz took Charlie out on another Jazz at the Philharmonic tour. Disc jockey
appearances were used to tie in with promotion of the new recordings. This time Granz hired a private detective to take care
of Charlie, beat off dope pushers, and see that the star of the
show was on time and ready to perform. Within a few days
Charlie had the guard conned and scoring for him.

After the road trip with Jazz at the Philharmonic, Charlie
opened December 10 at the Roost. The morale of the Quintet

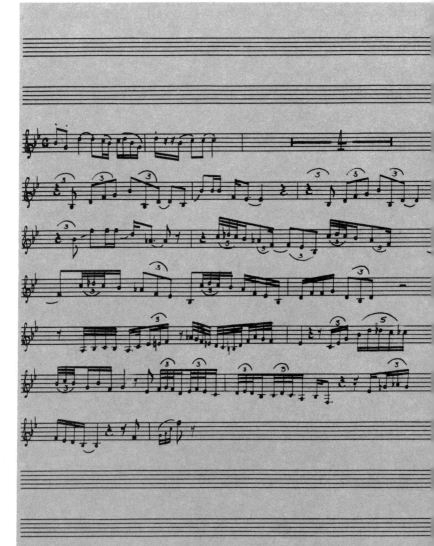

had suffered by Charlie's absences. Al Haig had replaced Duke Jordan on piano. Miles and Bird were hardly speaking. I caught the opening night and watched Charlie try to adjust from the concert hall to the intimate jazz club. The opening set was delayed while Charlie ostentatiously and in slow motion lighted and smoked a cigarette. A toy balloon was produced and inflated, and its air allowed to escape into the microphone. A toy cap pistol was used to shoot the piano player. Charlie was gaining weight. His jacket bunched over his shoulders. Christmas week the internal tensions within the group came to the surface. Complaining to me that "Bird makes you feel one foot high," Miles Davis stalked off the stand, not in an ordinary huff, but never to return. Max Roach quit the same night. When Charlie took his troubles to the agency, Shaw advised him not to worry. The woods were full of sidemen. Miles was replaced by McKinley Dorham, a sound if unspectacular trumpet player who said the appointment crowned an ambition of ten years. Max was replaced by Joe Harris, a big band drummer, formerly with the Gillespie Orchestra, not particularly suitable for a small combo.

Charlie forgot his troubles with the Quintet when the results of the *Metronome* poll were announced. He had won for the second straight year, this time by a large margin. He was also nominated for the alto sax chair in the all-star orchestra being assembled by *Metronome* for a special RCA Victor record. On Monday, January 3, 1949, Charlie reported to the RCA studios in midtown Manhattan for the session. The personnel read like a Who's Who of jazz: Dizzy Gillespie, Miles Davis, Fats Navarro, trumpets; J. J. Johnson and Kai Winding, trombones; Buddy de Franco, clarinet; Charlie Parker, alto saxophone; Charlie Ventura, tenor saxophone; Ernie Caceres, baritone saxophone; Lennie Tristano, piano; Billy Bauer, guitar; Eddie Safranski, bass; Shelly Manne, drums. The superstars were batoned by Pete Rugolo, arranger for the Stan Kenton Orchestra. The concentration of talents made it impossible for anyone to stretch out. Solos were so brief that they had the quality of curtain calls, but record buyers would get to hear everybody in jazz that year on a single record. The Metronome All-Stars recorded two sides, *Victory Ball* and *Overtime*. Each musician sat behind a music stand on which his name appeared in large letters, and the group was thus photographed for RCA publicity releases. Charlie Parker had arrived as a *figura* in the commercial music world.

21

Birdland

Early in 1949 Billy Shaw, having built up a strong position in the booking business and acquired a following of artists rapidly rising in popularity, resigned as vice president of the Moe Gale Agency and launched Billy Shaw Artists, Inc. With him Shaw took those who had been under his personal management. For each of his stars Shaw had a New Year's bonus, a booking in a desirable spot at better money, a new record contract. For Charlie he had a special plum—an invitation to the International Paris Jazz Festival. "Stay with me, Bird," he told Charlie, "and tend to the store. I'll put your name in lights all over the world."

Charlie set about the tedious business of securing passports, visas, and smallpox certificates with boyish enthusiasm. When he recorded next for Mercury he titled two of the sides *Passport* and *Visa*. They were not particularly good sides, but that wasn't his fault. Granz had restored the Quintet to grace but could not stop meddling with its personnel. To the pure sound of the five original instruments he added the rambunctious tailgate trombone of Tommy Turk, a recent crowd-pleaser on the Jazz at the Philharmonic tour. Ensemble lines were hopelessly blurred, and the quality of the music coarsened. It was like adding a tuba to a Beethoven quartet.

For the trans-Atlantic plane trip the Parkers joined Howard McGhee, Lips Page, Flip Phillips, Tadd Dameron, and others invited to the festival. Tall, thin, looking rather out of it, Doris was seen walking several paces behind the men, carrying the saxophone on its journey back to its homeland. The party arrived a day before the concerts, and Charlie at once made the round of Montmartre jazz clubs. French jazz musicians received him warmly. They were familiar with his style from records they had imported. Charlie was lionized; he sat in, jammed with French jazz musicians, lost sleep, and sampled the French heroin willingly supplied by new friends. He was bearded in his hotel room by a reporter for *Melody Maker*, the leading British music magazine. The writer had a lengthy list of questions on Charlie's analysis of bebop, his opinion as to whether it was actually jazz (British tastes were still mired in pre-war concepts), his evaluation of various traditional jazzmen, Louis Armstrong, Sidney Bechet, and others. Charlie was charmed by the Englishman's accent and studied it closely during the interview. To each of the questions he answered by reading a stanza from *The Rubaiyat of Omar Khayyam*. Finally the *Melody Maker* man gave up and wrote that Charlie Parker in person made no more sense than Charlie Parker the musician. English readers remained as ignorant as ever of the new style. When the reporter asked Charlie about his religious affiliation, Charlie replied, "I am a devout musician."

The concert took place in Salle Pleyel. Traditional jazz was represented by Sidney Bechet, the middle period by Lips Page, and the new wave by the Charlie Parker Quintet. Bechet was the hit of the festival. Playing nothing more harmonically advanced than seventh chords, sticking to such riverboat classics as *High Society*, filling the Salle Pleyel with his great skirling tone, the New Orleans veteran had the crowds dancing in the aisles. Lips Page was warmly applauded. Charlie's set was pure, definitive, almost private, too intimate for the huge music hall. It was warmly received by the avant garde claque and elicited from reviewers such comments as *"formidable"* and *"succes d'estime."*

Charlie jammed after the concert at the Club Germaine, where author-musician Boris Vian was master of ceremonies. Jean Paul Sartre, then first reaching the height of his fame, visited the club, and Vian asked the existentialist philosopher if he wanted to meet Charlie Parker. "Yes, of course," Sartre replied. "He interests me." Introductions were arranged. Charlie told Sartre, "I'm very glad to have met you, Mr. Sartre. I like your playing very much." According to Vian, Sartre stared at Charlie with expressionless dark eyes. But he remained for two sets of the music. Such was the oblique encounter between two men who, despite wide differences in race and culture, were leading exponents of the existentialist way of life, one on a theoretical, the other on a practical level.

When an admirer presented Charlie with a rose, he calmly ate the petals and stuck the stalk in his buttonhole. The next day Charlie met Charles Delaunay, son of the French painter, publisher of the world's first jazz discography (1938), and director of the French jazz magazine *Jazz Hot*. Charlie also met Andre Hodeir, then writing *Jazz: Its Evolution and Essence*. These cultured, intellectual men treated Charlie with the respect they felt was due an important artist. The reception given jazzmen in Europe was far different from that prevailing in America. The music was taken seriously, not as mere entertainment. The critics who covered the festival for the Paris papers were the same critics who reviewed important recitals, symphony concerts, and operas. New jazz records were reviewed with the same seriousness as new books. In Europe dark skins were a mark of distinction rather than a cause for suspicion and contempt.

Charlie had a long talk with Kenny Clarke, who had established a permanent residence in Paris and was planning to become a French citizen. They had not exchanged anything more than a "What happening, man?" since the old days at Minton's. Clarke had matured, both as a man and a musician. He was doing well as a radio and recording artist. He conducted a school for young drummers, lived in a suburb of Paris with a beautiful woman, attended concerts and art shows. He had come to definite conclusions about the status of the black artist in America. America had no respect for the artist. There was no solution of the race problem in the foreseeable future. "Bird, you're slowly and surely committing suicide over there," Clarke told Charlie. "So are Billie Holiday and many others. Come over here and *live*. You can stay with me until you get straight. You may never make a hundred thousand a year, but you'll be around a long time and people will appreciate your music. Over here you will be treated as an artist. The French understand these things." Clarke asked Charlie to think it over carefully.

Charlie returned to New York with a new opinion of himself and his music, and a determination to return to Europe. His marriage to Doris was breaking up, and he was dating Chan Richardson again. Billy Shaw was delighted with the results of the trip and had the reviews translated and included in Charlie's press book. According to the agent big plans were in the making. Shaw called them "colossal" but gave no hint as to their nature. For the present he wanted Charlie to reorganize the Quintet and mark time at the Onyx Club, where he could be pulled out on short notice. McKinley Dorham had left and the drummer's chair was open. Charlie hired a fast, young percussionist, Roy Haynes, and Red Rodney, a young trumpeter, excellent men who very nearly made good the loss of Miles and Max.

The Mercury contract was renewed under favorable terms. Granz had a new idea.* For the next session he would back

* Norman Granz, Billy Shaw, and Charlie Parker himself are given various roles in hatching the Bird with Strings idea. Parker had toyed with the idea of a quasi-symphonic background for his improvisations ever since Dizzy Gillespie had divulged similar plans a year or two earlier. There was no doubt that Granz and Shaw welcomed the commercial possibilities of the format.

Charlie with a studio orchestra of strings and woodwinds. It would be the most impressive presentation of a jazz artist in the entire history of recording: Charlie Parker with Strings. On November 3 Charlie recorded in the Mercury studios with a chamber orchestra hand-picked from the best studio musicians in New York, among them Bronislaw Gimpel and Mitch Miller. The chamber orchestra consisted of three violins, viola, cello, harp, oboe, English horn, and a three-piece jazz rhythm section. Charlie was proud and pleased to find himself in such distinguished company. At once he began talking about his new group with "the cats from Koussevitsky's band" (the New York Philharmonic Orchestra, then under the direction of Serge Koussevitsky). Charlie recorded *Just Friends, Everything Happens to Me, April in Paris, Summertime, I Didn't Know What Time It Was,* and *If I Should Lose You.*

The ballads were well played, and the work of the men in the string and woodwind sections of a very high standard. Other aspects of the session were less favorable. The scores by Jimmy Carroll were glib and without distinction. Charlie was overawed by a display of musicianship that was nothing more than routine for good legitimate professionals. But he felt that he had achieved a peak, recorded his best session, and made jazz respectable.

Just Friends was the best of the several sides. The alto saxophone soars majestically over the lush background. Its tone is brilliant and its virtuosity compelling. Enough of the original melody remains to sustain the interest of the man in the street. But the strength that Charlie had drawn from Miles and Max, and the freedom that he had enjoyed within the intimate, flexible setting of the Quintet, so essential to inspiration and real improvisation, had been lost.

Soon after the *Just Friends* session Charlie was called into the Shaw office and given the news about a new Broadway jazz palace to eclipse all others. Licensing and financing problems had delayed its opening, originally scheduled for September, but now the obstacles had been overcome and all was ready for a gala opening the week before the Christmas holidays. The new club was located at 1678 Broadway, near Fifty-third Street, and Shaw suggested that they walk over and look at it.

The new club, on which finishing touches were being applied by workmen, was impressive. Carpeted stairs led from Broadway to a landing with a checkroom and ticket booth. The club would operate on an admission policy, like the Roost. Another short flight led to the main room. The new club would accommodate four hundred persons. It would be the biggest and finest jazz club in the world. There were tables, booths, a big bar, and a bull pen. The booths were covered in imitation leather. The stage was large enough for a full-sized orchestra. There was a new piano. At the back of the room a sound studio had been installed behind thick plate glass. The well-known disk jockey Symphony Sid Torin had been engaged to broadcast his popular show nightly from the premises. Each night thirty minutes would be broadcast live from the bandstand. The walls were decorated with huge oil paintings in oval frames. They were larger-than-life portraits of the celebrities of the music world—Dizzy, Sarah, Eckstine, Torin, Max Roach, Bud Powell, and, occupying a place in the center, Charlie Parker himself. It had been drawn from an old publicity photograph showing him smiling boyishly over the curved end of a saxophone.

"Well," said Billy Shaw. "What do you think?"

"It's out'a sight," Charlie said. "Do I get to play in here?"

"We're going to open with six bands. I'm booking the entire package. Naturally you'll be here. And we'll do better than that! Did you see the bird cages?"

Charlie could see a number of empty cages hanging from the ceiling. There were twenty or thirty of them.

"There will be tame finches in every one of those cages," Shaw told him. "And a talking mynah bird in the one over the bar. Birds," Shaw said. Shaw took Charlie affectionately by the arm and led the way back upstairs. They crossed to the opposite side of Broadway. Now Charlie was able to see the large sign slung from a crane and about to be jockeyed into place over the entrance. The neon letters said: "BIRDLAND. THE JAZZ CORNER OF THE WORLD."

It was a signal honor for a jazz musician. When the owners

of Birdland contemplated the idea of naming the club after a practicing jazz musician, there had been no one else to consider. Big names of the past no longer held any box office allure. Of the contemporaries none, not even Dizzy Gillespie, possessed Parker's charisma, or could lend the weight necessary to launch a club that would in fact be the Jazz Corner of the World for two decades. Parker had dominated jazz since 1940, when he first appeared with the Jay McShann Orchestra, prompting veteran jazzman Cootie Williams to remark that Parker's influence as an innovator had exceeded that of Louis Armstrong. In Cootie's words, "Louis changed all the brass players around, but after Bird all of the instruments had to change—drums, piano, bass, trombones, trumpets, saxophones, everything." Before Charlie's time jazz had been heard in ballrooms as a music for dancers. With his advent jazz had moved from the larger arena of the ballroom to the intimate setting of the lounge. There it was no longer danced to, but listened to, and for the first time taken seriously as a musical genre.

Charlie's accomplishments were many. He had revealed new dimensions in saxophone playing, enabling the horn to complete its evolution from a fattener of orchestral textures to the most expressive of instruments. Charlie updated the timeless blues song, and contributed some of its finest performances. He had metamorphosed the Tin Pan Alley ballad into a tightly knit, often recondite composition based on the idea of the Kansas City riff, a repeated melodic figure underlined by a strong rhythmic pattern. With perfect taste and intuition he had abstracted the body of music before his time, purging it of anachronisms and irrelevancies, and endowed it with a compelling vocabulary. Almost every post-Parker innovation has been based on something of his own, for example the free-form passages heard on *Bird at St. Nicks* that lead to John Coltrane, and other musical signposts that point to the modal, jet-stream style of Ornette Coleman and the expanded tonal idiom of Eric Dolphy. A saxophonist, he was the inspiration of Clifford Brown, the most promising trumpeter after Roy Eldridge, killed in his twenty-sixth year in an auto accident. Parker's music was the alpha and omega of Miles Davis's trumpet

style and musical system. Even recent, controversial, icono-
clastic improvisers—Albert Ayler, Archie Shepp, and Sonny
Simmons—have their roots in Charlie Parker. Russell Procope,
forty-year veteran of the Duke Ellington Orchestra and a fine
alto saxophonist in his own right, said, "A Bird comes along
once every century." As the Forties ended with the opening of
Birdland, the queen of jazz lounges, Afro-American music was
about to extend its horizons and make its influence felt in the
rest of the world. As a counterpoise to European art music, and
the popular forms based on that tradition, jazz brought the
world a new set of musical values: fresh melodies, an intoxicat-
ing sound, and the irresistible kinetic qualities that flowed from
its polyrhythms.

Birdland opened December 15. The club was packed to capacity. The press, the public, and the entertainment world had
turned out to hear the greatest convention of talent ever
booked into a night club: bands led by the guest of honor, Charlie Parker, by Lester Young, Stan Getz, Lips Page, Max Kaminsky, and a new singing star, Harry Belafonte. There were
tame finches in the bird cages, except for the cage over the bar.
The mynah bird had not yet been booked. Pee Wee Marquette,
a midget, dressed in a custom-made white dinner suit, acted as
master of ceremonies, cranking down the microphone stand to
suit his tiny frame, haranguing the crowd with florid announce-
ments delivered in a flat, nasal falsetto. Miss Diana Dale, the
artist responsible for the garish likenesses of show business celebrities adorning the walls, was in charge of the hat-check concession. Behind the thick plate glass at the back of the club, in
the brightly lighted radio booth, like a goldfish in an aquarium,
basked radio's Mister Hip, Symphony Sid. WJZ had given him a
midnight-to-four schedule, direct from the Jazz Corner of the
World, in which hourly shows of jazz records alternated with
live broadcasts directly from the bandstand, both interlarded
with jivey commercials for Broadway clothiers, retailers of hi-fi
equipment, the Colony Record Shop directly across the street,
hip florists, barbers, even morticians. The one for Sunshine Funeral Parlors went:

"When Fate deals you one from the bottom of the deck, fall by the Sunshine Funeral Parlors. Your loved ones will be handled with dignity and care, and the cats at Sunshine will not lay too heavy a tab on you. Now I'd like to play a request, Cootie Williams's great record, *Somebody's Got to Go*."

For live broadcasts Sid's microphone cut directly into the Birdland public address system so that he could carry on a dialogue with the jazz greats of the world. On opening night he called out, "Bird, Bird—A gennulman just called in from the Bronx. . . . The gennulman wants to know if you'd play for him *A White Christmas*?" It was like asking Heifetz to oblige with *Play Fiddle Play*. But it was Bird's night. With the saxophone in the low register, sounding richly like a tenor, Charlie played the theme of *I'm Dreaming of a White Christmas*, then stretched out in a long, loving improvisation. The yuletide favorite played as no one had ever heard before. Big, buttery and luscious, the melody notes that everyone could hum bubbled from the saxophone like good home cooking. On those rare occasions when Charlie played straight, coloring the original notes with only the slightest changes of pitch and the faintest inflections of blue modality, he was a sumptuous player indeed, and one capable of powerfully affecting the square and the man in the street. Everyone listening who was past thirty knew the Bing Crosby vehicle that spun in record store doorways each Yule season and perenially sold hundreds of thousands of records. That night the case-hardened habitués—who else would be in a night club on Christmas eve?—experienced an involuntary moistening of the eye and thought back about Christmas eves at home, long ago, in better days, and reordered drinks. Thus ended the most turbulent decade in the history of popular music in America.

PART IV

22

Travels with a Genius

The second edition of the Charlie Parker Quintet was unique in that it contained two white jazzmen, Red Rodney and Al Haig. Haig was a veteran of the Parker-Gillespie band and one of Charlie's contemporaries. Rodney was seven years younger than Parker, barely twenty-two when he joined the band a few weeks before the Birdland opening. Many musicians wondered what a young man barely out of his teens, and a white one to boot, was doing in the most distinguished combo of the day. Rodney was Charlie's own choice. His trumpet style, with its broad, soft, clear tone and fluid, legato phrasing, was similar to that of Miles Davis. Events had proved that the presence of Miles in the same band with Charlie presented insoluble personality conflicts. What was wanted was a trumpeter who would fit, who could play, who would follow directions, and who thought Charlie Parker was God. Rodney measured up in every respect.

Born plain Robert Chudnick in Philadelphia, February 27, 1927, in a mixed Jewish-Irish-Italian neighborhood that had produced more than its share of jazzmen (Gerry Mulligan, Buddy de Franco, Bill Harris, Charlie Ventura), Rodney had begun his musical career as a piston bugler in a Jewish War Veteran's Youth Band. His father had fought with the British in the Palestine disorders of the Twenties. Rodney's first trumpet was a bar mitzvah present.

Bright, precocious, but badly motivated, he dropped out of regular high school to become a student at Mastbaum Trade, an institution for neighborhood delinquents. At Mastbaum he began to study trumpet and was soon at the head of his class. At sixteen he left Mastbaum to join a name dance orchestra. By the time he was eighteen Rodney had worked with Jerry Wald, Jimmy Dorsey, Gray Gordon, Elliott Lawrence, and the Casa Loma Orchestra.

His first model was the popular, sweet-toned Harry James. Then the boppers had gotten hold of him, advised that he get rid of his "funky Harry James sound," and turned him onto Dizzy Gillespie, Fats Navarro, and Charlie Parker. With that Rodney joined the modernists. Charlie Parker became his idol. When Charlie left for the famous engagement at Billy Berg's, Rodney accepted an offer from Gene Krupa solely because Krupa was booked into the Hollywood Palladium and he would be able to hear Bird and Diz every night after the Palladium closed. After a year with the drummer's band, Rodney continued his grand tour of major dance orchestras, playing with Woody Herman, Stan Kenton, and Claude Thornhill. Before his twenty-first birthday, Rodney had been with every important white jazz orchestra.

At the peak of his career Rodney turned his back on the big bands and sought employment on The Street, where he worked with Ventura, Mulligan, Chubby Jackson, Kai Winding, and other top white combos of the day. Mobile, aggressive, gregarious, popular, and capable, Rodney was a musician's musician. Now he had achieved his life ambition: to work with a black band and the man he considered the greatest musician jazz had produced.

Rodney was a small, thin, bouncy man, five-five, weighing a hundred and twenty pounds. He was freckled, red-headed, garrulous, and a sharp dresser. Outside of a casual acquaintance with marijuana, Rodney knew nothing of drugs, except that they were widely used and that his new employer was one of their notorious consumers. Charlie called his new trumpet man "Chood," a joke with mild anti-Semitic overtones, or "Junior." In addition to his musical duties, Red was asked to hail cabs, run errands, pick up laundry, and flush narcs. And, when necessary, to score for the boss. The relationship was closer than the one between Parker and Benedetti, because Red was a working musician, Bird's right-hand man onstage as well as off.

Onstage the master-disciple relationship was strict. When Red made mistakes he was chewed out and often fired, though always rehired the next day. Offstage, master and disciple became very tight, in the intimate way that is possible between men speaking the same dialect and engaged in the same pariah profession. When chicks were available Charlie would deal off the one he didn't want to his assistant and, in rare moments of generosity, let Red pick the one he preferred. Charlie taught Red the subtle art of the put-on. He taught Rodney the tricks of relaxation, of catching up on lost sleep with cat naps in a taxi cab or on a dressing room counter. The useful trick of "changing the scene"—altering the inner mood and therefore the creative output by engaging in various odd interludes between sets. Sometimes Charlie would take a cab to Fifty-seventh Street and commandeer a surrey for a brisk gallop through Central Park. One night Rodney found his employer stretched out on top of a large metal trash receptacle, staring at the sky. Charlie was shifting the inner scenery. The set before he had played with glassy brilliance. The next set his solos were starry, lyric, and wistful. Sometimes Charlie came to the bandstand with material gleaned from radio or television shows, or the sound track of a current movie. One evening he had improvised for twenty minutes on the Lone Ranger's theme song.

Charlie was obsessed with taxicabs. He used them to dose himself with pills, to write down occasional scraps of music, as his office, his waiting room and his bedroom. Rodney estimates that during this period Charlie put in almost as much sack time in the battered back seats of taxis as he did in apartments. Sometimes Charlie would keep the cab for an entire day, running up astronomical bills on the meter. His favorite cabby was a man named Ralph Douglas, who had become a Parker fan after hearing a recording of *Cool Blues*. He'd park in front of clubs where Charlie was playing so that he could slip inside and catch the sets. When Charlie saw Douglas he'd say, "Don't move, Baby, just wait."

Each day an unconscionable amount of time was taken up with the routine of obtaining drugs. Greater precautions were necessary when the police turned on the heat, and long trips had to be taken to obtain the daily ration, devious, costly trips by cab to obscure, sinister neighborhoods in north or east Harlem. Sometimes a pusher would discipline the client with a "burn," a bad dose that left Charlie unturned or ill. When the panic was on and Charlie dared not show his face, it was the clean, twenty-two-year-old Jewish kid from the good working-class tinsmith's family in Philadelphia that had to do the scoring.

Every night Rodney stood at the elbow of the musical colossus he admired more than anyone else alive and listened to a man bombed-out on heroin pouring forth his superabundance of beautiful sounds and original ideas. He could not help speculating, as so many others had done before, if the boundary that separated mere talent from true genius could not be crossed by means of those simple injections of clear liquid squirted into a vein.

One evening Rodney came into the dressing room to find the saxophone case lying open on the makeup counter. Tucked alongside the neck of the saxophone was a spoon, a candle and a hypodermic needle. Charlie banged the case shut. "That's something you don't want to mess with," he told Rodney.

A week later Rodney arrived to find Charlie cooking heroin in the old, discolored spoon. Charlie's sleeve was rolled to the shoulder and the upper arm tied off with a necktie. Charlie turned quickly, scowled and said in a gruff, nasty voice, "The door, man! Shut the motherfuckin' door! Twist the latch!"

Rodney did as he was told. Then he stood and watched Charlie go about the business of taking a daily fix. Charlie waited until the white powder in the spoon had turned to colorless liquid. He used the hypodermic needle to suck liquid out of the spoon and, when the reservoir was full, held the needle up to the light and said, "There's the cool world, man!"

Then he twisted his arm so that a vein rose from the flesh and slid the point of the needle into the vein. A few drops of blood, looking almost black against the dark skin, slid sluggishly down Charlie's forearm. Charlie slowly pushed the plunger of the needle until the clear liquid disappeared. His movements were as steady and precise as those of a chemist at work in a laboratory. When he was finished Charlie put his tools back in the saxophone case. He sat at the counter, smoking a cigarette in deep puffs, watching its end turn to ash, staring fixedly into the mirror. The injection seemed to have no immediate effect but within half an hour Charlie was relaxed, expansive, and ready to play.

Rodney was both fascinated and repelled. He knew that Charlie was addicted but this was the first time he had stumbled onto the grim business of preparing and taking a fix. Rodney was facing the same dilemma common to jazzmen exposed to Charlie's musicianship night after night. "To play like Bird, you had to go by Bird . . ." Or did you? Was heroin the passport to the forbidden inner world where Bird lived and created his music? Rodney's workingman's Jewish lower-middle-class background had conditioned him to shy away from narcotics with horror. The idea of puncturing a healthy vein was repulsive, almost obscene. He began to sniff cocaine. It was several weeks before he could bring himself to try heroin. Then he had to enlist the help of an old junkie who showed him how to handle the tools, raise the vein, and make the injection. The first time he was sick. Then he began to adjust to a small dose. Charlie jumped all over him. "Do as I say, not as I do!" he admonished. "For God's sake, man, quit, before you get hooked." The advice was repeated many times, but without effect. Within a month Rodney was addicted. Friends told him that he was playing well, but he didn't really know. Nobody played like Bird. It was an odd band—two junkies in the front line and behind them a rhythm section where everyone was clean. It was a very good band, every bit as good as the one with Miles Davis and Max Roach.

After a long stand at Birdland the Quintet went on the road with Jazz at the Philharmonic. The tour began inauspiciously at Buffalo with the hang-up of Charlie's not being able to score. The first concert was saved only because understanding upstate fans undertook to make the necessary arrangements. After a week of missed curtain calls, Granz offered Rodney one hundred dollars cash for each night that he produced Charlie, ready to play, at the scheduled time on the program. Rodney failed to collect a single bonus in the two months that the tour lasted. The Quintet appeared on that part of the program coinciding with Charlie's availability, usually at the end. But the audiences loved Bird, and Granz endured the arrangement. Charlie played with fresh ideas every night. Unlike others on the tour, who would keep playing clichés and meaningless riffs as long as they could stir the audience, Charlie never extended his solos beyond the scope of his ideas. On this tour, as on others, Charlie always made it a point to stop off in Detroit to see his son, Leon, who was living there.

The tour wound up in Minneapolis, and the Quintet returned to New York for a stand at Cafe Society Downtown. Rodney's friends told him he had aged two years in two months. The habit was tearing him up. Red decided to kick while he could, and promptly fell victim to what seemed unbelievably painful withdrawal symptoms. Charlie found him in bed, shivering and sweating, which was normal, and suffering from acute abdominal pains, which was not. Charlie prepared a light shot from his own supply, gave Rodney an injection, and stood by to observe the results. When the abdominal pains became worse Charlie knew they had nothing to do with withdrawal. He called a cab and rushed Red to the Columbus Hospital. Rodney was doubled up in agony by the time they arrived, suffering from acute appendicitis. Doctors told Charlie that the appendix would have burst in another few hours, and credited him with saving Rodney's life.

Charlie saw his trumpet player through a difficult convalescence, then helped him find a job at a summer resort in the Catskills where he could recuperate. The Cafe Society job was played with Fats Navarro as Rodney's replacement on trumpet. The village night club was the scene of a memorable jam session one night when Art Tatum appeared.

Billy Shaw asked Charlie if he would consider a short tour of the Southern states. "I don't have to tell you what the South is like. But the money is good. I'll set it up so you can come back with ten or twelve grand. It's up to you."

"I've been there before," Charlie said. "Book it!"

"Of course you'll have to get rid of that white trumpet player," Shaw said.

"I don't understand."

"You can't risk taking him through the South. They won't stand still for a mixed band down there."

"Ever heard of an albino Negro?" Charlie asked. Shaw was dubious. Charlie told the agent, "Go ahead and book the tour. We won't make any changes in the band."

"You're out of your mind!"

"We'll bill Rodney as Albino Red. I'll have him sing the blues every set."

The band traveled in two cars, Roy Haynes's medium-priced one and Charlie's new Cadillac. Charlie was such an erratic driver that only Rodney was willing to ride in the big car. The rest traveled with Roy Haynes—Johnny Roberts, the road manager and watchdog for Shaw's interests, Tommy Potter, and pianist Walter Bishop, who had replaced ofay Al Haig, too fair to chance the trip under albino guise. The weather was steaming and the schedule tight. Shaw had booked them out on eighteen straight one-nighters. The band played Jacksonville, Atlanta, Montgomery, Birmingham, and other large cities of the South. Only Mississippi was bypassed. Billed as "Albino

Red, Appearing Exclusively with the Charlie Parker Quintet,"
Rodney was made to stand up each set and sing the blues. Since
Rodney didn't know any real blues, an old hit, *The Boogie
Blues*, once featured by the Gene Krupa Orchestra, was resur-
rected. Each set, his face florid with heat, strain, and effort,
Rodney dutifully sang, "Oh, don't the moon look lonesome shi-
nin' up there through the trees," while Charlie honked outrageously funky figures in the background. Whether Southern
Negroes were deceived by this charade no one knew. If they
were not, they were too gracious and discreet to comment. As
for the whites, the masquerade was accepted at face value—
after all, who would want to pass himself off as black in the
South?

The ambiguous situation was good for its share of hazing
and variations on the racial theme. Rodney was required to perform flunky work usually handled by a band boy. "Hey, there,
Chood," Charlie would yell. "Get a move on. Hustle them instruments up to the stage. Get things set up. Give Roy a hand
with the tubs. And see to them bags." Rodney struggled with
tom-toms, instrument cases, and the string bass. At hotels and
rooming houses he struggled with two-suiters while Charlie
lorded it over him like a field boss. When Red protested, Charlie
said smoothly, "Now, Chood, can't afford to have any of these
peckerheads get wise to you being ofay!"

"It's a little more than I bargained for."

"Now you know how the other half lives. I'd forgotten how
bad it was myself."

Charlie did not hesitate to carry his relations with Southern whites to the point of brinkmanship. One favorite device
was to bait cab drivers by pretending that a piece of luggage
was lost. Onstage and for white audiences Charlie played the
role of the "educated nigger," making himself ridiculous with
big words and high-flown phrases. "Now, ladies and gentle-
mans," he would announce, "Our little group here will en-
deavor to give you our version of . . ." And, "Allow me to introduce the youngest member of our band, little ole Albino Red
himself! Let's bring this fine young artist on with a rousing
round of applause!" And Rodney would shuffle uncertainly to

the microphone to sing his ersatz blues in a small, truculent voice.

When black promoters told him, "Mistuh Parker, we understand up north you the Bebop King! That's mighty fine, but down here what people wants is——"

"Now, my man," Charlie would cut in omnisciently, "don't want you to worry about one thing. What we's gonna give you ain't gonna be nothing but them solid old, real-gone, red beans and rice-ly kind of music, kind ever'body can shake a leg to. Yes, suh, *we aims to please!*"

The first set would be as promised: *In the Mood, South, Caravan, Boogie Woogie Blue Plate*, a scattering of barrelhouse blues. Later the band would get into its own bag, The Street stuff. Whatever the Quintet played, for white crowds or black, the music swung, set feet shaking, and was thoroughly danceable. With Charlie blowing at full volume and Rodney filling out the line with his big, soft tone, and the rhythm section swinging like crazy, the Quintet sounded like a fifteen-piece orchestra. Charlie had long ago learned tricks of playing for dancers. He liked to feel their rhythm coming back to him. The tour was a great success. Charlie made the saxophone bleat and honk, fomenting the simulacrum of the gospel quartet and the rhythm and bues band. Funky and hortatory, Charlie blew it out for the dancers stomping and sweating in the hothouse halls of the Southern cities. On pop tunes he had a way of weighting the melody notes with rhythmic energy, so that they hung a fraction of a second longer than originally written, with an implication of urgency and double time. Of the tour and its performances Rodney said, "We had only five pieces, but we sounded like the Count Basie Orchestra."

The band played one dance for white folks and the other, either earlier or later, depending upon local curfew laws, for black people. Charlie received four hundred dollars for each dance job and the sidemen one hundred. Charlie argued that the hundred was for the whole evening's work, not each dance. Threatened with a mutiny, he backed down and said he was "just testing them." The tour did nothing to enhance Charlie's stature as an artist. He was a barnstorming entertainer, no more and no less. Working overtime to assure himself that he was a success as a man of the world, if not a musician, he elaborated the pattern of his play acting, roles, and disguises. "Bread is your only friend," he lectured his sidemen, and then made another effort to con them out of the extra one hundred dollars a night. With a single exception, the band received no attention from the Southern press. In North Carolina author and publisher Harry Golden turned out to hear them and gave them a nice little write-up.

In the course of a single day Charlie would go through half a dozen disguises, becoming by turn the buffoon, the uppitty bossman lording it over flunkies, the fake Louis Armstrong, a simpleton, a con artist, the Cadillac-borne Harlem bigshot adrift in the South. The inevitable problem of narcotic supplies arose before the trip was half finished. Since most of the doctors in the South were white, Red Rodney was elected to score. Charlie coached him on the technique. Rodney would approach medicos cold turkey and go through his act, describing a convincing chronic illness, the need for pain-killing drugs, and, when the doctor hesitated, drop the magic bill on the desk. Sometimes doctor and dispensing pharmacist would be one and the same person. After pocketing the bribe and writing the prescription the doctor would take off his white jacket and go next door to the pharmacy he owned and make up the package.

By far the most unpleasant part of the trip were the rooming houses and hotel accommodations available for "colored only" in 1950. White road manager Johnny Roberts registered downtown and had it good. For the same prices the rest of the jazzmen, including Albino Red, lived in a succession of badly ventilated rooms, stifling with humid summer heat. The rooms were furnished with broken-backed beds, mattresses with springs that stuck through the ticking, torn sheets, and pillows that felt like they were stuffed with broken crockery. Narrow hallways lit by single forty-watt bulbs led to bathrooms with broken toilets and ancient tubs ringed and yellowed with a decade's accumulation of dirt. Charlie told Rodney that this would be his last Southern tour, no matter how much money was guaranteed.

The tour worked up to Memphis. The accommodations there were unusually grim. Even Charlie had reached the breaking point. "Chood," he said conspiratorially, "tell you what. You go downtown to one of them oh-fay hotels—and *register*." The voice grew more confidential and a little humble. "I'll carry *your* bags and we'll both take a bath!"

The musicians returned to New York well-heeled, exhausted, and vowing never again to set foot below the Mason-Dixon line. A stand followed at Birdland, where Charlie celebrated his thirtieth birthday August 29 at a party laid on by Oscar Goodstein. Then, at Billy Shaw's direction, the Quintet was temporarily disbanded while Charlie fulfilled the first round of bookings for the string unit. Charlie Parker and Strings appeared at the Apollo and other theaters and made their concert debut at Carnegie Hall September 16. Charlie also appeared in a jazz documentary produced by Norman Granz and directed by Gjon Mili.

On tour with the strings Charlie made first violinist Teddy Blume his personal manager. Blume was a small, self-effacing man with a classical background, a first-rate if undistinguished violinist. Blume was responsible for leading the string section and taking care of the band book. Now he became responsible for getting Charlie to his place of employment on time and soon Charlie's instrument boy, valet, banker and go-between in love affairs. Blume was astonished at Charlie's sexual appetite. Charlie frequently indulged in sex three times a day, with different women, and seldom went a day without it. Star-struck girls followed Charlie from state to state. Young girls appeared who said they wanted autographs or interviews for school papers and it was Blume's job to screen these candidates for Charlie's attentions. After a pregnant teenage girl claimed that Charlie was the father of her unborn child, and had to be paid off, Blume was instructed to weed out the jail bait and pass along only those past eighteen years of age.

One night Charlie and his road manager were drinking and Charlie pointed to a woman seated on a barstool. Her appearance fitted the well-known line in a traditional blues lyric, "Big fat mama with the meat shakin' off her bones." She was the fattest woman Blume had seen outside a circus. Charlie began to speculate on her hidden charms and sexual endowments. An introduction was arranged and within a short time the road manager, his artist, and the fat woman were alone in Blume's room, chosen over Charlie's because of Jim Crow pressures and fear of interference from the hotel management. Charlie asked the woman to disrobe. She had huge rolls of fat everywhere and enormous breasts. At Charlie's insistence Blume watched an orgy that lasted for almost an hour. The fat woman was willing, experienced and sensual. When it was over she told Charlie that she would never be able to forget him and would buy every one of his records.

When Charlie could not sleep he ordered Blume to play the violin softly for him in the bedroom. There were bills for damage to rugs and bedclothes from the lighted cigarettes that dropped from Charlie's fingers as he fell asleep. There were near busts and skin searches as narcotics officers in various cities tried, without success, to catch Charlie with the goods. In public, Charlie bullied the road manager unmercifully and patted him on the head like a dog. When a scurrilous article giving details of Charlie's misadventures, sexual exploits, and narcotic addiction appeared in *Confidential* magazine Charlie threatened to sue. Blume advised him to forget the whole thing; every word was true. When Blume's tenure as personal manager ended with the dissolution of the string unit he told an interviewer that the period had been the most harrowing of his life and that "Charlie Parker was like having a terrible disease."

In November the tireless Shaw conjured up another unusual booking, a week's whirlwind tour of Sweden. Roy Eldridge would be co-featured. Each American jazzman would appear with a band of Swedish musicians. Attired in a new Harris-tweed overcoat, chosen for the cold weather ahead, Charlie boarded an SAS flight for Scandanavia.

Charlie arrived at Bromma airport outside Stockholm on Sunday, November 19, astonished to find a welcoming crowd of Swedish musicians, music critics, and jazz fans. Charlie took an immediate liking to Stockholm, with its bracing air, clean streets, old-world buildings, and friendly people. At his first press conference he was treated like a visiting celebrity. Asked to name his favorite classical composers, he gave Hindemith, Ravel, and Debussy, in that order, and named Jascha Heifetz as his favorite artist. Of the famous violinist Charlie said, "His phrasing is such that he swings. Heifetz cries through his violin." Swedish critics made it plain that they considered Charlie a concert artist of equal stature. About the various warring camps in jazz Charlie said, "There is no point in talking about different kinds of jazz. The everlasting fight between the old and the new jazz makes no one happy. The most important thing for us is to have our efforts accepted as music." Discussing the differences between jazz and European "art" music, he said, "There is no boundary line to art. Music is your own experience, your thoughts, your wisdom. If you don't live it, it won't come out of your horn. . . . Bebop," Charlie said, "is convenient only for small combos and ought to be played pretty fast. In a big orchestra arrangements suppress the spontaneous imagination." Asked to define his own aims, Charlie said, "I am aiming at beautiful tones." He said that he believed he had reached a new level of performance with the strings, and that his best single effort was *Just Friends*. Swedish critics demurred. They preferred his work with the Miles Davis and Red Rodney quintets. Asked about race relations in America, Charlie shrugged and refused to discuss the subject. Pressed to name his favorite jazz saxophonist, Charlie popped up with a curious though excellent choice, the late Leon "Chu" Berry, whose big soft tone and fluid style had been heard with many of the swing orchestras of the late Thirties.

The tour was sponsored by Nils Hellstrom, publisher of the Swedish jazz magazine *Estrad*, and opened at Konserthuset, a large hall in downtown Stockholm. To accommodate the demand for tickets, two concerts were given. Roy Eldridge appeared with a group of Swedish swing musicians and Charlie with a group of hand-picked "modernists," trumpeter Rolf Ericson, bassist Yngve Akerberg, drummer Jack Noren, and pianist Gunnar Svensson. Charlie opened with *Anthropology*, and followed with long versions of *Cool Blues, Cheers, Lover Man*, and *Stupendous*. The Swedish musicians were excellent, superior to those Charlie had heard in France the year before. Ericson had worked with Charlie Barnet and Woody Herman during a three-year stay in America. Svensson played in the George Shearing style.

As he left the hall Charlie was applauded by a group of Stockholm high school students clustered around a sandwich stand. Charlie, surprised that many spoke English, treated the crowd to refreshments and talked about jazz. Then he was triumphantly carried off to the national headquarters of the Swedish jazz clubs, permanently housed in a vaulted cellar in an old part of Stockholm. There he found extensive libraries of jazz books and records, listening and reading rooms, and current copies of jazz reviews published in Finnish, German, Swedish, Norwegian, French, and English. Back numbers were bound and covered many years of publication. The walls were filled with framed photographs of jazz personalities starting with Louis Armstrong. Charlie had never seen anything like this in his own country, where jazz of course had begun, and indeed he was right. There was nothing comparable in America. He was asked to autograph a picture of himself. The Swedes were pleased when he did. The picture was hung on the wall with those of Jenny Lind and jazz celebrities. After a sumptuous buffet, washed down with liberal amounts of Pilsner beer, wine, and Swedish schnapps, a jam session got under way, continuing until four in the morning. Charlie treated his ecstatic listeners to long improvisations of favorite compositions, already familiar to Swedish musicians from a study of records. Charlie charmed everyone with his personality, described by Swedish writers as "modest, good humored, and conciliatory." Apparently the Swedes had expected a prima donna or grand seigneur of music. That Monday in 1950 was one of the happiest and most fulfilling days of his life.

With two changes in personnel, Gosta Theselius for Gunnar Svensson and Thore Jederby for Akerberg, the tour of Sweden's principal cities began with a double concert at Gothenburg. Charlie and Roy Eldridge were photographed walking about in the first snow of the year in their "varnished shoes," which seemed to amuse the Swedes. Even though Charlie had been in Sweden only a day or two, he had already begun to receive a large number of letters from jazz fans, saying that they were honored by his visit to their country and praising his music. Most of the letters were written in English.

Wednesday the touring musicians played a matinee at Amiralen dancehall in Malmo, then drove a few miles north to the University of Lund, where a jam session was held at Akademiska Foreningen. The Swedish barnstormers were played out. Charlie improvised alone. He played a long solo in the blues pattern, described by one reporter as a "sermon never heard before or since." All the time he was drinking steadily, praising the Swedish schnapps. Once he borrowed Arne Domnerus's clarinet and played a few numbers.

During the tour Charlie handed two hundred dollars in krona to Carl-Erik Lindgren, critic for *Estrad*, asking Lindgren to buy something that he could take home. Lindgren had not the slightest idea of what to do with the money. Finally Lindgren bought Charlie a very smart hooded coat, considered *"le dernier cri* with snobs," and a Swedish peasant dress for Kim, the daughter of Chan Richardson, whom he had begun dating again before leaving for Sweden. Charlie discussed the possibility of living in Sweden with his new friends, noting that everything in Sweden seemed "cool" and the problem of race relations did not arise. He was told that he could establish a headquarters in Stockholm or Copenhagen and manage to keep busy playing clubs and concerts in Scandinavia, Poland, Germany, Yugoslavia, France, Belgium, and Italy. England was difficult because of the quota on foreign musicians imposed by the British musicians' union. Spain and Portugal were deaf to jazz. The money would be nothing like that in the States, but enough to live in reasonable comfort.

After the session at the University of Lund the musicians crossed the Sound to Denmark for a big concert at K. B. Hallen, where they were joined by the Norwegian Quintet of Rowland Greenberg, whom Charlie had met in 1949 at the Paris Jazz Festival. Benny Goodman, the one-time King of Swing, was in Copenhagen that night and took part in the jamming. From Denmark the musicians returned to Sweden for a matinee appearance at Folkets Park, a beer garden and dance pavilion in Helsingborg. Blind pianist Lennart Nilsson joined the party. Aware that a Negro was out of the ordinary in all-white Sweden, Charlie gently took the pianist's hand and placed it on his head. Nilsson felt the wiry hair and said that he understood, and Charlie was pleased.

As usual the concert was a sell-out in spite of the very high prices charged by promoter Hellstrom to cover expenses. After the concert the musicians adjourned to a nearby restaurant for a round of eating, drinking, and jamming that went on until the small hours of the next morning. According to Greenberg, Charlie played non-stop and "like a demon," all the time consuming large quantities of schnapps, obtained through various subterfuges, since strict alcohol laws prevailed in Sweden at that time. The jam session was recorded and later released on the Swedish label Sonet. The Helsingborg festivities marked the end of seven days' travel, concertizing, and jamming. Charlie told his Swedish friends he was "beat to the ground."

By contrast to his behavior on the Southern tour, with its sweltering heat, the Swedish tour, done in sub-freezing weather, showed the face of a new Charlie Parker to the public. Sensing that he was surrounded by jazz lovers and well-wishers at every stop, Charlie abandoned all pretense of play acting and became the artist that he was. Except for the damage done by the unending consumption of schnapps, his misadventures in Sweden were innocent.

A final concert remained, and it was with great difficulty that Greenberg and Lindgren were able to get him out of bed and on the road the next morning, a feat possible only after another bottle of schnapps had been scrounged from a room steward who proclaimed himself a Charlie Parker fan. That night Charlie was outplayed by Swedish altoist Arne Domnerus. Not until a second bottle of schnapps had been obtained and consumed did Charlie regain his old form. The musicians returned to Stockholm, where Charlie rested during his last day in Sweden. Charlie's playing during the Swedish tour was on a high, perhaps new level. Realizing that listeners were already familiar with his records and were ready to hear, not replays of a past success, but innovations, he stretched out. His tone was clear and singing and the saxophone under perfect control, even on pianissimo passages. At Malmo there was a superb *Lover Man*, lyrical, gentle, almost shy, full of lovely surprises, the performance he wanted desperately to give that fateful day in Hollywood. He made new discoveries as he responded to requests for *Cool Blues* and *Embraceable You*.

Charlie had reservations to leave Sweden on a Scandinavian Airlines flight to Paris on Sunday, November 26. Greenberg and Lindgren saw him off, and the last half hour was spent reminiscing at the airport bar. The three men were still laughing and joking when Charlie's flight was called. At the departure gate Lindgren embraced Charlie and said, "*Au revoir*, Charlie. Of course you know that means 'until we meet the next time.' I sincerely hope that will be in the very near future."

Suddenly Charlie became serious. He looked deeply into Lindgren's eyes and said, very slowly, in a gloomy voice heavy with meaning, "No, Carl, we will never meet again." Then he picked up his saxophone case and walked off to board the plane. The *alegría* of the lovely week in Sweden was not to be experienced again in his lifetime.

In Paris the SAS flight was met by Charles Delaunay, who asked Charlie if he would consider appearing at a concert scheduled for the following weekend. Charlie accepted the offer, asked for and was given an advance against his fee. He then spent the intervening time revisiting the various jazz bistros in Montmartre. At le Boeuf sur le Toit he ran into Kenny Clarke, who once again tried to persuade him to leave America and join the growing colony of expatriate American jazzmen. An encounter with emigré Don Byas was less pleasant. The two saxophonists, who had never been friendly during their days on The Street when Byas was trying to run with the boppers, became involved in a heated argument. Old hostilities flared, and Charlie pushed back the table, saying, "Come outside, Byas, and I'll try you." When Byas reached the sidewalk Charlie opened a knife. Byas, a small, wiry man, immediately pulled out one of his own. The two saxophonists faced each other under the street lights. When Charlie saw that Byas was deadly serious, he dropped his belligerent posture, laughed, and said, "Don, I really believe you'd try to cut me."

"You're so right, Bird," Byas replied. "I would."

Charlie folded up his knife and walked back into the club.

The weekend arrived, and with it the day of the Delaunay concert. Three days of carousing in Paris, on top of the Swedish tour with its excitements, new faces, places, and strange food had completely exhausted Charlie. His stomach, alternately bathed in Swedish schnapps and French cognac, had declared open rebellion. Charlie was sick. One thought entered his mind —to get home. He called the desk, asked that a porter be sent up to pack his bags, telephoned the airport, secured a reservation on a flight for New York via London, and within an hour was on his way back to the States. He did not trouble himself to call Delaunay. Without pills, drugs, or liquor, he suffered torments on the long flight home. Saturday evening in New York he was persuaded to appear on a Leonard Feather jazz show broadcast overseas. Through a special hook-up the audience at the Delaunay concert had the strange experience of hearing Charlie's voice, distorted by the trans-Atlantic transmission, addressing them during intermission, explaining his failure to appear on their program. "Sorry, folks," he told his French fans, as if he were apologizing for a missed dinner engagement, "it was '*Just One of Those Things.*' I . . . I had to cut out." To Feather's questions he answered that he had gone to Paris for a short holiday, but failed to mention the advance from Delaunay. In London, *Melody Maker* magazine savored the details of the fiasco in a front page piece headlined "THE INCREDIBLE STORY OF CHARLIE PARKER IN PARIS."

As had happened with bouts of stomach trouble in the past, this one didn't go away. After three days of misery, during which he vomited blood and was unable to retain food, Charlie went to Medical Arts Hospital in midtown Manhattan, where X-rays confirmed a preliminary diagnosis of acute peptic ulcers. Charlie was put on a special diet and placed in a private room with around-the-clock nursing. Drugs, pills, and alcohol were expressly forbidden. After a week Charlie began to improve. Bragging of his "remarkable powers of recovery," he said he was ready to leave the hospital, a plan quickly quashed by the doctor, who prescribed another week of intensive care and, after that, a strict regimen—above all, total abstinence from hard liquor in any form. Charlie did not agree but said nothing. That night, when his nurse had gone for coffee, he ghosted down a corridor, took a service elevator to the basement, reached the street, and hailed a cruising cab, directing the driver to Birdland. He found the Jazz Corner of the World roaring along in fine style. He borrowed money for cab fare from the box office and entered the club named in his honor. He was wearing hospital pajamas and cloth slippers. Manager Oscar Goodstein found him at the bar. Charlie was busy downing drinks concocted from a recipe he had just invented, milk laced with Scotch whiskey. In a jolly mood, he told Goodstein that the drink was a sovereign remedy for stomach ulcers. With a good deal of difficulty Goodstein talked him out of sitting in with the house band and persuaded him to return to the hospital.

23

A Queer Night in

Brussels

The Red Rodney period was notable for another change in Charlie Parker's lifestyle. During the winter of 1950 Charlie made his final break with Doris Sydnor. A quiet, conservative girl, devoted to Charlie not because he was a famous musician, but because she loved him, Doris was out of her element in the hectic life of night clubs, jam sessions, and road trips. Doris simply had not been able to cope, or keep up. Shortly after the Birdland opening Charlie began living with Chan Richardson and thus began the fourth important liaison of his life. Charlie took the trouble neither to divorce Doris nor to marry Chan. Requirements of the legal code were simply not for him. Chan and Charlie were first seen together in public at St. Nick's Ballroom, when Charlie played a one-night dance job with the Quintet. (The engagement was recorded by Joe Maini and Don Lanphere, two young West Coast musicians who were augmenting Dean Benedetti's efforts; the tapes were eventually released by Fantasy label as *Bird at St. Nicks.*)

In 1951 The Street no longer enjoyed a monopoly on the music. Its famous cellar bistros were giving way to the Broadway jazz palaces. Chan was no longer its Mesta-de Stael. When Chan and Charlie began seeing each other Chan was a ripe twenty-seven, Kim an adorable four, and Charlie Parker thirty-one. Charlie was no longer the young brown god of bebop. He was dangerously in peril of being named its elder statesman, as had happened to Lester Young. The mere fact that Charlie won every saxophone poll with monotonous regularity and was named musician of the year by jazz writers was in itself ominous, a sign that the music was now understood by the critics and wholly accessible to the public. At thirty-one, Charlie looked closer to forty. His weight had gotten out of control. He was five feet nine inches in height, and did not carry excess poundage well. The once muscular one hundred and fifty pounds had been blown up to more than two hundred, most of it padding. The once boyish, eager, ecstatic face now appeared thickened, coarsened, roughed over, insulated with fat, graven with lines that would not go away. He bulged in his suits. The new liaison had the quality of those mature, autumnal romances of middle-aged couples depicted in British novels. But it was a good arrangement, one that better might have begun in those years when The Street was roaring and life seemed an endless jam session. Of all Charlie's women, there had never been one with Chan's understanding of the music, the life, the pressures under which the creative artist worked. Allowing for the inevitable separations and defections, it was a marriage in kind if not in fact, and would last for the rest of Charlie's life.

As suited slightly aging hipsters, and to escape the hurly burly of the music business, they removed themselves from the usual neighborhoods—midtown, Harlem, The Street—and relocated in a five-room front apartment at 422 East 11th Street, in what was then a Polish-Jewish neighborhood and has since become the East Village. The apartment was comfortably furnished with odd pieces from second hand stores, from 7 West 52, and from Mrs. Richardson's home in New Hope, Bucks County, Pennsylvania. Charlie bought a phonograph and shelves for their combined record collections. For the first time since he had left the Olive Street house in Kansas City, Charlie had a real home of his own. It never became a crash pad. Invitations were extended to a highly select few among Charlie's friends. Charlie began spending a lot of time at home. He took Kim for walks and became friendly with neighborhood merchants. In a geographical sense the move from Harlem to the Lower East Side amounted to no more than the substitution of a black ghetto for a Jewish ghetto. The change was an important one in Charlie's life. It marked the first intrusion of a black culture hero into white Bohemia.

After a few months on 11th Street Charlie moved his wife and family to a larger and more luxurious apartment at 151 Avenue B, in the same neighborhood. He tried very hard to achieve the normal lifestyle that had eluded him. Sunday dinners *en famille* became important events with which no jam session might interfere. He looked forward to having Mrs. Richardson and Chan's Aunt Janet as guests. Charlie appeared at the table neatly dressed in a tie and fresh suit, and played the role of the solicitous, old-fashioned host. He was gallant toward Chan, and worshipped Kim. One night he brought Kim a five-foot stuffed rabbit on the train from Philadelphia. Charlie and Chan spent the summer at Mrs. Richardson's house in New Hope, Pennsylvania. Charlie gardened, took walks in the country, and called on neighbors. When Chan met the commuter train at Trenton he would walk up the stairs to the station wearing a dark vicuna overcoat and sneakers, a rolled copy of *The New York Times* tucked under one arm. He made a fetish of respectability. Chan thought that if the years could have been rolled back—and if Charlie had been white and without talent—he might have lived out the rest of his days as a "happy square."

In 1951 Charlie was at the peak of his commercial success. He was kept busy filling bookings with the Quintet and the string unit. His Mercury records were selling well, and the label had renewed his contract. An established draw on Jazz at the Philharmonic tours, he was as familiar to ticket buyers as Coleman Hawkins or Lester Young, those idols of his early years, but the one fatal flaw remained—Charlie's addiction to drugs, now in its fifteenth year. His system had become so conditioned to heroin that withdrawal bouts no longer held their old terrors. With Rodney he discussed the possibility of giving up the habit, and said that he was bothered by the example he had set for so many young jazzmen. "If I stop, maybe they'll stop," he told Rodney.

But that was not so easily done. The state of his health had grown more precarious. The ulcers had returned, and a visit to a doctor had disclosed early, disquieting signs of a heart condition. He told pianist Walter Bishop, "I go to this heart specialist and give him a hundred dollars and he treats me but it don't do no good. I go to this ulcer man and give him seventy-five dollars to cool my ulcers out and it don't do no good. There's a little cat in a dark alley and I give him five dollars for a bag of shit—my ulcer's gone, my heart trouble is gone, everything gone."

Interviewed by Leonard Feather on a New York radio show, he became involved in a discussion of a recent article appearing in *Ebony* magazine under the by-line of band leader Cab Calloway. Cab, one of those displaced by the boppers, blasted the new generation of musicians and pointed to the widespread use of narcotics in their ranks. Charlie was bombed on dope when he went to the studio. Speaking very slowly, in unctuous tones, he declared, "I never read such a violent, contemptuous thing against music today. It was poorly written, poorly expressed and poorly meant. It was just poor."

"Charlie, I certainly don't think that a musician necessarily plays better under the influence of any stimulus of any kind," Feather replied, "and I'm pretty sure that you'll agree with me, won't you?"

"Well, ah, yes," Charlie responded. "I'd rather agree with you to a certain extent. Nobody's fooling themselves, never—any more—anyway. We'll put it that way."

Feeling sorry for himself one night in the dressing room, Charlie rolled up his sleeves and, pointing to the needle marks on his arms, told a friend, "This is my home. This is my portfolio. This is my Cadillac."

Thanks to an acutely developed awareness of danger, acquired during fifteen years of living in the urban jungle, Charlie Parker had managed to preserve a remarkable record: Not once in his life had he been arrested on a narcotics charge. Charlie had survived countless pat-downs, raids, and ransacking of rooms. One night as Blume looked on to be sure that there would be no planted evidence, two detectives went through Charlie's luggage, instrument case, clothing, peered into his mouth, looked between his toes, examined the veins in his arms with a magnifying glass, and even poked an instrument up his rectum—all without finding anything incriminating. In New York Charlie knew most of the men on the narcotics squad by first name. He would greet them with sardonic effusiveness and offer to stand them drinks. Bantering with them and forecasting their next moves became an intriguing game to him. Although he was high on their list of suspects, so wary was Charlie in his arrangements for scoring and turning on that not once were they able to catch him with the goods. He always seemed to be one jump ahead of the "narcs." His luck, and supposed immunity from the bust, became part of the Parker legend. But there was more than one means by which the hunter might hamstring and bring down the quarry. In 1951, after he and Chan had been living together only a few months, the establishment finally got to him.

In New York City all performers working in places where liquor was sold were required to carry a "cabaret card," a license to perform issued by the New York State Liquor Authority. Without it no musician or entertainer could work in a night club. His engagements were restricted to theaters, concerts, and record dates. And of course he could work out of town. In 1951, at the recommendation of the narcotics squad, Charlie's cabaret license was revoked. Billie Holiday suffered a similar fate, as did many performers and musicians before and later, the last notable victim being Lord Buckley. Charlie learned the bad news shortly before Chan gave birth to a baby daughter, whom they named Pree.

When Charlie went to Philadelphia to play two weeks at the Club Downbeat, its proprietor was obliged to make a verbal agreement with the police: Charlie would not be molested for as long as he appeared, but he could arrive no earlier than the day of his opening and must leave Philadelphia no later than the day following his closing. The gray listing in New York had been leaked to the narcotics bureaus in other cities.

Charlie returned to New York and reassembled the Quintet for a Mercury record date. Red Rodney was located in the Catskills, cooling out at the Premier Hotel and rooming with Lenny Bruce, the establishment's director of recreation. Flown down by charter plane at Charlie's insistence, Rodney joined John Lewis, Ray Brown, and Kenny Clarke to record *Swedish Schnapps*, *Si Si*, *Blues for Alice*, *Back Home Blues*, and a long postponed remake of *Lover Man*. The remake invited comparison with the by-product of the nightmare session in Los Angeles. The notes were the same, but the performance was routine, uninspired, almost officious. It had none of the excruciating emotional intensity of the first version, and none of its apocalyptic vision. Rodney told Parker that the first *Lover Man* was still one of his most important recordings and an invaluable musical document, because it showed a genius at work in a moment of extremity, improvising on bare reflexes. Charlie flew into a temper, cursed the day he had made it, Dial Records, its partners, and said he wished he could destroy every recording, 78 or 33 rpm, pressed from that odious, accusing master.

Charlie continued to wear two hats. The out-of-town schedules were a nuisance and required a great deal of traveling. Road trips always meant greater living expenses, while maintaining a home in New York, not to mention higher prices for narcotics. Charlie's supplies were now furnished at inflated prices, like the fees of surgeons, adjusted by pushers to reflect his status. An occasional appearance at Carnegie Hall or the Apollo Theater only pointed up the awkwardness of the cabaret card situation. In the fall of 1951 Billy Shaw came up with another European junket. Parker and Rodney were flown to Europe to join Jazz at the Philharmonic, arriving in time to appear in Hamburg. After concerts at Frankfurt and Munich, the show moved on to Brussels.

There, backstage after the concert, the musicians were besieged by the usual crowd of fans, buffs, and emigré musicians. From this crowd came a slight, mysterious man with the confidential manner of a secret agent. He called himself Raoul, and called Parker "Shar-lee Par-kaire." There was an immediate understanding between them. After a brief conversation he took Charlie by the arm and, steering him through a path that opened in the press of people seeking to shake hands and obtain autographs, led the way to a black Mercedes. Raoul was a Parker fan. He had collected every one of Charlie's records on American and European labels. Raoul was something more, a businessman of a special sort. Raoul drove Charlie to an obscure neighborhood in downtown Brussels and parked the car in front of a small store, of which he was the proprietor. The store resembled an old-fashioned pharmacy where prescriptions were filled and proprietory drugs sold. Over the door a sign with gothic letters said "CHIMISTE." Raoul locked the Mercedes, escorted Charlie Parker inside, turned on the lights, and pulled down the blinds. "Now, Shar-lee," he said, "I have something interesting to show you. I think you will agree that you have never seen a store like mine."

One showcase displayed quarter and half moons of hashish. Cards, neatly printed in French, showed the places of origin: Iran, Turkey, Greece, Egypt. The pitch-black half moons came from Iran and were the most potent, and expensive. Prices were shown in Belgian francs, French francs, and English pounds. A matching showcase displayed marijuana. The selection was wide. There was marijuana from Mexico, Guatemala, Panama; from Morocco and Tunisia; from the famous growing areas of the Near East, Turkey, Lebanon, and Macedonia. Grass in varying hues of green, loden, and pale gray. On the opposite side of the room was displayed the hard stuff, cocaine, opium, morphine, heroin. Samples of white powder lay on clean rounds of chemist's filter paper, spotless and tempting. Wall shelves with glass fronts displayed hypodermic needles, syringes, hashish crucibles, cookers, opium pipes, hookahs, and other accessories for the addict who had—or wanted—everything.

Raoul explained that he was the largest retailer of narcotics in Europe. In 1952 all of this was perfectly legal in Belgium. (Newly enacted and restrictive laws would come in 1955.) Of course Raoul was greatly honored to have as his guest an internationally known addict. Raoul told Charlie that he himself was a controlled user, having become addicted after a long stay in a hospital where he learned he was suffering from osteomyelitis. Raoul suggested that Charlie call the hotel and invite other members of the Jazz at the Philharmonic troupe to the store for a party. Charlie called, woke Red Rodney, and persuaded him to dress and join them. Raoul said that it would give him great pleasure to have Charlie sample the specialties of the house. What would he like to try? Some of the Iranian hashish for a starter? No? Cocaine, perhaps? Only heroin interested Charlie. But of course, heroin was the specialty of the house. Raoul's heroin arrived in Brussels from such widely separated sources as Marseilles, Naples, Beirut, Istanbul, Basle, and Seoul. The South Korean variety was interesting but that from Switzerland, manufactured under close controls by one of the world's great pharmaceutical firms, was the purest and most trustworthy, something that he could recommend without reservation. Hypodermic needles were produced and sterilized, and injections prepared. Finally Rodney arrived by cab.

The party that began that night went on for thirty-six hours and was joined by various odd guests, all of them jazz buffs. The shop did not open for business the next day. The blinds remained drawn, and callers were ignored. It was Raoul's great honor, he said, to entertain the artist who had given him so many hours of pleasure. During the party jazz records were played endlessly on Raoul's expensive phonograph; the music was heard through a system of multiple speakers concealed in the walls and ceiling of the store. Raoul had copies of *Hootie Blues* and *Red Cross* that Charlie had forgotten. As to the almost-forgotten Jazz at the Philharmonic tour, that would now be playing Amsterdam. That could wait, Raoul insisted. There were others who could perform—Ella Fitzgerald, Gene Krupa, Oscar Peterson, Illinois Jacquet. Let them entertain the Dutchmen.

Out of this euphoric fog came the nagging thought that the next stop for JATP was Paris, at which a special concert featuring Charlie Parker was scheduled. A well-known French composer-conductor had been engaged to present a concert involving sixty symphony musicians and a long medley of Parker tunes. And Charlie would be the soloist. Yes, Charlie agreed, when Rodney reminded him of this commitment, they would have to break up this most beautiful of all parties. Raoul saw them to the airport and made sure that Charlie and Red had an ample supply of their favorite drug for the days ahead. Charlie and Red arrived in Paris the afternoon of the special concert. Both were exhausted.

The tall, austere Granz was in a rage. They had been lost for seventy-two hours, and Granz had engaged detectives to look for the missing musicians. The Paris concert was sold out, and there was a rehearsal scheduled for that afternoon. Charlie awoke ill and barely able to get out of bed. "See here, Chood," he told Rodney. "You'll have to go down there. Take a look at the scores. Dig the keys. Then come back and fill me in."

"Bird, you'd better pull yourself together and make it," Rodney said. "Snorg [Norman Granz] says this is a big one."

"What's he want of me?" Charlie groaned. "Now, do as I say." Charlie went back to sleep.

The conductor was furious when Rodney told him that Parker would not be available for the rehearsal. The scores looked difficult. The spelling was in European style, and Rodney wasn't sure of the keys. The tunes were copied out in English. The French couldn't change those. Rodney made a show of taking notes. He kept reassuring the conductor that there was no need for worry. Parker was used to this sort of thing. He would be able to cope with everything. He did make a list of tunes to be played: *Now's the Time*, *Cool Blues* (which had won a Grand Prix du Disque in France), *April in Paris*, *Klacto-veesedstene*, and so on. As an experienced band musician, he knew only that it was nothing he would have wanted to tackle without at least two rehearsals.

That night when the curtain went up, Charlie nodded genially at the conductor and waited for the downbeat and the opening fanfare. The symphonic orchestra began playing *Now's the Time*, with the melody carried on the strings pizzicato. It was a beautiful beginning but a tricky one. Leading to the first theme there was a deceptive cadence that promised to modulate but instead returned to the original key. At the first measure Charlie walked onstage, picked up the lead, and took over. The saxophone soared over strings, woodwinds, and brass. Charlie played the thirty-minute medley without a single mistake. In Rodney's three years with the boss, it was the most uncanny performance he had ever heard Charlie give.

The tour resumed. When Charlie and Red, spaced out on Raoul's heroin, missed the next two concerts, Granz put them on a trans-Atlantic flight for New York and announced that the tour would proceed without them.

After the excitements of the third, brief European trip, Charlie settled down to the inconvenience of playing everywhere in America except New York. Once again he won the polls. In January he cut four sides with the Strings, five more with the Quintet, augmented by conga drums. He recorded an additional four sides with Oscar Peterson and a big band. He played the Howard Theater in Washington, the Times Square Club in Rochester, Tiffany's in Los Angeles (with Chet Baker), Tootie's in Kansas City, the Glass Bar in St. Louis (with Jimmy Forrest), and Bop City in San Francisco, where he met poet Kenneth Rexroth. In Los Angeles on June 5 he made a session for which Granz rounded up four of the greatest saxophonists of jazz: Johnny Hodges, Benny Carter, Ben Webster, and Charlie Parker. Feeling the strain of working as a single, Charlie flew back to New York after the session. The Strings had become a little boring. Charlie wanted to get back to the intimate setting of the Quintet, and asked Shaw to stir up some bookings. Red Rodney was again located in the Catskills, and came down to New York to reorganize the band. The band played a week in Cleveland and another in Boston, and went to Philadelphia to work the Downbeat. There the roof fell in. Rodney was picked up for possession of narcotics and sentenced to five years in a federal penitentiary. Only by means of a last-ditch stand by attorneys was the sentence suspended and Rodney committed for six months to the federal narcotics hospital at Lexington, Kentucky. That was the end of the Quintet.

22

The Jazz Baroness

Shaken by Rodney's arrest, Charlie laid off drugs and went back to booze. He moonlighted on his valuable Mercury contract, recording for Prestige Records of Bergenfield, New Jersey, under the pseudonym Charlie Chan. To further mask his presence he used a tenor saxophone. Others on this odd date were Sonny Rollins, Miles Davis, Percy Heath, and Philly Joe Jones. During the warm-up period Charlie drank a fifth of vodka. The records were curiosities of the Parker discography, one of the two occasions when he recorded with tenor saxophone.

Toronto was the scene of a memorable concert sponsored by the New Jazz Society of that city. Presenting Charlie Par-

ker, Dizzy Gillespie, Bud Powell, Charlie Mingus, and Max
Roach, the concert was ill-advisedly scheduled for the same
night as the Rocky Marciano-Jersey Joe Walcott heavyweight
championship fight, and attracted only about seven hundred
people to the twenty-five-hundred-capacity Massey Hall. Charlie arrived in Toronto without his horn, and played with a white
plastic alto lent by a local music store. The old feud between
Charlie and Dizzy was revived. Acting as master of ceremonies,
Charlie affected a broad British accent. In an ironic tone he introduced Gillespie as "my worthy constituent." During the concert Dizzy lived up to his name by continually clowning and
leaving the stage to check on the progress of the fight, which
Marciano won by a knockout in the first round, much to Gillespie's displeasure. Bud Powell had just been released from a
Long Island sanitarium after undergoing a long regime of electric shock treatments and was drunk from the first number onward, leaving Mingus and Roach as the only undisturbed, sober
members of the band. At intermission fans and musicians alike
repaired to the Brass Rail opposite Massey Hall and drank until
the harassed promoters herded them back to the stage. The
crowd made up for its size by vociferous applause and shouts of
"Go!" and "Now!" In spite of distractions, revived enmities,
and general inebriety, the concert produced an electrifying
hour of music. When the box office receipts proved insufficient
to meet guarantees to the musicians, Charlie forced those responsible to write checks on their personal bank accounts and
saw to the collection of the money the following morning.

Mingus had taken the precaution of having the concert recorded. The tape sounded like one of the old hell-for-leather
cutting sessions at Minton's. Norman Granz thought it outstanding and suggested that with a little editing it could be released as a commercial record. He asked the men how much
they wanted as an advance on royalties. "One hundred thousand dollars," Charlie Parker told the promoter. The deal was
not consummated. After railing about white exploitation of
jazz musicians and white monopoly of recording facilities and
labels, Mingus launched a label of his own, Debut, with *Jazz at
Massey Hall*. The Charlie Chan pseudonym was used again to

conceal Parker's presence and fend off litigation by Mercury attorneys. Mingus' independent label, soon to include two other releases of on-site recordings featuring Parker, ran into merchandising problems and its distribution was eventually taken over by Fantasy-Prestige of Berkeley and are still carried in the catalog.

For Charlie the hassle of arranging his professional life around the periphery of New York City had become most burdensome. A second child arrived, a son, who was named Baird. There were now three people dependent on his earnings. Pree, aged two, was often ill, and strained finances sent the Parkers to free clinics as often as to doctors' offices. Charlie was losing out on what could have been top-paying engagements at Basin Street, the Aquarium, Bop City, and, ironically, the club named in his honor. Taking pen in hand, an extreme measure, since Charlie wrote letters only in moments of duress or dire need, he addressed the New York State Liquor Authority:

"My right to pursue my chosen profession has been taken away, and my wife and three children who are innocent of any wrong-doing are suffering. . . . My baby girl is a city case in the hospital because her health has been neglected since we hadn't the necessary doctor fees. . . .

"I feel sure when you examine my record and see that I have made a sincere effort to become a family man and a good citizen, you will reconsider.

"If by any chance you feel that I haven't paid my debt to society, by all means let me do so and give me and my family back the right to live."

It was the letter of a deeply frustrated man crying out in pain, but that did not prevent Charlie from dipping into his bag of guile and con and throwing out the gratuitous offer of voluntary imprisonment that could not possibly be accepted or discharged.

There was no response from the Authority. Through its attorneys, Billy Shaw Artists pursued the matter by less direct means. At this time Charlie met Baroness Pannonica de Koenigswarter, a wealthy, unconventional bohemian who had appeared on the jazz scene. A member of the English branch of the Rothschild family, she had survived a pampered childhood, a famous finishing school in Paris run by three Lesbian sisters, a coming-out ball in London, and a court presentation at Buckingham Palace. As an emancipated young sportswoman and aviatrix, she had met her husband, Baron Jules de Koenigswarter, a ranking official in the French diplomatic corps, on the tarmac of Le Touquet airport. During World War II the Baroness had continued her adventures as a decoder for De Gaulle's intelligence in Africa, a private in the Free French Army, a broadcaster for a propaganda station in Brazzaville, and a driver for the War Graves Commission. Her introduction to jazz had come about through her brother, Victor de Rothschild, Churchill's personal courier to the White House. During his trips to the United States Victor had visited The Street and studied piano with Teddy Wilson.

In 1951, imbued with an evangelical spirit and overwhelmed by the boredom of her life as a diplomat's lady at the French embassy in Mexico City, she left her husband and came to live in New York, in a suite luxuriously furnished with antiques and period pieces at the Hotel Stanhope on Fifth Avenue. The apartment soon became an elegant crash pad for a number of jazz musicians and was, on a more selective basis, a counterpart of 7 West 52nd. There the Baroness reigned, mixing highballs and ordering catered dinners for jazz musicians, mostly black and playing in the contemporary style. Their comings and goings, the playing of records at all hours, and an occasional orderly jam session kept the Baroness in constant hot water with the management of the hotel. Thelonious Monk was often seen loitering in the lobby, costumed in a red shirt and British hunting hat, wearing his black shades and carrying a white cane, much to the discomposure of the ancient dowagers who lived at the Stanhope. The Baroness avoided eviction only because of her title, influence, and force of personality. Eventually her rent was doubled.

Baroness Pannonica, called Nica by her friends, was a tall, well-fleshed woman with the face of an aging, irrepressible gamin. She was witty, sardonic, outspoken, and absentminded, seldom able to keep appointments. Cultured and intellectual, she was creative as well, and painted strange canvases using mixed media of acrylic, milk, Scotch, and perfume. She possessed a great simplicity and directness of manner that endeared her to jazzmen. Like many exposed to French culture, the Baroness was fascinated by African sculpture, Afro-American music, and negritude. She dressed carelessly in clothes bought from the most expensive shops. Her Rolls-Royce, which she called the "silver pigeon" and drove herself, her furs, jewelry, and gold pocket flask were familiar in the jazz clubs along Broadway, in Harlem and Greenwich Village. Her patronage of jazz places and players in the early years of the 1950s earned her the name of the Jazz Baroness.

Thelonious Monk was the Baroness's most intimate friend among jazzmen. His *Pannonica*, recorded for Riverside, was dedicated to the Baroness, as was *Nica Steps Out* by pianist-composer Freddie Redd. Monk first brought Charlie Parker to the Fifth Avenue salon. Charlie soon became a frequent visitor, dropping in at any hour of the day or night to talk, listen to records, and drink the liquor of the house. The Baroness urged Charlie to bring Chan, and the two women developed a close friendship. The friendship with Baroness Pannonica de Koenigswarter was another extension of Charlie's expanding social horizons. The ghetto hero had moved downtown and made himself an accepted figure by the poets and painters of Greenwich Village. Now Charlie was getting what he took to be an interior view of Fifth Avenue society and its haute culture. He was impressed by the luxurious appointments of the suite at the Hotel Stanhope, by the Rolls Royce, by the expensive clothes so casually worn, by the Baroness's politeness, her ease in dealing with servants, and that she did not have to work. She belonged to that very small class who were born cool and she had learned how to live. Charlie did not fail to note that all of her friends in the jazz business were black, starting with himself and his old comrade-in-arms from the Minton's wars, Thelonious Monk.

In the spring of 1953 Red Rodney completed his six months at Lexington and returned to the music business. Although

Rodney had undergone therapy with Dr. Joel Fort (now on the advisory board of the National Organization for the Reform of Marijuana Laws) and other psychiatrists experienced in handling addicts, the hoped-for cure did not take. Rodney was approached by a pusher on the train from Lexington to New York, a run much traveled by narcotics dealers. He was soon readdicted. The reconstituted Charlie Parker Quintet included Parker, Rodney, Haynes, Potter, and pianist Kenny Drew. Billy Shaw booked the group in clubs in Detroit, Cleveland, Boston, and Philadelphia. Again the Quaker City lived up to its reputation of a jinx town for users. During the first week Rodney was arrested for "sale and facilitating of drugs." Hauled before a notorious judge, A. Cullen Ganey of the United States District Court, Rodney pleaded guilty, only to hear the jurist order that he be sent to a federal penitentiary to begin serving his original five-year sentence. Rodney was remanded to Leavenworth, Kansas, where he became part of a huge penal community of five thousand felons that included some of the most hardened and vicious criminals in America. Once again, warned by his sixth sense, Charlie Parker avoided the bust, but that ended the Quintet for all time.

Charlie went back to the Strings. One night he ran into Duke Ellington, who asked Charlie how he liked working with this kind of a background. "Confidentially, Duke," Charlie told the famous orchestra leader, "it's getting to be a drag."

"Tell you what, Bird," Ellington said. "I'll make you an offer. How would you like to join my band?"

"What kind of bread, Duke?" Charlie asked.

"Seeing it's you, I'll pay top money. Three-fifty a week."

"But, Duke, only three and a half bills!"

"Every week of the year, Bird, whether we're booked or not. And it will be all yours, clear. No sidemen to pay. No ten percent to the agency."

Charlie shook his head sadly. "No way, no way, man."

"What kind of money did you have in mind?" Ellington asked.

"Make it eight hundred a week and you got a saxophone player."

Ellington smiled. "Bird, for that kind of money *I'd* work for you!"

After a great deal of legal maneuvering and wire pulling, the attorneys for Billy Shaw Artists managed to get Charlie's cabaret license reinstated and Shaw booked Charlie Parker and Strings into Birdland. Critical applause was cool. "Tasteless" appeared in one review of the opening. As a novelty, the act was wearing thin. Shaw set up a week at the Apollo Theater and two weeks at Lindsay's Sky Bar in Cleveland. Overweight, clad in a white suit that made him look heavier than ever, Charlie stood in front of the string unit—three violins, viola, cello, and harp, a skeleton version of the studio group that had backed him for the Mercury recordings. Night club owners balked at the price asked for the full unit. The act grew more boring by the week. What Charlie had not considered was that written arrangements, played exactly the same way, note for note, would soon grow monotonous, not only for the listener but also for the soloist. Symphony musicians were neither trained nor expected to improvise. They were skilled sight-readers, able to reproduce with precision the notes set on paper before them—and no more. There were no counter voices, no moving lines, no call and response figures to stimulate the soloist. No chase choruses. The repertoire of the string unit was limited to a dozen-odd tunes. New arrangements were expensive. Night after night, set after set, Charlie played the same repertory: *Just Friends, April in Paris, I Didn't Know What Time It Was, Summertime*, and the rest. It was like the reshooting of a scene in a motion picture, the same actors speaking the same lines over and over again. Bebop, he had told the Swedish critics, should be played fairly fast. He was playing everything at the same slow, dreary tempo. Tony Scott, a friend from the Minton's days, told Charlie that he was studying composition and counterpoint with Stefan Wolpe, a classical composer with an international reputation. Wolpe was impressed with the Parker recordings Scott played, and a meeting was arranged in Scott's loft apartment. Charlie bowed elaborately and in a stage voice told the European composer that he was greatly honored by the introduction and wished to commission him to compose a work for seventy-five pieces, which Granz would pay for and record. An enormous budget was indicated, and Granz refused.

As Charlie toiled with the Strings, he watched new names establish themselves in the jazz firmament, younger men who commanded high prices for their appearances. The Dave Brubeck Quartet had become a top attraction on the campus circuit. After years of obscurity John Lewis had realized his dream of organizing a jazz chamber group. Called the Modern Jazz Quartet, it featured one of Charlie's old colleagues, Milt Jackson. The four musicians dressed like career diplomats. They had no bad habits and were never late. MJQ contracts stipulated that the sponsor must have a Steinway grand piano tuned that day to 440 pitch, just like Horowitz or Gieseking. The Modern Jazz Quartet played two fifty-minute sets per concert and no more. Their fee was fifteen hundred dollars a night, not a week.

The most talked-of record of the early Fifties was not made by Charlie Parker, but by Miles Davis. Auspiciously titled *Birth of the Cool*, it presaged a new era in American jazz, sounds chilled to a gelid state, drained of every trace of funk. The one-time "Junior" of the first Charlie Parker Quintet, and the leader's unwilling errand boy, Miles was now artfully turned out in tailored British tweeds. Miles made *Playboy*'s list of best-dressed men, and drove an imported sports car. As a member of the Parker Quintet, he had found ample opportunity to study the art of the put-on from one of its masters. Miles now reshaped this experience to create the new image of the combo leader, aloof and *disengagé*. Miles did nothing so crude as to mistake a telephone booth for a men's room. He simply turned his back on the audience at the finish of his solos and walked off the bandstand to sit alone at a back table, indolently smoking a cigarette and staring with stony contempt at the customers.

Outwardly he seemed unemotional, unconcerned, and indifferent. Inside he seethed with hostility. He worked out with boxers so that he could take care of himself in a brawl, forgetting, until an agent put him wise, that one good belt in the kisser could end his career. Recovering from throat surgery, he permanently ruined his voice in a telephonic shouting match with his agent. One of his favorite ploys was to shake hands with an old colleague, apply an excruciating jiujitsu grip, and, as the other writhed in his grasp, hiss, "I never liked *you*." Or comment, in his snakey voice, "Man, you're getting old." The new Mr. Cool was small, tweeded, and nasty, the new culture hero, driving a sports car with a trunkful of custom-fitted golf sticks, playing as white a style as it was possible for any black man to play, with sumptuous phrases, with an endless stock of ideas edited out of the Charlie Parker system of music, in an iced tone, without vibrato.

A study of popular music shows that styles undergo a radical change about every four or five years, the time for a given group of teen-agers to attain a majority. The old generation does not change its tastes. Those remain constant. Twenty years from now middle-aged Beatles' fans will still be listening to reissues of Beatles' records, as those who dated to the music of Glenn Miller subscribe to new editions of Miller records or the Time-Life nostalgia swing series. What changes are the tastes of the upcoming generation, who want nothing to do with second-hand heroes and desire to create new ones. The hipsters of the 1950s had looked upon Charlie Parker as a classical figure, half man and half myth, but the palace revolution at Minton's and the great renaissance of music on Fifty-Second Street were now history.

Miles Davis' Juilliard background, the measured pace of his lifestyle, its lack of frenzy (outwardly), his mastery of the put-on, his contempt for bookers and audiences, his demand for high fees, his flair for good clothes, the cerebral nature of his music all appealed to the new generation. Miles had style. Once in St. Louis he was standing on a corner after an autographing appearance at a record store, surrounded by sycophants, talking in low, barely audible tones. Suddenly an old acquaintance came hurrying up like a lost puppy to shout out an enthusiastic greeting. Miles froze the man with a penetrating look. Realizing that he had committed a serious gaffe, one that might cost him his status and wreck his career in jazz, the other had the presence of mind to instantly withdraw and walk slowly around the block. He then approached the group from a new angle and stood at its edge for some time. Finally Miles' eyes met his and there was the briefest of nods. The other had been restored to grace, but it had been a very near thing.

Jazz, the fickle art, had never stayed with one of its heroes for more than a generation. They were like Sir James Frazer's priestly kings of the wood, enthroned until cut down by a successor. The same cruel cycle that had relegated Jelly Roll Morton, Louis Armstrong, Coleman Hawkins, Fletcher Henderson, Lester Young, and others to history was threatening to overtake Charlie Parker. Young jazzmen, moving into the scene, were often surprised to learn that he was still around. Alternately addicted to heroin, the vice of the Forties, and alcohol, the vice of the Thirties, Charlie Parker was, in a time when everybody was straight, an anachronism. Obese, wearing a rubbery mask of disillusionment, more often rhapsodist than improviser, Charlie appeared with his Strings, at Birdland, Lindsay's Bar, Bop City, it no longer mattered where, for the nth time working over the clever melodies crafted by the tunesmiths of Tin Pan Alley. Charlie confided to Lennie Tristano that he had extracted the last ounce of variation from the immemorial blues. The thirty-two-bar format, with the foursquare sections and AABA scheme, which accounted for the rest of his performances, had lost its allure. Like a thin man inside a fat man wanting to break out, he spoke of studying formal composition, and actually discussed such plans with Stefan Wolpe and Edgard Varese, but nothing ever came of them. If he was locked forever in the blues and the ballad, it was because his whole musical life had been concerned with those forms. He was an off-the-top player, telling the same story over and over again, each time with infinitely fresh variations. Of formal composition he knew nothing. He could hardly discipline himself to write a simple lead sheet for a recording session.

Charlie Parker had the feeling of a man who has raced against odds and time to arrive at a destination, a great international event, to find that it is just finishing. The Fifties found him a Pied Piper whose last fanatic follower had dropped by the wayside. Given the mood and opportunity, he was still able to blow down any musician in jazz, and to summon forth performances that made pallid anything Dave Brubeck, the Modern Jazz Quartet, or Miles Davis could produce, no matter how much they strained, how cleverly they planned, as he had proved at Massey Hall.

25

King Pleasure

It was 1954, a fateful year for Charlie, and it began well enough, though at the expense of another prominent jazzman. Charlie Parker was working at the Blue Note in Philadelphia when an urgent call came from the Billy Shaw Artists' Bureau in New York. Stan Getz, featured saxophonist with the Stan Kenton Festival of Modern American Jazz, then winding up a national tour, had dropped out of sight in San Francisco. An immediate replacement was needed. Shaw negotiated a favorable contract and Charlie took the first non-stop flight to the West Coast.

He got there in time to play at the concerts in San Francisco and Oakland. The show included June Christy, Dizzy Gillespie, Erroll Garner, and the Stan Kenton Orchestra. In San Francisco Charlie revisited his favorite jam spots and renewed his friendship with poet-author Kenneth Rexroth, a close observer of the jazz scene. To Rexroth, Charlie appeared in the summerset of his career. Rexroth saw Charlie and Dylan Thomas as the two beleaguered, tragic giants of his time: "like pillars of Hercules, like two ruined Titans guarding the entrance to one of Dante's circles . . . the heroes of the postwar generation, the great saxophonist, Charlie Parker and Dylan Thomas. . . . As the years passed, I saw them each time in the light of an accelerated personal conflagration. . . . Both of them were overcome by the horror of the world in which they found themselves, because at last they could no longer overcome that world with the weapon of a purely lyrical art."

When Charlie appeared with the twenty-piece Stan Kenton Orchestra, he would walk onstage holding his saxophone and, without recourse to the public address system, begin his solo, cutting through the screaming brass section with its five trumpets and four trombones, and the huge reed choir. "His sound was so strong," an observer remarked, "that it cut through all that triple-forte background. Bird wiped them right out."

In San Francisco Charlie ran into Hampton Hawes, whom he had known in Los Angeles in 1946. The young pianist, an avowed Parker worshipper, was beginning to get together an impressive personal style, developed from Parker's saxophone methods as they might be adapted to the keyboard. They jammed at Jumbo's and Charlie paid Hampton Hawes one of his highest compliments. "When Hamp took his solos," Charlie told friends later, "you could hear rats piss on cotton." At a rap session Hawes questioned Charlie about his own musical development. Charlie smiled and said, "I lit my fire. I greased my skillet. And I cooked."

The following night, with the Kenton tour still in the Bay Area, Charlie went out to jam and became ill. Sweating, suffering from dizzy spells and grinding stomach pains, he played far below his usual form. Irreverent San Francisco musicians began to say that the king had fallen and, as Charlie fumbled and missed his fingering, started to crowd him at the microphone and make him look bad. Charlie stopped playing and laid his horn on the piano. "Give me an hour," he told them. "I'll be back." An hour later he arrived by cab, all smoothed out, and proceeded to demolish the opposition, man by man, in a display of musical omnipotence.

Hampton Hawes, one of Charlie's greatest admirers, dated his own musical awakening from the opening night at Billy Berg's in 1945. "I went there with Sonny Criss. Bird played an eight-bar channel on *Salt Peanuts* that was so strong, so revealing, that I was molded on the spot, like a piece of clay, stamped out. Bird never once in his lifetime played a single bar of bullshit. The vibrations he started are still moving across the world. He was like going to the moon thirty years ago. Tatum had it all together musically but not in life. Tatum was blind, and withdrawn. Bird had it all together in music and in life. A jazz musician makes a total commitment, which is himself, his attitude, his sound, his story, and the way he lives. Bird was like a god. I never crowded him or got too close. He talked to us about things I wasn't to read until years later in books by Malcolm X and Cleaver. I heard all that in his music. Bird was a deeply frustrated man. Sonny said he was the most miserable man he had ever met. Bird felt deeply about the black-white split. He was the first jazz musician I met who understood what was happening to his people. He couldn't come up with an answer. So he stayed high. His only outlet was his music. The weird things he did . . . well, he had to have his fun some kind of way. He was telling the world, 'You don't dig me and you don't dig my music, so dig this shit!' Bird borrowed money from everybody, but I think I'm the only person who owes him money. I owe him fifteen dollars he laid on me in New York when I was broke."

The Kenton tour ended in Los Angeles with a final concert that filled the huge Shrine Auditorium to its capacity of 6,700, turned away 2,000 and grossed $16,000. Charlie's feeling of being stranded in Southern California was relieved by a booking at Tiffany's. After the job he lingered on, enjoying the good weather, but suffering a new bout of stomach ulcers. When he visited a Los Angeles general practitioner for treatment he was ordered to a hospital to explore the further possibilities of cirrhosis of the liver and a pre-diabetic condition. Charlie refused to go and continued to play doctor to himself, adjusting the heroin highs from his hoard of down pills, barbiturates, and amytal.

While Charlie was at liberty the jukeboxes of Southern California suddenly burst forth with a recording of *Parker's Mood*, by rhythm-and-blues vocalist King Pleasure. Note for note, the singer had taken the solo from the Savoy recording and, reversing the usual process, set the music to words of his own invention. King Pleasure had developed this technique after paraphrasing recorded solos by Lester Young and James Moody (*D.B. Blues, Moody's Moody for Love*). Now his subject was the most controversial figure in jazz, its most brilliant performer, and its most notorious junkie, whose playing during the last year had afforded only flashes of old brilliance. In taverns, clubs, restaurants, in barber shops and the shine parlors along Central Avenue, wherever Charlie went he heard the lyrics, sedulously clothed in his own solo line, words that only too accurately described his malaise. Charlie's original exultant two-bar introduction had been paraphrased as:

> Come——with——me-ee-ee,
> If-you-wanna-go-to-Kansas City——ee-ee-ee . . . .

The muzzein cry of the opening was followed by:

> *I'm feeling low down and blue, my heart's full of sorrow,*
> *Don't hardly know what to do; where will I be tomorrow?*
>
> *Goin' to Kansas City. Want to go, too?*
> *No, you can't make it with me.*
> *Goin' to Kansas City, sorry that I can't take you.*
>
> *When you see me comin', raise your window high,*
> *When you see me leaving, baby, hang your head and cry,*
> *I'm afraid there's nothing in this screamy, streamy town*
> *A honky-tonky, monkey woman can do.*
> *She'd only bring herself down.*

So long, everybody, the time has come and I must leave you.
So, if I don't never see your smiling face again.
Make a promise you'll remember, like a Christmas day in December,
That I told you all through thick and thin, on up until the end,
Parker's been your friend.
Don't hang your head when you see those six pretty horses pullin' me.

Put a twenty-dollar silver piece on my watch chain,
Look at the smile on my face,
And sing a little song to let the world know I'm really free.
Don't cry for me, 'cause I'm going to Kansas City.

*Come with me, if you want to go to Kansas City.**

Kansas City was a town that Charlie had come to dislike more with each visit. It was now an empty shell as a jazz center and represented the worst aspects of provincialism and Jim Crow, certainly the last place in the world that he would wish to end his days. The twenty-dollar silver piece device had been lifted from *St. James Infirmary,* where the dead gambler is described lying on a mortuary slab with a similar good-luck charm on his watch chain, to show that he "died standin' pat." For a deeply sensitive musician to hear his own music mockingly clothed in the garments of derision and doom was an unforgettable and deeply disturbing experience. Charlie was privately outraged that his pianist on the original recording, John Lewis, had made the new version with King Pleasure. Like a nightmare that returns as soon as one falls asleep, and like the haunting memory of the wasted corpse of his own father in the Kansas City funeral home, the new version of *Parker's Mood* was a mnemonic demon from which there was no escape. Charlie watched the record climb on the rhythm-and-blues hit list until it was lodged among the top twenty. It was the *in* record of 1954. Charlie called Chan and exacted her promise that, in the event anything ever happened to him, she would under no circumstances permit him to be buried in Kansas City.

Charlie stayed on in Southern California. With Lester Young and Earl Hines, he helped open a new jazz club in Holly-

* King Pleasure, *Parker's Mood*, Prestige 7586.

wood, the Oasis. Hines appeared with a Chicago-style group that well suited his own style. Fatha had given up trying to run with the boppers. Lester fronted a mediocre five-piece unit and was cordial when they spoke backstage. He told Charlie he was into new things, although Charlie heard only a weak carbon copy of one-time greatness. The time when Charlie had listened to Lester Young through the walls of the Reno Club seemed very far away. The once-dashing Lester, star of the Count Basie Orchestra, the first hipster, was now slow and unsteady of movement, detached from reality, sealed off in a private world of fantasy. As he waited in the dressing room for Fatha Hines to finish, he told Charlie, "Bird-baby, I feel just like some l'il two-dollar whore sittin' here waitin' for my call." Lester's dressing room table was lined up with unopened fifths of Gordon's gin. He was drinking them off at the rate of about two a day. He seldom bothered to eat. Charlie wondered how long Lester could go on. From Lester to Bird to Miles! It set Charlie to thinking. He was the middle link in that succession. But Pres was forty-three and that seemed very old. Charlie was only thirty-four and people kept telling him that the thirties were the best years of your life.

Afternoons during the Oasis engagement Charlie went to the studios of sculptress Julie MacDonald, an acquaintance from previous visits to Southern California, to sit for a head in wood. The sculpture, now owned by a retired Santa Barbara pharmacist, shows him fat, middle-aged, inscrutable. The MacDonald sculpture has the dual, magical, forbidding properties of an African mask. When Miss MacDonald took him to see a collection of sculptures beginning with early Egyptian pieces and ending with Brancusi, she was astonished at his ability to grasp the inner meaning of the artist. Like Kenneth Rexroth, Miss MacDonald thought Charlie one of the great contemporaries, who had "caught the pulse of our times, the pressure, confusion, and complexity . . . sadness, sweetness, and love."

In March, while he was Miss MacDonald's guest, Charlie received the overwhelming news that Pree had died of pneumonia. He burst into tears and sobbed uncontrollably. His first distraught reaction was to blame Pree's death on his failure as a husband, his next on the indifferent medical care Pree had received at clinics. As he realized, a fraction of the money spent on drugs would have obtained for Pree the finest medical attention. "Any man who makes himself a slave to heroin is a fool!" he cried out to Julie MacDonald. He was so overcome with grief that Miss MacDonald took over practical matters, communication with Chan and arrangements for his immediate return to New York. Crushed by the news, Charlie revealed his confusion and anguish in a series of four telegrams sent to Chan that night:

> MY DARLING. MY DAUGHTER'S DEATH SURPRISED ME MORE THAN IT DID YOU. DON'T FULFILL FUNERAL PROCEEDINGS UNTIL I GET THERE. I SHALL BE THE FIRST ONE TO WALK INTO OUR CHAPEL. FORGIVE ME FOR NOT BEING THERE WITH YOU WHILE YOU ARE AT THE HOSPITAL. YOURS MOST SINCERELY, YOUR HUSBAND, CHARLIE PARKER.

An hour or two later he wired;

> MY DARLING. FOR GOD'S SAKE HOLD ON TO YOURSELF. CHAS. PARKER.

This was followed by the cryptic:

> CHAN, HELP. CHARLIE PARKER.

Early the next morning, after reservations had been secured Charlie wired:

> MY DAUGHTER IS DEAD. I KNOW IT. I WILL BE THERE AS QUICK AS I CAN. MY NAME IS BIRD. IT IS VERY NICE TO BE OUT HERE. PEOPLE HAVE BEEN VERY NICE TO ME OUT HERE. I AM COMING IN RIGHT AWAY. TAKE IT EASY. LET ME BE THE FIRST ONE TO APPROACH YOU. I AM YOUR HUSBAND. SINCERELY, CHARLIE PARKER.

The telegrams reflected many emotions and facets of Charlie's complex character: despair, anguish, a belated sense of responsibility, awkwardness in the use of straight English, preacher-like inclination for heavy words (fulfill), guilt, vanity ("My name is Bird."), and the infantile non sequitur, "It is very nice to be out here." He lost no time in flying back to New York.

Charlie found Chan crushed by grief. He took over the funeral arrangements. After a simple ceremony at which piano pieces by Bartok were played, Pree was buried in a New York cemetery. The image of the child in her tiny coffin, like the image of his father, would remain with him for the rest of his life. For the first time Charlie decided to take stock of his contracts and copyrights, reasoning that there must be a large sum of money due him from various sources. He had seen royalty checks made out to other musicians. Often the amounts were in four figures. Charlie had composed more tunes and contributed more ideas than any other musician and recorded as extensively.

"Composing" for Charlie was a special process, somewhat different from what is imagined as the usual act of creating a normal musical structure. Essentially Charlie was an off-the-top player. But the act of improvisation called for a point of departure. The raw material of Charlie's compositions came from two convenient stockpiles, the blues with its timeless twelve-bar sequence (I-IV-I-V-I) and the thirty-two-bar popular song that appeared in abundance between the two wars. American popular song, its facile craftsmanship derived from European art music, held for Charlie an ambivalent fascination. Charlie recoiled from its gratuitous melodies but admired its pretty harmonic resolutions. He kept the harmony and composed new melodies of his own, stretched them like a fresh canvas over the framework of the original, later to be brushed in with further embellishments that would vary from night to night. *Now's the Time*, *Ornithology*, *Red Cross* were genuine compositions, comparable to *One O'Clock Jump* or *In the Mood*, standards used by countless other musicians. Charlie almost never put any of this material on paper. To do so seemed a waste of time. He had no need of musical notes. Anything that he heard, performed, or created could be summoned from his memory at an instant's notice—for example, the segment of an improvised solo on an early McShann record that was later grafted onto the harmonic framework of *How High the Moon* and became *Ornithology*.

A man as devoted and skilled as Dean Benedetti might have made both their fortunes had he been willing to play the role of musical secretary instead of amateur recording engineer, and set the nightly stream of ideas to paper and seen to their copyright. This was not done because Dean's contempt for the establishment carried over to the recording and music publishing industry, and the copyright office itself. Dean saw them all as rip-offs, in the language of his day, *hypes*, and wanted nothing to do with them. That would have degraded the purity of Charlie Parker's deathless music. Dean was a devoted menace, one of the sycophants who surrounded Charlie and made it very difficult for him to come to grips with the real world.

Upon Billy Shaw's recommendation Charlie consulted A. Allen Saunders, a New York attorney who specialized in handling the affairs of the music industry. Saunders at once set about the complex task of bringing order to the existing chaos. Telephone calls were made and letters written, individuals and firms were threatened with legal action. Mr. Saunders soon found the matter a hopeless tangle of unexecuted agreements, breached contracts, and uncopyrighted material. Those threatened said they would vigorously defend any action taken against them. After spending some time on the matter Saunders came to the conclusion that no attorney or accountant was likely ever to straighten out the chaos.

Charlie played a week at the Blue Note in Philadelphia and two at Basin Street in New York. With the money he took Chan, Kim, and Baird to Brewster on Cape Cod. There Charlie spent the time enjoying domestic life and taking the family for picnics and long walks among the dunes. He kept his hand in playing an occasional weekend gig at Brewster's Red Barn. Soon he was drinking again. In July, with funds low, Charlie called Billy Shaw to say that he wanted to go back to work.

Billy Shaw had very nearly approached the point of no return with the most difficult client in a stable that included more than its share of temperament. Shaw came up with three weeks, August 26 to September 15, at Birdland—Charlie Parker with Strings—the unit to be co-featured with Dizzy Gillespie and songstress Dinah Washington. There would be about a thousand dollars a week clear for Charlie, enough to liquidate his most pressing debts.

Charlie returned from the Cape suntanned, superficially healthy, and thirty pounds overweight. Moonfaced and stolid, wearing his white suit, Charlie opened to a sell-out crowd. Once again Charlie found himself back in the environment that had conditioned his life, exposed to its deadliness, tensions, interviews, conferences, invitations, to its autograph-seekers, artists and repertoire men, producers, back-slappers, journalists, song pluggers, pushers, pimps, prostitute, and call girls. "Balling chicks," unabashedly on the make, would wait for him at the end of the evening, in spite of Chan's presence and Charlie's obvious satisfactory relationship with his wife.

Backstage, Birdland simmered with temperament and high times. The star dressing room was occupied by Dinah Washington, then thirty, working her way through a fourth smashed marriage, one of the notorious alcoholics in show business, and only a few years away from suicide. The combination of Dinah Washington and Charlie Parker on the same bill was a booking oversight that Billy Shaw would never repeat. Dinah Washington ordered booze by the caseload. The singer held open house in her dressing room, hosting non-stop parties from which artists reluctantly took time off to perform their sets.

After a brilliant opening night, Charlie's playing drifted off into the routine. Nothing swung. Jazz buffs heard the rhapsodizing of an eminent saxophonist, now more virtuoso than artist. Critics panned the show and asked when Charlie expected to get back to playing jazz.

Before the week was out, Charlie had begun to quarrel with his sidemen. Sunday night, in the middle of a dispute, he lost his temper. As the public address system beamed angry words and recriminations for all to hear, Charlie summarily fired the entire string orchestra. Birdland became the scene of the wildest confusion, and another scandal. While the stage stood empty Charlie went to the bar and began drinking straight whiskeys. Members of the string orchestra, who had been engaged for three weeks under the terms of a union contract, followed Charlie to the bar and began to chivvy him about the wages due them. Oscar Goodstein told Charlie that he had played his last engagement in Birdland.

Tears in his eyes, Charlie walked out of Birdland, around the corner to the rival Basin Street club, and drank himself into a comatose state. Then he called a cab and was driven back to his apartment. There was a scene with Chan. She told him that she couldn't take his drinking any longer and that he was destroying the family. Charlie disappeared into the bathroom. Twenty minutes later Chan opened the door to see if he had fallen asleep. The medicine cabinet was open and bottles were strewn about. Charlie was sitting on the edge of the bathtub. He had drunk a bottle of iodine and swallowed a bottle of aspirin tablets. Chan called the police. A police car arrived, followed by an ambulance and a *Daily Mirror* photojournalism unit. A photographer took pictures of Charlie being placed in the ambulance. He was rushed to Bellevue Hospital, where his stomach was pumped out. He was placed in the semi-agitative ward. The grapevine buzzed with rumors and versions. The legend was passing from the bizarre to the genuinely tragic.

Down and Out in
New York

Prompt action by the ambulance surgeon and the staff in the emergency room prevented Charlie Parker's suicide. He remained at Bellevue for ten days. His vital forces rallied, and he began to recover. While he was at the hospital the musicians he had fired took their case to the union, and as soon as he was released he was summoned before the trial board to answer charges. Charlie could offer no defense. He had been the contractor and had willfully and capriciously breached the contract. Charlie was fined and ordered to pay back wages, a total of over three thousand dollars. Protesting that he was broke, he was told that deductions would be made from future performances until the balance was paid.

A first installment came from his fee for the opening Jazz at the Philharmonic concert of the season at Carnegie Hall, September 25. Charlie shared billing with Billie Holiday, Sarah Vaughan, John Lewis's Modern Jazz Quartet, and the Count Basie Orchestra. "Bird was not at his best," reported *Down Beat*, "but his dynamic professional skill occasionally shone through and indicated how Parker sounds on his more relaxed dates." It was the first time a reviewer had made excuses for his performance. The following night Charlie played the Boston concert, there escaping a union impound on his wages since Boston was outside the jurisdiction of New York Local 802. He did not join the concert tour but returned to New York, mentally and emotionally exhausted.

On September 28 Charlie voluntarily committed himself to Bellevue Hospital. He told the admitting physician at the Psychiatric Pavilion that he was severely depressed and feared for his own safety. The admitting diagnosis was "acute alcoholism and undifferentiated schizophrenia." It was noted that, when drinking, he had threatened his wife and children, exhibited suicidal tendencies, was disturbed by the death of his daughter and by the memory of his father's funeral. Charlie's personality was described as "ingratiating," and there were findings similar to those at Camarillo: "high average intelligence, a hostile evasive personality, primitive and sexual fantasies associated with hostility, and gross evidence of paranoid thinking." A spinal tap was made: collodial gold curve was negative. The blood Wasserman was 2-plus positive. According to the Bellevue report "there was a history given that the patient was treated in 1945 in Los Angeles for lues with penicillin, bismuth and arsenic." The plus 2 Wasserman did not indicate syphilis specifically and any such diagnosis of Charlie's condition in 1954 was negated by the gold curve reading. If the information he gave to the hospital about his treatments in Los Angeles was accurate, it was probable that he had been cured of the disease. There was no follow-through on the physical examination, and no general medical diagnosis. A neurological examination was negative.

Charlie was shifted from one ward to another, from doctor

to doctor, from psychiatrist to psychiatrist. He charmed members of the medical staff who did not know who he was and supposed he was an ordinary derelict. One psychiatrist told Chan that Charlie needed to be confined to a mental institution and gave it as his opinion that Charlie was insane, adding that electric shock therapy might be the last resort. When Chan protested, the psychiatrist asked her if she wanted a "husband or a musician."

Charlie remained at Bellevue a fortnight and was released when he agreed to report to the out-patient clinic for psychotherapy. Chan and Charlie moved into Mrs. Richardson's house at New Hope, Bucks County, Pennsylvania, although this meant daily trips to New York for the treatments at Bellevue. Family debts had mounted, and Charlie urged Billy Shaw to find him something that would raise a substantial sum quickly, preferably outside New York and the jurisdiction of Local 802. The long-suffering agent agreed to give Charlie one more chance, and made a determined effort to place him with an extensive jazz tour of Europe ready to leave in a few weeks. At the last moment the facts of Charlie's hospitalization and drinking problem leaked out; the contract was refused, and Coleman Hawkins signed instead. In a mindless rage, Charlie turned on his benefactor and signed with the rival Moe Gale Agency. The Gale Agency was less adept in handling controversial artists than was Billy Shaw. Club operators were hesitant to make commitments. The fiasco at Birdland finished the Strings as a club attraction. Charlie had no real small band, though he told Gale that he could produce one on the strength of a few telephone calls. The best Gale could manage was a scattering of bookings as a single, fronting local or house rhythm sections. One night Charlie put on his oldest and shabbiest clothes, so that he looked like a stage tramp, and stood on the sidewalk in front of Birdland, a toothpick in his mouth. When a particularly well-groomed customer approached, "dressed to the nines" in Broadway toggery, Charlie would stop the stranger, admire the outfit and drawl in a country voice, "Say, fella', you must be one of them jazz moo-sicians, all dressed up thataway."

Charlie played George Wien's Storyville, a new lounge in Boston. His performances were spotty, and he complained about the rhythm section, although he had worked with the same men previously. The day-to-day pattern of his life became increasingly erratic. One afternoon he paid a visit to the Boston morgue. Concocting a story that he was seeking to identify a friend believed to have been the victim of foul play, Charlie spent part of the afternoon viewing one corpse after another as it was pulled from the freezing compartment for his inspection. He joked sardonically with the morgue attendants, and that night recounted his experiences to the men in his band. Back in New York, Charlie appeared at a concert produced by Bob Reisner at Town Hall. The concert was poorly publicized and the crowd meager. At intermission a union patrolman turned up to impound a share of his earnings.

On November 5, Oran Lips Page, the trumpet soloist whose ride choruses had been a feature of the Count Basie band at the Reno Club, died suddenly of a heart attack. Charlie took one of his protégés, alto saxophonist Jackie McLean, to the funeral and spent a long time studying the body as it lay in the casket. "They fixed Lips up real nice," he told McLean. "His wig sure does look good." No more of a high-liver than many another jazzman, Page was forty-six at the time of his death. The body was flown to Kansas City for burial, and many in the music business were reminded of King Pleasure's lyrics in *Parker's Mood*.

Prowling the Village one night with McLean, Charlie organized an impromptu session at the Open Door, but only after having to persuade the owner to let them use the bandstand. Later that night Charlie told McLean, "Here I am begging pennies for drinks and putting myself down. I am Charlie Parker and I have to beg people to let me play. Kick me in the ass, Jackie." Charlie insisted that McLean follow his instructions, and there was an embarrassing scene in front of the Open Door that was witnessed by a crowd of people who recognized Charlie as the star of the Sunday afternoon jam sessions. In his deep voice, speaking in the tone of a man giving orders that he expected to be obeyed, Charlie repeated, "Jackie, you heard me. I want you to kick me in the ass."

Nervous and embarrassed, McLean nudged Charlie in the backside with a knee, but this would not do, either. Charlie wanted to be hurt and humiliated. He said once more, clearly and distinctly, "Jackie McLean, I want you to kick me in the ass for letting me get myself in this position." Finally McLean planted his foot in Charlie's backside and Charlie said, "Jackie McLean, don't you ever allow this to happen to you." A week after the ass-kicking incident, Charlie found himself without a saxophone to fulfill a one-night engagement. He borrowed McLean's alto. The next day Charlie pawned the instrument and spent the money.

On December 10, Charlie fulfilled his last date for Norman Granz and Verve. With a rhythm section (Bishop, Bauer, Kotick, Taylor), his thinnest instrumentation for that label, Charlie completed two takes of *Love for Sale* and two of *I Love Paris*. He was not well, and was in indifferent form. There was a large swelling on the back of his tongue. The date was abandoned before the three hours had expired.

Later that month, during Christmas week, I saw Charlie at a cellar cabaret that operated briefly on Eighth Avenue near 48th Street as Le Club Downbeat. Charlie was shabbily dressed in a suit I remembered from earlier years. The suit had not been to a cleaner in weeks. Dirt creases showed on the cuffs and collar of a rumpled white shirt. Charlie was wearing carpet slippers. His face was bloated and his eyelids so heavy that only half of the pupils showed. The first five minutes of the set were spent in slowly assembling the saxophone while fellow musicians, all of them unknowns, stood nervously on the bandstand. When Charlie got around to playing it was evident that he was having trouble getting air through the horn. The saxophone tone, normally so clear and brilliant, had flabby spots. The club was half-occupied and the management indifferent to the music. The musicians were trying hard to organize an old-fashioned jam session, Kansas City style, but the effort was obviously a failure. At tables customers talked over their drinks and cast vexed looks at the bandstand, indicating that the music was too loud, or unmusical for their tastes. The lines that Charlie played were strange and exciting, as if he were trying to press forward into a new and unexplored area of his music. The performance was painfully reminiscent of the *Lover Man* date in California. The tragedy of the jazz musician in America, and the tragedy of the black artist in an alien land was vividly presented by that drab tableau on the bandstand of Le Club Downbeat that night of Christmas week, 1954.

An attempt to talk after the set proved futile. He sat at the table, sullen and barely coherent, full of hostility, staring at me with heavy-lidded eyes. He demanded the usual large sum of money, and I gave him the few extra dollars I had with me. He dug into his coat pocket and brought out a large white pill and began munching it slowly, explaining that it was codeine and helped control the pain of his stomach ulcers. He launched into recriminations about the release of *Lover Man* and the arm twisting that he claimed had taken place before he was permitted to leave Camarillo State Hospital. During the next set a club employee came to the table to say that Charlie was carrying a gun and had threatened to shoot me and that it would be in everyone's best interest if I left the premises. That was the last time I saw Charlie Parker.

New Year's Day 1955 Charlie and Bob Reisner, producer of Sunday afternoon jam sessions at the Open Door, met on a street in Greenwich Village. "I never thought I'd live to see 1955," Charlie told the producer, then quoted a stanza from the *Rubáiyát:*

> Come, fill the cup, and in the fire of Spring,
> Your Winter garment of Repentance fling;
> The Bird of Time has but a little way
> To flutter—and the Bird is on the Wing.

He had memorized the stanza, and took a grim pleasure in emphasizing his nickname. "Come on, Bird, things aren't that bad!" Reisner said jovially. Charlie filled Reisner in on his activities and state of health. He was no longer living at New

Iope or with Chan. They had split. He was drifting around the
Village, shacking up with friends. His horn was in pawn. His
health was poor; there had been a series of ulcer attacks. Somebody had told him about a sure cure for his condition. You tied
a string to a piece of radium and lowered it into your stomach.
He was looking for the radium. There was talk of a new band
with bassist Ron Carter, trumpeter Conte Candoli, drummer
Louis Bellson, and Bellson's wife, Pearl Bailey, in 1955 already
a strong box office attraction. Pearl would front the group and
insure its commercial success. All of this was still in the talking
stage. Reisner offered Charlie a gig at the next Sunday afternoon concert.

He arrived at the Open Door to find that Reisner had made
him the featured artist and cut him in on a percentage of the
take. Charlie stationed himself at the door, collecting tickets,
keeping his eye on the till. Several times he took exception to a
would-be customer and told the promoter to throw him out. Before the first set Charlie took the microphone and solemnly told
the crowd, "In the event there may by chance be any federal
authorities in the house, I would like to announce that I do not
have any narcotics on my person."

The Gale Agency sent him to Chicago for a four-nighter at
the Bee Hive, where he worked with trumpeter Ira Sullivan.
On opening night he spent most of his time in the dressing
room. On Saturday a union patrolman told Charlie that if he
did not play, he would be fined. At midnight he had passed out
in the dressing room. A young jazz enthusiast named Joe Segal
tried to revive him. Charlie kept pushing Segal away, saying
"One moment, please." Segal suggested a hospital. Charlie refused. The next day, to everyone's surprise, he showed up an
hour early for the Sunday afternoon jam session and was found
by admirers seated at the bar, smiling and jolly, a drink in his
hand, eyes sparkling. That afternoon he sounded more like the
Charlie Parker of old. From Ira Sullivan, Charlie learned the
latest news of Red Rodney.

Released on parole from Leavenworth, Rodney had come
directly to Chicago and worked with Sullivan at the Bee Hive
the previous fall. Within a few weeks Charlie's former trumpet

player had become readdicted, arrested, and returned to Leav
enworth to finish serving his five-year sentence.

When Charlie returned to New York he ran into Sonny
Stitt, a remote rival as an alto saxophonist. "Sonny," Charlie
said cryptically, "pretty soon I'm going to hand you the keys to
the kingdom."

He rode the subways aimlessly at night, alone. He would
take the Independent line at the Eighth Street station, ride to
the end of the line in Queens or the Bronx, and then return to
his starting point. He was seen in all-night restaurants, diners
and small neighborhood bars. One cold afternoon at the end of
January, Charlie was seized by an ulcer attack while walking
through the West Village and passed out on the sidewalk in
front of a brownstone building at 4 Barrow Street. He was recognized by artist Harvey Cropper and Ahmed Basheer, who
lived in a one-room cold-water flat in the building. With the
help of passers-by, Basheer and Cropper carried Charlie up several flights of stairs and put him to bed, no easy job considering
his weight.

Charlie began to twist and turn. He slowly regained con-
sciousness. "Who is Muslim?" he asked. "Where is that fellow
who is a Muslim?" He sat up in bed, staring at the faces. He
had met Basheer at a Village costume party at which he had
come as a Mau-Mau. Basheer was an American Negro from St.
Louis who had accepted the Moslem faith and changed his
name from Thomas Henderson to Ahmed Basheer. He had held
several discussions about religion with Charlie. Basheer was
trying to convert him to the Ahmediyya Movement in Islam.
The Mohammedan faith would solve Charlie's problems, Basheer told him.

"I want to hear the scriptures from the Koran," Charlie
said. Basheer took the book and began reading in Arabic. "It's
too beautiful!" said Charlie, placing his hands over his heart.

He said to those around the bed, "I know you fellows are
trying to keep an eye on me because you don't want me to kill
myself, but regardless of what you say or do, I'll have to die."

"Bird, don't try to talk," Basheer told him. "Try to rest
now. You are among friends."

"There won't be anything to it. It will be very easy. I'll just simply maybe jump off a bridge or something some night, and you fellows will hear about it." Charlie twisted in the bed.

Basheer asked him, "Wouldn't it be better if we took you to a hospital?"

"No, I don't want that. I don't like hospitals. Nothing you two can say can save me. I've made up my mind to do it."

Harvey Cropper said, "Bird, don't say that. Look what you'll be doing to all of the people who love your music! You can best serve the world by remaining alive. Many people would listen to what you have to say."

"Do you really think so?"

"Of course, Bird."

Charlie groaned and went to sleep.

Basheer later said, "We knew that like all artists, the world's failure to receive the love he was trying to give and receive was weighing him down. He believed his own death would solve his problems."

For several weeks Basheer, poet Ted Joans, and Charlie shared the flat. Heat was furnished four hours daily. To keep warm, the men were obliged to sleep in the same bed, under a pile of overcoats and sweaters. When the heat went off Charlie would shout down the airwell at the janitor, "What do you think we are up here, Eskimos?"

To Ahmed Basheer, Charlie said, "Basheer, I don't let anyone get close to me. Even you. Or my wife."

"Why?" Basheer asked.

"It's a long story. Once in Kansas City I had a friend who I liked very much. A sorrowful thing happened."

"What was that?" Basheer asked, supposing the friend had betrayed Charlie in some way.

"His name was Robert Simpson," Charlie said slowly. "He died."

That had been twenty-one years ago, in 1934, when they were both members of the Deans of Swing, just before Charlie dropped out of Lincoln High School and took the job at Greenleaf Gardens.

When he was able to get out of bed Charlie walked the Village streets. Dressed in a parka with an attached hood, he roamed Washington Square, the lower Village and the East Side, visited bars and small night clubs and occasionally played with young musicians he scarcely knew, with no other compensation than a few drinks grudgingly poured by the management.

Idle hours took Charlie to an instrument maker's shop run by master craftsman Pietro Carbone. There he watched in rapt attention as repairs were made on violins, drums, lutes and zithers. "My head is too big for a saxophone," he told Carbone. The instrument maker compared him to his countryman, Paganini, whose dissolute life and legendary improvisational skill so closely paralleled Charlie's own.

Charlie dropped in on Edgard Varese and found the avant-garde composer packing for a trip to France. Charlie again discussed the never implemented plan to study with Varese. "Take me as you would a child," he told the Frenchman. "I want structure. One instrument is not enough. I want to write for a lot of instruments, voices, a symphony or an opera." "Of course, Bird," Varese replied. "I always told you I was willing. But you must promise to show up." Varese asked Charlie to call him when he returned to New York the week after Easter.

Basheer helped organize a one-week's stand at the Comedy Club in Baltimore and went along as Charlie's personal manager and bodyguard, to see that Charlie did not drink too heavily. There were hassles over missed sets and docked pay. The day had passed when night club operators would tolerate Charlie's temperament. The name on the marquee had lost its luster. The engagement was not extended and Charlie and Basheer returned to New York, to the cold-water, walkup flat on Barrow Street where heat was available four hours early each evening. They slept in their clothing, played records and drank wine. They attended the movie *Carmen Jones*, in which Max Roach had a small part, four times. They stayed up all night so that they could sit in Sheridan Square at dawn and watch the sun rise over the tall buildings to the east. As the sun rose, Charlie told Basheer, "Look how beautiful it is early in the morning. Do you want to see Allah? Look east, way down there by Broadway. See the sun already to come up. That's God. Everything that you can see and everything that you can't see is Allah."

One night Charlie visited the Bowery with artist Harvey Cropper. The painter watched Charlie approach an aged derelict who was soliciting alms and punch the man viciously in the stomach. The derelict groaned and staggered. Charlie collected their combined resources, five dollars and thirty-five cents, and pushed it into the derelict's hand. "That was the best thing we could have done for him," Charlie explained. "Now let me show you how it's done." Charlie began panhandling and within an hour had collected several dollars in silver which they spent on beer and whiskey shots in saloons along the Bowery.

Wrapped in his hooded parka, Charlie rode subways, visited neighborhood bars and diners, intermittently ate and doctored himself. He made hit-and-run visits to beats he hardly knew, retraced steps, stood idly on street corners. He stared at displays in the windows of antique shops, book stores, and pastry makers, trying to get pleasure out of little things once more. Winter streets were windy and cold. He was frequently alone, as he had been twenty years before as a teenage truant roaming the back alleys of Kansas City, but now in the alien metropolis he had adopted as his home, and set out to conquer, but whose night clubs and music halls looked askance at his artistry and fading image. The Village was alien, too. He was no longer a black man in a black ghetto. He had lost his health and his force. Music, the one avenue that had been the escape route for his frustrations, was no longer open or safe. His movements were mechanical, erratic, purposeless. They followed a mindless pattern of disorder and whim. High life had become low life. Benedetti had been replaced by Basheer. He had lost the trick of living off the top. He no longer had good solutions. He was un-cool.

On a cold damp day at the end of February, Charlie pulled himself together, left the cold-water flat, and went uptown to the Moe Gale Agency. He found his "judges" displeased and indifferent. Charlie fell back on his best manner and made a reform speech. Gale came up with two interim bookings, one at

Storyville in Boston as a single, and the other at Birdland. The Birdland booking was for the following weekend, for two nights only, Friday and Saturday, March 4 and 5. It wasn't much, but it would afford Charlie a chance to play his way back into the good graces of Oscar Goodstein. The band would include Bud Powell, Charlie Mingus, Art Blakey, and McKinley Dorham.

The weekend at Birdland began with an unfortunate altercation provoked by Bud Powell, who was still a very disturbed man. Charlie was sitting in a booth with Lennie Tristano when Powell came by, smiled, said hello, then grimaced and, for no apparent reason, went on, "You know, Bird, you ain't shit. You don't kill me. Man, you ain't playing shit no more."

"Bud," Tristano cut in. "Don't talk that way. Bird's your Poppa."

Charlie said nothing. When Powell left, Charlie told Tristano, "You think he's crazy? I taught him to act that way."

For this most important engagement Charlie arrived Saturday night thirty minutes late. A large crowd had gathered to catch the Charlie Parker comeback. The first set had begun. Bud Powell was drunk, and Mingus, Blakey, and Dorham were attempting to cover his mistakes. Notes tumbled out of the instruments, zoomed, dipped, swirled about in a bitter cacophony. In the huge underground room with its larger-than-life medallions of show business personalities and trembling bird cages a crowd had gathered to hear the stars of jazz. There was no love and no joy in the playing of these men. Instead, evil forces were being set loose in the room. Goodstein commented crossly on Charlie's tardiness. "Get yourself up there and start playing," Goodstein said.

"With what?" Charlie replied, indicating Powell, who was slumped over the piano.

"I know. Bud is sick. He'll have to go back to the hospital. But you're the leader. Get up there and pull things together."

Charlie ignored Goodstein and walked to the dressing room area in the back of the club. He did not play the first set. He sat in the dressing room and waited for the next set. When it was time, Pee Wee Marquette appeared on the bandstand and began in his nasal falsetto: "And now, ladies and gentlemen, the management of Birdland proudly presents the Charlie Parker All-Stars." The midget paused and waited for the musicians to appear. Bud Powell came on alone and the crowd clapped. Bud bowed elaborately, grinned, and, perhaps to satirize his role as a performer, attempted to perform a set of dance steps. Powell was so drunk that he nearly fell into the ringside tables. As the midget looked on impassively, Powell reeled across the stage, sat down at the piano bench, and began playing *Little Willie Leaps*, his head hanging over the keyboard and his fingers slipping ineptly from the keys. The tune was scarcely recognizable by Birdland customers, the most knowledgeable of jazz buffs. Conditioned as they were to the unexpected at the Jazz Corner of the World, they settled back to await developments.

Next to show were Mingus and Dorham. Without success they attempted to support the pianist, but Bud had lost all sense of time. Mingus cast anxious glances at the rear of the club. Hal Harewood, drummer with the co-featured Kai Winding group, took over the drums, and the trio carried on briefly. At last Charlie Parker appeared, chatting amiably with Art Blakey. Unaware of what had happened, anaesthetized by several straight whiskeys, feeling confident and ready to play, Charlie went to the microphone and told the crowd, "Ladies and gentlemen, the management of Birdland has gone to *enormous* expense to bring you our all-star band." He proceeded to introduce the musicians and the first tune, *Hallucination*, a new composition of his own. Charlie counted off the first measure. The band began to play *Hallucination*. Bud Powell again played *Little Willie Leaps*.

Charlie stopped and repeated his instructions. Everyone started all over again. The result was the same.

"Come on, Baby!" Charlie told Bud Powell.

Powell swung around on the piano stool, faced Charlie, grinned, and demanded, "What key, mother——?"

"The key of S [shit], mother," Charlie snapped back.

Leader and pianist began cursing each other. Bud Powell smashed the keyboard with his elbow and walked off the stage.

When he had gone Charlie said, "Ladies and gentlemen, I'm sorry to say our most brilliant member has deserted us." But instead of carrying on with the set, Charlie stood at the microphone. He called in an anguished voice: "Bud Powell! Bud Powell! *Bud Powell!*"

McKinley Dorham stood at a corner of the stage, trumpet tucked under one arm, trying to detach himself from the scene. Art Blakey played a drum pattern, trying ineffectually to create a diversion. Mingus had stopped playing altogether. Charlie continued to call Bud Powell's name, his voice dirgelike, sounding over the public address system, through Birdland. He called "Bud Powell" twelve or fifteen times, until the effect on listeners was unbearable. There was no answer. As people began to leave the club, Mingus came to the microphone. Mingus said, "Ladies and gentlemen, please don't associate me with any of this. This is not jazz. These are sick people."

Mingus grounded his bass and left the stage. Customers at Birdland had the queer feeling that they had gone to the wrong place of entertainment that evening and were watching a scene from the theater of the absurd, complete with mimes, masks, and buffoons.

Charlie closed the cover of the piano over the keys Bud Powell had smashed. He discarded his saxophone on top of the piano. Through no fault of his own that he could grasp the big comeback performance at Birdland had failed. Charlie stood alone on the bandstand and watched Birdland empty itself of customers. At the back of the club Powell sat alone at a deserted table. The other musicians had gone to the back bar. Slowly and heavily, Charlie climbed down from the bandstand and followed the customers up the stairway to the street. Then he walked south on Broadway to Basin Street. He found a corner of the bar and began drinking whiskeys, double whiskeys without chasers. Charlie kept drinking whiskey shots until he barely was able to stand. Staggering, he made his way back up Broadway toward Birdland. It was nearly four o'clock and time to close. The big sign that he and Billy Shaw had watched being constructed was still on, showering Broadway with its rain of light. Charlie stared up at the lights and the letters.

Then he went inside the club and saw Mingus at the bar. Charlie put a wet cheek alongside Mingus.

"Mingus," Charlie told the bass player, "I'm goin' to go someplace now pretty quick where I won't be able to bother nobody."

"Bird, don't talk shit," Mingus said.

"Yes, Mingus," Charlie said slowly, "I'm goin' someplace where I ain't ever goin' to bother nobody. Not any more."

27

At the Hotel Stanhope

Wednesday, March 9, four days after the affair at Birdland, Charlie Parker started for Boston, where he was to play a weekend engagement at Storyville. He had no more than left the Village when impulsively he decided to stop off for a visit with the Baroness. Charlie was not sure why he wanted to interrupt the trip before it had begun. He was lonely, depressed by the fiasco at Birdland, and feeling unwell. The stomach pains were back, familiar symptoms of another ulcer attack. There was trouble with his breathing, too. He felt old and tired, as if he had been in the music business for fifty years.

Charlie walked through the lobby of the Hotel Stanhope, ignoring the frosty stare of the desk clerk, whose animosity toward the Baroness's Bohemian friends was well known, and took an elevator to the upper floor. The apartment with its Oriental rugs, expensive period furniture, and soft lights gave off an atmosphere of luxury and comfort, starkly contrasting with the cold-water flat on Barrow Street. As usual, the Baroness offered him a drink, and for the first time since he had known her, he refused. "Nica, I'm on the wagon," he told her.

The Baroness found this difficult to believe. She had never known him to refuse a drink. Charlie Parker on the wagon! The Baroness didn't believe it.

Charlie winked. "I just went on," he said.

The Baroness came toward him for a closer look and studied his face. "Aren't you feeling well?"

"I'm all right. Just let me have a glass of ice water. A big glass, please."

She brought him a tall, frosted highball glass full of ice water and watched him drink it. Then she said, "Bird, you're in pain."

"It's just my stomach. The ice water will cool it down." But he had no sooner got the water down than he had to go to the bathroom to vomit. There was blood in the vomit. He had seen blood in his vomit before, but not so much blood. He began to feel dizzy. He went back and sat down on the luxurious sofa.

"You're ill," the Baroness said firmly, and insisted on calling a doctor.

"No, don't call a doctor," Charlie said. "I'll be okay in a few minutes." He explained he was on his way to Boston to play a gig at Storyville for George Wien. He would appear as a single, using a house rhythm section that Wien provided. He knew it wasn't much of a gig. The new agency had gotten it for him and he had to make good, show up for all the sets on time, and play well. He was going to play his way back into the good graces of his judges. The day before, he had run into Louis Bellson on the street and learned that the band to be fronted by Pearl Bailey was still a possibility. He had to get himself back together. That band would bail him out.

The Baroness was not to be sidetracked. Charlie watched her pick up the antique telephone and, without consulting a directory, dial a number. There was a brief conversation and she hung up. The Baroness told Charlie that the doctor was one of the leading practitioners on upper Fifth Avenue and her own personal physician and that Charlie would like him. The Baroness said that Dr. Freymann would be arriving in a few minutes.

Charlie didn't believe that. Doctors never came right away in New York, if they came at all. But with the Baroness, you never knew. She had money, influence, and a way with her. When she walked into a restaurant head waiters treated her like visiting royalty.

Dr. Robert Freymann arrived in not more than ten minutes. He was a tall, well-made man with graying temples and merry eyes. Charlie's natural aversion to doctors was dispelled by the Baroness's personal physician. Dr. Freymann had authority and style. He was exactly the kind of doctor you would have expected the Baroness to have.

Dr. Freymann smiled and began by saying that he had played a little himself at one time but in medical school had to give it all up. The bedside manner was smooth and practiced. From the bag the doctor took out a stethoscope, thermometer, apparatus for measuring blood pressure and one with a tiny bright light for looking into Charlie's eyes. While the Baroness looked on, Dr. Freymann went through a smooth, efficient routine. Then he rolled up the sleeve of Charlie's shirt. Smooth fingers, their nails nicely manicured, gathered the muscles of the forearm and kneaded them into a soft bundle of flesh, exposing the veins with the old needle scars. Those scars were a complete history of his addiction, going back to the first time L'il Phil had turned him on in Kansas City, when he was fifteen years old. Scars that stood for his Cadillac, his portfolio of stocks and bonds, the Steinway concert grand, the apartment house in Queens. There was the unavoidable, unpleasant discussion about drugs. Charlie told Dr. Freymann that he had been off heroin for more than a year.

"Yes, I can see that," Dr. Freymann replied. The doctor wanted to know how much Charlie drank.

Charlie winked over the doctor's shoulder at the Baroness.

"Sometimes, Doc," Charlie said, "I take a little sherry before dinner."

Neither Dr. Freymann nor the Baroness smiled. Charlie's joke had bombed.

The discussion continued. Charlie admitted that he was drinking a quart or more a day. He answered questions about his confinement at Medical Arts Hospital for the first big ulcer attack after his return from Sweden and described how the attacks had become more and more severe and closer together. Once he had been stricken in Detroit and the attending physician had diagnosed a probable heart attack. Charlie told Dr. Freymann about another diagnosis of cirrhosis of the liver. Talking to the doctor made Charlie feel more hopeful, and better. It was getting late and he had the trip to Boston ahead of him. He announced that he had to leave, had to get the show on the road.

The doctor said at once that there was no question of his making the trip to Boston, or playing the saxophone. Both were ruled out. The instruments went back in the doctor's bag. The doctor filled a hypodermic needle with clear liquid from two vials and gave Charlie an injection, saying that the liquid contained glucose and vitamins. The doctor closed his bag and picked up the telephone. "I'm going to call an ambulance," he announced.

"Ambulance!" Charlie exclaimed. "What for?"

"The ambulance will take you to the hospital. That's the only place you can receive proper treatment."

"Hospital! Are you kidding?" A hospital was the last place Charlie wanted to go. He hated hospitals. Charlie began arguing with Dr. Freymann. He said that he was feeling better, much better, and that he would be able to get to Boston under his own power, that he had walked off worse attacks before.

The doctor tried to calm Charlie down. He said that the stay in the hospital might only be for a few days. It would depend upon the results of the tests and the way Charlie responded to treatment. The doctor would see to it that there was no publicity connected with his admission.

Charlie stood up to assert himself. A man was always at a disadvantage sitting down. When Charlie arose the dizziness returned. In the pit of his stomach lay a burning chunk of metal. The pain in his stomach would not quit. His heart pounded slowly and heavily. There was a feeling of numbness in his shoulders and arms. The room began to spin. Charlie sat down.

The doctor was explaining that only in a hospital would there be the necessary equipment for tests and the means for proper treatment. That no doctor could assume responsibility for Charlie unless he let himself be admitted to a hospital. The Baroness was talking, too. The Baroness was trying to get Charlie to be "reasonable" and give in and go to the hospital as the doctor asked.

"That's out!" Charlie said. "I'm not going to any hospital!" He knew that it was not within the power of the doctor to make him go if he refused.

The discussion went on. Charlie listened wearily. Then the discussion took a new turn. The Baroness saw that Charlie was not going to change his mind and said, "Dr. Freymann, why can't he stay here?" The Baroness proposed that Charlie remain in the apartment until he was better.

"Mr. Parker requires hospitalization. Only in a hospital can he have the around-the-clock nursing he needs."

The Baroness pointed out that she could divide nursing duties between herself and her daughter. They could do just as good a job as professional nurses. And wasn't Dr. Freymann's office in the next building? In that case he could be reached on short notice. It would be easier all around and better for everyone concerned. The Baroness was very persuasive.

Dr. Freymann didn't like it and didn't want to buy the Baroness's plan. But he admitted that he did not have the power to force Charlie to obey his orders. Finally with obvious misgivings, remarking that short of hospitalization he could not assume responsibility for his patient, Dr. Freymann agreed to let Charlie remain at the Baroness's apartment. He sent out for a prescription of penicillin and left directions as to the dosage.

Before leaving, the doctor took the Baroness into the

foyer. Charlie could hear their voices. The doctor said once more that Charlie was a very sick man, that under no conditions was he to leave the apartment, except in an ambulance. He made it quite clear that he did not like the situation and that the Baroness should call him if there were any change, night or day. Charlie heard him say, "I have to warn you that this man may die at any moment. He has advanced cirrhosis and stomach ulcers. He must not leave here except in an ambulance." Then the door closed.

That night Charlie slept on the sofa, in a bed improvised by the Baroness and her daughter. During the night Charlie drank three or four pitchers of ice water. His thirst was terrible. The next morning the pains still raged. Charlie was very weak. Dr. Freymann came three times that day, administering injections of glucose and supportive vitamins, and continuing the dosage of penicillin. The doctor took Charlie's temperature and pulse rate. He poked Charlie in the chest and back with the stethoscope. Then he ended by making another effort to get Charlie to a hospital. Charlie again refused. Charlie was about as sick as he ever had been. The fire burned in his stomach. His chest was being squeezed. The pains in his arms had returned. But the next day there were signs of improvement. Charlie lost track of the days. The Boston job began either today or tomorrow. The Baroness had called the Gale Agency and let them handle the cancellation. Nica told him that Gale would send a substitute. On the next day the stomach pains subsided. The burning sensation had gone. And things began to go better between Charlie and the doctor.

Friday morning after the doctor left, Charlie and the Baroness planned a surprise for his visit that afternoon. They would play a few numbers from the album Charlie had recorded for Mercury with the strings and woodwinds. The album was titled *The Great Charlie Parker with Strings*. The front cover of the record jacket had a color photograph of Charlie, almost life size, taken at the RCA studios when the session was made. For the doctor they would play *Just Friends* and *April in Paris*. That afternoon when Dr. Freymann arrived, he was told that a surprise had been prepared. Dr. Freymann was shown the album. The Baroness put the record on the hi-fi. The doctor sat in a deep armchair, eyes closed, and listened with his full attention. And the electronic magic filled the luxurious apartment with crying woodwinds and the eddying glissandi of a string section. Over it soared the saxophone, painting its melodic variations on *Just Friends*. The sounds were scooped through the speaker of the hi-fi set. The tone of the saxophone was centered, tender and passionate. Charlie Parker was vividly present, just as he appeared on the cover of the record album, just as he had been that day five years before at the recording studios.

Dr. Freymann was impressed. Charlie could tell that the doctor had really reacted to the music. Dr. Freymann praised the playing and the arrangements and told Charlie that he was a true artist.

Then the doctor's manner changed and he said that only with proper treatment would Charlie be able to resume his career. Surely that must be important to Charlie. Now that they understood one another, he hoped Charlie would allow him to make arrangements for admission to a hospital.

"But I'm already better!" Charlie insisted. "You said so yourself."

"Slightly," Dr. Freymann replied. "Only slightly better." At this stage any improvement could be deceptive. Charlie was a sick man.

Charlie smiled. He said, "Doc, my powers of recuperation have always been considered remarkable." Charlie told how he had walked away from the auto accident in which Ernest Daniels was badly injured and Old Man Wilkerson killed. How quickly he had recovered from the ulcer attack at Medical Arts Hospital, even though he had gone night-clubbing when the nurses thought he was in bed.

Dr. Freymann was not impressed. He said that Charlie was too strong-willed for his own good and that he was disappointed because Charlie was so uncooperative. If Charlie refused to follow his advice, then he must remain in the apartment and follow instructions to the letter. Above all, Charlie must continue to rest. Under no circumstances was he to leave, except in an ambulance. That must be understood. Next week, if Charlie continued to improve, the rules might be changed. That was possible.

Dr. Freymann put on his coat and the Baroness walked with him to the door. They spoke in the foyer for a minute or two. Charlie could not catch the words. Then the doctor left. Charlie did not see him again.

It was Saturday, and Charlie had stopped drinking the quantities of ice water. The Baroness helped move him to another part of the room so that he would be closer to the TV set. The Tommy Dorsey Show was due on in a few minutes, and Charlie wanted to see that. Dr. Freymann had agreed that he could sit up and watch.

When Charlie arose, he realized that he had become very weak. But that was from the lack of food and was only natural. He would see the show and eat something and then he would feel better. Propped in an easy chair, bolstered with pillows, draped with a blanket, Charlie played two games of peggity with the Baroness's daughter. Then it was time for the show. Dorsey's theme was *Getting Sentimental Over You*. The way Dorsey played it, the tune didn't swing very much, but Charlie liked the silky sound that T.D. got from the trombone. Then a juggler came on. Charlie had seen the same juggling act in vaudeville as a boy in Kansas City. The same thing the juggler did on the Tommy Dorsey show with trick bricks had been done in 1933 in vaudeville. Charlie dropped the blankets aside so that he could sit up. Bricks were flying around on the screen. Two of the bricks stuck together and the third brick flew up and stuck to the first two, just as Charlie had expected. Charlie began to laugh. "Crazy!" He laughed aloud in his deep, hearty, uninhibited laugh. Ridiculous, but it still fooled people, just as it had back in Kansas City. He liked that. It broke him up. The laughter became louder. As he continued to laugh, there was an intense rush of pain and a giddy sensation. He began to choke. There was blood in his throat, and he was choking.

He tried to straighten up by pushing against the sides of the chair. The picture on the TV screen blurred. The room spun.

One of the pillows fell from the chair and tumbled across the Oriental rug, where it lay in a pool of light. He pushed with both arms against the chair, but his elbows caved in. He could see the pillow lying on the Oriental rug. Inside him there was a sensation of something vital giving way. Collapsing. Then the pain became overpowering. A massive, numbing impact of pain. Like a supershot of high-grade heroin.

Seven thousand gut-busting dinners, water-drinking contests, goof balls dissolved in Dixie cups, popped pills, whiskey shots with no chaser, nights on the road, nights in the band bus, shouting matches against Billy Shaw, two chicks balled in a single bed, pleasured in the back of a speeding cab, guffaws, belly laughs, put-ons, musical fire fights, jam sessions, chase choruses, concerts, record sessions, and foaming saxophone solos crashed to a climax as shattering as the cymbal thrown at his feet across the stage of the Reno Club twenty years before. Something broke—gave way, or out. The stomach wall perforated by the peptic ulcer. The heart driven to its final, spasmodic, locked systole. The answer would never be quite clear. The mechanism that enabled Charlie Parker to ball, scoff, jive, turn on, con, act, to play the saxophone, sustaining the column of air in the throat, controlling the stiff reeds, supplying the energy to the musical computer in the brain, driving the fingers as they rattled against the levers and keys—all came to a stop. The system was switched off instantly, as if a generator had failed. And Baroness Pannonica de Koenigswarter, former aviatrix, dilettante, connoisseur of the black arts, registered in the *Almanach de Gotha*, libelled in *Confidential* magazine, panicked, steadied, dialed the number she knew from memory, heard Dr. Freymann's voice come on after three rings, saying, yes, he would come immediately, to let the patient remain exactly where he had fallen, to hold on, he would be there in less than five minutes.

The Baroness put down the telephone. Charlie Parker had fallen awkwardly to one side of the easy chair, across the pillow. The Baroness seized Charlie's wrist, feeling for the pulse. There was a pulse there. It was not very steady. She could feel the pulse flickering.

"He's going to be all right, Mummy," her daughter said. "He's all right now, Mummy."

The Baroness could feel the pulse working feebly against her finger. Then the pulse again began its shadowy flickering. Charlie Parker was hardly breathing at all. His eyes were shocked and staring, without movement. The breathing was hardly more than a rattle. The pulse stopped for several seconds. The Baroness felt her own pulse and then felt Charlie's pulse again. It had stopped working. There was nothing there at all. The only sound in the room was the music being pumped out of the TV set. That was still going. The juggler had finished and Tommy Dorsey was back. There was a picture of Dorsey with the trombone. The Baroness recognized the tune. It was *Marie*. A foreshortened shot of Dorsey lipping the trombone. The Baroness crossed the room and switched off the TV set, watching the picture zoom out to a pinpoint of bright light and then go off. She opened the front door of the apartment, leaving it ajar for Dr. Freymann. As she did so there was a tremendous clap of thunder that seemed to shake the entire building. She didn't want to believe the thunder. That was really impossible. Like the clap of thunder said to have occurred at the moment of Beethoven's death, the noise was the final, implausible crash of stage machinery in the drama of Charlie Parker's life. The long road that had begun in the district of Kansas City had found its ending in the apartment on upper Fifth Avenue.

Dr. Freymann was there in less than five minutes. He confirmed what the Baroness already knew, that Charlie Parker was dead. The doctor at once called the New York coroner's office and reported a death at the Hotel Stanhope. Between the hours of eight o'clock, when Charlie Parker died, and midnight, the Baroness's apartment was a scene of tension and confusion. The Medical Examiner arrived within the hour. He at once took over. Dr. Freymann and the Baroness had nothing more to do with arrangements. The Medical Examiner was followed closely by police, detectives, men from the coroner's office and morgue attendants. The Baroness was questioned closely and at length. She was unable to give Charlie Parker's correct address. The Baroness named Chan as next of kin, but she did not know Chan's address. She said that Charlie Parker was a friend and related the strange sounding circumstances of his drop-in visit, confinement and death.

There was little information for the blank spaces in the official forms. No one knew Charlie Parker's correct age. Dr. Freymann estimated Parker to be somewhere between fifty and sixty years of age, basing the figure on his patient's medical condition and appearance. Dr. Freymann attributed his death to stomach ulcers and pneumonia, with a contributing condition of advanced cirrhosis and the possibility of a heart attack. In all, there were four possible causes of death for an autopsy surgeon to probe. Medically, as in every other way, Charlie Parker had pushed his fingers all the way into the glove.

Early Sunday morning the body was removed from the living room sofa, placed in a wire basket and taken off to the city morgue. When Baroness de Koenigswarter was excused from further investigation by the authorities, she at once set out for the Village. The thought uppermost in her mind was to find Chan. She did not want Chan to read of Charlie's death in the newspapers or hear it broadcast over the radio. The Baroness went to the Open Door, the night club that had been the scene of the Bob Reisner Sunday afternoon jazz concerts, and many of Charlie's last appearances. The Baroness spent the rest of the morning talking to various friends, acquaintances and musicians. She was unable to locate anyone who knew where Charlie had been living or obtain Chan's address. Nor did she tell anyone that Charlie Parker was dead.

28

Coda: Six Pretty Horses
Pullin' Me

Chan was eventually located by an attorney representing pianist Teddy Wilson who had recorded with Charlie on the *Slam Slam Blues* date and whom the Baroness thought to call after she had exhausted every other lead and contact. The news of Charlie Parker's death leaked out due to the chance remark a morgue attendant made to a newspaperman. Forty-eight hours after his death the daily papers of Tuesday, March 15, carried their versions of the story. The *Journal-American* hinted at mysterious circumstances under a headline that read "BARE DEATH OF BOP KING PARKER." The New York *Mirror* predictably played up the romantic angle, heading its story "BOP KING DIES IN HEIRESS FLAT." *The New York Times* said, "CHARLIE PARKER,

JAZZ MASTER, DIES." Its account was respectful and as factual as sketchy research materials permitted. His age, taken from the death certificate, as estimated by the coroner, was given as fifty-three. Charlie Parker was actually thirty-four years of age. He would not be fifty-three until August 29, 1973. According to Chief Medical Examiner Milton Halperin, the cause of death was lobar pneumonia. Dr. Freymann's diagnosis was not mentioned.

Chan was located just before the headlines appeared in the streets. She at once went to the morgue, claimed the body, and had it sent to the Walter Cooke Funeral Home on 72nd Street. With the help of friends Chan made arrangements for a modest funeral, at which a simple sermon would be delivered and a medley of Parker compositions played by Lennie Tristano and Charlie Mingus, the kind of funeral that seemed suitable for a jazzman. After the services the body was to be buried alongside Pree at Mount Hope Cemetery in Hastings-on-Hudson, New York. Chan's plans were overturned with the arrival of Doris Parker, whom he had hardly seen for five years and who had borne him no children. Waving her Mexican marriage license and threatening Chan with a restraining order, Doris took possession of the body and arrangements for the modest funeral at the Walter Cooke mortuary were canceled. No one was in a position to question her claim to being Charlie's last legal wife of record. The body was removed forthwith to the Unity Funeral Home and new arrangements for the funeral made at Reverend Adam Clayton Powell, Jr.'s, fashionable Abyssinian Baptist Church on 138th Street, the "in" church uptown, and not far removed from Monroe's Uptown House. It was announced that Charlie would be buried in Kansas City. Chan protested and told Doris that she had made a promise that under no conditions was she to let Charlie be buried in the town he hated. The argument had no effect, but in return for her "cooperation," Doris and Doris Parker's attorney made a verbal promise that, after Addie Parker's death, Chan would be free to remove the body to Mt. Hope if she so chose. Chan's request that jazz be played at the services, at least a slow blues, was dismissed out of hand.

The services were held at the Abyssinian Baptist Church on a rainy Monday afternoon, March 21. It was a social event. Instead of a Parker medley, Arthur Sullivan's *The Lost Chord* was pumped out on an electric organ, a performance Charlie would have thought the ultimate put-on. The theme of the sermon, delivered by the Reverend David Licorish, was Charlie's lifelong search for the missing chord. Striving hard to impress show folk, the Reverend Licorish referred to the deceased as "Charlie-Bird," a neologism of his own making. The body was laid out in a new pin-striped suit, purchased by Doris. There was a new white shirt and a conservative cravat, the latter tied with a haberdasher's skill, the final knot smooth and precise. At Doris's instructions a crucifix was ordered from a religious goods store and placed by the mortician in the fingers that had been wrapped around an alto saxophone for the greater part of Charlie's life. The inspiration for this surprising touch was Doris's recollection that as a child Charlie had been farmed out by Addie Parker on her work days to a Catholic day school in Kansas City, Kansas. A confirmed atheist, he had not been inside a church in years. The body lay in an expensive bronze casket under a protective shield of plate glass, from which light glanced. Members of the hipster community, seeing the specular reflections on the glass, attributed this natural phenomena to supernatural causes. "It looked like nothing so much as the shimmering radiance surrounding the head of a saint," one hipster related. Those viewing the body found Charlie strangely at peace, but shrunken, collapsed, inert, truly dead, his powerful life force fled. Pallbearers included trumpeters Charlie Shavers and Dizzy Gillespie, pianist Lennie Tristano, drummer Louis Bellson, journalist Leonard Feather, and huge, perspiring Teddy Reig, the hip artists-and-repertoire man, resplendent in a shiny gunmetal-blue silk suit. On the way out of church into the gray March drizzle, the pallbearers lost their footing; the casket was nearly dropped and was saved only by a Herculean effort on the part of the powerful Mr. Reig. Even at his own last rites, it seemed that nothing could go smoothly for Charlie. Overturn and irony continued to rule the pattern of his life. On one hand he was surrounded by hipster fanaticism, on the other by vulgarity, hypocrisy, and cant. The presence of two warring factions at the church, those loyal to Chan and those professing an allegiance to Doris, the elbowing for choice spots by the parasites of the music business, the activities of the press, the legend-mongering of the hipsters, and the circuslike atmosphere of the funeral amounted to the final absurdity of Charlie Parker's short, tragic life.

Following the ceremonies, against his often-expressed wishes, and in spite of Chan's last-ditch protests, the body was flown back to Kansas City for burial, this part of the expense generously borne by Norman Granz. In Kansas City there was a second set of services, attended by Addie Parker and boyhood friends. Those who truly loved Charlie could only recall the strange, foreboding words sung by King Pleasure in the oracular litany of *Parker's Mood*:

> *So long, everybody,*
> *The time is coming, I must leave you . . .*
> *Don't hang your head when you see those six*
> *Pretty horses pullin' me.*
> *Put a twenty-dollar silver piece on my watch chain,*
> *Look at the smile on my face,*
> *And sing a little song,*
> *To let the world know,*
> *I'm really free.*
> *Don't cry for me,*
> *'Cause I'm going to Kansas City.*

A benefit concert to defray last expenses was held at Carnegie Hall, April 2, running from midnight to four A.M., hours that Charlie would have liked, and there was a great deal of good music played with love by those who had worked with him over the years. Those donating their services included Sarah Vaughan, Billie Holiday, Dinah Washington, Pearl Bailey, Billy Eckstine, Herb Jeffries, Sammy Davis, Jr., Mary Lou Williams, Hazel Scott, Lennie Tristano, Stan Getz, Charlie Shavers, Thelonious Monk, Gerry Mulligan, and Baby Lawrence. Leonard Feather, Jazzbo Collins, and Barry Ulanov acted as masters of ceremonies. Lester Young opened, Baby Lawrence danced, a Parker tape was heard, and many of Charlie's own and favorite tunes were played. Twenty-seven hundred persons attended, and hundreds were turned away. The concert netted $5,739.96. A similar concert in Sweden raised over $1,000, as did a non-stop twenty-four-hour benefit in Philadelphia.

Within a few days of Parker's death there appeared among the graffiti on walls in the Village and in subways, scrawled in black crayon or squirted out of pressurized paint cannisters, the legend "BIRD LIVES!"

Moving tributes appeared in the world's music press, which for the most part had ignored Charlie until his eminence was long and safely established. *"Le Bird N'est Plus!"* wrote *Le Jazz Hot* (Paris): "Charlie Parker—*fragile, mysterieux, insaisissable* . . ." Said *Orkester Journalen* (Stockholm):

> Together with Jackson Pollock, Dylan Thomas, and James Dean he became a symbol of protest for a whole generation. It is easy to see how these four artists shared the same rebellious mind and desperation, expressed so clearly in their work in different arts. And it is still easier to find the common ground in their death: Pollock and Dean through a mania for speed, Thomas and Charlie Parker through alcohol and drugs.

Like Dylan Thomas, Charlie Parker had boldly crossed a well-defined frontier and freed the language of his art from dross and cliché, investing it with a new intensity, color, and significance. The magnificent openings of *Parker's Mood, Slam Slam Blues,* and *Bird of Paradise* were, for those responsive to black music, as charged and as evocative as Dylan's poetry. There was the same impression of a molten vocabulary cooled and fused into a new idiom. Dylan's tragic statement might have been Charlie's own:

> *The force that through the green fuse drives the flower*
> *Drives my green age; that blasts the roots of trees*
> *Is my destroyer.*

And I am dumb to tell the crooked rose
*My youth is bent by the same wintry fever.**

Dylan Thomas had died only sixteen months before, not far away, at St. Vincent's Hospital in Greenwich Village—at the age of thirty-nine, dead of cirrhosis of the liver, diabetes, and other ills connected with his chronic alcoholism.

After the funeral the Baroness was further harassed by a round of scurrilous articles in the now defunct gutter press. *Confidential* and *Lowdown* followed their earlier Bird stories with new and still more lurid ones, intimating "fowl play", and a romantic liaison between the jazz musician and the descendant of the Rothschilds. The *Exposé* story was headed "The Bird in the Baroness' Boudoir" and called Nica a "slinky, blackhaired, jet-eyed Circe of high society" who had lured the "fallen sparrow" to his doom. These magazines were then at their last and most flagrant stage of misreporting and mudslinging. A barrage of libel suits would soon account for their disappearance. Baroness de Koenigswarter was one of Charlie's very few real friends, perhaps the only one who had no personally possessive or mercenary interest in him. She was a patron of artists and the arts in the tradition of European women who had led the great salons of the nineteenth century.

While the jazz world lamented the untimely demise of the most recent, and imposing, of its *enfants terribles* (Bix Beiderbecke, Bunny Berigan, John Coltrane, to name three on a list that could be expanded readily to two score), there were those who said privately that Charlie had lived long enough. He had been twenty years on the jazz scene, for fifteen of them a moving force. By 1950 or 1951 there was evidence that the stream of ideas gushing from his saxophone had begun to thin and falter. As he admitted to Lennie Tristano, he had taken the blues and the ballad as far as he could. Despite vague plans to study with Edgard Varese, Charlie had no preparation, training, or real aptitude for formal composition. In part his loss of powers

---

* "The Force that Through the Green Fuse Drives," *The Collected Poems of Dylan Thomas, 1934–1952* (New Directions, 1971).

could be blamed on the worsening state of his health. When he collapsed in the living room of Baroness de Koenigswarter's apartment, he was not so much dead as used up. As John Lewis pointed out, "Bird had given so much of himself." Had the medical authorities been properly finicky in their duties, they might have found four possible causes to enter on the official death certificate: lobar pneumonia, advanced cirrhosis of the liver, a perforated peptic ulcer, or a fatal heart attack brought on by all three. Nor was medical science able to offer any useful opinion as to the effects of fifteen years of narcotics addiction on the chemistry of the human body.

The psychiatric picture was less clear. Psychiatrists saw a man with a hostile yet ingratiating personality. A man who was constantly late, strung out on heroin, booze, and pills, addicted to frequent and often incredible excesses of food and sex—double dinners, hamburger-eating contests, bacchanals with two and sometimes three willing, experienced women locked in a hotel suite for around-the-clock orgies of dope and carnal sport. Every experience was evaluated on a simplistic scale of values: either it was a "drag" or a "ball." Charlie Parker literally balled his way through life, leaving behind a hopelessly confused set of impressions on those who knew him, and a body of music that was less an accident than the result of a deep, lasting commitment to a culture he loved and understood, and an uncompromising self-discipline, the only one to which he submitted in his lifetime.

The final Bellevue report hints at a real psychosis (undifferentiated schizophrenia). Charlie Parker may have been one of those psychotics precariously but sufficiently in contact with reality to function, albeit badly, and materially assisted by his great talent, in the real world, for the most part under his own terms, and given to childish outbursts of temper when things went against him. Or he may have been the "classic psychopath" described by Dr. Richard Freeman, the one qualified practitioner who took the trouble to study this most elusive patient.

Psychotic or psychopath? How valid are the counters of the psychiatry game when applied to black Americans? How greatly has the predominantly white, middle-class psychiatric community taken into account a way of life that, in the past, at least, has made survival dependent upon con, guile, the put-on, acting, and mask-changing? Or considered a colonial sub-society that has elevated to hero roles not great surgeons or educators, but store-front preachers, flamboyant politicians, Cadillac-borne procurers and gamblers, blues singers—and jazz musicians. Hipster, hustler, cocksman, junkie, and songster, Charlie Parker bears a striking resemblance to the black urban-ghetto culture hero described with singular perception by Charles Keil in *Urban Blues.*

In the monumental disorder of Charlie Parker's life the one thing that always mattered and for which he lived obsessively was his music. There he was completely serious and disciplined. His place as a germinal figure in American music is only in the process of being realized. ". . . with Armstrong [Parker] is perhaps the only jazz instrumentalist to whom the word genius seems appropriate," writes European musicologist Wilfrid Mellers in his *Music in a New Found Land,* the best study to date of the immensely vital and innovative music with which America has endowed world culture. Jazz style from 1920 to World War II seemed to flow from Armstrong. Charlie Parker changed the course of that river and set up a new complex of forces. Almost singlehandedly he emancipated time and sound for those to follow. Beginning with Miles Davis, who bird-dogged Charlie Parker as a young man and played at his side during his formative years, every instrumentalist since 1950 is derivative of the Parker style. The list includes all of the important figures in jazz since 1950: Sonny Rollins, Ornette Coleman, Eric Dolphy, Sonny Simmons, Clifford Brown, Red Rodney, Barbara Donald, Bud Powell, Hampton Hawes, John Lewis, Cecil Taylor, John Coltrane, Roland Kirk, Pharoah Sanders, Albert Ayler, and Archie Shepp. In their playing there is more than the foundation of Parker's jazz style. In varying degrees one also hears the religious ecstacy of Parker's music.

The true jazz age was not the decade of Van Vechten, Fitzgerald and Paul Whiteman. It was the decade of the 1940s.

Charlie Parker was the first, the real jazz age hero. His passionate feeling for the blues, pervading every note of his playing, his toughness and resilience, were expressive of the Afro-American ethos that has now become the archetype of the loneliness and alienation of modern man, its universal nature suggested by the odd, oblique confrontation between Parker and Jean-Paul Sartre in Montmartre in 1949, a passing of ships in the night. Parker's message of alienation and his pained cries against the hypocrisy of the society in which he found himself, its false values, sentimentality, and absurd pseudo-nostalgia for innocence were already well understood by those oddly-dressed, long-haired hipsters, black and white, who followed Charlie Parker from Minton's Playhouse to Fifty-Second Street in 1944, before the war had even ended. There was a new awareness of life and concern with society even then, even though it was part of a peripheral, emergent sub-culture articulated by an explosive music that few could grasp. That generation of hipsters was clearly the forerunner of the Beats of the next decade and, in our own time, the generation that is changing the face of America.

A few months after his death *Down Beat* readers elected Charlie Parker to the Jazz Hall of Fame, the fourth musician so honored. And Charlie Mingus commented, "The musicians at Birdland had to wait for Charlie's next record to find out what to play. What will they do now?"

The struggle over Charlie Parker's body was followed by another for control of his estate. Chan again found her legal rights as a common-law wife tenuous, and Doris prevailed. With the assistance of attorney Florynce Kennedy, an early campaigner for black liberation and women's liberation, Doris was named administratrix of the estate and discovery proceedings launched in the New York Surrogate Court. Summons were served on sixty-nine incredulous and indignant persons and firms in the phonograph record, concert bureau, booking, and music publishing industries—in fact, on everyone and anyone who at one time had or was rumored to have had any dealings with Charlie Parker. Norman Granz, Charlie's most consistent and best-paying employer, was served eight times, individually and as an officer of seven affiliated firms. The man who had picked up the tab for hospital and burial expenses, along with Charlie's first major employer, Savoy Records of Newark, was accused of willfully altering contracts. Premier Albums, a large custom bindery whose closest association with Charlie Parker was the manufacture of sleeves for labels issuing Parker records, was served. So were Metro-Goldwyn-Mayer and the four major labels, RCA Victor, Capitol, Decca, and Columbia, although none had entered into direct contracts with the artist. Other actions were directed at firms in various states and in Europe. The malicious character of those in the international cabal was suggested in the opening paragraph of the petition, which declined to reveal Doris Parker's true address: "withheld out of fear of bodily injury and harm." The petition, filed in the Surrogate's Court of New York County, set the value of the estate at round $102,000. Although Addie Parker had often insisted that Charlie had no middle name, he was referred to as Charles Christopher Parker, Jr. In this amazing legal document it was alleged and the surrogate briefed that:

> Encouraged by judicial, administrative, executive and legislative laissez faire, the companies throw crumbs to the creative artist and sweepings to his or her estate, in the bland assurance that no sane inquirer will spend the time and money to embark upon a tour through the financial maze, which is blocked at every turn by subsidiary corporations, mergers, liquidations and blunt refusals to disclose accounting information or even to provide lists of distributors and retail outlets. . . . Separate corporations are formed to distribute records, whose books are closed to the artist, composer, or his estate representative. Foreign cartel arrangements are made which lead to a labyrinth of bookkeeping cartwheels and Panamanian and Swiss bank accounts.
>
> Records are sold, thousands of dollars worth of advertising is purchased to sell ten and fifteen records. In some cases, session costs are infinitely elastic so that just as royalties begin to close the gap, session costs, chargeable to the recording artist, rise ex post facto. Master tapes, transcriptions and indeed, entire record

catalogues are transferred, acquired, disposed of and re-released with a dizzying speed that makes the old army game seem like child's play.*

The noisy discovery proceedings soon encountered the obstacles that had discouraged attorney A. Allen Saunders. Many Parker compositions were still in the public domain, available for use without fee by anyone. They had never been copyrighted. This applied to originals on Dial; Charlie had never signed the agreement authorizing Dial to establish a publishing subsidiary, even though he had been promised eighty percent of the net proceeds. Some compositions had been sold outright for a few dollars and were free forever from royalty payments. A few, like *Now's the Time* and *Red Cross*, had been pirated. On many recording dates no agreement concerning mechanical royalties had been executed. Breached contracts had led to suspension of royalty payments. Such odd persons as Moose the Mooche had been involved in the web of transactions. The estate was an incredible confusion of Charlie's own making.

An all-out struggle for its control began March 5, 1957, when Chan petitioned the Surrogate's Court asking that Doris Parker's letters of administration be revoked. The long-rumored doubt over the legality of Doris' marriage to Charlie became an open charge in Chan's petition. Chan alleged that both she and Doris had knowledge that Parker's marriage to Geraldine Scott had never been dissolved. Chan also alleged that Charlie had named her, Baird, and Kim as his legal heirs in a last will and testament written in his own hand July 11, 1954, and sent by telegram to A. Allen Saunders. Doris was ordered to show cause why her authority as administratrix should not be revoked. At the hearing, which did not take place for fifteen months, Chan was unable to produce the will, adequate records from the telegraph company or substantiate the claim that Charlie and Geraldine had never been divorced. Her petition was denied, and Doris remained in control. At that time Doris was involved with an enterprise called the Charlie Parker Rec-

* Petition, Surrogate's Court, New York County, May 11, 1961, Index No. A. 670/1956, Florynce Kennedy, for Doris Parker, administratrix for Estate of Charles Christopher Parker, Jr.

ord Corporation, which produced six Parker releases, mostly air shots and tapes, but soon went out of business.

Charlie's missing second wife did not turn up until May, 1960, when she was located at Alderson, West Virginia. Her petition to revoke Doris' letters of administration came as the bombshell that broke the case wide open. A certified copy of the license for her marriage to Charlie at Washington, D.C., April 12, 1943, was produced, together with the sworn statement that the marriage had never been legally dissolved. Geraldine charged that Doris' letters of administration had been obtained "by fraud, misrepresentation of material facts and gross deception perpetrated upon the court" and that "substantial royalties together with other assets" were being withheld and unlawfully used. Again Doris was ordered to show cause.

During the next two years a parade of claimants, counterclaimants and their attorneys passed through the Surrogate's Court. Forty-four separate items appeared on the Estate docket—directed accountings, motions to post bond, amend, punish for contempt, dismiss, appeal, submit to examination, take depositions, appoint special guardians, pay federal and state taxes and attorneys' fees. At last, on October 17, 1962, the contesting parties met to sign a Stipulated Agreement. It provided that Doris would not be examined or held accountable for the monies used during her period of administration. A new division of the estate proceeds was arrived at granting Geraldine $27\frac{1}{2}$ percent; Leon, 25 percent; Baird, 25 percent; Addie Parker, $7\frac{1}{2}$ percent; Rebecca Ruffing Parker, $7\frac{1}{2}$ percent. The intriguing question of the legality of Doris' marriage was sidestepped, but significantly her share was cut to $7\frac{1}{2}$ percent. The percentages may be regarded as a fair indication of the respective positions of the contestants and the merits of their claims.

No figures are available for the amount of monies that have passed through the estate, although the sums paid out for administrative expenses and legal fees are given as $50,451.41 for the period August 8, 1965, through September 6, 1970. Nor has the matter found its final resting point. According to a letter received from Chan in the fall of 1972, Baird has received nothing from the estate and further legal action is being considered. Thus, eighteen years after Parker's death, the struggle continues, and the man who left in his path a monumental trail of debris continues to have the last laugh, although it is a bitter one, for neither Chan nor Baird has received a dollar of the royalties he promised would be available "if anything ever happened" to him.

Many of Charlie's old associates continue to pursue active careers—Jay Hootie McShann (in Kansas City); Kenny Klook Clarke (Paris); Earl Hines (San Francisco); Billy Eckstine, Ray Brown, Louis Bellson, Jesse Price, Jimmy Forrest, Jimmy Witherspoon, Stan Levey, Pearl Bailey (Hollywood); Dizzy Gillespie, Howard McGhee, Milt Jackson, John Lewis, Thelonious Monk, Sarah Vaughan, Max Roach, Miles Davis, Al Hibbler (New York). All remember Charlie Parker with awe and love. Geraldine Parker was last seen in Washington, D.C., and Rebecca, several times remarried, in California. Leon served in the Air Force and returned to Kansas City. Addie Parker died there in April 1967. Lester Young died of alcoholism, cirrhosis of the liver, and malnutrition in 1959. Dr. Richard Freeman was the victim of a sudden fatal heart attack several years ago. Marvin Freeman is now a member of the Superior Court of Los Angeles County, in charge of juvenile bench judges. Maynard Sloate, whose embryo firm, Sloate-Orr Associates, handled the publicity for Charlie Parker's Camarillo benefit in 1947, has for several years been producer of Folies Bergere at the Tropicana Hotel in Las Vegas. Pee Wee Marquette was last seen working as a doorman for a Hawaiian restaurant located a block or two away from his old stand at Birdland. The club itself, after undergoing a facelifting and reopening as a rock palace, is now dark.

A number of old Kansas City hands assembled at the Monterey Jazz Festival in September 1971 for a nostalgic program produced by the author. It brought together Jay McShann, Jimmy Forrest, Jesse Price, Claude Williams, Billy Hadnott, Paul Gunther, Clark Terry, Herman Bell, Mary Lou Williams, Big Joe Turner, Jimmy Witherspoon, and Al Hibbler, many of whom had not seen each other for years. Mary Lou played *Froggy Bottom*, Al Hibbler sang *Skylark*, Big Joe Turner shouted *Roll 'em Pete*, Spoon sang *Hootie Blues*, while Jimmy Forrest played Charlie's original solo from the old Decca record. Hootie sang *Confessin' the Blues*, in the Walter Brown style, accompanying himself at the piano, then belted out *Vine Street Boogie*. The Kansas City Six rocked the fairgrounds with *Moten Swing* and *Jumpin' the Blues*. The concert, titled "Kansas City Revisited," was enthusiastically received. Hundreds danced in the aisles, and a few on the stage itself. Critics voted Mary Lou Williams and Jay McShann the rediscoveries of the year.

Opera Without Banners, a folk-jazz opera dedicated to Charlie, had its première in 1966 in Kansas City, where the Charlie Parker Foundation for Performing Arts, established by public-spirited jazz and symphony musicians, offers free musical instruction to talented young people living in Charlie's old neighborhood. In Chicago Joe Segal stages a Charlie Parker Memorial Concert each summer; in 1970 it featured Sonny Stitt and Red Rodney. In August 1971 the Charlie Parker Memorial Foundation unveiled a bronze headstone with a stylized bird and aggregate curbing at Charlie's grave. Mayor Charles B. Wheeler of Kansas City was present and proclaimed 1971 "Charlie Parker Year." The ceremonies were attended by Milt Jackson, Max Roach, and veteran saxophonist Joe Thomas.

The whereabouts of the wire spools recorded by the indefatigable Dean Benedetti remains a mystery. In total the spools amounted to hundreds of hours of Charlie Parker in performance. Dean was last heard from in Italy, where he died in the late Fifties. The spools were his entire reason for being, and it is presumed that he took the collection with him. Despite diligent search and public advertisements in leading European jazz magazines, no trace of the collection has been found. Tapes recorded by the "second generation" of amateur engineers, Joe Maini and Don Lanphere, have come to light. In 1969 Lanphere's tapes yielded six hours of previously unknown Parker. This material is now traded internationally by collectors of tape and unissued recordings. Getting it into the proper legal and technical form for public distribution presents many problems. There are now about twenty-four hours of Charlie Parker on tape, most of it unknown to buyers of commercial records, in many instances of superior musical quality. New tapes continue to turn up from time to time. The official Parker discography, records made for commercial firms, runs to a total of 219 individual numbers. These performances were recorded for 21 prime labels and later released or reissued in the United States and foreign countries on a total of 91 secondary labels. Discographies of several jazzmen are greater—Duke Ellington, Louis Armstrong, and a few others—but none succeeded in so attracting amateur engineers. As this is written, the Verve and Savoy recordings are available. Charlie Parker on Dial has been issued in a series of six limited edition LPs by Parker specialist Tony Williams, 300 Brocklesmead, Harlow, Essex, England. (A discography of Charlie Parker recordings available at publication date of this book appears in the appendix.)

After the funeral Chan Richardson returned to New Hope to raise Kim and Baird, and began producing Sunday afternoon jazz concerts at a local tavern renamed Bird's Nest. There Chan met Phil Woods, a young jazzman from Springfield, Massachusetts. Woods had developed his style by memorizing all of Charlie's recorded solos, as Charlie had done with Lester Young. This friendship between the young Parker-inspired saxophonist and Charlie's widow led eventually to their marriage. For several years Phil and Chan Richardson Parker Woods lived in the house at New Hope. Phil became a foster father to Kim and Baird, and often performed on Charlie's saxophone. In the Sixties, feeling that it would be better to raise Baird in Europe, where he would never encounter racial discrimination, they moved to Paris. There Phil is a well-known recording artist and jazz personality and, as many believe, the keeper of the holy fire. Kim is now twenty-five and married. Baird, who strongly resembles Charlie, is a talented guitarist. Kim and Baird appear with a rock group called Tapioca, and were recently booked into Epace Cardin, Paris.

In Las Vegas a short, bouncy, freckle-faced man, growing plump, hair still a flaming red, though now sprinkled with gray and professionally set with spray, works the better lounges and show rooms. Once he was the precocious boy wonder of the brass sections of the big white bands (Kenton, Krupa, Herman, Dorsey, Thornhill). A clean kid with a lot of chutzpah and no vices. After a sizable fraction of a lifetime, six years and eight months, spent at various federal correctional institutions—the Lexington narcotics hospital, the federal prisons at Leavenworth, Kansas, at Lewisburg, at Terminal Island, at Fort Worth—for crimes against himself and against society, all of them rooted in his addiction begun as a member of the Charlie Parker Quintet of 1950, Red Rodney, née Robert Chudnick, is back in circulation. The man who was one of Charlie Parker's closest friends still plays with the same cool, shimmering, bluesy tone that graced the third edition of the Quintet. Now its heartbreak quality is blended with the sounds of the bands that back up the big shows—Juliet Prowse, Ella Fitzgerald, the Mills Brothers, Sammy Davis, Jr., Rusty Warren, Connie Stevens, Wayne Cochrane, Tom Jones. A member in good standing of Local 369 of the American Federation of Musicians, Red Rodney is a journeyman trumpet player in sufficient demand in Las Vegas, where musical contractors pay the highest wages in the world, $325 scale for two one-hour shows six nights weekly, $25 extra if a brassman doubles on flugelhorn. Rodney commutes to work in a cobalt blue 1969 Le Mans coupe from a four-bedroom stucco home in a new development in East Las Vegas to downtown Las Vegas, a town that hears little jazz these days and sees little birdlife.

Acknowledgments

The present biography is the product of an obsession, mine and that of others. It has occupied me for years. Of course it is absurd that the biography of one of the great figures of Afro-American music has been written by a white man, and a middle-class, western, establishment-educated white man at that, but no black writer or scholar has come forward to write about one of his own great culture heroes. Meanwhile, time is running out rapidly on the prime sources. Other views—black views, women's views—will be welcome, and perhaps forthcoming. Interest in Afro-American culture on the part of black intellectuals and scholars has been numbed by white prejudices imposed on the black middle class. One has only to recall that until rather recently jazz and blues were forbidden by the music departments of such leading Negro institutions as Howard and Tuskegee.

375

My own involvement with jazz began in Los Angeles in 1937, when I insinuated myself into the favor of an orchestra leader named Luis Russell, who found a certain interest in the sameness of our surnames and invited me to accompany his band on a week-long junket of one-nighters through California. That was a happy beginning. The band featured Pops Foster, Paul Barbarin, J. C. Higginbotham, Henry "Red" Allen, Jr., and Louis Armstrong, all subsequently members of or candidates for the Jazz Hall of Fame. That involvement, accelerated by the temporary illusion that I alone had discovered the flowers of a great folk art growing up at the back doorstep, has continued through three decades of collecting records, hearing jazz live, and meeting jazz musicians. My own tastes are predominantly black. I am convinced that jazz is a black man's game, and that with very few exceptions (Beiderbecke and Jack Teagarden, perhaps) white players have been imitators, codifiers, and exploiters. My involvement later included two years of managing a retail jazz-record store and ten of operating Dial, an independent record label. For two harrowing years of the ten, Dial held Charlie Parker under what was laughably called an exclusive artist's contract that somehow succeeded in producing seven recording sessions and thirty-five sides. When Dial lost Charlie to Mercury in 1948 I continued to see him, very often under strained circumstances, until the time of his death. Then I began assembling the puzzle pieces of his discography and his life. Between writing a novel and *Jazz Style in Kansas City*, and the traditional odd employments of a writer of my generation (advertising account executive, publicity director for a dragstrip, photographer for a bullfight monthly, teaching courses in Afro-American music at the University of California and continuation English to high school dropouts), the Parker project has occupied a great deal of my time, and I am happy to see it completed.

Research has led to interesting adventures and discoveries in areas rapidly becoming forbidden to the white man, and where were found Jesse Price, Big Joe Turner, Harlan Leonard, Billy Hadnott, and Jimmy Forrest, all of whom had known Charlie as a teenager in Kansas City. Jesse Price filled in many lost pages of the misty early years; the sequences having to do with the Reno Club, Old Man Virgil, and Kansas City jam sessions belong to Jesse. Without those insights we would have to guess even more wildly than we do as to the springs of Charlie Parker's genius. Jay McShann, Gene Ramey, and Al Hibbler furnished details of Charlie's tenure with the McShann orchestra. Entirely different insights came from younger and readily accessible jazzmen: Dizzy Gillespie, Woody Herman, Duke Ellington, Gunther Schuller, Andre Hodier, Thelonious Monk, Howard McGhee, Ray Brown, Carlton McBeth, Mundell Lowe, Tony Scott, Sonny Criss, Hampton Hawes, Slim Gaillard, Slam Stewart, David MacKay, Roy Porter, Dodo Marmarosa, Jimmy Bunn, Bob Kesterson, Jo Jones, Don Lanphere, Louis Bellson, Billy Eckstine, Shelly Manne, John Lewis, Dick Stabile, Dexter Gordon, Benny Harris, Red Norvo, Kenny Clarke, Cootie Williams, Russell Procope, Paul Gonsalves, Budd Johnson, Max Roach, Tommy Potter, Duke Jordan, Stan Levey, Al Haig, Kenny Dorham, Sonny Simmons, Prince Lasha, Jan Noordberg, Woody Isbell, Earl Coleman, Chubby Jackson, Georgie Auld, Allen Eager, Joe Albany, Roy Hall, Curly Russell, Flip Phillips, Shorty Rogers, Roy Eldridge, Milt Jackson, Red Callender, Erroll Garner, Chuck Wayne, Al Hall, Earl Hines, Vivian Garry, Calvin Jackson, Bob Hardaway, Chuck Kopley, Archie Shepp, Beaver Harris, Red Rodney, Charlie Ventura, Jimmy Knepper, Mel Broiles, Hal McKusick, Zutty Singleton, Jimmy Pratt, Russ Freeman, J. J. Johnson, Kai Winding, James Moody, Dr. Louis Gottlieb, Mary Lou Williams, Howard Brubeck, Lucky Thompson, Don Lamond, Barney Kessel, Pearl Bailey, Ed Fisher, Ted Muradian and Babs Gonzales.

Also the late Denzil Best, Doc West, Dean Benedetti, Bud Powell, Serge Chaloff, Shifty Henry, Billie Holiday, Carl Perkins, Fats Navarro, Coleman Hawkins, Clifford Brown, Clyde Hart, Tadd Dameron, Sonny Berman, Arvin Garrison, and Lester Young. And non-professionals Lee Phillips, Dick Carpenter, Norman Granz, Edie Young, Joseph Cornfeld, M.D., Thomas Munson, M.D., Teddy Reig, Renice Dubois, and Chan Woods.

The late Lenny Bruce, an improviser whose career ran closely parallel to Charlie's and whose verbal lines had the same high, uncompromising quality, gave me additional insights into his opposite number. Bruce's biography is now being written by Albert Goldman. In 1970 Albert called me from Los Angeles, where he had gone to do research on the Lenny Bruce biography, to ask how my own project was progressing. It wasn't. He rented a car, drove to Escondido, and spent two days there going over materials and manuscript. Without his help and encouragement this book might never have been completed.

Ernest Daniels furnished information about the Thanksgiving Day automobile accident. Richard Dickert of Kansas City conducted taped interviews with Tootie Clarkin, Milton Morris, and Joe Barone, all of whom operated cabarets in Kansas City during the Pendergast era and employed Charlie Parker. Morris began in 1933 with the Novelty Club and today operates a music bar in which jazz records, especially those of Charlie Parker and Lester Young, are played continuously. With book critic Thorpe Menn of the Kansas City *Star*, the veteran night club man checked galleys for addresses, dates, names and other details of life in the heavenly city during its musical renaissance.

Among my fellow writers, Ralph Gleason, Ira Gitler, Bob Reisner, Don Schlitten, Louis-Victor Mialy, Sidney Finkelstein, Dave Dexter, Mark Gardner, Rudi Blesh, Albert Goldman, Martin Williams, as well as the late Marshall Stearns, Alan Morrison, and George Hoefer, have been generous of time and help. Robert Erickson and Bertram Turetzky of the music faculty at the University of California at San Diego checked the manuscript for musical errors, a task shared by Dr. Shelton Hendler, biochemist at Salk Institute, La Jolla, and former jazz trumpeter. Tom Owens, who is completing a thesis titled *Charlie Parker's Improvisational Methods* for his doctorate degree at UCLA, has given permission to use solos transcribed from Parker recordings, a ticklish and time-consuming task. Charlie Parker's recrystalization of *Embraceable You* was transcribed by Ted Muradian.

With the author's permission I have drawn from and in some cases quoted from *Bird, The Legend of Charlie Parker* by Robert Reisner (Citadel Press, New York, 1962), with its eighty-odd interviews of persons who knew Bird, its material on his last days in Greenwich Village, the Bellevue Hospital medical-psychiatric report and the many remarks by Mr. Reisner who produced concerts at the Open Door from 1953 until the time of Charlie's death. Bob also generously offered me the use of his photograph file and four of those photographs are used here, again with his kind permission. The asskicking incident is quoted from A. B. Spellman's *Four Lives in the Bebop Business*, one of the few books on jazz by a black writer. The quotation from Kenneth Rexroth is from his *The Alternate Society*.

Red Rodney, now completely rehabilitated and playing better than ever, was the chief source of information for the 1950–1953 period, including details of the Southern tour and the third European tour, which got bogged down in the Brussels chemist's shop. Red also read and checked the manuscript. Details of the Swedish tour were worked up by Dr. Borje Raftegard of the University of Gothenburg. Dr. Raftegard translated many articles from *Orkester Journalen* and the now defunct *Estrad*, Swedish jazz magazines, and interviewed Swedish jazzmen who accompanied Charlie on the 1950 tour. Perhaps he will forgive me from quoting from his letter: "To me, Bach and

Parker are the Dioscuri of western music. Oh, yes, I know it may be regarded as a flippant opinion, but I seriously insist!" The point is that there are enthusiasts all over the world to whom Charlie Parker continues daily to bring happiness.

A gathering of Parker buffs meets once monthly at a pub called the Rising Sun in London to exchange tapes and records, and rap. Among its members, Gordon Davies, an airport traffic director, has compiled a chronology of Parker's movements, bookings, and band tenures, which runs fifty pages. Electronics worker Tony Williams has the world's largest collection of Parker records and tapes, has published the definitive Parker discography (tracing out master and catalogue numbers of releases on American and foreign labels), and has issued on his label, Spotlite, a series of Parker records, limited to ninety-nine pressings. That is legal in England because it is viewed as a service to collectors. Tony conducted the taped interview with Kenny Clarke during one of the latter's appearances at a London jazz club. Mark Gardner, the editor of a provincial newspaper, has issued privately taped Parker material on his similarly limited label, Klacto, and lives in a sixteenth-century house in Faversham which he calls *Klactoveesedstene*. In Bastia, Corsica, Louis Schiavo, a wholesale seafood merchant, amateur painter, and Charlie Parker collector, spends his Italian holidays looking vainly for the missing Benedetti tapes.

I am deeply indebted to the veteran editors of two leading European jazz magazines. Charles Delaunay, director of *Jazz Hot* (Paris), the oldest publication devoted to jazz (it was established in 1934 by M. Delaunay, son of the French painter Robert Delaunay), found and forwarded such valuable articles as *J'ai été le chaperon de Charlie Parker et l'un des rare amis de Lester Young*, an interview with Gene Ramey by Francois Postif (*Jazz Hot*, March 1962), typical of the serious interest in jazz on the part of European music journalists. M. Delaunay also generously placed the photographic files of *Jazz Hot* at my disposal, as did Harry Nicolausson of *Orkester Journalen* (Stockholm). *Jazz Journal* and *Jazz and Blues*, the leading British periodicals, furnished a few Parker references and many about Kansas City, the latter contributed by American jazz writer and record producer Frank Driggs. Dan Morgenstern of *Down Beat* (New York) also made several photographs available. In general the little jazz magazines have been far more useful as source material than books.

Down Beat, the first American jazz and popular music magazine, is also the sole survivor in a field that has included many short-lived, outstanding entrants: *Jazz Information*, published by Gene Williams and Ralph Gleason; *Jazz, A Quarterly of American Music,* Ralph Gleason; *Jazz* and *Jazz and Pop,* Bob Thiele; *Jazz Record,* Art Hodes; *Record Changer,* Bill Grauer and Orin Keepnews; and the late, much-lamented *Jazz Review,* perhaps the finest of them all, co-edited by Nat Hentoff and Martin Williams, now director of the jazz division of the performing arts at Smithsonian Institution, Washington, D.C. The quotations from Prof ("Buster") Smith are from the now rare copies of *Jazz Review* (February, 1960), and the letter from Charlie Parker to the New York Liquor Authority and the telegrams from Parker to Chan Richardson are quoted from the Parker Memorial issue of *Down Beat,* published March 11, 1965, ten years after his death, and made available to that publication through the courtesy of Parker's former attorney, Maxwell Cohen of New York City. Unless otherwise identified, all other quotations, statements, and sources for sequences are drawn from the author's interviews undertaken for this biography. And finally, a very special thanks to Chan Woods for permission to use in its entirety, without deletions, that beautiful, intimate, and evocative letter written in 1947, when the music that is now part of history was still a crusade.

R. R.
Escondido and San Diego
October, 1972

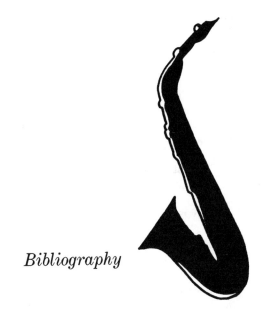

Bibliography

The bibliography of books that follows is selective and general. A bibliography of magazine articles is beyond the scope of this work, for there are a large number and in several languages. If one were new to jazz, interested in its mystique and stormy history, and willing to tackle four books, I think these might be Stearns, Leroi Jones, Hodeir, and Schuller, probably in that order. Stearns presents a good overview and is excellent on pre- and early jazz periods. Leroi Jones raises more questions than he answers, but is penetrating and provocative. *Evolution and Essence* is the work of a cultured, intellectual French composer, a fastidious view of the jazz scene and its major figures, including Charlie Parker, from the other side. Gunther Schuller's *Early Jazz* is the best work by an American scholar, but unfortunately ends where we wish to begin and, in view of Mr. Schuller's hyperactive present musical life, the sequel planned is not likely to be completed. Not one of these ambitious projects, which set out to tell the story of American jazz music, completes the job intended, probably because writing about jazz is something like playing jazz—a vocation without honor and frequently without profit in the country of its origin. The reason for this state of affairs is that jazz is a black art. This is no oversimplification. Throughout its life jazz has been continually, deliberately and literally denigrated. Still more indefensible is the fact that it continues to be. If one admits that black America has been able to produce a revolutionary and very important art, that is indeed a dangerous concession. Such an admission has never been made by the white establishment in America. Nor is it being made today.

The disturbing short story "Sparrow's Last Jump," written at and after the disastrous *Lover Man* session, may be found in Ralph Gleason's *Jam Session*. *Tom's Town* is a detailed study of the Kansas City body politic during the Pendergast years. My own *Jazz Style in Kansas City and the Southwest* explores for the first time the provincial culture that served as Charlie Parker's background. For the bebop era Ira Gitler's *Jazz Masters of the Forties* is the definitive work. Benny Green's *Reluctant Art* penetrates deeply wherever it touches, but does not have the grandeur of Hodeir's *Evolution and Essence*. *Studies in African Music* by A. W. Jones is the first scholarly approach to the music of tribal Africa, where it all began. Not to be overlooked is Wilfrid Mellers *Music in a New Found Land*.

SELECTED BIBLIOGRAPHY

BURLEY, DAN, *The Handbook of Harlem Jive*. New York: Dan Burley, 1944.

DEXTER, DAVE, JR., *The Jazz Story*. Englewood Cliffs, N. J.: Prentice-Hall, 1964.

Esquire's World of Jazz. New York: Esquire, 1962.

FEATHER, LEONARD, *Inside Bebop*. New York: Criterion, 1949.

FINKELSTEIN, SIDNEY, *Jazz: A People's Music*. New York: Citadel, 1948.

GITLER, IRA, *Jazz Masters of the Forties*. New York: Macmillan, 1966.

GLEASON, RALPH, *Jam Session*. New York: Putnam's, 1958.

GOLDMAN, ALBERT, *Freakshow*, New York, Atheneum, 1971.

GONZALES, BABS, *I Paid My Dues*. New York: Lancer Books, 1967.

GREEN, BENNY, *The Reluctant Art*. New York: Horizon, 1963.

HENTOFF, NAT, and ALBERT MCCARTHY, *Jazz*. New York: Rinehart and Co., 1959.

HERSKOVITS, MELVILLE, *The Myth of the Negro Past*. Boston: Beacon Press, 1958.

HODEIR, ANDRE, *Jazz: Its Evolution and Essence*. New York: Grove Press, 1956.

JONES, A. M., *Studies in African Music*. London: Oxford University Press, 1959.

JONES, LEROI, *Blues People*. New York: William Morrow, 1963.

KEIL, CHARLES, *Urban Blues*. Chicago: University of Chicago Press, 1966.

MELLERS, WILFRID, *Music in a New Found Land*, New York, Knopf, 1965.

MINGUS, CHARLES, *Beneath the Underdog*. New York: Knopf, 1971.

NEWTON, FRANCIS, *The Jazz Scene*. London: MacGibbon and Kee, 1959.

OLIVER, PAUL, *The Story of the Blues*. London: Cassell, 1968.

REDDIG, WILLIAM M., *Tom's Town: Kansas City and the Pendergast Legend*. Philadelphia: Lippincott, 1947.

REISNER, ROBERT, *Bird: The Legend of Charlie Parker*. New York: Bonanza, Citadel, 1962.

RUSSELL, ROSS, *Jazz Style in Kansas City and the Southwest*. Berkeley: University of California Press, 1971.

SCHULLER, GUNTHER, *Early Jazz*. New York: Oxford University Press, 1968.

SHAPIRO, NAT, and NAT HENTOFF, *Hear Me Talkin' to Ya*. New York: Dover, 1966.

SPELLMAN, A. B., *Four Lives in the Bebop Business*. New York: Pantheon, 1966.

STEARNS, MARSHALL, *The Story of Jazz*. New York: Oxford University Press, 1956.

ULANOV, BARRY, *A History of Jazz in America*. New York: Viking, 1952.

Discography

The discography that follows is divided into three parts. The first lists all Parker recordings available in catalogs of various labels at press time. The second lists recordings by Parker's contemporaries, sources, models, and musical companions. The third offers a convenient running discography of Parker performances discussed in the text, beginning with the Wichita *Lady Be Good* and ending with the final Verve session in 1954. Because of the rapidly changing fortunes and policies of the recording industry and label owners, discographies are notoriously short-lived. Experienced collectors usually pick up their records while they are offered. Unless otherwise indicated, all items listed in the discography are available upon publication of this book. In the summer of 1972, Bernard Stollman, president of ESP Records, New York, concluded an agreement with Robert Z. Dobrish of Hoffinger and Stuart, attorneys for the Charlie Parker Estate, wherein ESP would be authorized to release material formerly issued on the Charlie Parker, Le Jazz Cool and other now defunct independent labels, This material, most of it from air checks and on-site recordings, will appear in fourteen volumes (ESP–BIRD 1–14). Out-of-print items can often be found at specialty jazz and collector stores. Availability of catalog items can be checked by consulting the Schwann catalog, sold in large music stores. Fortunately all of the Savoy recordings are available, probably because Savoy has remained under one proprietorship, that of veteran independent label owner Herman Lubinski of Newark. Verve recently prepared a reissue of most of the Parkers in its catalog. As this book went to press arrangements were being made to distribute in America the Charlie Parker on Dial series reissued by Spotlite Records of England.

CHARLIE PARKER PERFORMANCES

Charlie Parker, Volumes 1–6, Saba ERO 8005, 8006, 8007, 8031, 8035, 8052 (imports)

Charlie Parker, Savoy, 12152

Charlie Parker (combining *Bird at St. Nick's* and *Bird on 52nd Street*), Fantasy 24009

Charlie Parker's Greatest Recording Session, Savoy 12079

Charlie Parker Memorial, Savoy 12000

Charlie Parker on Dial, Volumes 1–6, Spotlite 101, 102, 103, 104, 105, 106 (imports, limited edition)

Charlie Parker Story, Verve 68000, 68001, 68002

Charlie Parker World, Roost 2257

The Definitive Charlie Parker, 14 volumes, ESP–BIRD 1–14

Echoes of an Era, with Dizzy Gillespie, Roulette 105

The Essential Charlie Parker, Verve 68409

The Genius of Charlie Parker, Savoy 12009, 12014

The Genius of Charlie Parker, Verve 68003, 68004, 68005, 68006, 68007, 68008, 68009, 68010

Groovin' High, Savoy 12020 (Guild masters)

The Immortal Charlie Parker, Savoy 12001

Jay McShann, New York, 1208 Miles, Decca 9236 (*Hootie Blues, Confessin' the Blues, Sepian Stomp, Lonely Boy Blues, Swingmatism, Hootie's Ignorant Oil*)

Jazz at Massey Hall, Fantasy 86003

Yardbird, Pickwick S 3054

CHARLIE PARKER'S SOURCES,
MUSICAL REFERENCES, AND COMPANIONS

Louis Armstrong, Louis Armstrong Story, Columbia CL 851–4

Count Basie's Best, Decca DX S–7170 (including Lester Young)

Count Basie in Kansas City, RCA LPV–514 (Bennie Moten Band, 1930–32)

Sidney Bechet, *The Fabulous Sidney Bechet*, Blue Note 81207

Clifford Brown in Paris, Prestige S–7761

Don Byas Meets Ben Webster, Prestige S–7692

Charlie Christian, 1941, Counterpoint 554 (Minton's sessions)

Kenny Clarke, *Paris Bebop Sessions*, Prestige S–7605

Ornette Coleman, *Tomorrow Is the Question*, Contemporary 7569

John Coltrane, *New Thing at Newport*, Impulse S–94

Sonny Criss, *This Is Sonny Criss*, Prestige S–7511

Miles Davis, *Milestones*, Columbia CS 9428

———, *Sketches of Spain*, Columbia CS 8271

Eric Dolphy, *Where?* Prestige S 7843

Kenny Dorham, Prestige S 7754

Billy Eckstine Orchestra, Spotlite 100 (AFRS broadcasts 1945, import)

———, vocals. *Stormy*, Enterprise 1013

Roy Eldridge, *Nifty Cat*, Master Jazz J–8110

Duke Ellington, *Greatest Hits*, Columbia CS 9629

Erroll Garner, *Concert by the Sea*, Columbia CS 9821

Dizzy Gillespie, *Swing Low, Sweet Cadillac*, Impulse S 9149

Babs Gonzales, *Sunday*, Dauntless 6311

Dexter Gordon, *Our Man in Paris*, Blue Note 84133

Wardell Gray, Prestige S–7343

Al Haig, Prestige S–7841

Hampton Hawes, *High in the Sky*, Vault S–9010

Coleman Hawkins, *Pioneers*, with Mary Lou Williams, Prestige S–7647

Earl Hines, *Fatha Blows Best*, Decca 75048

Johnny Hodges, *Con-Soul & Sax*, Victor LSP 3393

Milt Jackson, *Bags and Trane*, Atlantic S–1368

Kansas City Jazz, Decca 8044. (Mary Lou Williams, Prof Smith, Big Joe Turner, Count Basie, Lips Page, Andy Kirk, et al.)

Kansas City Piano, Decca 79226 (Jay McShann, Mary Lou Williams, Pete Johnson, Count Basie)

Andy Kirk and the Clouds of Joy, *Instrumentally Speaking*, Decca 79232

Harlan Leonard and the Rockets, RCA LPV 531 (Leonard, Jesse Price, et al.)

Howard McGhee, *Maggie's Back in Town*, Contemporary 7596

Charlie Mingus, *Mingus Ah Um*, Columbia CS–8171

Modern Jazz Quartet, *Pyramid*, Atlantic S 1325 (John Lewis and Milt Jackson)

Thelonious Monk, *Greatest Hits*, Columbia CS 9775

King Pleasure, *Original Moody's Mood*, Prestige S 7586 (includes *Parker's Mood*)

Bud Powell, *The Amazing Bud Powell*, Blue Note 81503, 81504

Max Roach, *Percussion Bitter Sweet*, Impulse S 8

Buster (Prof) Smith, *The Legendary Prof Smith*, Atlantic S 1323

Sonny Stitt Plays Bird, Atlantic S 1418.

Art Tatum, *The Essential Art Tatum*, Verve 68433

——, *Piano Starts Here*, Columbia CS 8655

Big Joe Turner, *Jumpin' the Blues* (with Pete Johnson), Arhoolie R 2004.

——*Boss of the Blues*, Atlantic S 1234

Sarah Vaughan, *Golden Hits*, Mercury 60645

Chick Webb and his Orchestra, Decca 79223

Ben Webster, *Blue Light*, International Polydor S 623 209 (import)

Phil Woods at the Montreux Jazz Festival, MGM 4695

Lester Young at His Very Best, Emarcy 66010

Lester Young, *Giant of Jazz*, Sunset 5181

RUNNING DISCOGRAPHY OF
PRINCIPAL PARKER PERFORMANCES ON RECORD

Lady Be Good, Honeysuckle Rose, &c. (Wichita transcriptions). Wichita, November/December, 1940. Not available.

Hootie Blues, Swingmatism, &c. Dallas, April 30, 1941. Decca DL 79236.

Red Cross, Tiny's Tempo, &c. New York City, September 15, 1944. Savoy 12001.

I Want Every Bit of It. New York City, January 1945. Out of print.

Groovin' High, Shaw Nuff, &c. New York City, February/May, 1945. Savoy 12020.

Slam Slam Blues, Congo Blues, &c. New York City, June 6, 1945. Spotlite 106.

Now's the Time, Koko, &c. New York City, November 26, 1945. Savoy 12079.

Slim's Jam, Poppity Pop, &c. Hollywood, December 29, 1945. Savoy 12014.

Lady Be Good. Los Angeles, March 25, 1946. Verve MG Volume 1.

Ornithology, Moose the Mooche, &c. Hollywood, March 28, 1946. Spotlite 101.

Lover Man, &c. Hollywood, July 29, 1946. Spotlite 101.

Cool Blues, This is Always, &c. Hollywood, February 19, 1947. Spotlite 102.

Relaxin' at Camarillo, &c. Hollywood, February 26, 1947. Spotlite 103.

Chasing the Bird, Donna Lee, &c. New York City, May, 1947 (?). Savoy 12001.

Dizzy Atmosphere, &c. Carnegie Hall, New York City, September 29, 1947. Roost RLP 2234.

Embraceable You, Hymn, &c. New York City, October 28, 1947. Spotlite 104.

Klactoveesedstene, Out of Nowhere, &c. New York City, November 4, 1947. Spotlite 105.

Crazeology, Charlie's Wig, &c. New York City, December 17, 1947. Spotlite 105.

The Bird, Repetition. New York City, December 1947. Verve MG 8001.

Parker's Mood, Barbados, &c. New York City, August 29, 1948. Savoy 12009.

Slow Boat to China. Royal Roost, New York City, December 11, 1948. ESP.

Mango Mangue. New York City, December 20, 1948. Verve MG 8000.

White Christmas, New York City, December 25, 1948. ESP.

Slow Boat to China, Royal Roost, New York City, January 1, 1949. ESP.

Just Friends, &c. New York City, November 30, 1949. Verve MG 8004.

Move, Cool Blues, &c. Cafe Society, Greenwich Village, New York City, May 8, 1950. (with Fats Navarro). ESP.

Hot House, &c. St. Nick's, New York City, February 18, 1950. Prestige 24009.

Bloomdido, &c. New York City, June 6, 1950. Verve MG 8006.

Embraceable You, &c. Folkets Park, Halsingborg, Sweden, November 24, 1950. Sonet 27, Storyville 27.

Lover Man. New York City, August 8, 1951. Verve MG 8000.

Jam Blues, &c. Hollywood, June, 1952. Verve 8002.

The Serpent's Tooth, &c. New York City, January 30, 1953. Prestige 7044.

A Night in Tunisia, &c. Massey Hall, Toronto, May 15, 1953. Prestige 86003.

I Love Paris, Love for Sale. New York City, December 10, 1954. Verve MG 8007.

Parker's Mood (lyrics by King Pleasure). December 7, 1954. Prestige 7586.

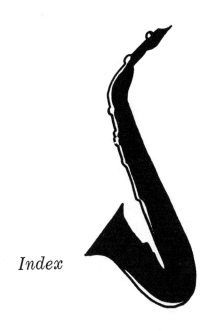

Index

Abyssinian Baptist Church (New York), 360–362
Adams Theatre (Newark), 126
Agnos, John (lunch wagons), 51–52
Ahmediyya Movement, 340
Akademiska Foreningen (Malmo, Sweden), 295
Akerberg, Yngve, 293–294
Albany, Joe, 167
Albert clarinet, 41, 45, 82–83
Albino Red. *See* Rodney, Red
Alexander, Willard, 77, 78
Allen, Jap (Cotton Club Orchestra), 37, 50
Allison, Tommy, 22
Almanach de Gotha, 356
American Federation of Musicians (AFM), 128, 147, 192, 249, 265, 333–334, 336, 339; *see also* Locals
Amiralen dancehall (Malmo, Sweden), 295
Ammons, Albert, 157
Ammons, Gene (Jug), 157
Amos and Andy (club, Kansas City), 30
"Amos and Andy" (program), 14
Anderson, Bernard (Buddy), 111, 114, 154, 157, 159–160
Antlers Club (Kansas City), 95
Apollo Records, 192
Apollo Theatre (New York), 127, 142, 148, 150–151, 196, 305, 317

Aquarium (club, New York), 264, 313

Argyle Lounge (club, Chicago), 242, 257–258

Arliss, George, 256

Armed Forces Radio Services (AFRS), 203

Armour Packing Company, 95

Armstrong, Louis, 36, 77, 103, 119, 131–132, 145, 172, 173, 194, 212, 220, 243, 256, 270, 275, 290, 294, 320, 366, 373

Asch, Moe, 208

Avakian, George, 208

Auld, Georgie, 261

Ayler, Albert, 258, 276, 366

Bach, J. S., 67

Bailey, Mildred, 164–165

Bailey, Pearl, 339, 349, 362, 371

Baker, Chet, 309

Bales, Walter, 109–110

Band Box. See Lucille's Band Box

Banjo Burney (Bernie), 106

Banks, Paul (orchestra), 49

Bar le Duc (club, Kansas City), 30, 71

Barefield, Eddie, 42

Barnett, Charlie (orchestra), 126, 160, 204, 239, 294

Barone, Joe, 96

Bartók, Béla, 209, 329; string quartets, 194

Basheer, Ahmed (Thomas Henderson), 340–343

Basie, Bill (Count, orchestra), 31, 32, 37, 42, 45, 49–56, 59–60, 66, 71, 76–78, 80, 83, 89, 90, 108, 109, 110, 111, 121, 122, 127, 135, 143, 158, 160–161, 165, 172, 174, 204, 289, 327, 334, 336

Basin Street (club, New York), 264, 313, 330, 332, 346

Bauer, Billy, 267, 337

Beatles, 319

Bebop style, 171–174, 244, 293, 317

Bechet, Sidney, 164–165, 270–271

Beckett, Fred, 94–95, 108, 135

Bee Hive (club, Chicago), 339–340

Beeks, Clarence. See King Pleasure

Beethoven, Ludwig van, 270, 357

Beiderbecke, Leon (Bix), 364

Belafonte, Harry, 276

Bell, Herman, 371

Bellevue Hospital (New York), 332, 333–335

Bellson, Louis, 339, 349, 361, 371

Beltone Records, 203

Benedetti, Dean, 1–25, 137, 170, 176, 181–183, 200–203, 207, 230, 235, 252, 283, 301, 330, 343, 372

Berg, Alban, 149, 209

Berg, Billy, 2, 7, 8, 17–18, 198; see also Billy Berg's

Berigan, Roland (Bunny), 364

Berlan, Alan J., 248

Berman, Saul (Sonny), 260

Berry, Leon (Chu), 135, 293

Billboard (magazine), 221–222

Billie's Bounce, 10, 195–196, 208

Billy Berg's (club, Hollywood), 1–25, 200–203, 205, 207, 208, 247, 282, 324

Billy Shaw Artists. See Shaw, Billy

Bird. See Parker, Charles, Jr.

Bird at St. Nick's, 301

Bird in the Basket (club, Los Angeles), 201

Birdland (club, New York), 264, 269–277, 281, 286, 299, 300, 313, 320, 330–332, 335, 344–347, 348, 367, 371

Bird's Nest, 239

Bird's Nest (club, Pennsylvania), 373

Birth of the Cool, 318

Bishop, Walter, 287, 303, 337

Black Deuce records, 248, 253

Blakey, Art, 158–159, 344–346

Bluebird records, 155

Blue Devils (Oklahoma City Blue Devils), 37, 42, 59, 94, 110

Blue Note (club, Philadelphia), 322

Blue Ribbon Salute, 151–152

Blume, Teddy, 291–292, 304

Body and Soul, 64, 67, 111, 113, 151

Boehm clarinet, 82

Boeuf sur le Toit (club, Paris), 297

Bolden, Charles (Buddy), 164, 172

Bop City (club, New York), 264, 313, 320

Bop City (club, San Francisco), 309

Bossa Nova, 250

Boston Conservatory of Music, 81, 85

Bothwell, Johnny, 207

Boulevard Lounge (club, Kansas City), 30, 47, 96

Bowman, Dave, 165
Boyley, Addie. *See* Addie Parker
Braddock's Bar (New York), 142
Brancusi, Constantin, 327
Brass Rail Bar (Toronto), 312
Brewster's Red Barn (Massachusetts), 330
Brice, Fanny, 106
Bridges, Henry, Jr., 42, 108, 135
Brockman, Gail, 146, 157
Bronson, Art (Bostonians), 58–59
Brooks, Shelton, 151
Brown, Clifford, 275, 366
Brown, Piney, 47–48, 61, 94
Brown, Ray, 3, 22, 198, 205, 305, 371
Brown, Walter, 110, 115, 118, 121–125, 127, 372
Brown Bomber (club, Los Angeles), 201
Brubeck, Dave (Quartet), 318, 321
Bruce, Lenny, 256, 305
Bucket of Blood (club, Kansas City), 30
Buckley, Lord (Richard Buckley), 304
Buckner, Christine, 50, 53–54
Bunn, Jimmy, 221–224
Burley, Dan, 100, 179
Burney, Banjo. *See* Banjo Burney
Burns, Ralph, 126, 207
Burton, Ellis (Chief, Yellow Front Saloon), 61
Butts, Jimmy, 167–171
Byas, Don, 4, 165, 192, 297–298
Byrd, Emry, 202–203, 211, 214, 217, 220; *see also* Moose the Mooche

Caceres, Ernie, 267
Cadet records, 193
Café Society Downtown (club, New York), 286–287
Caffrey, special agent, 40
Cagney, James, 219
California Supreme Court, 229
Callender, George (Red), 220, 238–241
Calloway, Cabell (Cab), 70, 137, 181, 303
Camarillo State Hospital (California), 229–234, 255, 338
Cannon, Jimmy, 173
Capitol Records, 73, 368
Capone, Al, 29, 40, 95
Carbone, Pietro, 342
Carmen Jones, 342

Carnegie Hall (New York), 247–248, 305, 334, 362–363
Carollo, Big Charley, 107
Carroll, Jimmy, 273
Carry, George (Scoops), 143, 146, 149, 152
Carter, Bennett (Benny, orchestra), 135, 137, 211, 309
Carter, Ron, 339
Casa Dell (club, Tulsa), 111
Casa Fiesta (club, Kansas City), 111
Casa Loma Orchestra, 282
Catlett, Sidney (Big Sid), 127
Cats and the Fiddle, 167
Central Avenue (Los Angeles), 19, 125, 201–203, 218, 325
Century Ballroom (Kansas City), 111, 115
Chaloff, Serge, 207, 260
Channing, Bill, 71
Chanticleer Club (club, Baltimore), 237
Charlie Chan (*nom de disque* for Charlie Parker), 311, 312
Charlie Parker Foundation for Performing Arts, 372
Charlie Parker Memorial Concert, 372
Charlie Parker Memorial Foundation, 372
Charlie Parker Record Corporation, 369
Charlie's Tavern (New York), 258
Chautauqua, 58
Cherokee, 18, 20–25, 75, 105, 116, 126, 137, 196; *see also Koko*
Cherry Blossom (club, Kansas City), 30, 47, 62
Chisholm, Shirley, 258
Chood. *See* Rodney, Red
Christian, Charlie, 78, 135–137
Christy, June, 322
Chudnick, Robert. *See* Rodney, Red
Churchill, Winston, 180, 314
Citizens' Fusion Committee, 95
Civic Hotel (Los Angeles), 224–226, 233
Clap Hands Here Comes Charlie, 126
Clarke, Kenny (Klook), 132–135, 137–139, 147, 151, 158, 164, 167, 171, 243, 272, 297, 305, 371
Clarkin, Tootie (Tutty), 38, 107, 111, 154, 156, 309

Clayton, Wilbur (Buck), 192
Cleaver, Eldridge, 258, 324
Clouds of Joy (Andy Kirk Orchestra), 42, 48, 60, 62, 78, 120, 121, 127, 149
Club Alabam (Los Angeles), 201
Club de Lisa (Chicago), 155
Club Downbeat (New York). See Downbeat Club
Club Downbeat (Philadelphia), 305, 310
Club Germaine (Paris), 271
Club Hi De Ho (Los Angeles), 235
Club Riviera (St. Louis), 160
Cochrane, Wayne, 374
Cole, Nat (King), 208, 239
Cole, William (Cozy), 193
Coleman, Earl, 239
Coleman, Ornette, 275, 366
Collected Poems of Dylan Thomas, 364
College Inn (club, Kansas City), 30, 61, 95, 111
Collins, Jazzbo, 362
Colony Record Shop, 276
Coltrane, John, 258, 275, 364, 366
Columbia Records, 167, 368
Columbus Hospital (New York), 287
Comedy Club (Baltimore), 342
Comet Records, 194–195
Commodore Music Shop (New York), 208
Commodore Records, 208
Como, Perry, 170
Condoli, Conte, 339
Condon, Eddie (Chicagoans), 165
Confessin' the Blues, 121–123, 125, 372
Confidential magazine, 292, 356, 364
Confirmation, 8
Continental Records, 152
Continental Room (Kansas City), 117
Cool Blues, 239, 260, 265, 284, 294, 297, 308
Cooper, Ralph, 151
Coquette, 112–113
Cornell University (Ithaca, New York), 216–262
Cotton Club (New York), 175
Coulsen, Vic, 137
C. P. MacGregor Transcription Studios (Hollywood), 221–224, 239–240

Crispus Attucks Grammar School (Kansas City), 33, 36–37
Criss, William (Sonny), 125, 207, 324
Cropper, Harvey, 340–343
Crosby, Bing, 170, 277
Cross, Red, 169, 186, 196
Crump, Tom, 157–158

Dale, Diana, 276
Dameron, Tadd, 135, 159, 193–194, 262, 270
Daniels, Ernest, 79, 354
Dan Wall's Chili House (New York), 105, 250
Davis, Angela, 258
Davis, Miles, 159, 195–198, 207, 208, 209–213, 220, 243–244, 246–247, 255, 257, 258, 267, 272–273, 275–276, 281, 286, 293, 311, 318–320, 321, 327, 366, 371
Davis, Sammy, 362, 374
Dean, James, 363
Deans of Swing (orchestra), 39–41, 43, 64, 70–72, 259, 341
Debussy, Claude, 293
Debut Records, 312–313
Decca Records, 77–78, 89–90, 115, 121–125, 128, 187, 203, 211, 368
Decca Sepia Series, 123
de Franco, Boniface (Buddy), 267, 282
De Gaulle, Charles, 314
Delaunay, Charles, 271, 297–298
Deluxe Records, 156, 161, 167
Denny, Al (orchestra), 111
Department of Internal Revenue, 95
Department of Mental Hygiene (California), 234
de Stael, Madame, 177, 301
Deuces. See Three Deuces
Dewey Square Hotel (New York), 243, 263
Dexter, Dave, Jr., 73, 117, 121, 208
Dial Records, 205–206, 207–217, 221–224, 233, 234, 238–241, 248–254, 369, 373
Dickert, Richard, 95
Dizzy Atmosphere, 8, 172, 178, 193, 198, 203, 207, 247
Dolphy, Eric, 275, 366
Domnerus, Arne, 295–296
Donald, Barbara, 366

Dorham, McKinley (Kenny), 267, 272, 344–346
Dorsey, Jimmy (orchestra), 58, 282, 374
Dorsey, Tommy (TD, orchestra), 173, 355, 357
Douglas, Buck, 42
Douglas, Ralph, 284
Douglas, Tommy (orchestra), 42, 81–83, 84, 86, 95
Douglas Brothers Orchestra, 42, 49
Down Beat magazine, 73, 76, 90, 117, 158, 160, 173, 197, 213, 233, 235, 367
Downbeat Club (New York), 163, 165, 237
Downbeat Club (Philadelphia). *See* Club Downbeat (Philadelphia)
Downbeat Room (club, Boston), 16
Downs, Chauncey (orchestra), 49
Drew, Kenny, 316
Dukoff, Bobby, 221–224
Durham, Eddie, 59, 78

Ebony magazine, 303
Eckstine, Billy, 98, 113, 143, 147–152, 154–161, 166–167, 169, 170, 186, 239, 243, 274, 362, 371
Eldon, Missouri, 79, 89–92
Eldridge, Roy, 112, 135–136, 139, 151, 224, 275, 292–295
Electro Broadcasting Studios (Glendale, California), 205–206
El Grotto Room. *See* Pershing Hotel, Chicago
Ellington, Edward Kennedy (Duke, orchestra), 36, 60, 81, 99, 128, 135, 138, 160–161, 174, 194, 220, 243, 276, 316–317, 373
Elmer Bean's Club (Kansas City), 30
El Sino (club, Detroit), 242, 252, 254
El Torreon (ballroom, Kansas City), 50, 81
Embraceable You, 250–251, 297
Embouchure, 82–83, 181
Emge, Charlie, 233
Enois, Leonard (Lucky), 110
Epace Cardin (club, Paris), 373
Epstein, Papa Sol, 49
Ericson, Rolf, 293–294
Esquire magazine, 206
Estrad magazine, 293, 295

Evans, Herschel, 30, 42, 44, 52–56, 62
Exposé magazine, 364

Fairyland Park (Kansas City), 111
Famous Door (club, New York), 163–164
Fantasy Records, 301, 313; *see also* Prestige Records
Feather, Leonard, 261, 298, 303, 361, 362
Federal Narcotics Hospital ("Lexington," Lexington, Kentucky), 310, 315–316, 374
Festival of Modern American Jazz, 322–324
Fields, Herbie, 137
Fifty-Second Street. *See* Street, The
Fifty Thousand Killer-Watts of Jive. *See* Leo Watson
Finale Club (Los Angeles), 206–207, 209, 211, 212, 218, 221, 224, 237
Finkelstein, Sidney, 261
Fitzgerald, Ella, 308, 374
Fitzgerald, Scott, 366
Fleet, Biddy, 105
Florentine Gardens (club, Hollywood), 207
Floyd, Pretty Boy, 40
Floyd, Troy (Dreamland Orchestra), 42
Folkets Park (Helsingborg, Sweden), 296
Forest Lawn Cemetery (Glendale, California), 205
Forrest, Jimmy, 309, 371
Fort, Joel, M.D., 316
Frazer, Sir James, 320
Free French Army, 314
Freeman, Lawrence (Bud), 165
Freeman, Marvin, 206, 208, 209, 211, 213–217, 221–224, 229, 233, 371
Freeman, Richard, M.D., 221–224, 226, 229, 230–234, 365, 371
Freymann, Robert, M.D., 349–358, 360
Fuller, Walter (Gil), 159

Gaiety Theatre (Kansas City), 39
Gaillard, Bulee (Slim), 179, 203
Gale, Moe (agency), 244, 248, 252,

255–256, 258–259, 263, 269, 335, 339, 343–344, 349, 353
Ganey, Judge A. Cullen, 316
Gardner, Goon, 98, 146–147, 149
Garner, Erroll, 167, 238–239, 323
Garrison, Arvin, 209–213
Garvey, Marcus, 104
General Amusement Corporation (agency), 125
Gershwin, Ira, 198
Getz, Stan, 206, 208, 276, 322, 362
Gibson, Harry the Hipster, 180
Gieseking, Walter, 318
Gillespie, John Birks (Dizzy), 3, 4, 18, 19–21, 22, 24, 114, 126–127, 139, 146–152, 154, 156–159, 167, 171–174, 180–181, 186, 188, 192–198, 200, 203, 205, 208, 230, 233, 237, 243, 247–248, 256, 257, 263, 267, 274–275, 281, 282, 312, 322–323, 330, 361, 371
Gimpel, Bronislaw, 273
Glaser, Joe, 30–32, 72
Glass Bar (club, St. Louis), 309
Golden, Harry, 290
Gonzales, Babs, 264
Goodman, Benny (orchestra, sextet), 76, 112, 135, 137, 194, 295–296
Goodstein, Oscar, 299, 332, 344
Gordon, Dexter, 192
Gordon, Gray (orchestra), 282
Gottlieb, Dr. Louis, 173–174, 207
Gould, Bud, 111
Grand Prix de Disque, 239, 308
Grand Terrace (club, Chicago), 146, 159
Granz, Norman, 203–205, 208, 237, 254, 265, 270, 272–273, 286, 308–309, 312, 318, 337, 362, 367–368; *see also* Jazz at the Philharmonic
Graves, W. W., 107
Gray, Wardell, 238–241
Greanleaf Gardens (club, Kansas City), 30, 71, 341
Green, Bennie (trombonist), 146, 156–158
Green, Benny (saxophonist, columnist *London Observer*, author), 196–197
Greenberg, Rowland, 295, 297
Greenwich Village (New York), 102, 333–344
Grennard, Elliott, 221–224

Grimes, Lloyd (Tiny), 164, 239
Guild Records, 193–194, 208
Gunther, Paul, 371

Hackett, Bobby, 165
Hadnott, Billy, 94–95, 371
Haggerty, Thomas, W., M.D., 234
Haig, Al, 3, 4, 21, 22, 24, 171–174, 198, 267, 281, 287
Halperin, Chief Medical Examiner Milton (New York), 360
Hammond, Dr., 231, 234
Hammond, John, 30–32, 76–78, 90, 121, 173
Hampton, Lionel, 135, 204
Handy, George, 205–206, 208
Harewood, Hal, 345
Harper's Magazine, 223
Harris, Benjamin (Little Benny, Benny), 143–144, 146–150
Harris, Bill, 282
Harris, Joe, 247–248, 267
Hart, Clyde, 126, 135, 167–171, 192
Harvard University (Cambridge, Massachusetts), 262
Hawes, Hampton, 207, 323–324, 366
Hawkins, Coleman (Hawk, Bean), 4, 30, 42, 58–60, 62–63, 83, 105, 113, 135–136, 164–165, 169, 186, 303, 320, 335
Hawkins, Erskine (orchestra), 127
Hayes, Thamon (orchestra), 42, 50, 51, 108
Haynes, Roy, 272, 287, 316
Headman, Mattie, 50
Heard, James Charles (J.C.), 194–195
Heath, Percy, 311
Hector's Cafeteria (New York), 195, 245
Hefti, Neal (orchestra), 254
Heifetz, Jascha, 277, 293
Hellstrom, Nils, 293, 296
Henderson, Fletcher (orchestra), 62–63, 99, 320
Henderson, Thomas. *See* Basheer, Ahmed
Henryson, Robert, 261
Herbert, Victor, 103
Herman, Woody (orchestra), 163, 187, 221, 233, 239, 260, 282, 294, 374
Hey Hay Club (Kansas City), 30, 95

Hibbler, Al, 120–121, 123, 125, 128, 371
Hi De Ho (club, Los Angeles), 235
Higgins, Otto (Kansas City police chief), 107
Higginson, Fred, 111
Hi Hat Club (Kansas City), 30, 63–64, 67, 83, 85, 154
Hill, Eddie (orchestra), 111
Hill, Teddy (orchestra), 131–133, 138
Hindemith, Paul, 209, 293
Hines, Earl (Fatha', orchestra), 98, 143–144, 145–153, 154, 155, 157, 161, 164, 326–327, 371
Hitler, Adolf, 180
Hodeir, Andre, 271
Hodges, Johnny (Rabbit), 60, 135, 138, 235, 309
Holiday, Billie, 194, 261, 272, 304, 334, 362
Holland, Herbert (Peanuts), 126, 135
Honeysuckle Rose, 65, 90, 112, 139, 172
Hootie Blues, 121, 122–126, 128, 137, 170, 187, 265, 307, 371–372
Hootie's Ignorant Oil, 115
Horowitz, Vladimir, 318
Hotel Cecil (New York), 131
Hotel Stanhope (New York), 314–315, 348–358
Hot Five. See Louis Armstrong
Hot Seven. See Louis Armstrong
Houston, Cisco, 208
How Deep Is the Ocean, 252
Howard Theatre (Washington), 132, 148, 309
Howard University, 155
Hunter, Lloyd (orchestra), 110
Hurst's Loan Office (Kansas City), 98
Hurwitz, Jerry, 102
Hyams, Margie, 261

I Got Rhythm, 75, 84–85, 92–93, 139, 172, 178, 198, 239
I Want Every Bit of It, 191–192
I'll Always Love You Just the Same, 168, 170
I'll Wait and Pray, 160, 168, 192
I'm Dreaming of a White Christmas, 277
Isbell, Woody, 208
Ives, Burl, 208

Jackson, Greig Stewart (Chubby), 126–127, 261, 282
Jackson, John, 111, 157
Jackson, Milt (Bags), 3, 21, 22, 198, 200, 261, 318, 371, 373
Jacquet, Illinois, 308
Jail (club, Kansas City), 30
Jam sessions, 42, 49, 57–65, 105, 127, 130–144, 337–338, 356
James, Harry, 135, 282
JATP. See Jazz at the Philharmonic.
Jazz: A People's Music, 261
Jazz at Massey Hall, 311–313
Jazz at the Philharmonic, 204–205, 254, 265, 270, 286, 303, 306–309; see also Norman Granz
Jazz Baroness. See Koenigswarter, Baroness Pannonica de
Jazz Hot magazine, 271, 363
Jazz Hall of Fame, 367
Jazz, Its Evolution and Essence, 271
Jazzman Record Shop (Hollywood), 207
Jazz Tempo magazine, 207
Jederby, Thore, 294
Jefferson High School (Los Angeles), 202, 216
Jefferson, Blind Lemon, 36
Jeffries, Herb, 146, 147, 155, 170, 362
Jenkin's Music Store (Kansas City), 61, 79
Jewish War Veterans' Youth Band, 282
Jimmy's Chicken Shack (New York), 99–102
Jive, 175, 178–179, 186
Joans, Ted, 341
Johnson, Albert (Budd), 42, 143, 155, 159
Johnson, Foster, 206–207, 218
Johnson, Gus, 110, 112, 121
Johnson, James Louis (J.J.), 252–253, 267
Johnson, Murl, 47–48
Johnson, Pete (Roll 'em Pete), 32, 47–48, 50, 68, 78, 93
Jolson, Al, 106
Jones, Jonathan (Jo), 83–85, 90, 92, 110, 133
Jones, Joseph Rudolph (Philly Joe), 311

Jones-Smith, Inc. (Basie pseudonym), 90
Jones, Tom, 374
Jordan, Ben, 221–224
Jordan, Irving (Duke), 243–244, 246–247, 267
Jubilee Junction (club, Jefferson City, Missouri), 125
Jubilee radio show (Armed Forces Radio Service), 203
Juilliard School of Music, 195, 243, 319
Jumbo's (club, San Francisco), 323
Just Friends, 273, 293, 317, 353–354

Kaminsky, Max, 276
Kansas City *Journal-Post*, 73
Kansas City Revisited, 371–372
Kansas City Six (Basie and McShann pseudonyms), 194, 372
Kansas City *Star*, 95, 185–186
Kapp, Dave, 77–78, 121–125
Kapp, Jack, 77, 122–123
Kaye, Sammy (orchestra), 197
Kaye, Sammy (Three Deuces), 164–165, 236–238
K. B. Hallen (auditorium, Copenhagen), 295–296
Keil, Charles, 366
Keith, Jimmy, 42, 48, 64, 94–95
Kelly's Stables (club, New York), 264
Kennedy, Florynce, 367–369
Kenton, Stan (orchestra), 22, 267, 282, 322–324, 374
Kessel, Barney, 239–240
Kesterson, Robert (Dingbod), 221–224
Kew Gardens, New York, 106
Keyes, Lawrence (88), 39, 64–65, 66, 70–71, 106, 259
KFBI, Wichita, Kansas, 111; *see also* Wichita tapes
Killian, Al, 126, 204
King Kolax (orchestra), 98
King, Dr. Martin Luther, 258
Kingfish, 14
King Pleasure (Clarence Beeks), 325–326, 336, 362
Kirby, John (sextet), 165
Kirk, Andy, 50, 51, 135, 159; *see also* Clouds of Joy
Kirk, Roland, 366
Klactoveesedstene, 148, 251–252, 260, 308

Knight, Walter, 42, 48
Knowles, Hattie, 50
Koenigswarter, Baron Jules de, 314
Koenigswarter, Baroness Pannonica de, 313–315, 348–358, 359, 364–365
Koko, 196, 208, 245; *see also Cherokee*
Konserthuset (Stockholm), 293
Koran, 340
Kotick, Teddy, 337
Krupa, Gene (orchestra), 22, 282, 288, 308, 374
Koussevitsky, Serge, 273

Lady Be Good, 90, 112–113, 205
Laguna, Eddie, 233
Lake Taneycomo, Missouri, 89–92, 120, 153–161
Lamond, Don, 239–240
Lanphere, Don, 301, 372
Lawrence, Baby, 362–363
Lawrence, Elliot (orchestra), 282
Lazia, Johnny, 40, 61, 107
Leadbelly. *See* Ledbetter, Huddie
Leavenworth penitentiary (Kansas), 316, 339–340, 374
Le Club Downbeat (New York), 337–338
Ledbetter, Huddie (Leadbelly), 208
Lee, George Ewing (orchestra), 38, 42, 49, 70–71, 81, 90–92, 95–106, 114, 120
Leonard, Harlan (Kansas City Rockets), 37, 42, 108, 110, 111, 114, 159
Levey, Stan, 3, 20–21, 22, 24, 167, 171–174, 193, 198, 200, 205, 206, 318, 371
Lewis, Alonzo, 37, 41, 45, 66
Lewis, Dave (orchestra), 49
Lewis, John (Modern Jazz Quartet), 126–127, 205, 220, 248, 264–266, 305, 326, 334, 365, 366, 371
"Lexington." *See* Federal Narcotics Hospital
Licorish, Reverend David, 361
Life magazine, 263
L'il Phil, 64, 73, 140, 350
Lincoln Gardens (club, Chicago), 172
Lincoln Heights jail (Los Angeles), 226
Lincoln High School (Kansas

City), 36–38, 39, 49, 50, 64, 69, 70, 71, 74–75, 108, 186, 341
Lincoln Theatre (Los Angeles), 132
Lind, Jenny, 294
Lindgren, Carl-Erik, 295–297
Lindsay's Sky Bar (Cleveland), 317, 320
Lindy's restaurant (New York), 249
Linguistics of jazz. See Jive
Little Tokyo (Los Angeles), 206–207, 218
Local 369 (AFM, Las Vegas), 374
Local 627 (AFM, Kansas City, "colored local"), 43, 50, 71, 75, 81
Local 802 (AFM, New York City), 131, 152, 334–335
Logan, Eli, 37, 48
Lombardo, Carmen, 113
London Observer, 196–197
Lonely Boy Blues, 128
Lone Star (club, Kansas City), 47
Los Angeles County Jail, 226
Los Angeles Fire Department, 224–226, 228
Los Angeles Philharmonic Auditorium, 204–205
Los Angeles Police Department, 219, 225–226
Los Angeles Superior Court, 371
Louis, Joe, 100
Love, Clarence (orchestra), 49
Lovejoy's (club, Los Angeles), 201
Lover Man, 193–194, 208, 223, 294, 297, 305, 338
Lowdown magazine, 364
Lowell, Fred, 50
Lubinski, Herman, 169
Lucille's Band Box (club, Kansas City), 30, 94–95, 109–110, 154
Lunceford, Jimmy (orchestra), 204
Lund, University of (Malmo, Sweden), 295
Lyons, Jimmy (Monterey Jazz Festival), 203

Mabane, Bob, 111, 112
McConnell, Shorty, 146, 157
MacDonald, Julie, 327–328
McElroy, Judge Henry, 107
McGhee, Dorothy, 219
McGhee, Howard, 126–127, 160, 164, 167, 196, 208, 219–227, 229, 235, 237, 241, 270, 371

Machito and his Orchestra, 265
McLean, Jackie, 336–337
McMillan, Vic, 211–213
McNeely, Shepherd, 50, 53
McShann, Jay (Hootie, orchestra), 8, 33, 39, 93–94, 109–116, 117–129, 135, 137, 140, 142, 153, 157, 158, 161, 211, 275, 329, 371, 372
Maini, Joe, 301, 372
Malachi, John, 157
Malcolm X, 258, 324
Malco Theatres, 51
Manne, Shelly, 22, 267
Marciano, Rocky, 312
Marden Hotel (New York), 263
Marmarosa, Michael (Dodo), 22, 209–213, 220, 239–240
Marquette, Peewee, 276, 344–345, 371
Martin's 210 (club, Martin's on the Plaza, Kansas City), 110
Massey Hall (Toronto), 311–312, 321
Mastbaum Trade High School (Philadelphia), 282
Mau-mau, 340
Mayfair Club. See Clarkin, Tootie
MCA. See Musical Corporation of America
Medical Arts Hospital (New York), 298–299, 351, 354
Mellers, Wilfred, 366
Melody Maker magazine, 270, 298
Mercury records, 265, 270, 272–273, 303, 311, 313, 317, 353–354
Messirolls (mezzrolls). See Mezzrow, Milton
Mesta, Pearl, 177, 301
Metro-Goldwyn-Mayer, 265, 368
Metronome magazine, 73, 126, 255, 267–268
Mezzrow, Milton (Mezz), 179
Mili, Gjon, 291
Miller, Glenn (orchestra), 175, 319
Miller, Mitch, 273
Miller, Verne, 40
Milligan, Maurice (United States attorney), 107
Millinder, Lucky (orchestra), 125–126
Million Dollar Theatre (Los Angeles), 219
Mills Brothers, 374
Mills, Jackie, 22

Mingus, Charles, 312–313, 344–347, 360, 367

Minor, Orville (Piggy), 111–114

Minton, Henry, 131–132

Minton's (Minton's Playhouse), 12, 130–144, 151, 166, 177, 179, 182, 196, 206, 207, 248, 312, 315, 317, 319, 367

Mister Behop. See Gillespie, John Birks (Dizzy)

MJQ. See Modern Jazz Quartet; Lewis, John

Modern Jazz Quartet (MJQ), 126, 205, 318, 321, 334; see also Lewis, John

Mohammedanism, 340

Monk, Mrs., 134

Monk, Nellie, 134

Monk, Thelonious Sphere, 133–136, 138, 195, 314–315, 362, 371

Monroe's Uptown House (club, New York), 99, 105–106, 136–138, 140, 143–144, 151, 177, 182, 360

Monterey Jazz Festival (Monterey, California), 203, 371–372

Moody, James, 325

Moore, Slim, 196

Moose the Mooche, 211–213

Moose the Mooche, 202–203, 216, 369; see also Byrd, Emry

Mop Mop, 169; see also Red Cross

Morris, Milton, 61

Morris, William. See William Morris Agency

Morrison, Rudy, 157

Morton, Ferdinand (Jelly Roll), 81, 320

Mosk, Stanley (judge, California Supreme Court), 229–230

Moten, Bennie (orchestra), 37, 42, 49, 59, 108, 110

Mount Hope Cemetery (New York), 360

Mouse (drummer), 180

Mozart, Wolfgang Amadeus, 34, 142, 149, 170

Muehlebach Hotel (Kansas City), 43, 60, 77, 95

Mulligan, Gerry, 207, 208, 282, 362

Mundy, Jimmy, 147

Music Corporation of America (MCA), 77–78

Musicians' Protective Association. See Local 627

Music in a New Found Land, 366

Musicraft records, 194–195

Musser, Mr. 79

Mussolini, Benito, 180

Nance, Ray, 146

Napoleon, Teddy, 22

Nash, Frank, 39

National Association for Reform of Marijuana Laws (NORML), 316

National Conscription Act, 127

Navarro, Theodore (Fats), 114, 244, 260, 267, 282, 287

Newark Zion Baptist Church, 150

New Jazz Society, Toronto, 311–312

Newman, Jerry, 136, 170

New Mexico, University of, 126

New York Amsterdam News, 100, 179

New York Journal-American, 359

New York Mirror, 332, 359

New York Philharmonic Orchestra, 273

New York State Liquor Authority, 304, 313

New York Surrogate Court, 367–371

New York Times, The, 302, 359–360

New Yorker, The, 263

Nica. See Koenigswarter, Baroness Pannonica de

Night in Tunisia, 148, 150, 158, 171, 212–213, 247

Nilsson, Lennart, 296

Nola Studios (New York), 157, 168–171, 264–265

Noone, Jimmy, 104

Noren, Jack, 293

Norvo, Kenneth Norville (Red), 164–165, 194–195

Norwalk State Hospital (California), 229

Novelty Club (Kansas City), 30, 61

Now's the Time, 8, 196–198, 207, 245, 248, 253, 265, 308–309, 329, 369

Oasis Club (Los Angeles), 326–327

Oliver, Joe (King), 59, 131–132, 172

On-site recordings, 1–4, 19–25, 136–137, 182–183

Onyz Club (New York), 151–152, 163–164, 165, 186, 259, 261–262, 272

Onyx Records, 253
Open Door (club, New York), 336–337, 338–339, 358
Opera Without Banners, 372
Orchestra World, 73
Original Handbook of Harlem Jive, 179
Orkester Journalen (Stockholm), 363
Ornithology, 8, 10, 128, 175, 211–213, 221, 233, 240, 250, 329
Orr, June, 233
Ory, Edward (Kid), 208
Oxford University (England), 152

Paganini, Nicolò, 342
Page, Oran (Lips), 32, 52–56, 59, 77, 111, 114, 135, 270–271, 276, 336
Page, Walter (Big Four), 37, 45, 52–56, 59–60, 71, 84, 90, 110
Palestrina, Giovanni Pierluigi da, 149
Palladium Ballroom (Hollywood), 22, 282
Palladium Ballroom (New York), 265
Panama Club (Kansas City), 30
Paradise Theatre (Detroit), 125, 148, 161
Paris Jazz Fair, Festival, 263, 269
Parisien Ballroom (taxi dancehall, New York), 102–106, 137
Parker, Addie, 32, 36–45, 46, 74, 79, 98, 153–154, 161, 360, 361, 362, 370–371
Parker, Baird (Laird Baird), 313, 330, 369–371, 373
Parker, Chan Richardson Woods, 174–177, 231, 236–238, 246, 272, 295, 300–302, 305, 315, 326, 328–329, 330–332, 335, 338–339, 341, 358, 359, 362, 367–371, 373
Parker, Charles, Jr. (Charlie, Yardbird, Bird)
    acting, 94, 119–121, 238, 246, 262, 267, 288–290, 297–298, 312, 335, 336–337, 339, 343, 350–351
    alcoholism, 101, 141–142, 219, 220, 222, 235, 245, 259–261, 296, 299, 311, 320, 330–332, 342, 345–347, 348–351, 356, 363, 365
    boyhood and youth, 32–75, 341
    composing, 169–170, 197–198, 320, 329–330, 342, 364, 369

discovery and use of upper intervals, 105, 250–251
doubling of time, 64, 83, 93, 112, 196, 264–266
dress style, 18–19, 22–23, 185, 256, 302, 317, 331, 337, 343, 361
drugs, 73, 74, 75, 139–141, 154, 184, 187, 192, 200–203, 216, 218–219, 222, 224, 236–238, 245, 249–250, 259–261, 264, 284–286, 290, 292, 303–308, 311, 320, 328, 337–338, 350, 356, 363, 365
embouchure, 82–83, 181, 337
gourmandising, 5–9, 68, 184–185, 235, 356
health, 73–74, 139, 219, 221–223, 232, 234, 263, 298–299, 308, 327, 338–343, 348–356, 365
improvisation, 62–65, 83–85, 93–95, 100, 116, 138, 169–170, 196–198, 239, 250–251, 265–266, 277, 289, 296–297, 308–309
modal approach to music, 63–65, 66–69, 75, 205
negritude, 22–25, 46–56, 62–63, 255–258, 262, 287–291, 302, 315, 365–367
Olive Street house, 33, 45, 69, 74, 106, 153, 196, 302
Parker quintets, 243–246, 249–252, 255, 257–259, 261, 263, 266, 270, 272–273, 281–290, 301, 302, 305, 309–310, 316, 318, 374
Parker string units, 272–273, 291, 309, 316–318, 320, 330–332, 335, 353–354
psychiatric evaluations, 231–232, 334–335, 365–366
reeds, 9, 11, 67–68, 182, 195, 247
rules for living, 69–70
sexuality, 105, 116, 141, 186–187, 245–246, 291–292, 365
style (saxophone), 123, 138, 170, 181–182, 223, 265, 273, 275, 277, 289, 293, 297, 309, 317, 323, 337–338, 354, 356, 363
typical day in the life, 4–25, 185–187
Parker, Charles, Sr., 32, 35–36, 56, 106, 326, 334
Parker, Doris Sydnor, 174–175, 231, 233, 235–236, 240–241, 243, 246, 254, 256, 263, 270, 272, 300, 360–362, 367–371
Parker, Geraldine Marguerite Scott

(Gerry), 143, 246, 254, 369–371

Parker, Kim. *See* Richardson, Kim

Parker, Leo, 157

Parker, Leon, 75, 97, 143, 153, 238, 286, 370–371

Parker, Pree, 305, 313, 327–329, 360

Parker, Rebecca Ruffing, 74–75, 79, 97, 143, 153, 246, 370

Parker's Mood (music), 264–266, 363

Parker's Mood (lyrics), 325–326, 336, 362

Patton State Hospital (California), 229

Paseo Hall (Kansas City), 50, 70, 81–83

Paseo Park (Kansas City), 43, 90

Paul, Ebenezer, 106

Pendergast, Tom, 31, 32, 33, 40, 49, 51, 59, 95, 107, 130–131, 163, 166

Perkins, Red (orchestra), 110

Pershing Hotel (El Grotto Room, Chicago), 148, 182–183

Peterson, Oscar, 308, 309

Petrillo, Ceasar, 156

Pettiford, Oscar, 126, 148–149, 151–152

Philharmonic Auditorium. *See* Los Angeles Philharmonic

Phillips, Joseph (Flip), 194–195, 270

Pincus, Mayor, 165

Playboy magazine, 318

Plantation Club (St. Louis), 159

Pollack, Jackson, 363

Porter, Cole, 103

Porter, Roy, 211–213, 220, 221–224

Potter, Tommy, 157, 243–244, 246–247, 287, 316

Powell, Carrie, 90–92

Powell, Earl (Bud), 274, 312, 344–346, 366

Powell, Reverend Adam Clayton, 360

Premium Album Company, 368

Premier Hotel (New York), 305

President, Pres, Prez. *See* Lester Young

Prestige Records, 311, 313; *see also* Fantasy Records

Previn, Andre, 208

Price, Jesse, 45, 52–56, 60–61, 83, 92, 94, 106, 108, 114, 371

Price, Sam, 60

Price-Smith Band, 94–95

Prince Stewart Orchestra, 94

Procope, Russell, 276

Prowse, Juliet, 374

Psychopathic Ward (Los Angeles County Jail), 226–227, 228–230

Radio Recorders (Hollywood), 209–213

Raeburn, Boyd (orchestra), 22, 158, 205, 208, 212

Rainey, Gertrude (Ma), 36, 52

Rameau, Jean Philippe, 67

Ramey, Gene, 39, 71–73, 83–85, 92–93, 110, 112, 116, 121, 142

Raoul, 306–308

Ravel, Maurice, 293

RCA (RCA-Victor) Records, 108, 155, 253, 267–268, 353, 368

Recording ban, 136, 149, 156, 249

Red Cross, 169–171, 172, 182, 192, 196, 198, 208, 307, 329, 369

Redd, Freddie, 315

Regal Theatre (Chicago), 125, 132, 148, 160

Reig, Teddy, 168–171, 195–198, 253–254, 264–265, 361

Reisner, Robert (Bob), 336, 338–339, 358

Relaxin' at Camarillo, 240, 265

Reno Club (Kansas City), 30, 31, 42, 49–56, 59–60, 62, 68, 76–77, 83–85, 89, 90, 92, 96, 154, 204, 327, 336, 356

Rexroth, Kenneth, 309, 323, 327

Richardson, Chan. *See* Parker, Chan Richardson Woods

Richardson, Kim, 236, 238, 295, 301–302, 330, 369–371, 373

Richardson, Mrs., 175, 237, 302, 335

Richetti, Adam, 40

Rico Reeds, 9, 11, 195

Riddick, Dave, 106

Riley, Jack, 193

Ritz Hotel (Chicago), 148

Riverside Records, 315

Roach, Max, 164, 195–198, 243–244, 246–247, 255, 267, 272–274, 286, 312, 342, 371, 372

Roberts, Johnny, 287, 290

Robinson, Bill (Bojangles), 146

Robinson, Earl, 208

Rockets (Kansas City Rockets). *See* Leonard, Harlan

Rodney, Red (Robert Chudnick, Chood), 22, 207, 208, 272, 281–291, 293, 300, 303, 305, 310, 315–316, 339–340, 366, 372–374
Rogers, Milton (Shorty), 207
Rollins, Theodore (Sonny), 311, 366
Romance without Finance, 168, 170
Roosevelt, Franklin Delano, 63, 180
Roseland Ballroom (Kansas City), 78
Roseland Ballroom (New York), 102
Ross, James, 64
Rothschild family, 313–315
Rothschild, Victor, 314
Royal Roost (club, New York), 263–264, 274
Royal Theatre, 148
Rubaiyat of Omar Khayyam, 270, 338
Ruffing, Rebecca. *See* Parker, Rebecca
Ruffing, Mrs., 74
Rugolo, Pete, 267
Rumboogie Club (Chicago), 156
Ruppert Stadium (Kansas City), 49
Rushing, Jimmy, 32, 59, 110
Russell, Charles Ellsworth (Pee Wee), 165
Russell, Dillon (Curly), 167, 171–174, 264–265
Russell, Dorothy, 253
Russell, Ross, 205, 207–217, 218–227, 228–241, 337–338
Ryan's (Jimmy Ryan's, club), 163–164

Safranski, Eddie, 267
Salle Pleyel (Paris), 270–271
Samoa Club (New York), 163, 165
Sanders, Pharoah, 366
San Juan Hill, 134
San Quentin penitentiary (California), 217
Sartre, Jean Paul, 271, 367
Saunders, A. Allen, 330, 369
Savoy Ballroom (New York), 99, 125–127, 196
Savoy Records, 167–171, 192, 194, 195–198, 239, 246–247, 248, 249, 253, 264–266, 368, 373
Savoy Sultans (orchestra), 127
Sax, Adolphe, 80

Saxophone, 9–11, 42, 80–81, 100–101, 141, 181–182, 252
Schlitten, Don, 253
Schoenberg, Arnold, 196, 207, 209
Scott, Cecil (orchestra), 127
Scott, Clifford (Scotty), 154
Scott, Geraldine Marguerite. *See* Parker, Geraldine
Scott, Hazel, 362
Scott, Howard, 157
Scott, Tony (Tony Sciacca), 317
Scott, William J., 111, 112
Segal, Joe, 339, 372
Selassie, Haile, 180
Selmer (Selmer et Cie.), 9, 80–81, 85, 252
Seven West 52nd Street (7 West 52), 175–177, 236, 301, 314
Shavers, Charlie, 135, 361, 362
Shaw, Artie, 135
Shaw, Billy (Billy Shaw Artists Bureau), 152, 154, 156, 158, 160–161, 172, 195–196, 198, 244, 248–249, 252, 254, 257–259, 263, 265, 267, 269, 272–274, 287, 292, 305, 313, 316–317, 322, 330–331, 335, 346, 356
Shaw, William, 71
Shearing, George, 294
Shepp, Archie, 258, 276, 366
Shrine Auditorium (Los Angeles), 324
Simeon, Omer, 146
Simmons, Sonny, 276, 366
Simpson, Robert, 41, 341
Sims, Arthur (Zoot), 206–207
Sinatra, Frank, 167, 170
Singleton, Arthur (Zutty), 164
Sipple, John, 160–161
Sissle, Noble (orchestra), 156
Sixty-five Club (65 Club, Chicago), 98, 113, 146
Skeat's Etymological Dictionary, 252
Slam Slam Blues, 194, 265, 359, 363
Slim (band boy), 221–224
Slim and Slam (Slim Gaillard and Slam Stewart), 203
Slim's Jam, 203
Sloate, Maynard, 233, 371
Sloate-Orr Associates, 233, 371
Smith, Bessie, 36, 52
Smith, Bryce, 107
Smith, Cladys [*sic*] (Jabbo), 146
Smith, Henry (Prof, Buster), 42,

44, 49–56, 59, 94–95, 97–99, 106, 109, 114, 154
Smith, Hezekiah Leroy Gordon (Stuff), 165
Smith, Major N. Clark, 37
Smith, Talmadge (Tab), 126
Smith, Tatti, 90
Smith, Willie, 135, 204, 235
Sonet Records, 296
Spaeth, Sigmund, 173
Sparrow's Last Jump, 223
Spirits of Rhythm, 165
Spitz, Eddie, 61
Spoon. *See* Witherspoon, Jimmy
Spotlite Club (New York), 163, 165, 230, 237
Spotlite records. *See* Williams, Tony
St. Nick's (ballroom, New York), 300–301
St. Vincent's Hospital (New York), 364
Stabile, Dick, 60
Stacy, Jess, 135
Stage Door Delicatessen (New York), 180, 184
Stalin, Josef, 180
Stearns, Marshall, 261–263
Steinway pianos, 134, 318, 350
Stevens, Connie, 374
Stewart, Dee. *See* Prince Stewart Orchestra
Stewart, Leroy (Slam), 164, 194–195, 203
Stitt, Edward (Sonny), 340, 372
"Stomach that Walks like a Man, The," 203
Stone, Jesse (Blues Serenaders, orchestra), 49
Storyville (club, Boston), 336, 344, 348–349
Stravinsky, Igor, 201, 209
Street, The (Fifty-second Street), 8, 23, 151–152, 154, 161, 162–177, 180, 194, 195, 198, 207, 222, 245, 261–262, 264, 282, 301, 319, 367
Subway Club (Kansas City), 30, 94
Sullivan, Arthur, 361
Sullivan, Ira, 339
Sunset Club (Kansas City), 30, 33, 36, 38, 43, 47–49, 61, 68, 154
Sunset Records, 233
Sunshine Funeral Parlor, 276–277
Svensson, Gunnar, 293–294

Swope Park (Kansas City), 105
Sydnor, Doris. *See* Parker, Doris Sydnor

Tapioca (rock group), 373
Tate, George (Buddy), 42
Tatum, Art, 29, 31, 100–102, 104, 112, 135, 146, 164, 167, 287, 324
Taylor, Art, 337
Taylor, Cecil, 366
Tempo Music Shop (Hollywood), 207–210, 233–235, 240
Terrell, Pha, 120, 122, 147
Terry, Clark, 371
Tharpe, Sister Rosetta, 126
Theselius, Gosta, 294
Thomas, Dylan, 261, 323, 363–364
Thomas, Joe, 372
Thompson, Charles Phillip (Sir Charles), 152
Thompson, Eli (Lucky), 3, 4, 19, 21, 209–213
Thornhill, Claude (orchestra), 282, 374
Thorton, Argonne, 195–198
Three Bips and a Bop, 264
Three Deuces (club, New York), 9, 23, 163, 164–165, 171–174, 175–177, 179, 183–184, 187–188, 236–238, 243–246, 249, 251
Tic Toc Club (Boston), 158
Tiffany's (club, Los Angeles), 309–324
Tijuana, Baja California, 254
Time-Life series, 319
Times Square Club (Rochester, New York), 309
Tiny's Tempo, 168–171
Toffinetti's restaurant (New York), 263
Tommy Dorsey Show, 355–357; *see also* Dorsey, Tommy
Tootie, Tootie's Mayfair. *See* Clarkin, Tootie
Torin, Symphony Sid, 172, 274, 276
Towles, Nat (orchestra), 110
Town Hall (New York), 336
Tristano, Lennie, 244, 267, 320, 344, 360–361, 362, 364
Tropicana Hotel (Las Vegas), 371
Truman, Senator Harry, 107
Trumbauer, Frankie, 58
Tumino, John (Tums), 111, 115, 117, 121, 123
Turk, Tommy, 270

Turner, Joe (Big Joe), 32, 47, 78, 371
Tuskegee Institute, 57

UCLA, 207
Ulanov, Barry, 126, 261, 362
Union Station (Los Angeles), 200
Union Station Massacre (Kansas City), 40
United Sound Studios (Detroit), 254
United States District Court, Philadelphia, 316
Unity Funeral Home, 360
Urban Blues, 366

Valentine, Jerry, 158
Vanity Fair Club (Kansas City), 30, 51
Van Vechten, Carl, 366
Varese, Edgard, 193, 209, 320, 342, 364
Variety magazine, 152
Vaughan, Sarah, 150–152, 155, 157–158, 160, 168, 170, 192–194, 254, 274, 334, 362, 371
Ventura, Charlie, 204, 207, 267, 282
Verdi, Giuseppe, 181
Verve Records (Norman Granz label), 337, 373
Veterans' Administration Hospital (Los Angeles), 224
Vian, Boris, 271
Virgil, Old Man, 44, 69–70, 73, 106, 153
Vocalion Records, 77–78, 90, 194
Volstead Act, 30

Wainwright, Connie, 157
Walcott, Jersey Joe, 312
Wald, Jerry (orchestra), 282
Walder, Herman, 42
Walder, Woody, 42
Walker, Jim Daddy, 48, 78
Waller, Thomas (Fats), 135–136, 165
Wall's Chili House. *See* Dan Wall's Chili House
Walter Cooke Funeral Home, 360
War Graves Commission, 314
Ware, Efferge, 78, 90–92
Warren, Rusty, 374
Washington, Dinah, 330–331, 362
Washington, Jack, 52
Waters, Ethel, 100, 146

Watkins, Ralph, 264
Watson, Leo, 165
Webb, William (Chick, orchestra), 99, 127
Webster, Ben, 30, 42, 62, 83, 135, 165, 309
Webster, Freddie, 126
Wells, Dickie (Harlem figure), 100
Wells, Dickie (trombonist), 135
West Bottoms (Kansas City), 95
West, Harold (Doc), 138, 167–171, 238–239
West, Odel, 94–95
Wettling, George, 165
Wheeler, Mayor Charles B. (Kansas City), 372
White Rose Bar (New York), 165, 186
Whiteman, Paul (King of Jazz), 366
Whitman, Bubbles, 203
Whittier, John Greenleaf, 179
Wichita tapes, 33, 111–114, 137, 170
Wiedoeft, Rudy, 60, 113
Wien, George, 336, 349
Wilder, Lee, 234
Wilkerson, George, 79, 354
William Morris agency, 156, 158, 160–161
Williams, Charles (Cootie), 135, 275–277
Williams, Claude, 371
Williams, John, 100, 146, 149
Williams, Junior, 158
Williams, Mary Lou, 60, 134–135, 362, 371–372
Williams, Rubberlegs, 192
Williams, Tony (discographer), 203, 373
Williams, Winston, 95
Wilson, Gerald, 207
Wilson, Richard (Dick), 42, 135
Wilson, Rossiere (Shadow), 147, 157–158
Wilson, Theodore (Teddy), 135, 194–195, 314, 359
Winding, Kai, 267, 282, 345
Witherspoon, Jimmy (Spoon), 371
WJZ radio, 276
Wolpe, Stefan, 317–318, 320
Woods, Phil, 373
Woodside Hotel (New York), 105
WOR studios (New York), 249–253
Wright, Lamar, 37
W9XBY radio (Kansas City), 76

Yacht Club (trio, Billy Eckstine), 154, 157

Yardbird. *See* Parker, Charles, Jr.

Yardbird Suite, 118, 211–213, 245

You Are My First Love, 151

Yellow Front Saloon. *See* Burton, Ellis

Young, Billie (orchestra), 57–58

Young, Billie, Mrs., 58

Young, James (Trummy), 146, 192

Young, Lester Willis (Pres, Prez, President, Red), 14, 30, 32, 42, 44–45, 52–56, 57–60, 62–63, 67–68, 80, 83, 89–92, 93, 94, 105, 111, 112, 113, 119, 127, 135, 138, 166, 186, 204–205, 208, 220, 239, 243, 244, 250, 256, 258, 260, 276, 301, 303, 320, 325–327, 363, 371, 373

style, 91–92, 113

Zeidler and Zeidler (Z and Z), 235, 241

Ziegfeld Follies, 175

About the Author

A native of Los Angeles and educated at UCLA, Ross Russell has followed a dual career in music and writing. Author of two hundred magazine articles and stories, he became a contributor of critical and biographical pieces to *Down Beat, Jazz Hot, Orkester Journalen, Jazz Review*, and many other music publications. He is the author of *The Sound*, a jazz novel, and the scholarly *Jazz Style in Kansas City and the Southwest*. He has lectured on jazz at New York University and Bucknell University, and has conducted courses in jazz, blues, and Afro-American music at University of California (San Diego, Riverside, and Palm Springs) and Palomar College.

In the commercial music field Mr. Russell has been president and director of artists-and-repertoire of Dial Records, Inc., proprietor of a jazz retail store, producer of jazz festival concerts, and for the two years that Charlie Parker was under contract to Dial, the artist's personal manager. Mr. Russell was also a member of the extension music faculty at University of California at San Diego, and of the international critics' committee of *Down Beat* magazine. He currently divides his time between London and California.

Other titles of interest

A CENTURY OF JAZZ
From Blues to Bop, Swing to
Hip-Hop: A Hundred Years
of Music, Musicians,
Singers and Styles
Roy Carr
256 pp., $9^5/8 \times 11^1/2$
350 illus., 200 in color
80778-5 $28.95

BLACK BEAUTY, WHITE HEAT
A Pictorial History of Classic
Jazz, 1920–1950
Frank Driggs and Harris Lewine
Foreword by John Hammond
360 pp., 1,516 illus.
80672-X $29.95

ORNETTE COLEMAN
A Harmolodic Life
John Litweiler
266 pp., 9 photos
80580-4 $14.95

TALKING JAZZ
An Oral History
Expanded Edition
Ben Sidran
535 pp., 20 photos
80613-4 $16.95

'ROUND ABOUT MIDNIGHT
A Portrait of Miles Davis
Updated Edition
Eric Nisenson
336 pp., 27 photos
80684-3 $14.95

ASCENSION
John Coltrane and his Quest
Eric Nisenson
298 pp.
80644-4 $13.95

BIRD: The Legend
of Charlie Parker
Edited by Robert Reisner
256 pp., 50 photos
80069-1 $13.95

FREE JAZZ
Ekkehard Jost
214 pp., 70 musical examples
80556-1 $13.95

THE FREEDOM PRINCIPLE
Jazz After 1958
John Litweiler
324 pp., 11 photos
80377-1 $13.95

IMPROVISATION
Its Nature and Practice in Music
Derek Bailey
172 pp., 12 photos
80528-6 $13.95

JAZZ MASTERS OF THE 40s
Ira Gitler
298 pp., 14 photos
80224-4 $12.95

JOHN COLTRANE
Bill Cole
278 pp., 25 photos
80530-8 $14.95

MILES DAVIS
The Early Years
Bill Cole
256 pp.
80554-5 $13.95

STRAIGHT LIFE
The Story of Art Pepper
Updated Edition
Art and Laurie Pepper
Introduction by Gary Giddins
616 pp., 48 photos
80558-8 $17.95

MINGUS
A Critical Biography
Brian Priestley
320 pp., 25 photos
80217-1 $11.95

Available at your bookstore

OR ORDER DIRECTLY FROM

DA CAPO PRESS

1-800-321-0050